I0815433

Tulsa 2021

RANDY KREHBIEL

TULSA 2021

A MASSACRE'S CENTENNIAL AND A NATION'S RECKONING

UNIVERSITY OF OKLAHOMA PRESS : NORMAN

Publication of this book is made possible in part through the generous assistance of the Wallace C. Thompson Endowment Fund, University of Oklahoma Foundation.

Library of Congress Cataloging-in-Publication Data

Names: Krehbiel, Randy, author.
Title: Tulsa, 2021 : a massacre's centennial and a nation's reckoning / Randy Krehbiel.
Description: Norman : University of Oklahoma Press, [2025] | Includes bibliographical references and index. | Summary: "An account of a city under inordinate pressure, Tulsa, 2021 offers a behind-the-scenes view of how Tulsans and Americans met a cluster of overlapping crises—COVID-19, a combustible presidential visit, and a nationwide explosion of racial tension—and what their experience can tell us about racial politics today"—Provided by publisher.
Identifiers: LCCN 2024038179 | ISBN 9780806195322 (hardcover ; alk. paper)
Subjects: LCSH: Tulsa Race Massacre, Tulsa, Okla., 1921. | African Americans—Violence against—History—20th century. | Tulsa (Okla.)—Politics and government—21st century. | Tulsa (Okla.)—Social conditions—21st century. | United States—Politics and government—21st century. | United States—Race relations—Political aspects.
Classification: LCC F704.T92 K75 2025 | DDC 976.6/8600496073—dc23/eng/20241219
LC record available at https://lccn.loc.gov/2024038179

The paper in this book meets the guidelines for permanence and durability of the Committee on Production Guidelines for Book Longevity of the Council on Library Resources, Inc. ∞

1 2 3 4 5 6 7 8 9 10

For Addie, James, Nash, and Walker

CONTENTS

PREFACE

COVID-19. George Floyd. Seattle. Portland. Washington, DC. A tumultuous presidential campaign with an unprecedented aftermath. Climatic catastrophe. The years 2020 and 2021 stressed every American and every American community to the breaking point. In that respect, one might argue this book could have been written about any medium-sized US city.

To be sure, Tulsa was in some ways representative of America as a whole. But Tulsa was also unique. It has been since the early twentieth century, when oil and ambition turned a dusty cowtown into one of the fastest-growing and wealthiest cities on earth. And then, on a bright spring morning in 1921, it became unique for the wrong reason, even in an era of undisguised and sometimes unbridled racism. That reason was the Tulsa Race Massacre.

Besides everything else, Tulsa in 2020 and 2021 found itself trying to come to terms with this past, as well as the present. To a large degree, this involved a fight, sometimes ferocious, over who got to tell the story and how they told it, not only the story of the massacre but of Tulsa itself. This is hardly new or unusual, but in Tulsa during this period the struggle was undisguised and on display for the world to see.

Among the challenges of writing about events such as the Tulsa Race Massacre—or Wounded Knee, or Babi Yar, or Nanjing, or history's countless other outrages of violence and destruction—is providing context without minimizing specific incidents. Tulsa's massacre fit a particularly intense pattern of racial violence in the United States during and after World War I. This is important because, I would argue, this is a period in our history the average American knows least about. More than once, I have been asked how Oklahomans, and especially Tulsans, could have suppressed almost all memory of the Tulsa Race Massacre for so long. Part of my answer is to ask the questioner what they know of similar incidents near their homes: Elaine, Arkansas; Washington, DC; the eastern Oregon wilderness. More times than not, the answer is a blank stare. So yes, it is important that people understand that racial violence is part of their history—of our nation's history—and not just Tulsa, Oklahoma's.

But it is also important to acknowledge the singular aspects that set the Tulsa Race Massacre apart. This is necessary not only to understand the massacre's place in history, but to properly acknowledge the lives so catastrophically changed, if not ended. For its intensity, for its combination of death, injury, and destruction, Tulsa seems to be unmatched or nearly so. And, for generations, those with an interest in doing so were able to all but expunge the massacre from public awareness. Thus, its national and international rediscovery as the 2021 centennial approached intensified scrutiny of a town struggling with many of the same problems as other cities, plus a few more.

A series of recent, high-profile shootings by law officers still rankled many Tulsans, especially Black Tulsans. Nearby, in the Osage Hills northwest of Tulsa, filming had begun for *Killers of the Flower Moon*, a big-budget motion picture depicting another example of racial violence, the oil-induced exploitation and systematic murder of the Osage people during the early twentieth century.

Then came word, in June 2020, that President Donald Trump had chosen Tulsa as the place for his first large in-person rally since the onset of COVID. Trump may have been popular in the Tulsa area and in the state and region in general, but this announcement generated a fear and dread perhaps not felt since the race massacre itself. The prospect of tens of thousands of people descending on downtown Tulsa—some passionately in support of the sitting president and some just as passionately opposed—in the middle of a pandemic, heightened anxiety for some to the point of hysteria. And while the moment passed without serious incident, the city's blood pressure hardly had time to recover as one nerve-racking episode after another turned life in Tulsa into a real-time streaming service drama.

The crises of 2020–21 passed, as crises do, but they exposed Tulsa to a degree of scrutiny and self-examination few cities, especially cities its size, ever experience. It was a time of jangled nerves, strong words, and stronger emotions. This is a reporter's attempt to tell that story, based on interviews, observations, contemporaneous reporting, and publicly available data. It does not present an academic thesis and is not intended as advocacy. It is, as Philip Graham put it, a "first rough draft of history."

ACKNOWLEDGMENTS

As a reporter, I learned long ago that every relationship and every morsel of information to come my way fit into not only a story, but the story—the story of who we are as Tulsans, as Oklahomans, as Americans, as human beings. That makes acknowledgments difficult. The list of people who informed this book and my reporting is virtually endless; even those who declined active participation in my search for understanding have, in their own ways, contributed to it.

Particularly generous with their time and thoughts were Philip Abode; Phil Armstrong; Kojo Asamoa-Caesar; Tyrance Billingsley II; Mayor G. T. Bynum; Venita Cooper; state representative Regina Goodwin; George Kaiser; former state senator Judy Eason McIntyre; Freeman Culver; Raymond Doswell; Reuben Gant; Bob Jack; Hannibal Johnson; Quraysh Ali Lansana; state senator Kevin Matthews; state representative Monroe Nichols; Rev. Ray Owens; Greg Robinson; Kavin Ross; Rev. Anthony Scott; Ashli Sims; Rev. Robert Turner; Kristi Williams; and Kajeer Yar.

Of great assistance, especially on the technical front, were those involved in the search for unmarked burials from Tulsa's 1921 Race Massacre. This included State Archeologist Kary Stackelbeck, senior researcher Scott Hammerstedt, University of Florida forensic anthropologist Phoebe Stubblefield, and independent researcher Betsy Warner. As always, historian Scott Ellsworth was an invaluable resource. The grave search oversight committee, chaired at various times by former state senator Maxine Horner, Brenda Nails Alford, and Kavin Ross, provided a good deal of insight into the varied perspectives of the community.

I am very much indebted to the fellow journalists whose reporting on this tumultuous period was indispensable to me and to the world at large. I, of course, include my coworkers at the *Tulsa World*, but also reporters and editors at the *Oklahoma Eagle*, the *Black Wall Street Times*, KOTV, KJRH, KWGS, KTUL,

KOKI, the *Washington Post*, the *New York Times*, and many others. I include in this group author and journalist Victor Luckerson, with whom I shared beneficial conversations over the course of several years.

The *Tulsa World* has long given me the latitude to pursue my whims, including the reporting that became the foundation of this book. I must thank Editor Jason Collington, City Editor Paul Tyrrell, former company president Bernie Heller, and many other reporters, photographers, and editors past and present, including but not limited to Kevin Canfield, Andrea Eger, Corey Jones, Ginnie Graham, Curtis Killman, Tim Stanley, Kelsy Schlotthauer, Samantha Vicent, Lenzy Krehbiel-Burton, Wayne Greene, Mike Simons, Ian Maule and Stephen Pingrey.

In *Tulsa, 1921: Reporting a Massacre*, I acknowledged the passing of several people influential in my understanding of the city and its history. Since that book was published in 2019, this in memoriam list has grown to include Julius Pegues, Eddie Faye Gates, Marc Carlson, Kavin Ross, Dwain Midget, former senator Maxine Horner, and Ed Wheeler, among others.

This book grew from discussions with University of Oklahoma Press editor Kent Calder and would not have happened without him. With Kent's retirement, the project passed into the capable hands of others at the Press, including Editorial Director Andrew Berzanskis, Managing Editor Steven Baker, and Acquisitions Coordinator Upuli DeSilva, and finally to independent copyeditor Susan Walters Schmid at Teton Editorial Services. Every good reporter knows he's only as good as his editor.

PART ONE

TULSA, 2020

1

SETTING THE SCENE

BLACK LIVES MATTER

Stenciled in bright bold letters down the middle of Greenwood Avenue, big enough for President Donald Trump to see as Air Force One circled downtown Tulsa, the words had been laid down in the middle of the night as both a message and an act of defiance. The forty-fifth president had chosen Tulsa to resume his COVID-delayed reelection campaign on June 20, 2020, because it seemed the safest of safe harbors, a Republican town in a Republican state surrounded by Republican states. He expected the downtown BOK Center (Bank of Oklahoma Center) and the streets surrounding it to be teeming with adoring supporters. And yet, had Trump looked out of the window, the only visible acknowledgement of his arrival would have been this phrase he had grown to despise.[1]

Whether President Trump actually saw the street painting is unrecorded; almost certainly, it would not have improved his mood. He had already been told the huge crowd he and his advisors had expected never materialized. Instead of the 100,000 or more people predicted, 10,000 at most had turned up. A planned overflow event outside had been canceled at the last minute. Instead of enthusiastic supporters swarming the streets, jamming into the arena, and perhaps scuffling with opposing demonstrators, Trump was being met by a half-full arena and a giant Black Lives Matter sign. Reportedly, some of his advisors feared Trump would order Air Force One to turn around and fly back to Washington.[2]

Some thought that was exactly what he should do.[3]

Trump had come to Tulsa to get away from such reminders of discontent. Less than a month earlier, a nation already on edge because of COVID-caused disruptions and racial and political tensions had ignited like dry kindling, ignited by the death of George Floyd, a Black man suspected of passing a counterfeit bill, at the hands of Minneapolis police. Riots broke out across the country, including in Louisville, Kentucky, where two months earlier police had shot to death a Black emergency room technician named Breonna Taylor. In Washington, DC, some 7,600 regular military and National Guard personnel, plus more than 2,300 law officers, were deployed against mostly peaceful protestors in and near Lafayette Square, across the street from the White House. Massive, weeks-long demonstrations in Portland and Seattle had turned violent and destructive as civil rights activists, counter protestors, anarchists, and others clashed with each other and law enforcement.[4]

There had also been protests in Tulsa, largely culminating with a march on the evening of May 31 that veered onto a downtown highway and into an incident involving the driver of a pickup truck pulling a horse trailer. Over several days, there had been some arrests and serious damage to a few businesses. Police deployed tear gas at least once.[5]

As a whole, though, the activities in Tulsa were less violent and less confrontational than in many other places. But Tulsa, probably more than most cities, was aware of where such passions could lead. During a roughly fourteen-hour period spanning May 31–June 1, 1921, racial conflict had turned into a conflagration that destroyed thirty-five square blocks of Tulsa's thriving Black neighborhood, including the commercial district along Greenwood Avenue known as Black Wall Street. No exact death toll has ever been determined but the belief, then and now, is that the thirty-seven for which death certificates are known were likely only a fraction of the true total. Thousands of Black Tulsans were left homeless. Financial losses were in the millions.[6]

The May 31, 2020, Tulsa march began as a ninety-ninth anniversary commemoration of this conflagration—now called the Tulsa Race Massacre—as well as of Floyd's killing a few days earlier. It was also a more general expression of both protest and unity in the face of rising discontent. Black Americans were not the only participants in this and the earlier demonstrations. So, when on June 10, the Trump campaign announced its first live rally would be held in Tulsa on June 19, many Tulsans were outraged. And not just for political reasons. After a brief slowdown, COVID-19 cases were again on the rise and public health experts warned the rally could turn into a "super-spreader" event. Black Tulsans were particularly angry. Their own Juneteenth celebration—observed in Tulsa for decades—had been canceled in deference to the pandemic. Now a man many of them considered the epitome of racism in America planned to appropriate their holiday by ignoring the safety protocols that had shut them down.[7]

"It feels like an insult, like a deliberate insult at worst and insensitive, unthinking and calculated at best," said Alicia Andrews, the Black Tulsan chairing the Oklahoma Democratic Party.[8]

Whether the choice of dates was intentional or simply uninformed is unclear, but Trump moved the rally back a day, reportedly after a Secret Service agent explained to him the significance of Juneteenth. That Trump then took credit for making the day better known did not endear him to Black Tulsans.[9]

"These types of things happen when you don't have diversity at the table," said state senator Kevin Matthews, a Tulsa Democrat and one of the state's few Black legislators. "For those who say they didn't know, or that it wasn't intentional, it is intentional . . . if you didn't include (Black Tulsans) in the discussion."[10]

Then came the news that Gov. Kevin Stitt had invited Trump to visit Greenwood.[11]

Greenwood has been synonymous with Black life in Tulsa since the early twentieth century and extends far beyond the mile-long street that bears the name. It is not hyperbole to say that many consider it a sacred place, consecrated not only by the blood of the massacre, but by the sweat and tears of generations of Black men and women fighting to realize dreams long deferred. President Trump may have been popular in Oklahoma as a whole, and even in the Tulsa metro area, but he had few fans in Greenwood. With the announcement that Trump might visit Greenwood, panic infused their anger as community leaders heard from groups offering up busloads of protestors and the Trump campaign bragged that the number of tickets requested for the BOK Center rally was approaching one million. Visions not just of Seattle and Portland, but of Tulsa nearly one hundred years earlier, filled Tulsans' minds and their nightmares.[12]

"My messages are flooded with people who have said, 'We're coming down to help you protest.' We never said we'd be protesting," said Sherry Gamble-Smith, a prominent figure in Tulsa's African American community.[13]

"We're trying to figure what we can do to keep people organized," said Gamble-Smith. "We want to make sure people's voices are heard but in a safe way."[14]

Downtown businesses closed and boarded up their windows. Locally based convenience store chain QuikTrip, whose Ferguson, Missouri, location was burned in the unrest that followed the 2014 shooting death by police of Michael Brown, closed five of its stores near downtown Tulsa. The Reverend Jesse Jackson joined Tulsa leaders in urging those unhappy about Trump's rally to stay clear of it.[15]

"Stay at home," Jackson said. "That's a form of protest, too."[16]

"I'd tell people he's not worth it," state representative Monroe Nichols (D-Tulsa) said, referring to Trump.[17]

Even after it was announced that Trump would not be coming to Greenwood—Vice President Mike Pence wound up meeting a sympathetic Black minister several miles from the heart of the district instead—Black Tulsans remained on guard. An old truck left idling on Greenwood Avenue during a hastily organized Juneteenth celebration was suspected by some participants of being a car bomb; the day after, some were concerned that an attempt would be made to break up a gathering a few blocks away at John Hope Franklin Park. For the most part, though, the protestors and counter protestors stayed away, or at least apart. The Juneteenth celebration turned into a two-day street festival that began a day before Trump arrived and was still going after he departed. It was during this event that a silent multiracial crew dashed onto Greenwood Avenue during the wee hours of June 19 and painted BLACK LIVES MATTER.[18]

So it was that on a street in a city where nearly a century earlier Black lives had mattered so little, they mattered enough for at least a few days for many to feel some sense of triumph. They had not wanted Trump in Tulsa, had feared what it would mean to their community, and though he had come anyway, it was not in the time or manner he had first chosen.

They had mattered. Maybe not as much as Black Tulsans wanted or deserved, but more than all those years earlier when standing up for just one Black life had been answered with death and destruction on an apocalyptic scale.

This was, though, only one victory out of many battles. And, like most such victories, it ultimately would come at a cost. In life as in movies, the empire always strikes back.

Matthews, while relieved, said as much.

"There's no victory until we have equity," he said. "I'm excited no one was harmed. But there is no victory . . . until Black lives matter like everyone else's."[19]

Tulsa's race massacre of May 31–June 1, 1921, is regarded as among the deadliest and most destructive episodes of racial violence in US history. Marauding whites, angry because armed Black men came to the Tulsa County Courthouse to assure the safety of an African American teen accused of attacking a young white woman, retaliated with an early-morning invasion. There may also have been an element of greed. White real estate interests wanted Deep Greenwood for commercial and industrial development and there had been a campaign to smear the neighborhood as crime- and sin-infested; some believe Greenwood's destruction on June 1 to have been part of a larger plot. In any event, the white mob swept in, killing Blacks who resisted and no doubt many who did not. Homes and businesses were looted and put to the torch, burning Greenwood to the ground, and leaving thousands of men, women, and children not only homeless, but in many cases penniless as well. It was a national scandal, an embarrassment and humiliation to white Tulsa, and a tragedy of unimaginable proportions to what had been one of the nation's most financially successful Black communities.[20]

Attempts by property owners, white and Black, to gain compensation for their losses failed because the incident was put down to civil disobedience—a riot, in other words. In an era when such acts of destruction had grown disturbingly common, insurance policies rarely covered the resulting damage. Somehow, Greenwood rebuilt anyway, reaching its zenith after World War II. Ironically, the loosening of segregation, coupled with the general wane of the small-scale "mom and pop" operations upon which Greenwood's business district depended, contributed significantly to rapid decline in the 1960s; urban renewal and a highway through the middle of the neighborhood virtually assured the old Greenwood would never return.[21]

And so, as the massacre's centennial approached, old and new grievances blended in a bubbling cauldron of emotions, aspirations, and motives. Many saw the approaching anniversary as an opportunity, as leverage to further particular causes: reparations, reconciliation, policing reform, inequity, community development, binding up old wounds, and perhaps even personal and political gain.

For others, the anniversary loomed as a thunderhead on the horizon, a storm to be weathered and survived. Tulsans, and principally white Tulsans, no longer denied the fact of 1921, but that did not mean they wanted to be reminded of it. Perhaps more to the point, they resisted and resented the idea that the Race Massacre had anything to do with them or held much relevance in the present. But there was no escaping.

The Tulsa Race Massacre was no longer an obscure historical footnote that embarrassed whites and traumatized Blacks conspired to keep quiet in hopes it would be forgotten. The subject of numerous television reports, newspaper stories, books, documentaries, television programs, podcasts, and every other sort of media conveyance, the massacre had come to epitomize America's racist past. In the fall of 2019, the nine-episode HBO miniseries *Watchmen* put a widely viewed fantasy twist to the story. Now, in microscopic detail, the world wanted to see how Tulsa had and would respond.

May 31–June 1, 2021, had been circled on calendars for years. In May 2016, ahead of the massacre's ninety-fifth anniversary, Republican senator James Lankford memorialized the event on the Senate floor, saying, "Five years from now we as a nation will talk about this even more when it's the 100-year anniversary. Who are we as a nation? How far have we come? And what do we have left to go to make sure that we really are one nation under God, indivisible."[22]

At about the same time, Matthews was formulating plans for a centennial commission.

"We can't rewrite the past, but we can build a brighter and more prosperous future," Matthews said when he and Lankford formally announced the commission the following February. Besides Lankford and Matthews, who was listed as chair, the membership included Republican first district congressman Jim Bridenstine, Republican mayor G. T. Bynum, a Republican county commissioner, and more than twenty-five other state and local officials and members of the community.[23]

In most obvious ways Matthews and Lankford seemed an unlikely pair, but they agreed on a desire to revive Black Tulsa's entrepreneurial traditions. Matthews had become a believer in entrepreneurship as a Tulsa firefighter, when department veterans schooled him on the sideline businesses many of them ran on their days off. As he worked his way into the upper ranks of the Tulsa Fire Department (TFD), Matthews invested in real estate and operated several businesses of his own. Entering politics upon his retirement from the fire department, Matthews began a crusade to rekindle the entrepreneurship for which Greenwood had once been known. In this he was not alone. Many other Black Tulsans wanted more control of their own circumstances by being their own bosses.[24]

The commission's purpose, Matthews said, was to "facilitate activities and events that will educate Oklahomans and Americans about the 1921 Tulsa Race Riot, its impact on the state and nation; to help remember its victims and survivors; and create an environment conducive to fostering sustainable entrepreneurship and heritage tourism within the Greenwood District and North Tulsa."[25]

More to the point, the commission was an attempt to formulate and project a coordinated, coherent message. "This should be about how we can and should celebrate what can and does unite us, not what divides us," Matthews assured fellow Tulsans and the world at large.[26]

By the time President Trump arrived in Tulsa in June 2020, though, disagreements about what the message of the massacre centennial should be were evident. These differences would grow over the next year as competing perspectives, opinions, agendas, and, at times, egos sought to define the story and ultimately the race massacre's legacy.

The century-long fight to control the message—how the story is told and by whom—is as important to understanding the lingering effects of the Tulsa Race Massacre as the massacre itself. The same is true of just about all history. The fights over the story—any story—are often as brutal in their own way as the events they are ostensibly intended to describe. As Sir William Francis Butler wrote of the carnage at Culloden, "It is the victor who writes the history and counts the dead,"

For decades, the victors of Tulsa's Race Massacre wrote the history by keeping it silent and counted the dead by pretending they never existed. Even after the past began to reemerge, the struggle over the story continued and in some ways became more complicated. It was no longer simply Black versus white, winners versus losers. No one really disagreed that a terrible wrong had been done in 1921, or that preceding and subsequent wrongs had compounded that damage. The city had been largely past that for years. As the massacre approached, the festering dilemma was what to do about it.

Some things change. Some things remain the same.

So it is with Tulsa.

The US census of 1920 describes a young, rapidly growing Tulsa with a population of 72,075, a more than three-fold increase from ten years before. It was overwhelmingly white and native-born; less than 3 percent of the residents were recorded as immigrants, with Russia the leading country of origin. African Americans accounted for 12.3 percent of the total. Nearly 85 percent of the population was under the age of forty-five.[27]

Tulsa in 1920 was a compact little island of urban life in a vast sea of farms and ranches. The city measured at most only a few miles in any direction from its center—the crosshairs intersection of Main Street at the Frisco Railroad tracks. Its 72,000 residents—many of them rural transplants—accounted for just 3.6 percent of Oklahoma's two million people.[28]

Politically, Tulsa was divided not only by party but by factions within the parties. City and county elections were every two years, and turnover in administration was frequent. After the 1920 election, the mayor, city auditor, and three of four city commissioners were Republicans, all elected by citywide vote. Intended or not, this system of electing officials at large assured Tulsa's municipal government would be white and mostly male, then and for decades to come.[29]

A century later, the 2020 census documented a much larger and more mature and diverse metropolitan area. Less than half the population identified as non-Hispanic white, and by one measure, Tulsa's demographics were among the most rapidly changing in the country. After a decade or more of stagnation, the city's population had grown to 413,000, spread over 200 square miles. The metropolitan area had surpassed one million, a full quarter of the state's population; more than half of Oklahomans now lived in the Oklahoma City and Tulsa metropolitan areas. Almost one in five Tulsans identified as Hispanic, and significant Asian communities had arisen where virtually none existed in 1920. In some area schools, one of the most common languages was Zomi, a Southeast Asian tongue spoken by immigrants from Myanmar.[30]

The 2020 census also found that Tulsans, like Americans as a whole, were more inclined to identify as belonging to two or more racial groups. While Tulsa's non-Hispanic white population declined by 12 percent during the decade from 2010 to 2020, to just over 200,000, the Hispanic (regardless of race) category grew 43 percent, to nearly 80,000. People identifying with the non-Hispanic, two-or-more category nearly doubled during the same period to about 38,000. That may explain, at least to some extent, why the non-Hispanic Black and American Indian categories were slightly lower than ten years before.[31]

City government and politics only partly reflected this growing diversity. A new city charter in the early 1990s had replaced the five-member commission consisting of a weak mayor and four commissioners elected citywide with a strong mayor and nine city councilors elected from districts. This led to somewhat more diverse representation. While only one Black Tulsan was ever elected to the city commission, since 1990, the city council has always had at least one Black member and sometimes two. Hispanics and Native Americans have also served.[32]

The biggest change, though, has been women's involvement in city government. In 1920, city auditor Mary Seaman became the first woman elected to Tulsa city government; she was defeated for reelection two years later. Not until 1980 would a woman, Patty Eaton, be elected to the city commission. In 1992, Susan Savage became the first woman to serve as mayor. Savage would remain in office ten years—the longest of any mayor in the city's history. A second woman, Kathy Taylor, was elected mayor in 2006, and while men regained the office in 2009, by 2020 six of the nine city councilors were women.[33]

Still, with all of these changes, many of the city's major issues remained the same: infrastructure, schools, jobs, policing, public welfare, and—yes—race.

Modern Tulsa began in 1882 as a few tents pitched along the course of the St. Louis-San Francisco Railway, better known as the Frisco, which was being built from northeast to southwest across what was then Indian Territory. This little tent city followed the railroad crews as a sort of traveling business district, usually moving every day or two. When they reached the Arkansas River, though, the tent city remained in place while the crews bridged the river near the juncture of the Cherokee, Osage, and Muscogee nations. This site was a little more than a mile north of the place where, nearly fifty years earlier, Loachapoka Muscogees had ended a forced march from their ancestral home in Alabama under a big oak tree on a bluff overlooking the Arkansas River. They called the place Tallasi, meaning old town. Tallasi largely disappeared during the American Civil War, which devastated Indian Territory, but in the 1870s a post office several miles away on the Perryman Ranch was given the name Tulsa. This post office was later moved to the railroad settlement and gave it its name.

Oil turned Tulsa into the Magic City, a place of instant fortunes and huge ambitions, but with the unsettling knowledge that for every boom comes a bust. The bloom of the first big strikes was still fresh when city leaders, in the early 1900s, began asking the question: What do we do when the oil runs out?[34]

More than a century later, Tulsa was still working on it. Oil and gas remained foundational to the city's economy, but now aerospace and healthcare were, too. The University of Tulsa, long known for its petroleum engineering program, had become a national leader in cybersecurity. Regionally, the manufacturing of electric vehicles and components was beginning to catch hold. Music, long a bright thread in the city's fabric, was becoming a marketable commodity. Two major motion pictures, *Minari* and *Killers of the Flower Moon,* were shot largely in and around Tulsa. The George Kaiser Family Foundation, which had already spent hundreds of millions of dollars on early childhood education, an internationally acclaimed park called Gathering Place, and other philanthropic enterprises, in 2018 undertook a program that paid high-tech transplants $10,000 each to work remotely from Tulsa.[35]

The Tulsa of the early 1920s was a spectacular place, but also a grim one. In early 1921, a report commissioned by Republican mayor T. D. Evans described neighborhoods rife with poverty, disease, and despair. Social workers Gertrude Vaile and Hilda K. Wills laid out a long list of recommendations to better meet the needs of poor and working-class Tulsans. Near the top of that list was housing. "Contrary to supposition," a newspaper quoted the report, "Tulsa has an unusually large and greatly neglected 'slum' district in which large families are living in one-room tents or shacks and where moral standards are shattered by promiscuous association of children of opposite sexes."[36]

Nearly a hundred years later, another Republican mayor acknowledged the same differences between rich and poor, and to some extent among races, still existed in Tulsa. In 2017, under Mayor G. T. Bynum, Tulsa became one of five cities nationwide to adopt the Equality Indicators, a fifty-four-item measurement for assessing inequalities and developing policy to address them. Tulsa's baseline score was below forty on a one-hundred-point scale. Wide discrepancies in housing and economic opportunities were documented.[37]

"It is very damning for our community," said Bynum.[38]

Bynum comes from a long lineage of moderate Republicans. His maternal grandfather and a maternal cousin were mayors of Tulsa. A paternal great-great-grandfather was mayor in the town's early rough-and-tumble days. Bynum himself had worked for Oklahoma Republican senators Don Nickles and Tom Coburn before returning to Tulsa and winning a city council seat in 2008. A coalition of moderates and liberals that cut across party lines helped elect him mayor in November 2016 on his promise to pursue a broad, aggressive agenda that acknowledged racial issues but did not single them out as a particularly high priority.

"I have no interest in just being mayor," Bynum said when he announced his candidacy in late 2015. "I would only want to run . . . if I think we can accomplish some big things. The dynamics are in place to really unify the city and push toward a couple of big goals."[39]

Bynum's pitch was not so much that he would do things radically different than his predecessor, Dewey Bartlett Jr., but that he would do them better. The agenda Bynum announced just before taking office in December 2016 included mentions of the city's growing Hispanic population and persistent inequities in disproportionately Black areas of North Tulsa, but the focus was largely on Tulsa's political constants—education, economic development, public safety, infrastructure, and, to some extent, taxes.[40]

All of that changed six months into Bynum's first term with the acquittal of former Tulsa police officer Betty Shelby in the shooting death of an unarmed Black man, Terence Crutcher.

The shooting had occurred the previous September on a north Tulsa street. As evening approached, Shelby came upon Crutcher's vehicle in the middle of the road and Crutcher himself wandering about, apparently in a daze. With police dash cams and a camera in a Tulsa Police Department (TPD) helicopter overhead recording, Crutcher walked toward his vehicle, an SUV, while Shelby ordered him to stop. When Crutcher reached the SUV, Shelby fired one shot, killing him on the spot. Shelby said she believed Crutcher was going for a weapon, even though she had checked the vehicle earlier and found none.[41]

Shelby said she suspected Crutcher was under the influence of the powerful drug PCP, a suspicion later supported by a postmortem. He had not been combative, but he was a big man—a big Black man—a fact commented on by one of the police officers in the helicopter. Did that add up to justification for killing him? Would the outcome have been different for a 110-pound white high school girl in a cheerleading uniform? Those were the questions asked in the months leading up to Betty Shelby's trial.[42]

Crutcher's was the third high-profile killing of an unarmed black man by Tulsa law officers in less than three years. One, in which an off-duty Tulsa police officer killed his daughter's boyfriend, had not yet come to trial (but would eventually lead to conviction). The third had resulted in a second-degree manslaughter verdict against a seventy-three-year-old Tulsa County Sheriff's Office reserve deputy who said he shot a suspect by mistake. The reserve deputy, an insurance executive, said he mistook his gun for his Taser. Some thought Shelby might offer a similar defense—that she shot Crutcher by accident—but she did not. She said she had simply done what she had been trained to do.[43]

It worked.

Jurors wept as their verdict was read; later it was revealed they had included a memo in the case file saying they could not believe Shelby's conduct met the legal definition of first-degree manslaughter, but some of them did not hold her blameless, either:

> While Officer Shelby made a justifiable decision at the moment she pulled the trigger according to her training, when reviewing the moments before she discharged the weapon, the jury wonders and some believe that she had other options available to subdue Mr. Crutcher . . . but due to the lack of

> direct or even circumstantial evidence that she was acting outside of her training . . . the Jury was forced by rule of law to render a not guilty verdict.[44]

In other words, Tulsa Police Department training—in essence a part of its culture—was more responsible for the killing of an unarmed man than the officer who pulled the trigger.

The Crutcher family and its supporters were understandably upset; Shelby and those on her side celebrated in a luxury downtown hotel. Largely lost in the furor was the fact that the jury had enunciated something Black Tulsans had been saying for more than a century, and that Black Americans had been saying for much longer than that. In 1921, at the time of the race massacre, Tulsa's police force was under investigation by the state attorney general's office for a variety of alleged misdeeds, including some white officers' treatment of Black people. After the massacre, Black and white witnesses would testify that Tulsa police helped set the fires that burned Greenwood to the ground. The distrust and suspicion of law enforcement had never gone away, and the Shelby verdict seemed to only confirm Black Tulsans' doubts about the justice system in general.[45]

The next morning, Bynum told reporters that Tulsa's racial disparities are the "great moral issue of our time in this community." He laid out policing reforms either underway or planned, and he and Police Chief Chuck Jordan suggested that the city got through the previous night without violent confrontations between protestors and law enforcement in part because of these changes, although Bynum also credited Black Tulsans.[46]

"Our history shows us African Americans in Tulsa have not been the instigators of lawlessness and riots," he said. "They have been the victims of them. So I would ask that we not keep assuming the worst from a part of our community that has been exposed to the worst in this city's history."[47]

Tiffany Crutcher, Terence Crutcher's twin sister, challenged Bynum to make good on his promise. A few days later she said:

> At the end of the day, we don't want Terence's name to be remembered as just another hashtag. We want for Terence Crutcher's name to invoke change, to bridge the fear and the mistrust that we're dealing with in the city right now. We believe that if [Bynum] turns his affirmations into action, and he helps us and locks arms with us to implement these reforms, we believe that then, and only then, real change can take place and true healing will be able to overflow and cover this entire community and this city.[48]

Three months later, Tiffany Crutcher launched a foundation in her dead brother's name, dedicated to policing reform but also social justice in general. At the launch, Sherrilyn Ifill, president and director-counsel of the NAACP Legal Defense Fund, was the keynote speaker and civil rights attorney Ben Crump emceed.[49]

The Crutcher verdict and Tiffany Crutcher's unwillingness to let it be forgotten, combined with a rising national tide, moved policing reform from its perennial spot on the back burners of city politics to a rapid boil front and center. Three years later, as Tulsa prepared for the Race Massacre centennial and President Trump was greeted with a half-empty arena and a Black Lives Matter mural painted in the street, it was just one of many issues ripping at the city.

2

PRIORITIES AND PERSPECTIVES

In 2000, not long after I'd been assigned to cover the state commission investigating what was then called the Tulsa Race Riot, state representative Don Ross asked me to meet him for dinner at a steakhouse called McGill's, a block from Tulsa's tony Utica Square and sandwiched between two trendy neighborhoods less than two miles from the intersection of Greenwood and Archer.

The commission had been Ross's doing. A few years earlier, he and Senator Maxine Horner had managed to get the enabling legislation through an almost entirely white legislature that, politically, had no incentive to poke at the embers of what was then a seventy-five-year-old fire. A Republican governor had been persuaded to sign the bill. Now that the commission had been assembled, it was gathering information and attracting national attention, and Ross wanted to make sure I understood some things. He also wanted to find out about me.[1]

Don Ross grew up in Greenwood in the 1950s and 1960s. He often told a story about being introduced to the race massacre by a teacher, W. D. Williams, who had survived it. After a stint in the Air Force, Ross became involved in civil rights activities and was a journalist for the *Oklahoma Eagle* and *IMPACT Magazine*, a publication he edited and that, on the fiftieth anniversary of the massacre, published Ed Wheeler's carefully researched account of it. Ross worked for a newspaper in Gary, Indiana, for five years in the 1970s, and later said that was where he first learned about politics. Returning to Tulsa, in 1982 Ross was elected to the Oklahoma House of Representatives from one of the three "Black" districts—out of a total of 101—created when US Supreme Court decisions of the 1960s established the one-man, one-vote standard of representation.[2]

Canny, direct, and funny, Ross had a way of cajoling concessions from his conservative white colleagues, most of whom were still Democrats at that time. In 1987, long before such things surfaced as an issue elsewhere, the Confederate flag disappeared from a display outside of the state capitol after Ross complained. Exactly what transpired remains unclear, but the flag never returned despite sporadic efforts by white lawmakers over the next fifteen years to reinstate it. Ross also was instrumental in Oklahoma acknowledging Martin Luther King Jr. Day, and in directing public works money to North Tulsa.[3]

When we met at McGill's that night in 2000, Don Ross was nearing the end of a twenty-year political career. But he had one more mission—to get what was then called the Tulsa Race Riot Commission across the finish line. Ross did not say so, but I understood that the purpose of our dinner was to determine whether I would be a help or a hindrance.

We talked for two hours or more, my appreciation of Don Ross growing by the minute. He had been in the arena, as Theodore Roosevelt might have put it. He had been in the fight, not only in the legislature but in the community. He understood the angles and knew all of the players. He knew their stories. One bit of our conversation particularly stands out, even now.

We were discussing the six airplanes that authorities deployed during the attack on Greenwood on the morning of June 1. Some people believe the planes were used to drop incendiary devices; others contend this would have been unlikely given the planes involved and the circumstances on the ground. I thought arguments over what seemed to me a relatively minor detail distracted attention from more salient and indisputable points.[4]

"What difference does it make," I asked Ross, "if the fires were set from the air or on the ground? The result would have been the same. An entire neighborhood burned, and a lot of people killed."

With just a look, Don Ross let me know just how wrong I was. The airplanes mattered. They mattered much more than whatever tactical purpose they served in the attack on Greenwood.

Over the years I have come to understand the planes—and most everything else—in two ways. One is material. The planes existed. They played some role in the attack on Greenwood. The other is symbolic. The planes represent, then and now, real and perceived power. In this context, they represent the advantages and control of whites over people of color. Oral histories going back generations have maintained that Black Tulsans were winning the battle for Greenwood until the airplanes appeared and the machine guns were unlimbered. Whites have always had the airplanes, figuratively speaking. They have always had the machine guns. They have always had the money and the law and, most of all, the power.[5]

The same is true in the broader struggle, then and now.

That is what I saw in Don Ross's face that night in McGill's. It jolted me into a realization of just how little I understood. The differences in white and Black Tulsans' lives and perspectives were not an abstraction. They were real and largely unacknowledged, especially by people like me.

The Frisco tracks (now owned and operated by BNSF) still run through Tulsa, bisecting downtown at an angle that deviates from east-west almost imperceptibly until viewed from height, where the correcting jogs in every downtown street can be observed marking the original townsite boundaries. In 1921, the tracks divided most of Tulsa but not necessarily Black from white. Black Tulsa—Greenwood—was a slice of what was then the northeast quadrant of the city, pinched between another set of tracks, the Midland Valley angling in from the northeast, and high ground on the west. Whites lived on both sides of Greenwood and were the majority of north Tulsans. North Main Avenue was still part of the downtown Tulsa business district, although its prominence was fading.[6]

Today, most Tulsans probably would say the city's north-south divide is Admiral Boulevard—originally the boundary between the Muscogee Creek and Cherokee Nations and known as the Federal Road—or Interstate 244 (I-244), also known as the Crosstown Expressway, which for the most part parallels Admiral. The twin lines divide Tulsa in two, but not in half.

South Tulsa stretches more than ten miles until it collides with the former farm communities that have become suburbs. Except along arterial streets, North Tulsa peters out into rolling prairie and densely wooded hills within a few miles of the nearest I-244 exit ramp. The gritty coming-of-age film *The Outsiders* was set and shot almost entirely in North Tulsa; the little house where the Curtis brothers (played by Patrick Swayze, C. Thomas Howell, and Rob Lowe) lived is still there, tucked away in a dilapidated neighborhood that has not changed much since *The Outsiders* was filmed in the 1980s—or, for that matter, since author S. E. Hinton created the novel upon which the movie is based in the 1960s. That pretty well summarizes the dichotomy between North and South Tulsa. South

Tulsa is where the insiders congregate. It has the nicest neighborhoods, the best stores, the swankiest clubs, and the finest restaurants.

North Tulsa is for outsiders.

That is the message anyone who spends any time in Tulsa receives: North Tulsa is full of crime, rundown neighborhoods, and undesirables—especially undesirable minorities. To the rest of Tulsa, North Tulsa means Black Tulsa, even though most North Tulsans are Hispanic and non-Hispanic White, with Black majorities in only a few census tracts north of downtown. In fact, the share of Tulsa's Black population living in North Tulsa declined from 52 percent in 2010 to 41 percent in 2020. While the total population of North Tulsa increased by about one thousand, the African American population dropped by about 5,300 during that time. The number living in the rest of Tulsa increased by almost the same amount.[7]

Tulsa south of the I-244/Admiral Boulevard dividing line is not all mansions and Mayberry. Some of the worst crime rates in the city are in sections of South Tulsa. There are poor and working-class neighborhoods, just as in North Tulsa, and strip malls and industrial parks. Thousands of people of color live in South Tulsa. But there are also vast neighborhoods of great wealth whose residents are almost all white.[8]

There are no obvious indicators of great wealth in North Tulsa. A few old mansions are tucked away in enclaves near downtown, relics of a halcyon era that ended nearly a century ago; solid middle-class homes of varying ages and architecture lend respectability to several neighborhoods. But in North Tulsa there are no exclusive addresses—white, black, or otherwise.

"The thing that strikes me about Tulsa is I don't know that I've ever lived any place that is as racially segregated as Tulsa, Okla.," said Rev. Ray Owens, pastor of Metropolitan Baptist Church, "By that I mean the sense that there are well-formed lines, the demarcation that divides people by race in terms of how they move around the city, in terms of the places people choose to eat and play and shop."

Owens grew up in South Central Los Angeles and Austin, Texas, graduated from Princeton Theological Seminary, served a church in Trenton, New Jersey, and worked in New York City, among other places. His move to Tulsa in 2006 included one of those everyday events that become defining experiences. Needing a mattress for an apartment, he found his way to a big box retailer deep in South Tulsa. When he called a church member for help hauling it, he was told, "What are you doing out there?"[9]

Owens learned that many North Tulsans, especially Black North Tulsans, do not venture any farther south than necessary. And the opposite is even more true: self-respecting whites do not go north.

"I began to make lots of relationships with white colleagues . . . and formed a lot of cool friendships," Owens recalled. "They always invited me to meetings at their churches somewhere in South Tulsa. And I said, 'Hey, guess what? I want to flip the script here. I'm going to host the next meeting.'"

"The Met," as Metropolitan Baptist Church is known, is a long-time congregation that in the early 2010s moved to the edge of the Osage Hills in northwest Tulsa.

"I mean, we're talking about race and reconciliation and how to bring this community together," Owens continued. "All those conversations happen in white churches in South Tulsa. We've got a fellowship hall; we've got a building—you guys come up here. And so, I stood at the door and greeted people. And I don't think it's an exaggeration at all when I say at least every third person said, 'I've never been up here. I've never been this far north.'"

Rev. Robert Turner of Vernon AME had a slightly different perspective. He moved to Tulsa in 2017 and over the course of a few years came to understand Tulsans as separated by more than geography. "I thought Tulsa was a breath of fresh air, coming from Alabama," Turner recalled in 2022. "I love my home state, but white people were a lot nicer to me initially [in Tulsa]."[10]

Eventually, though, Turner concluded this was largely because Oklahoma's relatively small Black population was not perceived as a political or economic force. It could be safely ignored and occasionally humored but did not require much consideration. Turner concluded many whites thought of Blacks as "not in large enough numbers to be a threat, so we can be nice—as long as they kind of stay in [their] place. Now, once I started doing activism work, then that warm greeting kind of changed in certain quarters."[11]

When Tulsa's first Equality Indicators report came out in 2018, Mayor G. T. Bynum said it did not reveal anything "that people might [not] have [already had] a gut feeling for but never knew the true, unvarnished, numbers-backed facts." Tulsa's overall score of 38.9 out of 100 is difficult to meaningfully translate, except to say that it was not flattering. More easily understood were comparisons among the various ethnic, gender, and geographic groups for almost all of the study's fifty indicators. Black and other minority Tulsans were at a marked disadvantage, and so were North Tulsans.[12]

The study divided Tulsa into four regions. North Tulsa was essentially the same area described earlier: everything above the I-244/Admiral line, except for the eastern-most census tract. That was included in East Tulsa, a mostly blue-collar area with large Hispanic and Asian populations. West Tulsa was the area south and west of the Arkansas River, where a string of separate communities had been absorbed into the city during the 1920s and 1930s. Tulsa's refineries and railyards are in West Tulsa, and neighborhoods still have a small town, working-class feel. North Tulsa's median household income of $28,867 was more than $12,000 less than the next closest, East Tulsa, and half that of South Tulsa. According to the report, a small business was almost four times more likely to be located in the Midtown area than in North Tulsa, and Midtown had three times as many jobs per capita.[13]

Median income for Black households was about 60 percent of Asian and white households, and $9,000 less than for Hispanic and Native American families. Black public school students were seven times more likely to be suspended and five times more likely to change schools during the academic year. Black juveniles were three times more likely than whites to be arrested; Black adults were arrested at two and a half times the rate for white adults.

The data point most often cited by Bynum: life expectancy in South Tulsa was on average eleven years more than in North Tulsa, with a maximum difference among city zip codes of sixteen and a half years.

Perhaps nothing more exemplifies Bynum's data-heavy management style than his embrace of the Equality Indicators project. Originally funded by the Rockefeller Foundation through City University of New York's Institute for State and Local Governance, it attempts to quantify inequity in a form conducive to policy fine-tuning.

"I think this allows us to have a much more educated discussion about how we address these issues and what the solutions are, rather than having philosophical ones that are based on broad assumptions," said Bynum.[14]

In a forward to the first Equality Indicators, Bynum wrote: "We have a responsibility to ensure that regardless of the area of town you live in, everyone has equal access to safety, education, and healthcare features that are vital to the quality of life in our city."[15]

A few months later, Bynum announced a forty-one-point initiative, called Resilient Tulsa, to address the issues highlighted in the Equality Indicators report. These "visions" were categorized under "an inclusive future that honors all

Tulsans"; "equip all Tulsans to overcome barriers and thrive"; "advance economic opportunity for all Tulsans"; and "transform city and regional systems to improve outcomes for all Tulsans."[16]

While eyes may have rolled at some of the highfalutin language, the report addresses, with a frankness unusual for official Oklahoma, such issues as systemic racial inequality, underfunding of public education, and implicit bias in the criminal justice system. Resilient Tulsa's goals were not the brick-and-mortar public works projects often used to measure civic progress, but less-quantifiable objectives such as improved communications, implicit bias training, and neighborhood engagement.[17]

But by the start of 2020, skeptics were restless. They were tired of speeches and detailed plans that never seemed to go beyond the talking stage. They wanted action, and they especially wanted action on policing reform.

On a humid July night in 2019, several cruisers carrying members of the Tulsa Police Department (TPD) Gang Unit pulled into the Town Square Apartments in North Tulsa. This was not unusual. The unit had been there at least once the day before and police had been called to the complex 260 times during the first six months of the year. Separated by a high fence from Booker T. Washington High School, a magnet school drawing top students from all over the Tulsa district, Town Square had a reputation for criminal activity. Police had investigated 456 incidents there in 2018, including 9 assaults, 4 shootings, and 3 stabbings. The Gang Unit, specializing in high crime areas, began dropping in on the complex as part of a community policing initiative advocated by Mayor Bynum. According to some, these visits were known in the community as "Task Force Tuesdays" because of the day they usually occurred. Officers spent time talking with residents, ostensibly to win their trust but also to gather intelligence. They passed out coats in winter and informally followed up on minor disputes and disturbances. But they also kept their eyes and ears open and asked a lot of questions.[18]

On this particular evening, four officers were drawn to a car backed into a parking space. From the four bodycam and dashcam videos later released by the police, it is unclear what attracted their attention, but over the course of about fifteen minutes one officer questions two young men, one in the car and one outside it, while Corporal Rusty Brown stands to one side. A third officer shuttles back and forth between the first officer—identified by his bodycam video and by himself as Officer Barnhart—and a cruiser, where he appears to enter information into a laptop computer. A fourth officer stands about thirty feet from the car in question without otherwise becoming involved in the engagement.[19]

Also present were several policing reform advocates, including Tiffany Crutcher. The Crutchers had grown up in Tulsa; their family had been in the city since before the race massacre. After Betty Shelby was found not guilty in Terence Crutcher's death, Tiffany Crutcher closed her physical therapy practice in Alabama and moved back to devote full time to policing reform and social justice. As word of "Task Force Tuesdays" had gotten around, Crutcher and others, as part of a group called Demanding a JUSTulsa, began showing up to keep an eye on the police and advise residents of their rights.[20]

In Corporal Brown's bodycam video, he appears to be in a discussion with Crutcher and two other activists, Kristi Williams and Nat Wachowski-Estes. The first thirty-four seconds of the video has no sound, however, and by the time it is activated the discussion is winding down.

BROWN: "Who are we harassing?"
CRUTCHER: "I didn't say you were harassing anything. . . . So you can keep that little snide tone."
BROWN: "Wow. Just asking a question."
CRUTCHER: "You're being sarcastic, is what you're doing."

After Williams encourages her friend to "move along," Brown says, "OK. Well, have a good day, OK?"

CRUTCHER: "You have a good day, too."
BROWN: "Thank you, ma'am."[21]

Officer Barnhart, meanwhile, questions the two young men, beginning with the one in the car. Barnhart maintains a casual, almost palsy tone but is unrelentingly persistent.

BARNHART: "How's it going man? Have I ever met you before? [headshake] You stay out here? [headshake] No, you're just visiting?"
SECOND OFFICER: "Hey, what's your first name?"
MAN IN CAR: "What's my first name? Juan."
SECOND OFFICER: "Juan? [nod] Juan Guzman?"
OFFICER BARNHART: "All right. Where you staying at, man?"
JUAN: [unintelligible].

OFFICER BARNHART: "Oh, all right. Up north? [gestures to other young man] How do you know this guy? [unintelligible answer]. How do you know this dude? . . . Okay, Juan. You got a last name?"

JUAN: [unintelligible].

BARNHART: "Huh?"

JUAN: "Martin."

BARNHART: "Martin? Man, I swear I met you before."

JUAN: "You don't know me."

BARNHART: "I was out here yesterday. . . . Oh, yeah, I'm sorry. I was rude. I didn't introduce myself. My name is Barnhart."

A woman who has gotten into the car on the driver's side can be heard saying, "I know. You're here all the time." Barnhart acknowledges he comes through "every once in a while" and moves as if to walk away but turns back and resumes his questioning.

BARNHART: "What's your real name? You know I'm not going to sweat you."

JUAN: "I gave you my name, Juan Martin."

BARNHART: "Martin? That's your real name?"

JUAN: "Juan Martin."

BARNHART: "What's your middle name? You got a middle name?"

After a few more minutes of this, Barnhart again makes as if to leave only to resume his questioning, this time about what the man plans to do the rest of the evening and how long he plans to be at the apartment complex. He also asks about the car's contents.

BARNHART: "I just like talking man. Nothing in here [the car] that shouldn't be? That you know? I know it's not even your car. Nothing—What you got an ankle [monitor] for? Dude [points] what you got an ankle for? What did you do? You got in trouble for that? What did you go in for?"

JUAN: "You probably already know."

BARNHART: "I don't even know who you really are."

JUAN: "I told you. [The second officer] is probably running it right now."

BARNHART: "That's who you really are? You got any ID or anything?"

JUAN: "Yeah, but it's in my shoe."

BARNHART: "You mind getting it for me?"

Barnhart soon wheedled the ID from Martin and turned it over to the officer running checks through the cruiser laptop. Clearly, Barnhart is suspicious about the car and the occupant, but the second officer comes back and says "I thought he was somebody else"—a remark that may explain some of the officers' initial interest. The car has an expired paper tag, though, and that has also raised flags. So does the fact that the vehicle identification number plate on the dashboard is covered by papers.

After about six and a half minutes, Barnhart gives up on Martin and goes around the car to talk to a tall, slender youth who apparently got out from behind the steering wheel as Barnhart's cruiser pulled up. The young man eventually identifies himself as Eddie Townsend.

With Townsend, Barnhart takes a different angle.

BARNHART: "Hey, this your car?"
TOWNSEND: "Nah."
BARNHART: "This is not your car? Whose car is it?"
TOWNSEND: "It's my mama's."
BARNHART: "Why she got the VIN covered up?"
TOWNSEND: "I don't know. Her name is [gives name]. Look it up."
BARNHART: "It looks suspicious, man. A lot of stolen cars, they do that. They cover up the VIN. I'm not saying it is [stolen], I'm saying that's why [it's suspicious]. No big deal, though."

As Barnhart goes back to the car and peers in the rear driver's side window, Crutcher can be seen in the background, apparently speaking into her phone, saying, "This is what we're fighting for, guys. This is why we're at city hall. They're looking at their [car] tag. This is what you call [unintelligible]."

Townsend, meanwhile, wants to know what the officers are looking for.

TOWNSEND: "Can I ask what was wrong for you to approach the car like that?"
BARNHART: "No, we're just talking to you. We talk to a lot of people."
TOWNSEND: "Yeah, but you just be pulling up on people, like not even talking to them, just running up on them."

Barnhart responds by asking Townsend, who to this point has identified himself only as "Eddie," if he has a last name. Townsend gives it to him and says, "You can look me up. I'm clean."

Instead, Barnhart continues to ask Townsend about his name and whether he's related to a person whose name cannot be clearly heard on the video. He seems to be trying to place Townsend among people the officer knows. Barnhart asks if he can check the VIN number; Townsend agrees to move the papers covering it.

While the VIN is being checked, Crutcher tells Townsend he needs to know his rights.

"I don't even know none of them," he says.

Crutcher tells him to be respectful, but that he does not have to consent to searches or to give his identification.

Townsend, who is shirtless, calls to Barnhart: "You see any gang tattoos? You all are the Gang Unit. You see any gang tats? I'm not in a gang. Come on, now, that's my mama's [car]."

A woman, possibly the one in the car, says, "Why do we need all of these police just for a VIN number? Why do we need all of you police?"

Barnhart finally says nothing is coming back on the VIN, which means the car has not been reported stolen, but it also has not had the title or tag updated. Townsend asks again if he should call his mother.

"Naw, it's all good, man," Barnhart replies, then adds. "You got nothing in there you shouldn't have, though, for real?"

"No," says Townsend.

"You telling me the truth?" Barnhart asks one more time.

"Yeah," Townsend says.

The two shake hands, Barnhart thanks Townsend for talking with him, and recommends his mother get the car properly tagged and registered.

"That way she don't get any tickets," Barnhart says. "Or you, if you're driving it."

Corporal Brown, on the other side of the car, tells Townsend the car is likely to be towed if he's stopped by a patrol officer.

With that, all of the officers except Brown get in their cars and drive away. The entire episode spans less than fifteen minutes. No one has been arrested. No one has been ticketed. Was anyone harassed? Intimidated? No, the officers insisted. Yes, said the advocates.

Some residents, interviewed several days later, seemed mostly annoyed, but said they were being singled out for a level of questioning and surveillance other segments of the population would not have experienced or tolerated. One agreed that police tended to approach residents as suspected criminals instead of ordinary citizens. Another said police seemed to assume he was up to something he should not be.

"It feels like when they put on that badge, it's like they're above somebody," he said. "As a citizen, can I get out of my car and approach you to ask what your name is or do you have drugs on you for the hell of it? That is why the police do not get any respect. We don't care about them riding through here. But if there isn't any crime going on, we don't need them here."[22]

On July 10, the day after the incident at Town Square, Crutcher and several others came to a city council meeting to complain about the unit's behavior, which one described as "terrorism."[23]

"Burned in my memory is a police officer looking into . . . the car trying to read a VIN number because they are harassing teenagers about a parked car that they are sitting in where a young man is telling them, 'This is my mom's car. If you have these questions, call her,'" said Gregory Robinson II.[24]

The sort of questioning conducted by Barnhart, no matter how low key, was a form of harassment and intimidation by white law officers against poor, largely powerless Black people, the group said in an open letter issued a few days later.

"These young people were targeted, peppered with questions, and accused of being dishonest simply because they sat in a parked car in a particular neighborhood," they wrote.[25]

In front of the council, Crutcher said Brown, in particular, was "very condescending to me and talked down and said, 'I am not going to get into a debate with you.'" Crutcher later told a reporter that exchange occurred separately from the one partially captured by Brown's bodycam.[26]

Unexpectedly, yet another viewpoint emerged during this meeting when Bynum chimed in to say he, too, was present during the episode, sitting in one of the cruisers and observing while on one of his periodic police ride-alongs.

"I saw everything that happened, and it happened five feet away from me," Bynum said. "And I had a very different take on what I saw than what I have heard about tonight."[27]

Town Square residents did not appear particularly distressed by the unit's visit, Bynum said, and the officers conducted themselves professionally during several interactions with young African Americans that evening. He acknowledged having a different perspective than Town Center residents, but said, "I did not see terrorism last night. I did not see harassment of teenagers. I saw a very different dynamic occur once folks started showing up and telling people in that complex that this is racially biased policing."

Later, as the discussion spilled into the hallway outside the city council chamber, Crutcher told Bynum, "What would you feel if all of these (police) cars came from nowhere and swarmed round one car? Does it take six officers to check a VIN number? . . . That's excessive force. That's what we're talking about."

Bynum, after viewing the police videos, reiterated his earlier statements. JUSTulsa, in its letter, said "Residents reported feeling 'terrorized' by task force officers."[28]

Referring to the first Equality Indicators report, Robinson told a reporter, "For us, this is not about having a gotcha moment. It's not about having an us-vs.-them or getting rid of certain officers. This is about getting to the root cause of why these inequities exist."[29]

Interviewed several days later, Sergeant Brian Hill of the TPD Gang Unit said questioning residents was an aspect of "proactive policing" in high crime areas.

"As far as our mere presence being a harassing-type of deal, then if that's harassment, I'm not quite sure how we go about police work," Hill said. "How in the world are we going to get anything done? How in the world are we going to do any education or prevention if our mere presence is considered a type of activity that people do not like?"[30]

Underlying these faceted interpretations of those fifteen minutes at Town Square Apartments are layers of human emotions, of individual and collective biases born of disparate experiences, of sometimes slippery motives, egos, and perhaps even self-interest. Politics and social justice are ultimately about distribution of power and control. They are about who makes the rules that largely determine who gets what. These are things about which humans have difficulty being objective, and over the coming years claims and counterclaims of exploitation, opportunism, and self-dealing would grow in number and volume.

By mid-2019, Bynum and Crutcher were getting national attention: Bynum as a moderate Republican mayor willing to acknowledge issues of equity, race, and policing; Crutcher as a tireless advocate for social justice and the perspective of Black Americans. The Town Square incident, though, illustrated the deteriorating relationship between Bynum and Crutcher, Robinson, and others who viewed his talk of a fair and just city as just that—talk. Tenuous anyway because of many Black Tulsans' long-standing and understandable distrust of city government, communications soon broke down almost entirely amid accusations of bad faith.[31]

In response to a string of police-involved deaths including Terence Crutcher's, Bynum had promised policing reforms that, by early 2019, included a proposed Office of Independent Monitor (OIM). Modeled after Denver's OIM, it was intended to give citizens more say in use of force policy and discipline. Bynum's proposal immediately ran into opposition from the Fraternal Order of Police (FOP) local, which had endorsed Bynum in his mayoral campaign three years earlier. By the time of the Town Center incident, Bynum's plan was taking fire from all sides, with reformers complaining it did not go far enough and the FOP and law enforcement advocates dead set against it.[32]

Also simmering was the Crutcher family's wrongful death lawsuit against the city, Shelby, Police Chief Chuck Jordan, and Officer Tyler Turnbaugh, who was present when Terence Crutcher was shot. In addition to financial damages, the suit demanded concessions and reforms that, if won, would make it a landmark case. Many of the demands would not or could not be met by the city, while the plaintiffs' side remained adamant.[33]

Even before the Town Square incident, Bynum and Damario Solomon-Simmons, the lead attorney in the Crutcher case, were bickering openly. In early March 2019, Solomon-Simmons, Tiffany Crutcher, and others put together a community meeting on the now year-old Equality Indicators report and specifically the city's low score—twenty out of one hundred—for police use of force. The city had not held public meetings on the report, and some people—not just Solomon-Simmons and Crutcher—questioned the city council's and Bynum's commitment to addressing the issues raised by the report.[34]

Bynum's response: "Whether hearings are serious fact-finding sessions by city councilors or PR stunts by trial lawyers suing the city, we are going to stay focused doing the hard work of making Tulsa a place of equal opportunity for everyone."[35]

The following week, Crutcher came to a city council meeting with a box containing her brother's blood-stained clothes and other effects turned over to the family by Tulsa Police.

"Mayor Bynum," said Crutcher, "you said [the community meeting] was simply a PR stunt. You think my brother being slaughtered by a killer cop is a PR stunt? Do you think my parents coming up here every single week is a PR stunt?"[36]

Later, Bynum told a reporter, "I was not talking about the whole event. I was talking about [Solomon-Simmons'] comments at, before and during, the event."[37]

After the other officers got into their cruisers, turned off their bodycams and drove away that July evening, Corporal Brown remained behind, his camera still rolling. After trying, without much success, to open a conversation with some women to whom he had apparently spoken the previous day, Brown walked around to the back of one of the apartment buildings where he had left his vehicle. There he encountered Nat Wachowski-Estes, who a few minutes earlier had been with Tiffany Crutcher, Kristi Williams, and another woman. Brown stops Wachowski-Estes, asks his name, introduces himself and urges Wachowski-Estes, who is white, to continue distributing JUSTulsa's informational leaflet.

"Like I said," Brown tells Wachowski-Estes, "we come through here at least once or twice a day because we get a ridiculous amount of shootings, robberies, stabbings out here. A lot. Probably one of the most in all of Tulsa."

The two proceed to talk for around ten minutes, with Brown trying to convince Wachowski-Estes that the unit's primary mission is preventing serious crime by taking guns away from people who shouldn't have them.

"We've got numerous guns off certified gangsters, felons quite frequently, actually," Brown says.

> What we do is we go to the parts of Tulsa that have the highest rates of violent crime. Our main goal is to get guns off the streets from people that aren't allowed to have them. Convicted felons, people possessing them while committing other felonies. That's who we get the guns off. . . . If we're taking guns away from people who are shooting people, we're going to lower the number of homicides in Tulsa, we're going to lower the number of people that get shot, and most of them are the innocent victim.

"Look," Wachowski-Estes says, "I get it. And look, I know things get heated, but none of us think every cop is bad or that everything cops do is bad. It's just we talk to a lot of people—I have a lot of friends . . . who get stopped, just traffic stop after traffic stop, no ticket, no warning, just pulled over all the time going home."

Later Wachowski-Estes says these stops have been without any explanation.

Brown is clearly skeptical that "a lot" of people are being pulled over for no apparent reason but encourages JUSTulsa to request dashcam and bodycam video from the stops and to file complaints with internal affairs. Wachowski-Estes says people in North Tulsa fear retaliation if they do that.

"A lot of people report stuff and nothing ever happens or they end up having patrol cars roll by their apartment or their house all the time," he says.

Brown seems to think such things are rare. He invites Wachowski-Estes and Crutcher to accompany the unit on patrol.

In the heart of the conversation, Wachowski-Estes stops Brown's explanations and says, "I'm going to tell you something. I'm not trying to piss you off, but you're talking to me in such a different way than you were talking to Dr. Crutcher. Why?"

Brown, perhaps a little taken aback, replies, "Uhh, Dr. Crutcher came at me pretty irritated or upset. Maybe a little bit. I don't think I, uh—I think she's on Facebook or . . . something and she's sitting there trying to—oh, I don't know what the word is. The way she's talking about us, talking about the way we're harassing people. We're not harassing anybody."

Wachowski-Estes clearly believes Black people are being harassed, although he does not claim to have personally experienced or witnessed it. Brown clearly believes such incidents are exaggerated, or perhaps perceived in the heat of the moment as more confrontational than intended. He rejects the idea that almost daily episodes such as the one that has just occurred fit the definition of harassment or intimidation.

"I promise you," Brown says, "the cops in our department do not want cops out there going rogue, doing stupid things, violating people's rights."

"But there has to be some little give from your point of view," Wachowski-Estes replies. "I get that the way Dr. Crutcher came at you (she) was obviously irritated and upset. But also I get that her brother's dead. No matter how you feel about how that situation went down, he's dead. . . . And that entire moment changed her life completely. And that's true of a lot of people."[38]

Each of the police videos from that evening provided a different view of a single brief interaction; one can only imagine the perspectives of the dozen or more other people present—the two young men, the three women with their children watching from nearby, the children themselves. And this from one fifteen-minute snippet in the life of a city, multiplied by the number of bodycam and dash cam videos, amplified by days of controversy and turmoil. And the worst was yet to come.

3

THE PLAGUE YEAR

The first Tulsan to die was Merle Dry, a 55-year-old Oral Roberts University groundskeeper and Pentecostal pastor. He developed a fever on Sunday, March 15, 2020; by evening he could hardly breathe. His wife, Carrie, acting quickly, drove him to a hospital emergency room. On Monday evening, hospital staff told her she would have to leave Merle's bedside as a precautionary measure. On Tuesday, Merle tested positive for COVID-19. On Wednesday, he died.[1]

"My last image of him was shortly before I left," Carrie Dry, a public school teacher, said. "He was in a full-face oxygen mask and was struggling to breathe. I held his hand, prayed with him and told him I loved him. I never saw him alive again."[2]

Hers would be a tale told many times in the coming years, across the United States and around the world. But in these early days, when so little was known about COVID-19, about how to prevent it and how to treat it, such stories were especially terrifying. A plague unlike any known in most Americans' lifetimes was rolling across the country in silent, unseen waves. At first the epidemic seemed to unite communities, including Tulsa, psychologically and emotionally, even as it drove individuals into personal isolation. Soon, however, it became one more wedge levering the joints of society, politicized and even racialized. In Tulsa, as elsewhere, local officials butted heads with state and federal counterparts, surrounding communities, business owners, and the citizenry on how best to contend with the virus. In many respects, Tulsa was similar to most other cities.

COVID-19 and the fight against it sapped communities' energy, upended social and economic life, and strained resources and relationships. But Tulsa was also unique in at least two respects: the international political and media event that President Donald Trump's June visit became, and the stress of the approaching race massacre centennial.

Word of what would become known as COVID-19 first reached the United States in December 2019, after officials in Wuhan, China, reported several patients with "an atypical pneumonia-like illness that does not respond well to standard treatments." On January 13, 2020, Thailand reported the first case outside of China. On January 20, the Centers for Disease Control and Prevention (CDC) reported the first known cases in the United States, from tests taken two days earlier in the state of Washington. On January 31, as cases multiplied across the globe and were confirmed in Illinois, Arizona, and California, Secretary of Health and Human Services Alex Azar declared a national public health emergency.[3]

COVID-19 seems to have arrived in Tulsa—and Oklahoma—on February 23, brought from Italy by someone identified only as a man in his fifties. He did not become symptomatic until February 29, and confirmation of the virus was not announced until March 6. At the time, some officials naively—or perhaps wishfully—suggested the illness could be contained. The infected man worked from home, which meant fewer contacts outside of his immediate family, all of whom were under quarantine.[4]

"In the United States there's [*sic*] been 14 deaths from COVID-19. That's nationwide, while at the same time there's been 18,000 deaths from the seasonal flu," Gov. Kevin Stitt said at a press conference announcing the state's first positive test. "Here in Oklahoma we have one confirmed case of COVID-19 and zero deaths. In Oklahoma alone we've had fifty-three deaths from the seasonal flu."[5]

Bynum was a little more cautious.

"The most important thing for all of us as Tulsans to do is to focus on what we can control, and that is preventing infection," the mayor said. "Not just for this, but for any other number of respiratory viruses.

"We all should avoid contact with sick individuals. We should wash our hands frequently. If we are sick, we should stay home. Don't try to tough it out and go to work and make everyone else sick."[6]

Even at this early date, the differences in approach to COVID were noticeable.

Stitt, a self-made millionaire who had barely voted, much less held public office until elected governor in 2018, thought like a businessman. Commerce, not public health, came first to mind. Publicly, Stitt minimized the threat posed by the virus.

A week after that first positive test, and three days after being present when an NBA game in Oklahoma City was cancelled because a visiting player tested positive (the entire league suspended play later that night), Stitt tweeted a photo of himself and his family at a crowded Oklahoma City restaurant, with the message "Eating with my kids and all my fellow Oklahomans at the @CollectiveOKC. It's packed tonight! #supportlocal #OklaProud." Ridiculed in the way only the Twitterverse can, the tweet was quickly deleted; the next evening, with positive test results popping up, Stitt declared a state of emergency. Initially, he took several strong steps to contain the spreading contagion. Throughout the pandemic, though, business-as-usual—or at least as much as possible—was the priority.[7]

Coming from a long line of Chamber of Commerce Republicans with multi-generational ties to oil and gas, Bynum was sympathetic to business owners. But he also came from multiple generations of civic involvement and administration. His own career was principally in public policy. On almost every issue, he gave considerable weight to subject matter experts, and this was no different. While Stitt churned through public health officials until he found some who agreed with him, or at least did not disagree publicly, Bynum worked closely with Tulsa County Health Department Executive Director Bruce Dart and the city's hospitals. The same weekend as Stitt's tweet, Bynum followed CDC guidelines and limited gatherings within the city limits to first two hundred fifty and then fifty. On Monday, March 16, the city of Tulsa and Tulsa County declared emergencies, and the next day Bynum ordered bars, restaurants, gyms, and entertainment venues closed by midnight.[8]

"I hate the impact that this will have on our city. . . . But there are no good options in this situation. There are only decisions about which options do the least harm," Bynum said.[9]

Initially, just about everyone, including Stitt, embraced fairly strict containment policies. By the end of April, though, political leadership was ready to declare victory and go back to more or less normal. Despite the warnings of medical professionals, the state activated a three-step phaseout of COVID restrictions, beginning April 24 and ending June 1. Bynum and his friend, Oklahoma City mayor David Holt, soon found themselves increasingly isolated, talking with each other as much as three or four times a day as they tried to keep the contagion from overwhelming their cities' health care systems.[10]

"Tulsa does not exist in a bubble," Bynum said after Stitt ignored White House recommendations and ended most state-mandated prevention measures effective May 1, 2020. "Tulsa's [COVID-19] cases will not go down, they will increase."[11]

At this point local governments could still enact stricter ordinances, but Bynum said it would be pointless.

"I can't ask people who work at a restaurant in Tulsa to remain unemployed while we pursue a fourteen-day decrease when . . . for one hundred miles around us, people can go to work, contract the virus and bring it to our community," he said.[12]

Looking back some time later, Bynum said, "You had different philosophies. That was something I struggled with in the first wave. The governor and I, I think, just had a different approach. I think he was very concerned about the whole long-term impacts on the economy of having people out of work for a prolonged period of time. That's an entirely fair concern to have. I think it caused him to be much more hesitant implementing restrictions than Mayor Holt or I were in our cities."[13]

Bynum was less forgiving of some others.

"As a Republican, I don't understand fellow Republicans . . . encouraging people to use horse [medication] . . . but not listen to hospital personnel who tell you you should wear a mask," he said. "That made no sense to me [to believe] something you see on social media or the internet" instead of people "trained over decades in health care."[14]

Increasingly, though, those were exactly the people to whom some politicians, including President Trump, were appealing during the 2020 election campaigns. When, on June 10, Trump announced he would resume campaign rallies in Tulsa, new COVID-19 cases for the city and state were trending upward; in two days, on June 12, they surpassed the previous one-day highs set in early April. But hospitalizations were down and most of the state's political leadership seemed to believe the worst had past. Bynum did not.[15]

"There was this false sense of 'Okay, we got through this. And then the next wave—omicron—hit and things started getting bad again," Bynum later recalled. "That's when I thought it became more partisan and political in that second wave than it had been in the first."[16]

The mixed messages sent by leadership, the media and sometimes the medical community jaded the public, Bynum said. He told his communications team to figure out who had the most credibility and get them in front of an audience.

"At the national level and the state level and the local level, you didn't have the leaders saying the same things," Bynum said. "You had different people saying different things. And it wasn't, I think, out of any malicious intent. Nobody knew everything about COVID in the beginning. But when citizens are seeing different officials saying different things it causes distrust to develop."

That distrust delayed a mask order for Tulsa, even though by mid-June—just ahead of Trump's rally—Bynum had concluded one was necessary.

"We knew we were going to need to do it but we had to spend like a month building the case with Tulsans as to why we should do it," Bynum said. "We spent about a month in meetings where we had the medical personnel from each of our major health systems get up and talk about why we needed to have people masking up in Tulsa, and the impact this was having and what they were seeing in their emergency rooms."

Through polling and other means, Bynum said, the city concluded "the most-trusted people to talk about these issues weren't elected officials or even Dr. Dart at that point. It was hospital personnel. So they were the ones who made the case before the council and I ultimately adopted our mask ordinance."

But that would not be until July 16, or almost a month after President Trump came to town.[17]

If not for COVID-19, President Trump probably would not have come to Tulsa during the 2020 campaign. Almost certainly, such a visit would not have been the international media event and local flashpoint the rally became.

Little if anything consequential to presidential campaigns had ever happened in Oklahoma. Its middling electoral vote total, now seven but previously as many as eleven, had not been in play since 1976, when Republican incumbent Gerald Ford edged Democrat Jimmy Carter. A Democrat had not carried the state since Lyndon Johnson's 1964 landslide, or even a county since Al Gore in 2000. Trump received almost two-thirds of the vote in 2016 and would get an almost identical percentage in 2020. So, while candidates often visit the state ahead of the early spring presidential primary, nominees for the fall general election do not.[18]

Trump himself had visited Tulsa as a candidate in January 2016. At that time the city was so far off his campaign's radar the event location was spelled "Tusla" on press credentials. As would be the case four years later, predictions of an overflow crowd—on this occasion at the Oral Roberts University (ORU) 11,200-seat Mabee Center—proved overly optimistic. But this one was close. Perhaps as many as ten thousand people were in the building through the course of the lengthy event. About a dozen high school students managed to unfurl a handmade banner reading "Trump Makes America Hate Again" before getting the bum's rush, and Trump ordered a man whose shirt he did not like thrown out, but the event otherwise went off in fairly routine albeit boisterous fashion.[19]

Trump finished a respectable second in the 2016 Oklahoma primary to Texas senator Ted Cruz, who had worked the state harder than Trump. Four years later, after Oklahomans had gotten to know Trump better, they either really liked him or really hated him. Polling by Oklahoma City-based Amber Integrated consistently pegged his approval rating at just under 60 percent through all of 2020, with a disapproval rating of just under 40 percent. That left very few in the undecided category.[20]

On this trip, though, Trump did not have to worry about winning the Oklahoma primary (although he did) or Oklahoma votes. After months of being cooped up by COVID, he needed attention. He needed a crowd. Trump had tried to make do after the pandemic shut down his live rallies by frequenting the White House Press Briefing Room, but that had not worked out well. Once, he suggested injecting disinfectant into the bloodstream to ward off COVID. Another time, he ridiculed a 75-year-old man who police had beaten during a protest in Buffalo. By May, according to ABC News' Jonathan Karl, the president was "desperate" to get back on the road, in front of adoring admirers instead of reporters. To his campaign team, fretting over falling poll numbers, Oklahoma's 60 percent approval rating looked pretty good.[21]

Why Tulsa was chosen for this coming out party is unclear. A spokesman for Governor Stitt said Oklahoma was picked because state leaders had lobbied to move the National Republican Convention there when Charlotte, North Carolina, the planned site, announced COVID restrictions. Karl says Brad Parscale, Trump's campaign manager, pitched at least twelve possibilities including a sort of regatta off Mar-A-Lago, Trump's oceanfront Florida resort. One rumor was that the Trump campaign wanted to go to Oklahoma City, but that Bynum's friend David Holt said no. Holt had made no secret of his distaste for Trump but denied any involvement in the rally. Trump nearly lost Oklahoma County, where most of Oklahoma City is located, in 2016, and would come even closer to losing it in 2020, so that could have been a factor in not going there.[22]

Tulsa, too, was fairly lukewarm on Trump. But in its suburbs and for hundreds of miles in all directions lived millions of his most ardent fans. Somebody seems to have told Trump about the Bank of Oklahoma (BOK) Center, which is annually ranked among the top large performance venues in the country; in announcing the rally, he referred to the arena as a "beautiful new venue, brand new," although it actually had been open for thirteen years. The venue had been dark for months and had cancelled all bookings through the end of the year because of COVID-19, but on June 9 the Trump campaign contacted the arena's management company and the doors were thrown open.[23]

A few days later, Parscale said more than one million tickets had already been requested on-line. Ironically, those tickets came with a disclaimer of liability for COVID-19 contracted at the rally.[24]

Nationally, the press and Trump's political foes played up the rally's racial angles, even after the date was moved back from Juneteenth, as well as the potential for it to become a COVID "super-spreader."

"This rally is really shaping up to be a teeming petri dish inside a wrecking ball inside a juggernaut," the *Los Angeles Times*' Virginia Heffernan wrote, referring to the COVID threat.[25]

In many reports, Trump's decision to reopen his campaign in Tulsa was juxtaposed with the 1921 massacre, the deaths of Terence Crutcher and others killed by local law enforcement, and what was described as Tulsa's racist history.

The *Washington Post*'s Colbert I. King, in a column headlined "The Most Racist President in Modern History Revels in Violence," suggested Trump was going to Tulsa looking for a fight, figuratively and literally. A *Post* story by DeNeen L. Brown was headlined, "Trump Rally in Tulsa, Site of a Race Massacre, on Juneteenth Was 'Almost Blasphemous,' Historian Says." In the *New York Times*, then-Congresswoman Val Demings said, "Tulsa was the site of the worst racist violence in American history. The president's speech there on Juneteenth is a message to every Black American: more of the same."[26]

"This isn't just a win to white supremacists—he's throwing them a welcome home party," said then-US senator Kamala Harris.[27]

Trump, his camp, and more-sympathetic media largely ignored the rally's racial and public health implications. They said the event posed no greater COVID risks than the protests and in some cases riots following George Floyd's death a few weeks earlier, and grimly reported Bynum's decision to declare a precautionary civil emergency in downtown Tulsa as a harbinger of antifa and Black Lives Matter mayhem.[28]

In dismissing the COVID threat, Stitt summarized the attitude of many Oklahomans—and Americans—who took personally the virus' disruption of their lives and the steps taken to contain it.

"That is the thing about our society," Stitt said. "We are a free society. You are free to come to that event. If you are immune compromised in any way, we suggest you wouldn't come. You are free to come. You are free to stay home. But we have to learn how to deal with this."[29]

For many, masks and social distancing, and later vaccinations, were understood as a personal choice to protect oneself rather than to protect others, and as shameful and ultimately futile measures, against fate or God or whatever decided who succumbed to the virus and who did not. If, that is, the virus existed at all.

Stitt never went that far, although he came to insist that COVID was not as dangerous as most medical experts said and that the number of deaths attributed to the virus was greatly inflated.[30]

"We need to continue to be vigilant and continue to take precautions, but we also have to learn how to deal with COVID," Stitt said ahead of the rally. "It is in the United States. It is in Oklahoma. And we can't let it dictate our lives. We have to go about our lives, but we are going to do it with every precaution possible," he said.[31]

By "every precaution," Stitt apparently meant every precaution each individual person chose to take, not every precaution that needed to be taken to protect the most people possible. Bruce Dart, executive director of the Tulsa County Health Department, was not of the same mind. Dart, with more than thirty years in public health administration, warned that Tulsa's trend lines—contrary to the assurances of Stitt, Vice President Mike Pence, and others—were all headed in the wrong direction.[32]

"It's an honor for Tulsa to have a sitting president want to come and visit our community, but not during a pandemic," said Dart. "I'm concerned about our ability to protect anyone who attends a large, indoor event, and I'm also concerned about our ability to ensure the president stays safe as well."[33]

Two days later, at a Tulsa Public Schools board meeting, Dart said, "I'm extremely concerned. . . . I think we have the responsibility to stand up when things are happening that I think are going to be dangerous for our community, which it will be. It hurts my heart to think about the aftermath of what's going to happen."[34]

"I'm a little angry," Dart told the *New York Times*. "It's like seeing the train wreck coming."[35]

Dart was not alone, but neither was everyone on his side. He and Bynum were berated from all sides, both by those who wanted the rally stopped and those who did not. The invective against Dart became such that the police were brought in. A lawsuit to force compliance with "government mandated social distancing protocols, including the required wearing of masks and reducing attendance so that at least six feet separates each rally-goer while in the arena" was turned down by the courts.[36]

"Prayer is our only recourse," said attorney Paul DeMuro.[37]

Bynum met Air Force One at Tulsa International Airport, along with other leading state Republicans, but spent the night with Tulsa police instead of at the rally. Having been elected on a nonpartisan ballot, he said, he did not think it appropriate for him to attend a partisan event. This did not spare him from criticism. In an extreme case, a Virginia man who wanted the rally stopped sent Bynum and his family forty-four email messages and called fourteen times over a twelve-day period.[38]

"Gov. Kevin Stitt and Mayor G. T. Bynum failed in the most important function of government: to protect the health, safety and welfare of the public," said one letter to the *Tulsa World* from a local resident. "The rally for President Donald Trump on June 20 constituted a public health nuisance that could cause many Tulsans to catch the disease and possibly die. . . . I have never seen such weak leadership from our city in its most important duty to protect the public."[39]

Bynum insisted he had little authority in the matter.

"It was presented to me not as, 'Hey, this is your choice,'" Bynum said in a later interview. "It was, 'The president is coming to the BOK Center and they want to confirm we will provide police protection while he's here.'"[40]

Bynum maintained then and has ever since that he did not know Trump was coming until told by ASM Global, which managed the BOK Center and adjacent convention facilities under contract with a city trust authority. That contract gave ASM sole authority to book events into the venues.[41]

Confronted by perturbed members of that trust, ASM Executive Vice President Doug Thornton's story differed from Bynum's. Thornton did not dispute that Bynum learned of the rally from ASM but said the company "immediately contacted the city when the Trump campaign approached [ASM] about holding a rally at the BOK."[42]

"We would never book a show or an event of this magnitude that would have the impact on the public infrastructure outside the facility without advising the police chief, the mayor, those officials," Thornton said.

"We were told at the time by city officials there were no concerns from a public safety standpoint. We were advised to support the event to the greatest extent that the state and the president would allow."

Bynum later said he told ASM officials, "'If you don't feel safe, you are the experts we trust to operate this facility. You are one of the top event management companies in the world, one of the largest. If you don't feel that this can be conducted safely, then you should not do it, and I will have your back.'"[43]

In any event, Bynum said the only way he could have blocked the Trump rally was by declaring a state of emergency, and he did not have sufficient cause to do so. He initially imposed a downtown curfew but dropped it, apparently at Trump's urging.[44]

"There were [initially] a lot of concerns about doing it around Juneteenth," Bynum recalled. "I give Senator Lankford a lot of credit for kind of back-channeling with the White House to help them realize that was not a good idea, which caused them to change the date. After that, then the questions began to come up, 'Why don't you prevent this from happening?'"[45]

Many of those questions were coming "from a lot of the people who had been most helpful for me in advocating the mitigation processes that we had been implementing in the early going of the pandemic," Bynum said.

Bynum said he couldn't justify shutting down the Trump rally, despite the dire warnings of public health professionals. The campaign had agreed to safety protocols (most of which were ignored once the doors opened); furthermore, Bynum had refused to clamp down on George Floyd and anti-Trump protests in the preceding weeks.

> The challenge for me . . . is I had right wing Republicans asking me, "Why aren't you out shutting down all of these Black Lives Matter protests? We [aren't] supposed to have gatherings of people." My answer to that was, we need to allow people to voice their beliefs freely. In a democracy, that's how democracy works. As long as they're peaceably assembling, we shouldn't be preventing them from engaging in political free speech.
>
> And then, immediately, the very people [whose free speech] I'd been protecting . . . were the ones dog-piling me, saying, "You need to prevent Donald Trump from coming to Tulsa and having this deal at the BOK Center." The problem with that was that they were in compliance with every single one of the state's reopening regulations around events. We were in a moment when hospitalizations were at record lows for the pandemic, so there wasn't a justification for preventing it.[46]

The entire city seemed to be on edge in the days leading up to the rally. Aside from the fear and anger surrounding COVID-19 itself, the pandemic had created economic and social uncertainty. Stuck at home with little to do except fret about their own personal safety and financial futures, Tulsans had more time than ever to watch cable news and dive into internet rabbit holes. Civil disorder in cities across America, especially in the wake of George Floyd's death, deepened divisions and intensified emotions. On Greenwood Avenue, monuments and landmarks were covered to prevent Trump or Vice President Mike Pence from using them for photo ops. Sheets of plywood covering downtown windows were turned into murals by a dozen artists.[47]

Some of the tension in Tulsa was mitigated by the Trump campaign's decision to push back the rally a day to avoid Juneteenth. This seems to have been at least partly the result of Lankford's intercession, at Black Tulsans' urgent request, although bad press may have also been a factor. Lankford also acted as intermediary in convincing all concerned that Stitt's tone-deaf invitation for Trump to tour Greenwood was disaster in the making. Both situations, though, illustrated just how little Oklahoma's political leadership or the White House understood about Black America. Many Black Tulsans were convinced Trump intentionally chose Tulsa as the place and June 19 as the date of his rally to humiliate and provoke them. They viewed Bynum's refusal to stop it as another betrayal. [48]

"I do think that all of it was intentional in terms of selecting Juneteenth . . . during the centennial year" of the race massacre, said Quraysh Ali Lansana, a journalist, poet, scholar, and educator. "He chose Oklahoma because it was 'friendly confines' for him. So it did not help the [Black] community feel any better about the state of Oklahoma. It did not help the community feel anything better about the mayor of Tulsa. It further fractured the community, and it was a very, very tense and intense few days."[49]

Instead of direct confrontation with Trump and his supporters, alternative events were organized. This included a hastily assembled Juneteenth celebration along Greenwood Avenue, less than a mile from the BOK Center, with the Reverend Al Sharpton as featured speaker. Attendees arrived Friday morning to find the Black Lives Matter message stenciled on the street and something of a carnival atmosphere that lasted far beyond the scheduled close Friday night and into the next day and night, long after Trump had come and gone.[50]

In a Friday tweet, Trump sounded almost hopeful someone would start something, saying, "Any protesters, anarchists, agitators, looters or lowlifes who are going to Oklahoma please understand, you will not be treated like you have been in New York, Seattle, or Minneapolis. It will be a much different scene!'" But Black Tulsans and like-minded friends had accepted Trump coming to Tulsa as long as he did not come to the part of Tulsa they held most dear, or violate a holiday observed by the city's African American population at least as far back as 1905.[51]

"By and large, most of the Black community just wanted to be in Greenwood and be left alone," said Lansana.[52]

Trump supporters did not seem that keen on a fight either. Gathering downtown days ahead of the rally, they set up booths and roamed the streets in a festive mood. Arguments developed on the day of the rally, prompting police to separate the Trump and anti-Trump elements, but no serious violence occurred.[53]

Tulsa World reporter Michael Overall compared the scene a few blocks from the BOK Center to a popular annual street fair:

> A grown man walked past wearing an American flag onesie. A street preacher dragged a wooden cross down Boulder Avenue. And thousands of Make America Great Again hats flooded the streets of downtown Tulsa.
>
> For several blocks near the arena, the early afternoon atmosphere seemed like a surreal alternative Mayfest, complete with food vendors and street performers but where every booth sold Trump gear.
>
> "We just wanted to come hang out and show our patriotism and show our support for the country and for the president," said [one woman], decked out in red, white and blue. "We're having a great time just being around like-minded people."
>
> Not everyone was like-minded, however.
>
> Half a block [away], a shouting match broke out between Trump supporters and two women holding their fists in the air and chanting "Black lives matter." A crowd quickly swelled around them, the chants growing louder from both sides.
>
> "Stop spreading hate," one of the women shouted.
>
> "Nobody here hates you," responded a man with a Trump flag wrapped around his shoulders like a superhero cape. "We love you, and Donald Trump loves you."
>
> The chants only kept getting louder from both sides, with the crowd growing large enough to block Boulder Avenue until Tulsa police separated them: Black Lives Matter on one sidewalk, Trump supporters on the other, shouting across the street from each other.
>
> Dirk Baker blamed Trump for dividing the city so close to the centennial of the Tulsa Race Massacre.

"It was the worst decision he ever made to come here," Baker said. "This isn't the right time. Tulsa is very emotional right now. We're very emotional right now over what happened in 1921. It's not the time for Trump to come here."

Urged by the street preacher with the wooden cross, Baker paused to hold hands and pray with a Trump supporter. But the shouting continued around them.

Cheyenne Roberts stood nearby, quietly holding an American flag and two rainbow placards.

"Make the United States united again," one said.[54]

Bynum realized the predicted hordes were not descending on his city after all while driving toward downtown with Police Chief Wendell Franklin. It was the afternoon of June 20, and the freeways were almost empty.

"We were prepared." Bynum recalled. "They were saying we were going to have 100,000 people at this rally and the stuff outside. We were prepared from a law enforcement standpoint for that to be the case."[55]

Law enforcement had been brought in from throughout the region. The National Guard was on alert. Bynum says he "spent the whole day with Chief Franklin and the TPD leadership" at a command post.

"We came into downtown to kind of check everything out midday," he said. "I remember driving on the highway into downtown Tulsa . . . and there was like one pickup with a Trump flag on the highway and nobody else. I turned to Chief and I was like, 'Chief, I've driven into Norman [University of Oklahoma] and Stillwater [Oklahoma State University] on game day. This does not feel like game day traffic.' He said, 'I was thinking the same thing.'"

By late afternoon, the outdoor stage around which the expected overflow crowd was to assemble had been shut down and would soon be taken apart. Campaign workers inside the BOK Center were pulling off stickers affixed to seats that instructed people to maintain social distancing. According to Jonathan Karl, Parscale informed Trump, still aboard Air Force One, that the inside of the arena "looks like Beirut in the eighties."[56]

The fire marshal said 6,200 tickets were collected. People familiar with the 19,000-seat arena thought 10,000 people might have been inside, which would have been on par with Trump's 2016 appearance. Fox News, which broadcast the rally, logged its best Saturday prime time ratings ever with a total audience of 7.6 million, and the campaign claimed four million watched its livestream of the event. But there was no denying Tulsa had been a massive disappointment to Trump and his team. It had spent $2.2 million for a half-empty arena that more than anything gave hope to Trump's opponents. Bynum later observed the rally was not even the largest indoor event in Tulsa that Saturday; a home and garden show at the fairgrounds drew far more people, he said.[57]

Trump's campaign first tried to blame the turnout on "radical protesters" it said kept supporters out of the rally, but that notion was quickly shot down. About a half-dozen arrests were made in the vicinity of the arena in the hours before the rally, and only two of those seem to have been inside the block-wide security perimeter set up around the arena. One was a 74-year-old freelance photographer who told police he was sympathetic to Black Lives Matter; the other was a 62-year-old art teacher wearing an "I can't breathe" t-shirt who refused to leave the secure area when officers told her to do so, even though she had a ticket to the event. Police later confirmed the order to remove the teacher, Sheila Buck, came from the Trump organization, which prompted questions about why police were taking orders from a political campaign.[58]

Trump's team and supporters also blamed the media for scaring people away with their reporting on the COVID-19 threat and the possibility of violence. Here they may have had a point. Combined with the campaign's own boasting about a large turnout, some people may have concluded the possibility of being one of the 19,000 to actually get in the arena was not worth the hassle, not to mention risk, and watched from home instead.[59]

"It turned out that Donald Trump supporters were pretty much like most other people," Bynum said later. "They wanted to let somebody else try it out first.

"When we were walking around out there, these were not the orcs they were being made out to be by the media," he said. "These were largely good old boys and gals who were happy to be out of their house but were still being pretty cautious. . . . Even the president's supporters, they were happy to let somebody else try it out first rather than risking it themselves."[60]

Bynum said not opposing the rally was a factor, too.

"My belief is that if I had tried to prevent [the rally] without proper grounds for doing so, the president's supporters would have thought they needed to turn out in droves to stick up for their guy," Bynum said. "Because we . . . allowed them to exercise the same free speech rights we [allowed] the other end of the political spectrum the [previous] few weeks, they didn't feel like they had to turn out for their guy."[61]

Bob Jack, then the Tulsa County GOP party chair, said many local Republicans were frightened away—but he also thought organizers erred by not making tickets more easily available to local party members.

"It was all screwed up," Jack said later. "We were getting calls at the party about tickets and we could never get anybody to respond to us from the Trump organization. Even from the state [party], we couldn't get good responses."[62]

Jack believed there was something to the notion that people with no intention of attending the rally jammed up the online ticket system with thousands (or hundreds of thousands) of bogus orders while discouraging people who would have actually gone.[63]

"We were never contacted," Jack said. "We never were called. Matter of fact, I had to beg to get tickets, me as the chairman of the party. [I obtained] tickets through the . . . state chairman. He weaseled two tickets for me.

"The ticket deal was a complete debacle. Just a complete debacle."[64]

Even without the pandemic, G. T. Bynum likely would have had an opponent for reelection in 2020. Tulsa mayors always have reelection opponents. But COVID-19 added another subplot—especially after Bynum signed into law on July 16 an ordinance mandating distancing and face masks in most public settings within the city.[65]

"My approval dropped twenty points the moment I signed that," Bynum said. "I had been steady at 72 to 75 percent, and then I signed the mask order and it dropped to 52 percent."[66]

The August 25 municipal elections, in which Bynum had seven opponents and seven of the nine city council seats were on the nonpartisan ballot, were just forty days away. Bynum was still the favorite, but he needed a majority in the first round to avoid a runoff. In a runoff, anything was possible.

Bynum's chief rival was Greg Robinson, the 30-year-old African American who had joined with Tiffany Crutcher, Kristi Williams, and others pressuring Bynum for policing reforms and a commitment for race massacre reparations. At the other end of the political spectrum, a 37-year-old firebrand named Ken Reddick appeared unlikely to win but capable of siphoning off enough conservative votes to deny Bynum the majority the city's charter required.

The June 8–10 filing period followed the first months of COVID uncertainty and fear, the accompanying economic upheaval, and national and local civil unrest related to police use of force; it coincided with the announcement of the

Trump rally and a Bynum misstep on national TV. In a June 7 appearance on CBS' *Sunday Morning*, Bynum said he believed Terence Crutcher's death was "more about the really insidious nature of drug utilization than it is about race." The comment went over like the proverbial lead balloon.[67]

"When your friends start calling you and repeatedly use the phrase, 'I know your heart,' it is a good indicator you've screwed up," Bynum posted a few days later on Facebook. A recent rapport with his most vocal critics was shattered. Tiffany Crutcher told writer Victor Luckerson that Bynum's remark was one of the most disheartening moments in her crusade to change policing.[68]

And it got worse. The day after Bynum's CBS interview, TPD Major Travis Yates remarked on a local conservative radio talk show that "all the research on this says . . . we're shooting African-Americans about 24% less than we probably ought to be based on the crimes being committed."[69]

There was more to Robinson's entry into the race than just those two incidents, of course. His father, also named Greg Robinson, was a vocal and sometimes controversial community leader and local government critic. "I believe people have lost control of government, and it needs to be put back in their hands," the elder Robinson told the *Tulsa World* in 2002, not long before his death from a heart attack at age forty-eight. The younger Robinson had worked in Democrat Kathy Taylor's 2012 mayoral campaign and in Hillary Clinton's presidential bid four years later. In 2020, he was using the skills and knowledge he had acquired in those jobs to organize Black Tulsans behind a theme very similar to the one his father voiced nearly two decades earlier. He and his allies accused Bynum of talking a good game on race and equity but not actually doing much. Rev. Robert Turner of Vernon AME Church told Bynum "you have shown yourself to be just another White man in power" after Bynum complained about Turner leading marchers to the mayor's house over the weekend of May 30–31.[70]

By this time, Turner had spent every Wednesday late afternoon for more than a year and a half in front of Tulsa's city hall, holding a Bible and arguing through a bullhorn for reparations to descendants of those affected by the 1921 Race Massacre. Reparations had been an issue since at least the 1990s and had even been proposed—some would argue promised—by white civic leaders in 1921. As a way of rectifying the obvious discrepancies highlighted by the Equality Indicators, Bynum said he favored greater economic opportunities and quality of life for Black Tulsans but opposed individual payments for Race Massacre families. This was one bone of contention between the mayor (and just about all white politicians) and at least some of those Bynum called "the activists."[71]

Another immediate point of conflict was the police department's participation in a cable network program called "Live PD." The program consisted of several studio moderators, including TPD Sergeant Sean "Sticks" Larkin, commenting on video feeds from several law enforcement agencies, including Tulsa police. Opponents said the program exploited people "on their worst day." Many of those shown interacting with officers were impaired; others just happened to be in the wrong place at the wrong time. Some observers thought "Live PD" was simply bad publicity for the city. Bynum, perhaps prodded by police, maintained just the opposite, saying it allowed Tulsans to see the challenges law officers face.[72]

So, as in many cities, the pot was already bubbling when George Floyd died at the hands of Minneapolis police on May 25, only a few days before the ninety-ninth anniversary of the race massacre.

"I've spent the better part of my life in the civil rights movement," said Rev. Warren Blakney, a long-time Tulsa pastor, during a press conference held by several Black Tulsans after Floyd's death. "And I've seen violence over and over again. But watching [the Floyd video] has probably moved me more than anything I've seen in the last 20 years."[73]

On May 30, a Saturday, Tiffany Crutcher, Robinson, and Turner led a multiracial group estimated at about one thousand through the business district of Brookside, a popular south Tulsa neighborhood on the east side of the Arkansas River, obstructing traffic and trying to get the attention of Tulsans "out to brunch," as Turner put it. Eventually they blocked Interstate 44, the main freeway through the city, where one of the protesters was injured by an automobile.[74]

"Before COVID-19, America's virus was racism," Turner told the demonstrators at one point. "We are sick and tired of this disease. We demand a vaccine. Social distancing can't kill racism. A face mask can't kill racism. Nothing but the truth can cure it."[75]

Leaving the highway, the protesters headed toward Bynum's house about two miles away. According to Bynum, TPD had just ended more than a month of around-the-clock guard duty at his home, the result of threats arising from, as he put it, keeping bars closed on St. Patrick's Day because of COVID-19. Now the police were back to hustle Bynum and his family away before the marchers, with an entirely different set of grievances, arrived. He would later describe that Saturday, "when my family got run out of our house," as one of the worst days of the worst summer of his life. The Bynums would soon sell the house and move to a less-known location. If anyone found irony in a Tulsa mayor fleeing his home the way Greenwood residents had fled theirs almost a century before, no one mentioned it.[76]

While ostensibly about the killing of George Floyd and policing reform in general, the protest's real target was Bynum. Organizers made this clear at the top.

"We're not out here just marching for no reason," Robinson said. "We're not out here because we just woke up mad today. We've been mad. We've been going to city hall. Everybody loves you, Mayor Bynum, because you talk good. But your actions don't match your talk."[77]

Tiffany Crutcher asked the crowd to "just scream at the top of your lungs and let Terence know that you still care, that you haven't forgotten."[78]

But they also wanted Bynum to hear. The protesters called upon him to settle the Crutcher family's lawsuit against the city; a week later, in discussing the protest, Tiffany Crutcher said, "I hope that Mayor Bynum acknowledges that Terence's civil rights were violated and that my family can get some closure in this matter as it relates to making sure Terence's kids are taken care of."[79]

But Bynum was unlikely to acknowledge anything given the pending lawsuit. And he viewed the march on his residence, for what he considered personal gain, a breach of trust. In a long Facebook post that evening, Bynum wrote:

> I respect the Tulsans who used their time today to show other Tulsans that they care for the lives of their neighbors—that they want this to be a better city and that every life is sacred.
>
> I want to thank the men and women of the Tulsa Police Department who worked throughout the day to keep the protesters safe as they voiced their beliefs.
>
> I've been asked if I will meet with activists to discuss their aspirations for our city. My answer: Of course.
>
> I've tried throughout my time in public service to keep an open door and engage a broad range of viewpoints in order to make the best decisions possible. I've met many times with the leaders of today's protest, and remain eager to work with any Tulsan who wants to build a better city for the next generation.
>
> What I will not do: Agree to a list of demands because people block streets, shut down highways, or come to my family's home. Change occurs in Tulsa through collaboration, deliberation and thoughtful action—not through attempts at intimidation.[80]

Turner quickly responded.

> Tulsa thought we had a leader in you. Instead, you have shown yourself to be just another White man in power who characterizes the peaceful actions of African Americans as intimidating. That is how our people die while jogging. That is how our people die while eating ice cream on their couch. That is how our people die while sleeping in their own bed. Being Black is not a crime. The color of our skin should not be equated with aggression, anger, or intimidation. Shame on you, Mayor Bynum.[81]

The next day, May 31, a crowd numbering in the thousands gathered for what was billed as a Black Lives Matter march beginning in an open space adjoining Vernon AME on North Greenwood Avenue. Except for its basement, Vernon had been destroyed in the 1921 race massacre and rebuilt in the same spot. When Interstate 244, also known as the inner dispersal loop or IDL, was built around downtown Tulsa in the 1960s and 1970s, it passed close enough for traffic to rattle the stained-glass windows of both Vernon and another historic Black church, Mt. Zion Baptist, two blocks away. Captured on film, the fiery destruction of Mt. Zion—brand new in 1921 and said to be "the finest church for colored people in the state"—proved an everlasting image of the massacre's wantonness and horror. Like Vernon, Mt. Zion had rebuilt slowly and painfully over decades, and refused to move despite the dislocations of time, modern highways, and urban renewal. On this day, as people of many ethnicities gathered in Greenwood to remember past racial atrocities and protest present inequities, the two old churches stood silent watch over a neighborhood no longer recognizable from a century before. The houses and small businesses that replaced those destroyed in 1921 had themselves disappeared. For decades much of the old Greenwood laid fallow, a wasteland of empty buildings and vacant lots. By 2020 it was again coming to life, although not in a way that suited those who saw what was happening as just another way to transfer what had been Black Tulsa to non-Blacks. Across the highway from Vernon and Mt. Zion, new buildings were going up and old ones were being refurbished. A baseball stadium had been shoehorned into what had once been a Black neighborhood adjoining Greenwood Avenue. Directly south of Mt. Zion, on the other side of I-244, sat John Hope Franklin Park, created in response to the work of the race massacre commission two decades earlier, with meticulous landscaping and signature sculptures by African American artist Ed Dwight.[82]

It was to this park the protesters were headed late on the afternoon of May 31. The original plan was for them to go there from Vernon AME, a distance of a quarter mile, by crossing under the inner dispersal loop; somehow, though, they wound up *on* the highway instead of under it as Oklahoma Highway Patrol troopers and Tulsa police scrambled to stop traffic. A least two vehicles got caught up in the milling protesters. One, a car, was let through after the driver convinced the people surrounding her that she had an emergency. A pickup truck pulling a long horse trailer then began forcing its way through after the car; when two or three protesters began banging on the hood, the driver held up a gun and placed it on the dashboard. Someone lit what appeared to be a flare but that, through retelling, was soon dubiously described as an attempt to set the trailer on fire. In the confusion, a protester toppled from an overpass, suffered a broken neck, and was paralyzed. The pickup driver was briefly detained by officers of the Oklahoma Highway Patrol at the scene but was then waved on as angry protesters approached. No one was cited but the incident became the justification for a new state law granting motorists immunity for driving over people blocking a street or highway.[83]

After leaving the highway, the protesters marched to the Tulsa County jail, less than a mile away on Denver Avenue, then south to Riverside Drive, which runs along the east bank of the Arkansas River, and from there back to Brookside. Until this point, the protests had been mostly contained and law enforcement had kept its distance except for traffic control. That changed as evening descended and a crowd gathered on South Peoria Avenue between 36th and 38th Streets refused to disperse.[84]

South Peoria is Brookside's main thoroughfare, with the stretch from 32nd to 38th featuring the most popular boutiques, eateries, and shops. These include not only such national brands as Trader Joe's, Urban Outfitters, and Lululemon, but local favorites such as an old dry cleaners converted to a sushi restaurant and an eccentric gift shop called Ida Red's. Shortly after 9:30 p.m., police told the crowd to disperse within the hour or face arrest; some in the crowd responded by throwing water bottles and other objects at officers. According to police and a television reporter, members of the crowd hurled paving bricks from a center median at cars. Police twice answered with tear gas and pepper balls. A bank and several businesses were vandalized and broken into.[85]

Following a pattern seen in other cities, the protests had now taken on a different character, apparently under different leadership. The original organizers, and perhaps many of the original participants, seemed to be no longer present.[86]

"Are people really out here to riot or are they out here to support Black lives?" said one man as he came out of a Brookside restaurant. He and his companion, he said, had been among the earlier Black Lives Matter marchers.

"Are they out here to cause destruction or are they here for the cause?" asked the second man.[87]

By about 11:30 p.m., the remaining protesters had moved more than a mile south, to the parking lot of a shopping center at the intersection of Peoria Avenue and Interstate 44, where Turners' group had blocked highway traffic the previous day. Law enforcement closed the interstate, but, except for some plainclothes officers, kept its distance. This arm's-length approach frustrated some protesters who wanted a confrontation with police. Now they forced one. Windows of a pawn shop and a consignment furniture store were smashed, with damage to the latter estimated at $10,000. Police again moved in with tear gas and pepper balls, and this time the crowd did break up.[88]

Turner, Crutcher, and state representative Regina Goodwin all denounced the violence, and in some cases questioned the motives behind it.

"They've been doing it ever since Martin Luther King's marches," Goodwin said. "They infiltrated those marches and destroyed property. If you're going to stand with us, stand correctly. Because we want to keep moving on."[89]

Police Chief Wendell Franklin blamed the vandalism, which he said included the destruction of a highway patrol vehicle, on "rogue groups," and said the original BLM organizers had worked with police to avoid serious conflict.

"It was some individuals who wanted to take advantage of what was taking place—a peaceful protest—and be a part of destruction and chaos," said Franklin, only a few months into his job as Tulsa's first Black police chief.[90]

On Monday—the 99th anniversary of the destruction of Greenwood—Bynum, Franklin, Crutcher, Robinson, City Councilor Vanessa Hall-Harper, about three dozen policing reform advocates, and Franklin's senior staff emerged from a three-hour meeting to announce they had reached an agreement on several issues. Tulsa would end its participation in Live PD (which was soon cancelled, anyway), Bynum would continue to pursue creation of an office of independent monitor based on the one in Denver, Franklin would institute certain internal police department reforms, and Bynum promised to meet with the Crutcher family.[91]

Franklin said he would work with Tiffany Crutcher and a few others on policy and discipline, including use of force, but indicated he was already taking internal steps to address the issues.[92]

"I want to just pause for a moment and honor the lives lost," Tiffany Crutcher said. "I mean, we are standing here on the day the smoke cleared, and today the smoke has cleared. . . . I really don't know what to say. I am quite emotional."[93]

Franklin, who had been promoted to TPD's top leadership position a few months earlier, after twenty-three years on the force, chafed under the conditions of an FOP contract and civil service protections that prevented the chief from directly firing officers. At the press conference announcing the agreement, he noted Tulsa officers could not be immediately dismissed as those involved in George Floyd's death had been.[94]

"For us in Tulsa, we would suspend that officer with pay," Franklin said. "I would love for us to work on some other avenue, because I think that if that were to happen here and that we announced that we suspended a person and they were being paid, then it just continues to fester. That continues to draw undue scrutiny of the Police Department."[95]

Franklin expanded on that a few days later, telling a reporter, "From my perspective, I'd like to have more flexibility to act more swiftly."[96]

But that did not happen, and neither did the office of independent monitor. Two of Bynum's OIM proposals had already been shot down in a crossfire between the police union and the reformers, including Hall-Harper, who said it did not go far enough. Now Bynum's "Denver model" would be dead before the summer was out. Bynum blamed Hall-Harper and the reform advocates for refusing to meet with the FOP; they accused Bynum of hiding behind the police union.[97]

"If he is serious . . . about having an OIM, he can do that right now," said Hall-Harper, whose husband Marcus Harper was a TPD officer who had been in some hot water with the department and possibly the FOP. "He can also move ahead with addressing those issues that must be addressed in the collective bargaining process."[98]

Meanwhile, the FOP President, Jerad Lindsey, boasted in a podcast about how the union mobilized public opinion on the issue to "flip the vote" on the city council.[99]

Thus, the optimism of June 1 evaporated like a summer morning mist. Three days later, on June 4, white members of TPD's Organized Gang Unit handcuffed two black teens and arrested one of them after the pair was stopped for jaywalking on a deserted North Tulsa street. Two days after that, a white former Tulsa County jailer working as a motel security guard pepper-sprayed, then shot and killed the brother of a Black TPD officer. Then came Bynum's CBS interview, and the day after that Yates' declaration that, statistically, Tulsa police were not shooting as many Black suspects as they "probably ought to." Also that day, protesters marched the short distance from Greenwood to City Hall in support of police reform.[100]

"Coming together sounds cool," Greg Robinson told the crowd at the courthouse. "Unity sounds good. You know what sounds better? Justice. What sounds better than a false peace is justice."[101]

Two days later, on June 10, Robinson filed for mayor.[102]

Changing Tulsa's form of municipal government in the early 1990s led to more diverse representation but also lessened the chances of a Black person winning citywide office, in large part because it reduced the number of elected citywide offices from six to two—mayor and auditor. One is the city's most high-profile elected office, the other its most obscure. There is no intermediate step for norm-defying candidates to introduce themselves to voters citywide. The only African American ever elected citywide in Tulsa was Ron Young, a Republican who in 1979 was appointed finance commissioner in the old system and then won in his own right in 1980 and 1982. Although virtually unknown to the public when appointed, Young became popular enough that some thought he might become mayor. That possibility ended in 1983, when Young abruptly resigned and ultimately left town after admitting he had made several thousand dollars' worth of personal calls from his office telephone. It was not the biggest scandal ever to hit Tulsa city government by any stretch, but it was enough to end the promising career of a Black man.[103]

That history did not bode well for Greg Robinson and he knew it. As he tells it, he did not even want to run for mayor in 2020. But he strongly believed someone from his political side of the street should and he could not find anyone else who would. Everyone he and Tiffany Crutcher approached, including state representative Monroe Nichols, said no.

"I looked, begged, and pleaded, I will say with older, more mature, more seasoned politicians," Robinson recalled later. "They felt like it wasn't their time for whatever [reasons]. And in the 11th hour, no exaggeration, it was around midnight [the last day before filing] when essentially we had gotten off the phone with the last politician, who goes 'No, I'm not going to do it,'" he said.

"At that point, I was asked by a group of—my mentors, really—if I would be willing to run. . . . And so that's where that came from. I wish that there was a more planned-out reasoning and rationale, but the reality was, you know, there wasn't. I ran because I felt like somebody needed to run."[104]

Robinson was actually the third Black candidate in the mayoral race, which in itself was noteworthy. Ty Walker, a Republican, owned a restaurant in the one hundred block of North Greenwood; Democrat Ricco Wright had an art gallery a few doors down from Walker's establishment. Walker, who had previously run for city council from a South Tulsa district, seemed unlikely to get enough Black Democrat votes or draw enough GOP votes away from Bynum to be a threat. Wright lacked Robinson's political experience and public speaking skills and dropped out after being accused of sexual assault.[105]

If, as Bynum said, his COVID shutdown order cost him twenty percentage points, the most likely beneficiary would seem to have been Ken Reddick, a favorite of antiestablishment Republicans and a vocal opponent of pandemic precautions. But it was Robinson who immediately emerged as Bynum's most troublesome opponent.[106]

"We have a mayor right now who has spoken well about issues of racial justice but has not acted on it," Robinson told *Mother Jones*. "This is a mayor who has called reparations divisive. This is a mayor who has said Terence Crutcher's death was not due to racial bias, but due to his inability to control his drug addiction. This is the mayor who got a large percentage of African American votes, and yet has not done right by African Americans in the city of Tulsa."[107]

"To say racism is the city's No. 1 issue and then to say there is no racially biased policing doesn't make sense," Robinson told the local press after filing. "We're sick and tired of [the city] acting as if racism doesn't exist. If that scares some people, I certainly understand. But these things need to be addressed. We don't want to force anything down people's throat; we want to build consensus."[108]

Democracy requires consensus, or at least acquiescence, from those governed. That may be better than the alternative, but majority rule can be a form of tyranny all its own if not exercised with a sense of fairness. It is that sense of fairness to which Robinson, Crutcher, Turner, and many before them have for decades appealed in regard to the race massacre specifically and social justice in general. A century ago, the race massacre became a symbol of a majority run amok. By 2020, Terence Crutcher's death, largely through his twin sister's efforts, became another example of the never-ending struggle between those who are in charge and those who are not. Although this struggle is often portrayed as a racial one, race in America is almost wholly a political and economic construct, originally invented by people in power to justify exploitation of those who are not.

"We still don't have justice in Tulsa," Robinson said in the *Mother Jones* interview. "We don't have reparations for the victims. We don't have anyone brought to justice. Right now we are trying to have a conversation about it. But what we have to do as a city is push beyond and understand that just having a conversation is not going to be enough. As long as Greenwood is not owned by the descendants of the race massacre, we still have not received justice. There's buildings popping up, developments being made—they are not owned by the descendants. How can you take land, kill people and then those people don't have land anymore? And then they are supposed to be looking at you building wealth on it and . . . be okay with that?"

The transfer of what might be called "old" or "original" Greenwood from mostly Black owners to others occurred over decades and completely within the law—which in some ways is precisely the point Robinson and others have argued for many years. In their view, laws are too often written with favor, not fairness, as the guiding principle. The system thus created pressures or even forces some landowners—in this case, the Black property owners of Greenwood—to sell at distressed prices for the benefit of others. Things do not always work out that way, and the payoff can be generations away, but the bottom line is that property that mostly belonged to Black people well into the 1960s no longer does.

Policing reform got a lot of attention in Greg Robinson's 2020 mayoral campaign because it was the topic of the moment. In reality, he was in the race to promote a much broader social justice agenda that included reparations and targeted some of the persistent inequities documented in the annual reports so often cited by Bynum. Broadly, their stated goals were much the same. Robinson, with little to lose by doing so, advocated a much more direct and immediate approach that reflected Black Tulsans'—and Black Americans'—frustration at always being told to be patient, that change is hard, that it takes time. But Robinson also hoped to appeal to whites and others with similar complaints who, he said, should be united by their circumstances, not divided by race.[109]

"Oklahoma is a state where, frankly, you have a ruling class politically [whose] policies are not in the best interest of poor people, white, black, brown or whatever," Robinson said.[110]

Days before the election, he said it was up to the mayor to sometimes go against the prevailing powers that be.

"The mayor's job, as the leader of our city, is to make decisions that protect the safety and prosperity of Tulsans regardless of the political blowback," Robinson said. "I am not concerned about reelection; I am not concerned about the political blowback that I get."[111]

Bynum, though, said, "Greg wants it to be a fight where his side wins and the other side loses, and I don't think that that is a sustainable way to grow a city or to bring people together and build the kind of Tulsa we want it to be."[112]

In Bynum's view, things like individual reparations and some of the policing reforms could not be implemented from the top down without acceptance from the community as a whole, or at least a large majority of it. As a practical matter, that may be true, but from the perspective of Robinson and his followers, that also means doing nothing, or doing it at a glacially slow pace. Outlawing slavery in American took more than two hundred years, and another hundred to begin addressing oppression and exploitation that fell just short of forced servitude. Another sixty years on, the United States still struggles with racial, social, and economic inequities.

"If you think about the differences between molding consensus and searching for consensus, I think most of our politicians . . . search for consensus," Robinson said in 2022. "I think we hide behind consensus. 'This is what my, my constituents want.' . . . You can be informed by constituents. Absolutely. You should be. Your actions should always be informed by constituents. But if we go by that token, the majority of constituents are white. So every time I hear that, as a Black man I hear, 'Well, this is what the white people wanted.'"[113]

No polling data exists on the racial breakdown of voting in Tulsa's 2020 mayoral race, but it seems fair to say that a majority of white people wanted Bynum. In the final count, he received 52 percent and avoided a runoff against Robinson, who came in second at 29 percent. Reddick, the far-right candidate, finished with 14 percent.

In a way, the election was a victory for both Bynum and Robinson. Bynum got another term, and Robinson got a platform.

"As a mayor I've governed as a non-partisan centrist," Bynum reflected. "The most gratifying thing about winning and winning by the largest re-election percentage [margin] a mayor has had in three decades—even in a summer when pretty much everything that could go wrong did go wrong—is that the center held in that majority. The extremes get a lot of attention, and they make a lot of noise, but they don't represent a majority of the people."[114]

Robinson might argue that it is the pressure and persistence from outside the center that forces reexamination of the status quo and, ultimately, change.

"I think that we grow through discomfort," he said. "The reality is that we like to talk about being in the center and in the middle, but frankly, the center . . . can be just a very convenient place to hide from progress."[115]

In retrospect, Robinson questions whether he was ready, at age thirty, to take charge of the city. But as a Black candidate with a strong message on race, he is proud to have gotten 29 percent of the vote in a city that's about 15 percent African American.

"With a sixty-day campaign we got almost thirty percent of the vote. During a pandemic," Robinson said. "The city of Tulsa is not 30 percent Black people—and certainly not 30 percent of the people voting are Black." [116]

With everyone watching Bynum and Robinson, few noticed at least two other salient points. One was the turnout: more than 65 percent of the city's registered voters did not cast a ballot, despite a year of almost unprecedented turmoil. The other was how poorly the conservative candidate Reddick fared under circumstances that could hardly have been more favorable for an antiestablishment conservative. Bynum claimed his approval rating fell twenty points—from 72 percent to 52 percent—when he signed the July masking ordinance. If so, those twenty points clearly did not go to Ken Reddick. He finished a distant third with 14 percent of the total vote.

Bob Jack, the Tulsa County Republican party chair, said he came under intense pressure to endorse Reddick, largely from the vocal suburban tea party alumni and MAGA enthusiasts who had wrested the GOP away from the downtown Chamber of Commerce Republicans. He refused.

"I didn't think Ken was the right guy for the job," said Jack. "And we sure didn't want Greg Robinson. So I said, 'Guys, the lesser of all these evils is G. T. We need to support G. T.' Well that didn't go over well with a lot of Republicans. They feel like G. T. is a RINO."[117]

But Tulsans kind of like RINOs—who, despite digs from the new right about being Republicans in Name Only, are really closer to the Tulsa Republicans of the past. Some cities or states are purple because half of their residents are dark blue and half are deep red. The election results suggest Tulsa is purple because a lot of its voters are purple. But the election results also add to the evidence that the middle Bynum spoke of is edging leftward compared to Tulsa's suburban neighbors and all of rural Oklahoma. This deepening cleft, observed across the United States, has had, and continues to have, important consequences for Greenwood and all Tulsans.

4

SEEKING JUSTICE

While a city councilor, before becoming mayor in 2016, G. T. Bynum recalls, he became convinced the city had an obligation to do all it could to find the remains of everyone killed in the 1921 Tulsa Race Massacre. In October 2018, nearly two years after taking over the city's executive suite, Bynum announced an initiative to do just that.[1]

"If there are mass graves . . . the citizens of Tulsa deserve to know and the victims and their families deserve to know it," Bynum said.[2]

Bynum announced the project on Facebook, saying he "did not intend to make this public until we had [a] plan in place," but that circumstances had persuaded him otherwise. Those circumstances included the publication of a *Washington Post* story a few days earlier and a meeting in a North Tulsa church during which Reverend Turner, the Vernon AME pastor, pressed him on the issue.[3]

Turner was relatively new to Tulsa, having arrived about a year earlier to pastor the historic but financially challenged old church on North Greenwood. Like many older congregations, Vernon was declining in active membership and had difficulty maintaining a nearly one-hundred-year-old building that was, according to Turner, "literally falling in."[4]

Turner said he spent his first year in Tulsa "going to school."

"I studied where I was, studied the people," Turner said in 2022. "Studied the community, studied the church. I wasn't coming to Tulsa to be anybody important. I was coming to pastor a church and to love on the people within the four walls of the church."

As he studied, Turner realized some of those killed or financially ruined in the massacre had been prominent Vernon members, and that survivors among the membership had been largely responsible for rebuilding the church afterward. His initial warm impression of Tulsa, he said, was cooled by the city's refusal to make good the massacre victims' losses and the immediate change of attitude he sensed when the subject was broached.

On September 12, 2018, Turner made the first of what became weekly appearances in front of Tulsa City Hall at Second Street and Cincinnati Avenue, usually with a bullhorn, lobbying for reparations ahead of his church's Wednesday prayer meetings.

"They have city council meetings on Wednesday night," Turner said. "That's the time traditionally in the church when we have Bible study. So that's kind of like an affront to God to me. And so, if they don't want folks to come to Bible study, I decided to take the Bible to them."

About three weeks later, Turner raised the issue of mass graves during a meeting with Bynum at Morning Star Baptist Church.

"I'll never forget it," Turner said. "They were taking questions . . . to the mayor. It was my first time physically being in the mayor's presence. He had seen me outside his office [protesting] every week, but this was my first time in his presence."[5]

The *Washington Post* story "They Was Killing Black People" had just been published, and in it, Hall-Harper said she would be pressing the city to carry out the investigation suspended nearly twenty years earlier. Turner "was hoping that somebody would ask the mayor a question" about it. When no one did, said Turner, "God was like, 'That's why I have you here, for you to [ask].' I still didn't want to ask, but the facilitator said, 'Okay, we have time for one more question,' so I raised my hand and took a deep breath."[6]

Turner says he asked Bynum about reparations and mass graves.

"The mayor did not respond to my question on reparations," Turner recalled. "I wasn't surprised. But he did respond to my question and concern about mass graves. He said, 'You know what? You're absolutely right. I just talked to my staff this morning.'"[7]

Turner said he does not know if he believes the last part—"If you have news like that for a predominantly Black crowd, you lead [with it.] That type of stuff, that's like red meat." But he credits Bynum for following through. Within a few months, a group of subject matter experts was lined up to search for remains under the supervision of a citizen oversight committee. Turner, who until that point had been fairly anonymous, was appointed to the oversight committee. He said that one question he had asked soon had reporters calling the Greenwood Cultural Center, across the street from Vernon and at that time the Race Riot Centennial Committee's home base, looking for Turner.

"At the time, nobody knew who I was," Turner said with a laugh. "That [question] made history and the mayor kept his word."[8]

But finding the remains of an unknown number of people disposed of a century ago in unknown ways in one or more unknown locations is not easy. That may sound self-evident, but to a lot of people it was not. Some thought the city already knew, quite literally, where the bodies were buried; others were convinced they knew themselves, if they could only get the authorities to look.

How many died as a result of the massacre, and what happened to all of the remains, is one of 1921's enduring mysteries. A round figure in the hundreds is usually given but the truth is that no one really knows. Around three dozen death certificates have been connected to the massacre but almost everyone who has looked into the matter believes the actual number of deaths was probably higher, and perhaps much higher. People suspected as much even at the time.[9]

A *Tulsa Tribune* headline, published on the afternoon of June 1—the very day of the disaster—estimated the dead at sixty-eight Blacks and nine whites; a bulletin on the same page quotes National Guard Major Charles Daley as saying he expected at least 175 bodies to be found in the smoking wreckage of Greenwood.[10]

The next morning, under the headline "Dead Estimated at 100; City is Quiet," the June 2, 1921, *Tulsa World* reported:

> The difficulty of determining the number of dead negroes is caused by the fact that the bodies were apparently not handled in a systematic manner. [Major] Byron Kirkpatrick, aide to Adjutant General [Charles] Barrett, said last night that none of the bodies had been handled by [National] guardsmen, but that it had been reported a number of bodies were removed in motor trucks operated by citizens. Kirkpatrick said he does not know where they were taken—whether they were placed at some specific point for later attention, if they were dumped into a large hole, or thrown into the Arkansas River.
>
> Fifteen bodies of blacks are in a local undertaking establishment. Reports heard over the city indicates [*sic*] five to eight times that number of negroes were killed during the riots.[11]

Hours later, however, the *Tribune* reported the death toll as only twenty-seven, and that Daley and another National Guard officer had found "not one charred body" in the "devastated area."[12]

The June 3 *World*, published the next morning, gave the confirmed dead as thirty—ten whites and twenty Blacks. That toll grew over the summer as others died from their injuries.[13]

Those were just the confirmed deaths. No one, it seems, really believed that was all of them. Maurice Willows, who the American Red Cross sent to manage relief efforts, wrote in his final report, dated December 31, 1921, that estimates of the dead ranged from fifty-five to three hundred. NAACP investigator Walter White, who arrived in Tulsa several days after the massacre, said he was told 120 Blacks were buried in unmarked graves at a secret location. James Leighton Avery, whose father Cyrus Avery would be largely responsible for the creation of the famous Route 66, said in 1980 that he had watched from the roof of the downtown high school building as trucks "drove up and down Tulsa streets filled with dead bodies, black and white, all headed in different directions."[14]

Variations describe uncounted dead, unmarked graves, and grisly disposal of human remains. Bodies were incinerated, thrown in the Arkansas River, dumped in a mass grave (or graves), laid out in a great trench, tossed into nearby abandoned coal mines, hauled away in trucks and rail cars, scattered out in cemeteries across northeastern Oklahoma. Most of the speculation, then and now, focused on Blacks, but at least some African Americans believed that white fatalities were more underreported. Taken together, it is a confused and confusing narrative that reveals no clear answers about how many actually died and what ultimately happened to their remains.[15]

Ed Wheeler, who interviewed about ninety people for a story published on the fiftieth anniversary of the massacre in 1971, concluded that probably around forty people died. Scott Ellsworth, whose 1982 book *Death in a Promised Land* was the first on the subject, thought the number was at least twice that and probably more. The legislative commission of 1997–2001 insisted the death toll had been in the hundreds.[16]

Ellsworth had grown up in Tulsa; he not only interviewed but became friends with many massacre survivors in the early 1980s. He left Tulsa for college and graduate school but remained in touch with some of his old contacts and became a protégé of John Hope Franklin, a Tulsan who became an internationally acclaimed historian. When the state commission was formed in 1997, Ellsworth signed on and led the first real search for the massacre's unaccounted dead. He and Dick Warner, a retired accountant and Sherlock Holmes devotee, conducted dozens of interviews and tracked down countless leads. At several sites, engineers from the University of Oklahoma and state archeologist Bob Brooks employed an early form of what is often called ground-penetrating radar, adapted from technology used to hunt for oil and gas deposits far underground. As information accumulated, Ellsworth became particularly interested in three locations: Newblock Park, Oaklawn Cemetery, and Rolling Oaks Cemetery.[17]

About a mile west of downtown along the Arkansas River, Newblock Park had been a city dump in 1921 and the site of the city's waterworks. Wheeler said he had been told, while researching in 1970, that immediately after the massacre bodies had been laid out along the river, or possibly on a sandbar, but soon disappeared. Wheeler was never able to confirm the story. Later, Ellsworth became intrigued by the tale of a boy who said he took a human skull from a work site at the park in the 1940s. That and other information persuaded Ellsworth that Newblock Park was a likely place to look, but a thorough search in 1998 yielded no results.[18]

Rolling Oaks Cemetery is now encircled by the city of Tulsa with a turnpike running nearby, but in 1921 it was part of a rural Black settlement called Rentie Grove (also known as Rentie's Grove and Rentie) about ten miles southeast of the city. Several cemeteries from that era are there, but Rolling Oaks was of particular interest. It was originally known as Booker T. Washington Cemetery and for many years was a Blacks-only burial ground. Stories Ellsworth and Warner heard caused Ellsworth to think there was a good chance massacre victims had been brought there, probably with the consent and approval of their families. But, again, a search of the most likely locations turned up nothing—although a few years later abandoned graves dating from a few years after the massacre were uncovered during a construction project.[19]

These graves appear to have had no connection to the race massacre, but they momentarily brought to the fore another aspect of broader race issues in Tulsa and eastern Oklahoma, involving not only Blacks and whites but tribal nations as well, and the mingling of ancestry among all three. Rentie Grove itself was never more than a store, a school, and a couple of churches—and the cemeteries—but it was the hub around which a Black agricultural community revolved. These farmers were freedmen and descendants of freedmen of the Muscogee Creek Nation. Some also had Creek forebears; many were combinations of multiple ethnicities. Family histories were tangled and often not well-documented. In any event, they were entitled to shares when the tribal holdings were broken up and individually allotted to Muscogee citizens in preparation for Oklahoma statehood. Between the communities of tribal freedmen in the east and Black homesteaders in the central and western parts of the new state, Oklahoma had more than fifty all-Black towns in the early 1900s. Some consider Greenwood to have, in effect, been the largest of them.[20]

Small farms are a tough way to make a living and as Tulsa grew, the children and grandchildren of the allottees sold out and moved away, often to Greenwood. The segregated school closed in 1955, after the *Brown v. Board of Education* decision, and the children were sent to Jenks, a few miles west across the Arkansas River. The last four allotment acres were sold in 1984. Black people have not disappeared from Rentie Grove. The 2020 census counted more than eight hundred African Americans in the tracts comprising the community of a century earlier, probably not far from the population in 1921. But of course, it is not the same. Today they are a small percentage rather than the exclusive majority. And when graves and later bones of Black folks were turned up while making way for an upscale development where freedmen and their families once eked out a living, it touched a nerve. The term "gentrification" had not yet come into common use, but that is what it seemed like to some. The land was bought, not stolen. Everything was legal and above board. But somehow, as often seemed to be the case, the modest homes and farms and businesses of poor Black folks had eventually turned into big money and big houses for somebody else.[21]

"This is . . . what they have always done to Black people," said Bishop Thomas Smith of the Church of the Living God, "They find a way to do what they want to do, and they make sure it's legal."[22]

The third site, Oaklawn Cemetery, was one of the most and least likely places to find uncounted burials. Adjoining the southeast corner of downtown, it is Tulsa's oldest public cemetery. In 1921, it was separated from the city's core by the Midland Valley Railroad tracks running roughly north and south. Today the east leg of the inner dispersal loop—the same IDL cutting through lower Greenwood—follows the same general course as the Midland Valley once did. What is now 11th Street runs along the south edge and in 1921 was one of the main roads out of the city.

The fundamental argument for and against Oaklawn as a likely place to look is more or less the same: it is a cemetery. If you did not care whether people knew what you were doing and the main concern was burying decaying remains as quickly as possible, the cemetery is a likely choice. It was close at hand—only about a mile from where the deadliest fighting occurred—and funeral home records and newspaper reports indicate between thirteen and eighteen African

Americans killed in the massacre were, in fact, buried there. Two headstones bearing the names of massacre victims Reuben Everett and Eddie Lockard are in what is generally described as a Black potter's field. Whether the headstones mark the actual burial places of the two men was, and to some extent still is, unclear.[23]

But if you *did not* want the general public to see what you were doing and public health and sanitation were not your overriding concerns, Oaklawn makes less sense. It could be clearly viewed from rail cars passing on the west and by traffic along 11th Street, which in 1921 was a main road in and out of town. It did not, and does not, fit the description of a secret and remote location.

But several pieces of information persuaded Ellsworth that perhaps at least some victims besides the thirteen to eighteen in the records might be interred at Oaklawn. One was a 1971 interview with Eunice Cloman Jackson, wife of Black undertaker S. M. Jackson, in which she said her stepfather had helped dig graves for Black victims at Oaklawn. Then Ellsworth and Warner talked to Clyde Eddy, a white man who said that as a boy he saw crates holding bodies buried at the cemetery. Finally, there were ground radar readings that showed an anomaly roughly corresponding to Eddy's memory, near the cemetery's southern border in an area with only scattered headstones. Excavation was planned for early 2000, but then delayed and ultimately cancelled. The initial postponement occurred after city officials said they had found records indicating unrelated burials in what, in 1921, was the white paupers' field; later, the commission itself shut down the search for good, with Don Ross saying that since Black race massacre victims were already known to be buried there an excavation seemed unnecessary.[24]

Underlying this and almost all of the commission's work was the struggle to shape and control the story. Sometimes the struggle was between the commission and outside forces. Sometimes it was within the commission itself. The latter most often erupted in disagreements about what to include or feature in the final report and what to leave out or minimize. Some favored a narrative built around clearly established and accepted facts. This, they argued, would prove sturdier against the criticism of naysayers and nitpickers out to discredit the commission's work. Others were more aggressive. The case for reparations, it was said, required the story to be as compelling as possible. But there was more to it than that. Aside from some commissioners' lack of enthusiasm for anything called "reparations," the elements most difficult to document tended also to be stories told and retold by Black Tulsans for decades. Those fighting hardest to include these oral histories considered it a moral obligation to see them made part of the official record. As Don Ross had made clear to me, these stories mattered and on more than one level.[25]

Bynum may not have fully understood this when he made public his plans to relaunch the search the original commission had given up eighteen years earlier. If he expected to be hailed as a great hero, he was disappointed. While many Tulsans cautiously praised the announcement, there was also a good deal of skepticism. Disagreements about where to look, who would do the looking, and who would be in charge flared quickly.

"The thing I did not know, in terms of the difficulty, was that the technical side would actually be much more straightforward than the human side," Bynum said in 2022. "I also made the mistake of expecting the most fervent opposition to the search to come from white Tulsans who thought it was a waste of time. In reality, that has been almost completely non-existent. Most criticism of the search has come from Black activists who don't trust the city."[26]

Bynum understood that, he said. Black Tulsans had plenty of reason to be suspicious. But, from his viewpoint, it made an already difficult task more so.

Putting the band back together after nearly two decades was not easy. Clyde Snow, the internationally known University of Oklahoma forensic anthropologist who had contributed important research and technical expertise to the original study, had died. So had Dick Warner. Alan Witten, the OU geophysicist who had conducted the seismic scans of the three locations in 1998–2000, was also dead and his data had disappeared. Most of the witnesses, including Clyde Eddy, were gone. Bob Brooks, the state archeologist, had retired. Eddie Faye Gates, who had interviewed just about all the race massacre survivors still living in the late 1990s, was in declining health and would die in 2021.

Still, a few key individuals remained. This included Ellsworth, now a University of Michigan history professor, and forensic anthropologist Phoebe Stubblefield, whose family had roots in Greenwood. Warner's daughter Betsy had all of his notes and was added as a researcher. Also on board was Kavin Ross, who had operated the equipment for Gates' interviews two decades earlier and as a writer, journalist, and photographer had continued poking about the area for clues to the missing dead. The son of Don Ross, it had been Kavin, acting on a tip from Dick Warner, who had brought to public attention the lost cemetery in south Tulsa.

"It's a difficult situation," Kavin Ross said in 2022, describing the search for race massacre burials. "A 100-year-old whodunit. One of the greatest history's mysteries."[27]

The search team was organized into three committees: Public Oversight, Historical Context and Narrative, and Physical Investigation. The Public Oversight Committee would eventually grow to two dozen or more members, initially chaired by 85-year-old former state senator Maxine Horner. It included Turner, Kristi Williams, Greg Robinson, state senator Kevin Matthews, state representative Regina Goodwin, Tulsa City Councilor Vanessa Hall-Harper, and Smithsonian official John W. Franklin, son of John Hope Franklin. Kavin Ross was soon added and eventually became chair. The Historical Context and Narrative Committee included several historians. Physical Investigations consisted of Ellsworth, Stubblefield, state archeologist Kary Stackelbeck, and a small number of others.[28]

The Oversight Committee's first public meeting was to have been in May 2019, but record spring rains forced postponement. Torrents upstream took the Arkansas River far out of its banks, straining an aged levee system and inundating low-lying areas from Keystone Dam, west of Tulsa, to the downstream narrows of Van Buren, Arkansas. Adding to the mayhem were a record fifty tornadoes in Oklahoma during May. Thus, cascading weather disasters eclipsed what would have been a momentous rollout of the grave search.[29]

The rescheduled meeting on June 27, at a north side event center, was long—more than two hours—but relatively uneventful.[30]

"If you get murdered in Tulsa, we have a basic contract with you that we will do everything we can to find out what happened to you and render justice for your family," Bynum told the gathering. "That's why we are treating this as a homicide investigation for Tulsans who we believe were murdered in 1921."[31]

Hall-Harper, already at odds with Bynum over the first Equality Indicators report and policing reform, said, "It is my goal that our ancestors—who were brutally murdered and placed in mass graves—are given to their families and receive a proper burial so we as a city can have closure. It is the work we must do and achieve together. It is work that must be done."[32]

There were some indications of what was to come. Several people called attention to alternate sites, a few specific but most too vague or general for immediate action. But it demonstrated what many observers already knew: Black Tulsans' generationally ingrained distrust and even hatred of Tulsa's city government was far more profound, and would be more difficult to penetrate, than Bynum and most other Tulsans comprehended.[33]

Tensions were a notch or two higher by the next public meeting on July 18, just a few days after Bynum and some Public Oversight Committee members clashed over the Town Square incident. The July 18 meeting, featuring subject matter experts explaining the technicalities of the undertaking and trying to temper expectations, did not do much to satisfy the skeptics.

Scott Hammerstedt, the senior researcher at the Oklahoma Archeological Survey in charge of the subsurface scanning at Oaklawn Cemetery, Newblock Park, and Rolling Oaks, described the specialized instruments to be used. The machines were a great advance from those Alan Witten had improvised from oil and gas-seeking seismic equipment twenty years before. Nevertheless, Hammerstedt cautioned, they would not produce the kind of images television and movies had conditioned the public to expect.

"You are not going to get (an image of) an actual skeleton," Hammerstedt said.[34]

Ellsworth said he and Dick Warner were told of at least twenty-five possible sites, but that pinpointing specific locations was difficult if not impossible.

"If you don't have a piece of land you can point to . . . in a pretty finite area, you're not going to find anything," said Ellsworth. "In an area this size [about 200 square feet] you could bury 100 bodies. Imagine how many areas there are this size in this building [or] in the parking lot outside. The world gets very big early on.

"We might not find anything at [the chosen] sites," he said. "We might not find any mass graves. We might find the remains of three people, or five people."[35]

Stubblefield, the voice of experience in the sort of field work being contemplated, told the audience to "be realistic."

A century had passed, she said. Remains decay, even those that have been embalmed. Instead of needles in a haystack, the team would be looking for needles in a pile of needles—bodies among many other bodies, buried in a cemetery. Conclusively proving remains were from the race massacre would likely be difficult.

"I present this not to be a killjoy for those eager to get these stories told," Stubblefield said. "It's really to frame a timeline."[36]

As a graduate student, Stubblefield had conducted skeletal analysis for the original commission. In the years since, she had become one of the nation's leading forensic anthropologists. She was a professional. She would not be rushed or cut corners, but neither would she be waved off. Her goal, Stubblefield said, was "to send these people home . . . and I hope to be able to identify them enough to know [whether they are] . . . a race massacre victim."[37]

Ellsworth tried to put the project into perspective.

"This is really unprecedented work that we're doing," he said. "I really can't think of anywhere in the country where there's already been so much effort put in; there's ongoing effort, and please know that even though you may not hear from us for a few months, we're not lying around. We're committed to this."[38]

In late September, it was announced that scanning would begin the second week of October, and that a fourth site, called "The Canes," had been added to the list. The Canes was a homeless camp along the Arkansas River at the foot of Crosbie Heights, an old neighborhood between downtown and Newblock Park. The location roughly corresponded with photographs of a mass burial that a former Tulsa Police officer said he'd seen in the early 1970s.[39]

In the end, Hammerstedt and his team scanned at Oaklawn Cemetery, Newblock Park, and The Canes, but not Rolling Oaks. Unlike the other sites, Rolling Oaks was privately owned and not inclined to throw the cemetery's gates open without a firm agreement about what would and would not be allowed. All four sites demonstrated some of the limitations and challenges of this sort of project, even with improved technology.[40]

For technical reasons, including interference from a high-voltage transmission line, only one of the three scanners employed by Hammerstedt was much use at Newblock Park. He and Oklahoma Archeological Survey Director Amanda Regnier reported detecting "human-made features, pipes or filled-in ditches," but "[n]o anomalies consistent with graves." Considerable "land modification" over the years, the report says, further lessened the likelihood of finding anything. "[W]e do not believe that any intact burials are located at Newblock Park" the report concludes.[41]

Metal debris and sandy soil again limited scanning of the nearby Canes site to one instrument, and even it was limited by terrain and groundcover. Still, two potential areas, each about six and a half feet by ten feet, were identified.[42]

Even Oaklawn was less than a perfect test site. Interference from power lines and the nearby highway, and to some extent from the sheer volume of people with electronic devices who came to watch the crew work, invalidated the first scans and the work had to be repeated, this time under more controlled conditions—in other words, with the cemetery closed and spectators at a distance. Hammerstedt also had to explain that his equipment could not scan under the adjoining elevated highway, where Goodwin, Turner, and fellow Oversight Committee member Chief Egunwale Amusan said they believed the remains of massacre victims may have been entombed.[43]

"We have heard from too many witnesses, and there is too much oral history," Goodwin said, adding that she believed the team should also be looking in

Crown Hill Cemetery beyond the city's northern boundary. Crown Hill was not a cemetery in 1921, but that did not eliminate it as a possible mass burial site.[44]

The east leg of the inner dispersal loop—the same IDL slicing through Greenwood—was built mostly in the 1960s and 1970s. As far as can be determined, no human remains were found during the considerable earthwork done to raise the highway above the surrounding neighborhood. A small sliver of Oaklawn was deeded to the state for the right-of-way, however, which may have necessitated moving some burials. Perhaps more to the point, a rail line had passed along the same general route in 1921, which feeds the notion that perhaps rail cars were used to transport bodies to a spot near the cemetery. Why these bodies would have been left along the tracks or buried there, instead of either in the cemetery less than a hundred yards away or, alternately, left on the rail cars and taken to a distant site where they would not be seen, is unclear.[45]

To a large extent, these complaints and disagreements were as much about the long struggle over control of the story—the history—as anything else. Except for Stubblefield, the most visible members of the on-site scientific team were white. They had been hired by the city. The city could not be trusted. And it was not as if those most invested in the grave search had no reason to hold such a view.

A lot of people wanted to control or at least influence the narrative. Bynum wanted to persuade not only Tulsans but the world that, as the Race Massacre centennial approached, the city was making a good-faith effort to locate these long-neglected burials. Individual reputations, friendships, emotions, and even careers were at stake. Most public officials watched warily from a distance, concerned that they might be dragged into political quicksand.

Despite the complications, the October 2019 scanning produced some startling results. In mid-December, at a community meeting in the auditorium of Carver Middle School just off North Greenwood Avenue, Hammerstedt announced indications of a "pit" measuring twenty-five feet by thirty-two feet, in an area a previous Oaklawn sexton thought might be the site of a mass grave. Another area of interest, a short distance to the south near Lockard's and Everett's headstones, showed indications of many single, unmarked graves.

"I'm as confident as I can be in the results that this is a very big candidate [for] something associated with the massacre," Hammerstedt said.[46]

Stubblefield, ever cautious, said the discoveries probably meant "tens, not hundreds" of bodies, but an important development nonetheless.[47]

Perhaps fueled by the popularity of the HBO series *Watchmen*, which had debuted a few weeks earlier with a fictionalized but credible imagining of the destruction of Greenwood, Hammerstedt's announcement made national and even international headlines. But it was not the main topic of discussion that night in the Carver Middle School auditorium. Turner and other vocal members of the Public Oversight Committee wanted Hammerstedt to go back to Newblock Park and find something; they also demanded the city get immediate access to Rolling Oaks Cemetery and produce the photographs the former police officer claimed to have seen.

"The next time we meet, I don't want my ears to hear that we have not gotten legal permission to survey [Rolling Oaks]," Turner said. "The next time we meet, as God is my witness, I don't want my ears to hear that we're still waiting on the Tulsa Police Department to find the pictures from 1973."

TPD has long denied knowledge of such photos, including to the author in 2000. Turner said the denial, and the delay in scanning Rolling Oaks, indicated a "cover up" or "some sort of obstruction."

"We are actively pursuing the truth on this, wherever it leads us, in a transparent way," Bynum said. "The sad reality is that the better part of a century went by in which the people of Tulsa didn't want to talk about this. People actively worked to cover it up . . . and very nearly succeeded."

Less than two months later, Stackelbeck announced that a test excavation in Oaklawn's so-called Sexton site, where the large anomaly had been detected, would begin in April. If anything, that only intensified the pressure from skeptics who maintained the search was being purposely misdirected.[48]

The meltdown occurred at a March 3, 2020, meeting. In a packed auditorium at Rudisill Regional Library, Turner jumped from his chair in protest and then stretched out on the floor to signify riot dead possibly interred at Rolling Oaks. He harangued Deputy Mayor Amy Brown as incompetent because scans at the south Tulsa cemetery had not yet been arranged and declared the grave search a sham. Results were wanted, not foot-dragging and doubletalk.

Stackelbeck appeared shocked and Stubblefield, attending via a remote hookup before all but a very few Americans had heard of Zoom, sounded appalled.[49]

"We're not covering anything up. We're just not," said Stubblefield. "We've made great progress. . . . I assure you we are one hundred percent on board with finding these individuals, with finding our dead. We're not trying to jerk anyone around." she said.

When Bynum tried to convince Turner and the others that taking the Rolling Oaks owners to court, as they were demanding, likely would be counterproductive, Stubblefield noted the meetings were livestreamed and said, "I, for one, would not be surprised if part of our difficulty with getting a signature has something to do with watching the response every time this committee has to report we don't have that signature."

Ten days later, President Trump declared a public health emergency. Tulsa, and Oklahoma, recorded its first COVID-19 death on March 18. On March 22, the city announced that the Oaklawn excavation was suspended indefinitely, and that it had reached an agreement with Rolling Oaks' owners.[50]

In the weeks and months ahead, the world experienced an upheaval like few living Americans ever had. Public gatherings were banned or sharply curtailed. Businesses closed. Jobs evaporated. Supply chains dried up. The city of Tulsa announced 1,000 of its employees would have to take seventeen unpaid furlough days by the end of the year. The death of George Floyd fueled the protests in downtown and Brookside and the march on Bynum's house. Human Rights Watch called for race massacre reparations. The mayoral campaign began. Donald Trump came to town. COVID cases soared. And in the early morning hours of June 29, two police officers were shot trying to wrestle a reluctant motorist out of his car. One of them, Sgt. Craig Johnson, died. The other, rookie Officer Aurash Zarkeshan, was seriously wounded but somehow survived.[51]

Bynum describes the shooting as something close to a breaking point for him. He, his wife, and their children had gone to a family lake house to get away from the calamities of the past few weeks, only to get a 3 a.m. call from Chief Franklin telling him two police officers had been shot in the line of duty.

"That was the first time in all of this that I just broke down sobbing," Bynum said. "My predecessors as mayor had all told me the worst call you will ever get is that an officer has been shot," Bynum recalled. "To have two officers shot at the same time was hard to comprehend. And it was then that it was all too much. Everything kind of added up, but that was the last straw. So I pulled it together, got in my car, and drove to Tulsa in the middle of the night."[52]

Aside from the sobering nature of the tragedy, the shooting took the air out of the police reform movement that had been building since Terence Crutcher's death and found full voice after George Floyd's. Instinctively, the community rallied behind the police. His funeral filled the 4,500-seat sanctuary of one of Tulsa's megachurches and thousands of people lined the route from there to the cemetery ten miles away in Broken Arrow.[53]

Poignant, somehow calming after the clamor of the Trump rally, the Black Lives Matter demonstrations and marches, and the disruptions and fear caused by COVID-19, Johnson's death and funeral reminded Tulsans that as much as they had been through, they still had their lives and they still had each other.

"I remember coming out of Sgt. Johnson's funeral and we're going to have a funeral procession to the gravesite and pulling out of that parking lot and thinking, 'Oh, it's really nice, there's some people here,'" Bynum said. "Flags and signs to show they appreciate the officers. And that route was—ten miles? I think it's ten miles from that church to the cemetery and it had people lining the streets the entire way. I've never, and I lived in D.C. for six years, seen anything like that that was completely spontaneous."[54]

In that environment, with COVID-19 in full bloom and mid-summer temperatures approaching triple digits, the excavation at Oaklawn Cemetery began on the morning of July 13, 2020, a four-hour rain delay further heightening anticipation of a major find. The "sexton site" had been chosen because of the subsurface scan results, and because of the story that a sexton had planted crepe myrtles along that section of the western boundary in the belief riot victims were buried there. Researchers had also noted that while the cemetery had essentially been full for decades, that particular plot seemed to have never been used. On hand were Stackelbeck and a team of archeologists, Stubblefield, Angela Berg from the state medical examiner's office, Public Oversight Committee members, and a city public works crew. The cemetery was closed, and the press and the public were kept behind the fence separating Oaklawn from a bike trail along the highway embankment and the cemetery. Still, spectators could see most of what went on—which, as it turned out, was not a lot.[55]

A city backhoe operator scooped out a ten-foot by twenty-foot plot to a depth of three feet, and then a trench down to seven feet, without reaching a foundational layer of soil or finding any sign of human burials. Stubblefield and the archeologists sifted through each bucketful by hand, but the only thing turned up was "fill"—soil and other materials, including what appeared to be a door to an old boiler, dumped into a depression in the topography. Stackelbeck said the researchers were still optimistic, but this was not what had been expected.[56]

And so it went for more than a week. The test excavation got wider and deeper but ultimately no closer to the mass grave the science and the history said should be there. A pair of shoes discovered ten feet below the surface on July 21, eight days into the dig, created brief excitement but proved to be nothing more than what they seemed. By then, the researchers had concluded the anomaly detected by subsurface scanning was an old creek bed filed in decades before. The lack of maps and photographs made it difficult to determine when and had prevented the researchers from realizing they were making a mistake in the first place. One day after the shoes turned up, the excavation was shut down with the promise that the search would resume in the fall.[57]

"Unfortunately, things did not transpire the way that we hoped they would," said Stackelbeck. "We are able to confirm this is not the location we are looking for."[58]

State senator Kevin Matthews took some difficult votes during the 2015 session and heard about it from his North Tulsa constituents. The result, six long and tortuous years later, was one of the country's most heralded new museums, situated at the corner of Greenwood and Archer.[59]

As Matthews remembers it, his constituents wanted to know why he had voted for $25 million bond issues for two languishing projects—an American Indian museum in Oklahoma City and a popular culture museum in Tulsa—and not gotten anything in return. Being Black and a Democrat in the Oklahoma legislature is a double disadvantage and so the rare occasion when a vote matters is an opportunity for the old-fashioned horse trader politics that minorities of all kinds depend upon for any sort of concessions from ruling majorities.[60]

Matthews grew up poor in North Tulsa. He was working as a hospital orderly, barely getting by, when a friend named Terry McGee suggested he apply to the fire department. That suggestion changed Matthews' life. Twenty-five years later he retired as administrative chief—the top personnel officer—and along the way acquired the firefighters' penchant for side businesses. He has had dozens of them, he figures, from dry cleaners to real estate to remodeling. He has sponsored mentoring and entrepreneurship programs for young Black Tulsans. But on this occasion, he said, he was struggling to come up with "something big" that would help his Black Democratic constituents and that the white Republican majority would go for.[61]

Matthews said the answer came from Lester Shaw, a musician and educator who for years had been trying to restore the Big 10 Ballroom, a one-time Chitlin Circuit hotspot on Apache Street, about three miles northeast of Greenwood and Archer. In its post-World War II heyday, acts playing the Big 10 included Ray Charles, Ella Fitzgerald, Count Basie, Ike and Tina Turner, Little Richard, B. B. King, Fats Domino, Jackie Wilson, James Brown, Bobbie "Blue" Bland, Sam and Dave, Dinah Washington, and the Temptations. The Big 10 had been empty for decades and had not been a music venue since the 1960s when Shaw bought it in 2007. He envisioned it as a showplace for Pocketful of Hope, his nonprofit music-centered youth program. Shaw also thought it might appeal to a Black middle class in search of its heritage.[62]

"He said, 'Have you heard of this term called cultural tourism?'" Matthews recalled.[63]

Matthews says that caused him to reflect on Tulsa's and Oklahoma's Black heritage, particularly Greenwood and the state's all-Black towns. In 2022, he said:

> I started to think, wow, you know, we have a rich culture here, African American culture that hadn't really been touted. . . . And so how could I garner resources? At that time, I was the only African American man in the Senate. We had one African American woman, one African American man, and there were only seven Democrats [out of forty-eight state senators]. And so, it was like, what could I do to increase my odds of making this happen? I thought, "The only way that this is going to happen is to create some bipartisanship, and why not get input from elected officials at every level?"

Two key connections were Ken Levit, the executive director of the George Kaiser Family Foundation, and Maressa Treat, at that time a field representative for US senator James Lankford but also the wife of one of Matthews's colleagues, Oklahoma City Republican Greg Treat, who was on track to become the Senate's top-ranking officer, the president pro tempore.

To understand Tulsa, it is important to understand the extent to which it has depended, and still does, on the philanthropy of a small number of Jewish families who owed their fortunes to oil and gas. At the top of the list are the Kaisers, the Schustermans, and the Zarrows. George Kaiser, Charles Schusterman, and Henry and Jack Zarrow were all born in the United States to immigrant parents fleeing deadly oppression—the Schustermans and the Zarrows in Russia and the Soviet Union, the Kaisers in Nazi Germany. Sam and Ruth Zarrow arrived first, around 1916, and were said to have harbored Black Tulsans during the race massacre. They were originally in the grocery trade but with their sons and another relative eventually gravitated to oilfield salvage and then pipelines. Sam Schusterman also started in the oilfield salvage business. Herman Kaiser, who had been an attorney in his native country, was yet another Jewish immigrant to Tulsa who began as a pipeline supplier before starting a small oil company in 1949. From these hard-won footholds, the first American generation of the three families launched extraordinary careers, in both business and philanthropy. The foundations they and their spouses established continue to underwrite a wide array of services from childcare to homeless shelters to mental health facilities and even a Veterans Administration hospital, the only one of its kind in the United States.[64]

The biggest of these philanthropic organizations is the George Kaiser Family Foundation (GKFF). With assets of more than $5.2 billion, according to the nonprofit watchdog GuideStar, GKFF and its namesake founder often seem to have a hand in almost everything that happens in Tulsa. Certainly there are Tulsans who believe that to be true. The executive director of the GKFF-affiliated Tulsa Community Foundation is a long-time city councilor, and a senior GKFF officer is in the Oklahoma legislature. George Kaiser describes GKFF as an "operational" foundation, as opposed to "distributional." It does not just mail out checks. It hires talent and puts it to work for the community. As much as cash, GKFF contributes expertise and connections. And that can be perceived as intrusive and even self-serving.[65]

In an email, Kaiser said such considerations have been "top of mind for GKFF" and that suspicion of "wealthy, white, self-described liberals coming to a community with ideas for improvement when they do not have the lived experience to justify having their ideas considered or, worse yet, imposed" has at times been difficult to overcome.[66]

"It helps once people realize that everything I have is committed to GKFF; my children (who are very well provided for) do not seek any inheritance (as I didn't) and are fully supportive," Kaiser wrote. Except for him and some personnel, he said, "There is no mix of our for-profit and not-for-profit activities."[67]

Even the skeptics have to admit GKFF has done extraordinary things for the city. Its early childhood education centers are considered among the best in the country. Its Tulsa Remote program, which offers a $10,000 stipend to remote workers who move to the city, became a model for similar incentives nationwide. The $400 million Gathering Place is a state-of-the-art park carefully planned down to every leaf and piece of playground equipment; GKFF was also behind Tulsa securing the archives of singer-songwriters Woody Guthrie and Bob Dylan. The BOK Center is named for Kaiser's Bank of Oklahoma, the largest financial institution in the state. Less conspicuously, GKFF's involvement in economic development, particularly in emerging technologies, seems to be growing rapidly. Its 36 Degrees North and Build in Tulsa initiatives, for instance, foster startups and small—often one-person—businesses, with Build in Tulsa specifically geared for Black entrepreneurs. So, establishing a relationship with Levit, GKFF's top officer, was no small thing for Matthews's blossoming plans.[68]

"It didn't get real legs until I talked to Ken Levit . . . about how hard it was for me to vote for the (popular culture museum), and I needed help with Greenwood," Matthews said. "And he committed to help."[69]

Matthews recruited Hannibal Johnson, a Tulsa attorney, historian, and author, to help craft a message. Glenda Love, who had extensive nonprofit experience, advised Matthews on how to set up what became the Race Massacre Centennial Commission.

In the meantime, Matthews had gotten to know Lankford through Maressa Treat. Oklahoma's white Republican politicians tended to keep their distance from Black Democrats but Lankford, said Matthews, was different.

"He was very supportive and very accessible, and we built a relationship," Matthews said. "As Senator Lankford met certain people in the community, he would try to show his support by having events or press conferences with us, and basically it felt like he wanted to be more inclusive than we had seen in the past."

Their friendship would eventually carry a cost for both, but when they launched the commission in February 2017 those consequence were still years in the future. GKFF, already involved in developing a North Tulsa industrial park, had agreed to pay for a fulltime centennial commission staff member. Shaw's Pocketful of Hope received a GKFF grant as it continued to restore the Big 10 Ballroom. In October, Lankford held a community meeting in the venue.[70]

The commission's original mission statement did not say anything about a museum or history center, but by early 2019 it clearly was headed in that direction. Matthews said a 2018 trip arranged by Lankford to see the newly opened Smithsonian Institution's National Museum of African American History and Culture, with its exhibit on Greenwood and the massacre, convinced him Tulsa should do something similar.[71]

"It was amazing to me to see the Greenwood story told so well in Washington, D.C., even at a higher level than it was told right here in our own city," Matthews said.[72]

A $16 million capital campaign begun in fall 2018—when the commission changed its name to use the word "massacre" instead of "riot"—had grown to $25 million by April 2019. Matthews said the biggest share of that would go for renovations to the Greenwood Cultural Center, including an adjacent "world class museum experience" devoted to the full history of Greenwood, from its origins to the present. The campaign's cochair was GKFF's Monica Basu, who said $9 million had already been raised, including $2 million from GKFF. In May, GKFF paid for a contingent of Tulsans, including Matthews, to visit the race- and civil rights-related museums in Montgomery, Alabama.[73]

"Other states have documented the trauma that has taken place across the country with race relations to give a better perspective how to display and teach around the issue of the race massacre," Matthews said upon return. "The commission itself is motivated by the fact that we're coming up on the anniversary of the race massacre. Very little has been done to tell the story. The whole idea of the commission is based on that fact."[74]

The idea of a Greenwood museum was far from new. Vernon AME had been suggested as a location in the early 2000s, and plans were actually drawn up for an $18 million archives, museum, and memorial on the site that became John Hope Franklin Reconciliation Park. Although the impetus for such a museum came from interest in the race massacre, the expressed intent had always been a comprehensive retelling of the community's history. That such a project was still in discussion nearly two decades later owed largely to reluctance on the part of potential funders and a lack of agreement within Greenwood about what such a museum would look like, what it would say, and whether it was even appropriate.[75]

At a May 9 event at the Greenwood Cultural Center, Kristi Williams and Councilor Hall-Harper asked similar questions about this latest proposal. They especially wanted to know about community input and to what extent GKFF would control the project. Over the next two years, a sharp museum-reparations dichotomy emerged. Generally speaking, those behind the museum said they supported reparations in some form but thought the cash payments to race massacre survivors and descendants sought by others unlikely under current conditions. Those prioritizing reparations thought a museum—and especially one largely funded (and therefore probably controlled) by white people—a dubious half-measure, if not an outright misdirection. They wanted the centennial's focus on those most affected by the massacre. This disagreement on how best to tell Greenwood's story exacerbated existing conflicts over leadership and control. Entwined were other social, political, and economic factors, including the battles over police reform, economic development, and the other discrepancies highlighted in the Equality Indicators report. The split deepened and became more embittered after Solomon-Simmons, who also represented the Crutcher family, filed suit on September 1, 2020, against the city and others on behalf of Lessie Benningfield Randle as a 105-year-old race massacre survivor. Viola Fletcher, 106, was soon added, and her 100-year-old brother Hughes Van

Ellis joined the plaintiffs a few months later. Among other things, the lawsuit turned up the volume on the argument that families most directly affected by the massacre had been cut out by the centennial commission and that some or all of the money raised for the museum should go to them instead.[76]

But back in May 2019, when Williams and Hall-Harper were asking their questions at the Greenwood Cultural Center meeting, the museum drive appeared to be full speed ahead. Matthews managed to get $1.5 million for the commission into that spring's general appropriations bill. The John Hope Franklin Center for Reconciliation and Greenwood Cultural Center were on board, and so was Bynum, who backed a $5.34 million line item for the cultural center in a proposed city bond issue package. Meanwhile, GKFF was opening doors in the nonprofit world, and the involvement of Lankford, then arguably the state's most popular political figure, lent some credibility on the right. It also helped that the state's new Republican governor and lieutenant governor were both Tulsans and both supportive—at least in concept.[77]

At the end of May, work began on an associated project particularly favored by Matthews—the Pathway to Hope, a series of outdoor exhibits linking the Greenwood Cultural Center and Vernon AME with John Hope Franklin Park. In July, the commission named New York-based Local Projects, whose credits include the National September 11 Memorial & Museum and the Legacy Museum of African American History in Montgomery. In September, Hannibal Johnson, who had become interim curator of the still-unnamed museum, and Local Projects representatives met with the public in the same Carver Middle School auditorium where, three months later, Scott Hammerstedt would announce the discovery of a promising anomaly at Oaklawn Cemetery. For the first time, the designers described the interactive virtual barber shop that would become one of the museum's singular features. Bynum and Gov. Kevin Stitt were given their own presentation the following day.[78]

But strains were developing in the partnership, particularly over the future of the Greenwood Cultural Center. Created largely by state representative Don Ross and state senator Maxine Horner, the center began in the mid-1980s when the post-massacre brick home of survivor Mabel Little was moved a short distance down Greenwood Avenue, across the street from Vernon AME, and restored. A modern gallery and event center were erected alongside a few years later. The center received a small but vital state subsidy as long as Horner, Ross, and their fellow Democrats controlled state government, but that went away when Horner and Ross retired and Republicans ascended to the majority in the mid-2000s. It did not help that Oklahoma had trouble paying its bills for the first two decades of the twenty-first century. Amenities and local attractions, from community centers to state parks, were cut off. So, it is not surprising that when Matthews managed to get $1.5 million for the centennial commission, his counterpart in the other chamber, state representative Goodwin, wanted to know why the Greenwood Cultural Center was left out.[79]

The Greenwood Cultural Center has some important exhibits and once housed the Oklahoma Jazz Hall of Fame but is mainly a space for community events. In the Centennial Commission plan, the Center would have remained as part of a larger complex that included—and some believed would be dominated by—the history center and, more to the point, the history center's funders. They viewed the museum as a Trojan horse, a creaking monstrosity concealing a new wave of invaders who, one way or another, would take over another piece of Greenwood. To people associated with the cultural center, and to some influential Black Tulsans, this was unacceptable.[80]

Work on the history center was to have begun by the end of 2019 in order to have the building at least erected by the time of the race massacre centennial. Even that was going to be a tight fit. But when the new year came and went without even a spadeful of dirt turned, it was apparent something was wrong. Ostensibly, the hang up was legal. The Greenwood Cultural Center leased the land on which it sat, and on which the history center would sit, from the city. It was a complication that, again, boiled down to primacy: Who would lease from whom and under what conditions? The point was a genuinely important one, but almost certainly not as important as the fact that quite a few people associated with the Greenwood Cultural Center did not want a museum in the parking lot—and especially one built by outside interests they did not control and did not trust.[81]

"I am a 23-year resident of Tulsa, and in my time being here, you have a community that the mindset overall is, 'Promise made, promise broken. Promise made, promise broken,'" said Phil Armstrong, who was essentially acting as the commission's executive director, after an early March meeting involving the cultural center board of directors, the commission, and city officials including Bynum.

Armstrong had been the cultural center's board chair the previous year and understood its reservations. The center, he said, "is an icon, it is the legacy of Sen. Maxine Horner and Rep. Don Ross." Protecting the center's name and prominence in the community mattered.[82]

Although Armstrong did not become the commission's full-time director until August 2019, he was involved from the start. He was on the 2018 trip to Washington with Matthews and a few others and also remembers it as a transformative moment.

> They came back, and then they held a donor-fundraiser . . . at Greenwood Cultural Center," Armstrong recalled. After a presentation on the Tulsa exhibit in the African American History museum, the question was asked, "'Why do people have to go to Washington, D.C., to learn about our history? Why can't we fill a history center or something of that nature here, right where it took place?' That was the electrifying, lightbulb, open-your-eyes moment. [The commission] walked out of there with almost seven, eight million dollars in pledges.[83]

According to Armstrong, the Kaiser, Schusterman, and Zarrow philanthropies all pledged at least $1 million each that night. So did ONEOK, the Tulsa-based natural gas giant.

"The big funding came from that meeting," Armstrong said. "'Oh, you're going to build something like that?' 'Yes.' We didn't know it was going to be called Greenwood Rising, we didn't know where we were going to build it. It was just the fact that it was something that could really move the needle forward in terms of 'Wow, what if we could build something like that here?'"[84]

But if that meeting launched what became Greenwood Rising, it also galvanized opposition. By the time Armstrong became project director the following August, it was in danger of losing public support—and not just from leery African Americans. A few months after taking over, Armstrong said "Sometimes it is challenging."

> You are dealing with . . . white people who are thinking, "Let's get past this. Why do we have to keep dragging back through history?" [African Americans saying] "You know what, that was a long time ago, it's traumatic, I don't really want to talk about it," to the younger generation that says people were never paid, [they deserve] reparations. There are a lot of voices, a lot of emotions, and rightfully so.[85]

Looking back three years later, Armstrong said, "My perception is that we had two tracks of thought. One, you had the white community, who . . . have the concern that this is maybe another round of trying to make white people feel guilty about what happened one hundred years ago. Why can't we get past it? Why do we keep going back to it? Every time we try to go forward, you've got to pull us back into the anguish of what happened. And there's nothing we can do about it."

> And then from the Black community's side, this has never been addressed fully. There's been, of course, small . . . things to address it, but nothing in a full, community gathering around this initiative to say we're going to acknowledge and atone in a way that allows us to move forward.
>
> For a lot of Black citizens . . . we've been down this road before. We've heard this tune sung. And nothing really happens. Nothing ever really changes. . . . And now this commission comes along and says they're going to do it. So there was a lot of distrust. There was just a lot of mistrust on both sides. Because here we are, almost a hundred years later, and what's changed? So the pushback was, "Why are we going down this road again? Who is this centennial commission that says it has the answers to make this a moment in time when we really start getting down to substantive work to make change?" That was difficult. That was very, very difficult. I cannot overstate how difficult it was to just get people to sit down and then trust everyone to go in the right direction.[86]

The commitment of the foundations and Lankford was key to answering skeptics outside the Black community.[87]

> Doors were opened that otherwise would not have been opened because James Lankford was so up-front in saying, "This is the right thing to do. Politics aside, this is the right thing to do." There are those I know for a fact would not have answered a call from Senator Matthews, that would not have answered a call from Phil Armstrong, but when James Lankford picked up the phone and said, "I believe in this. I'm a part of this. And I want you to work with us on this," they answered.[88]

But the involvement of Lankford and other non-Black supporters, financial and otherwise, also heightened suspicion within the African American community. And understandably so. Recent development in the portion of Greenwood inside the inner dispersal loop was almost all by non-Blacks and the city. At least as far back as 2006, the Greenwood Chamber of Commerce lodged a formal complaint against the city's urban renewal agency, claiming favoritism for non-Black investors. The agency, which acts as a gatekeeper for much of that development, says access to capital is the biggest obstacle for Black developers. Some would answer that lack of access is another manifestation of the systemic racism that many, including at high levels in Oklahoma, resolutely maintain does not exist.[89]

"It came down to, 'What the Greenwood Cultural Center's role would be if this [history] center is placed there,'" Armstrong said. "There was a fear that Greenwood Cultural Center would pretty much go away. Some in the community raised a concern that this new center is just going to take over and the Greenwood Cultural Center is just going to go away . . . that someone is going to take over the Greenwood Cultural Center and if we don't stand up we're going to lose our center."[90]

By mid-April 2020, the commission decided it could not wait any longer if it hoped to at least have a building to show for the race massacre centennial a little more than a year away.[91]

"The architects and construction folks said if you have any hope of finishing this building in time, which was the goal, you've got to make a decision," Armstrong said. "So the commission notified the mayor—the mayor was trying to broker those discussions—the commission said we have no hope but to pull out and try to find an alternative."[92]

Cultural Center board chair Sherri Tapp issued a statement saying, "We completely support the efforts of the commission and what they are trying to do . . . and we look forward to opportunities to work with them in the future."[93]

At the time, it seemed as if yet another attempt to memorialize Greenwood's story was headed for the ditch. As it turned out, it was probably the best thing that could have happened for both the museum, which by now was being called Greenwood Rising, and the Greenwood Cultural Center.

Less than two weeks after ending negotiations with the Greenwood Cultural Center, the commission announced it would be building Greenwood Rising on the southeast corner of Archer and Greenwood, the iconic crossroads where Black Wall Street began, and that Bob Wills and the Texas Playboys introduced to a new audience in the 1941 hit "Take Me Back to Tulsa." Kajeer and Maggie Yar, who had built a mixed-use development on the intersection's southwest corner and were starting work on the southeast corner, volunteered to move the latter seventy-five feet south, hard against what are now the Burlington Northern Santa Fe tracks, to make room for Greenwood Rising.

"The Hille Foundation and 21 North Greenwood, LLC, already in the process of developing the land, halted construction and moved the site of a planned mixed-use building to donate the land to the Centennial Commission," Matthews told commission members in an April 27, 2020, email. "What an amazing gift and amazing show of support for our efforts.

"We will be able to begin construction immediately."[94]

In fact, groundbreaking would not occur until August, but Greenwood Rising got a prime location and the Greenwood Cultural Center kept its identity.[95]

The Yars' involvement brought another dimension to the evolving Greenwood story. Both had grown up in and around Tulsa. Like Charles Schusterman, George Kaiser, and Henry Zarrow, Kajeer Yar was the son of immigrants, in his case from Afghanistan, who arrived in the United States when he was a toddler. Maggie Hille Yar's father, Jo Bob Hille, was a successful independent oilman. Maggie had graduated from Booker T. Washington High School, as had Kevin Matthews, which meant both belonged to a far-flung and influential alumni network. But being a white BTW alum can be both a plus and a minus with Black Tulsans. Not only integrating Booker T. and nearby Carver Middle School but turning them into magnet schools attracting students from all over the city likely saved the schools from closure, the fate of most historically Black schools in the wake of *Brown v. Board of Education*. Booker T.'s status among white Tulsans, and even nationally, soared. But the change also meant some neighborhood Black students could no longer go there, and this produced another sense of loss, of invasion, and reinforced the feeling that the few things that Black Tulsans could call their own were being taken away. Some thought the way in which Carver and Booker T. were integrated constituted a form of scholastic gentrification.[96]

For those concerned about what was beginning to be called the gentrification of Greenwood, the Yars did not exactly fit the mold. Kajeer was not Black but he was not white either. Maggie was white but a Booker T. grad who had maintained strong connections with the school. The Yars, through the Hille Foundation, had seen to it that a memorial to Booker T. Washington's legendary founding principal Ellis Walker Woods was erected on the OSU-Tulsa campus, near the school's original site. Maggie belonged to the centennial commission. The Yars were both essentially sympathetic to Black Tulsans and their hopes for Greenwood, and by signing over the land for Greenwood Rising, the Yars gave the history center something the Greenwood Cultural Center did not have—a deed to its own property.[97]

"We care a lot about making sure the story of the massacre, and not just the massacre, but the story of Greenwood and Deep Greenwood and Black Wall

Street specifically is being told," Maggie Yar said soon after the transfer. "That is very important to us."[98]

"They have to own their land," Kajeer Yar said in 2022, referring to Greenwood Rising. "They have to not be beholden to anyone, not to the city, not to the county. That organization needs to be able to speak on its own behalf . . . because the neighborhood has never been able to have its own voice about what happened and what it wants to happen."

Of course, anything that increases traffic to the intersection of Greenwood and Archer was likely to enhance the Yars' investment in the GreenArch Building, across the street from Greenwood Rising, and 21 North Greenwood, the building they moved to make room from the history center. That fed the growing criticism of Greenwood Rising as just another step in the takeover of Greenwood.

"We get that a lot," Kajeer Yar said in 2022. "I don't think [the museum] hurts. I don't know that we've seen a massive increase, though."

Yar is a defender of Greenwood but also a critic, especially of those who presume to speak for it without putting in what amounts to sweat equity.

> I've told people over and over again, if I see you here, your boots are on the ground, you've attempted to run a business in Greenwood, or you've shopped here, you've done business here, then criticize us all you want. But if you're here in an attempt to shake someone down . . . I don't have any time or place for that. And honestly, that's such an affront to the people that lost their lives here, and also the people who struggled here.
>
> The people that predominantly stayed and rebuilt, they don't get enough attention. To say, "Despite the worst parts of humanity being shown to us, we love this place enough that we're going to rebuild." Those have always been . . . my inspiration just to say, you know, if people stuck it out with that kind of nonsense, we owe their legacy the same amount of stick-to-itiveness.[99]

The story of how the Yars—or, more precisely, the Hille Foundation—became involved in GreenArch, and then by extension 21 North Greenwood and Greenwood Rising, is an example of how byzantine Greenwood development can be.

GreenArch actually evolved from a proposal by Reuben Gant, then executive director of the Greenwood Chamber of Commerce, in the mid-2000s. Although the Greenwood Chamber of Commerce had been around since the 1930s, it was reorganized and repurposed in the 1980s to facilitate the rescue and management of the ten buildings in the 100 block of North Greenwood. These were all that remained of the old business district after the economic and social changes of the 1950s and 1960s, urban renewal, and construction of the inner dispersal loop; in 2000, the Greenwood Chamber acquired sole ownership of the buildings from the city. In 2006, the Chamber's economic development arm, Greenwood Community Development Corp., put in a bid on 5.8 acres of long-vacant land on the north side of Archer west of Greenwood, with Gant proposing a mixed-use development to be called Franklin Square, after John Hope Franklin. At the time, not much was going on in that neighborhood, although development of what would become known as the Arts District was inching eastward from North Main Street.[100]

The Tulsa Development Authority (TDA), the city's urban renewal agency, twice extended bid deadlines but did not receive any others, and after more than a year, finally agreed to sell to Greenwood Community Development Corp. for $1.8 million. Just five months later, in June 2008, Mayor Kathy Taylor decided that very site would be perfect for a new baseball park to keep Tulsa's minor league affiliate in town, and persuaded Gant to trade his tract for one on the southeast corner of Greenwood and Archer.[101]

"When you have 400,000-plus people coming into the area, it's going to really expose the district, not only to out-of-towners, but Tulsa residents that have never been north of the tracks," Gant said at the time.[102]

But while Gant and the Greenwood Chamber of Commerce now had the land, they had no money to do anything with it—a familiar dilemma for Black would-be developers.

That is where the Yars came into the picture. They brought the capital with the idea of taking advantage of some government programs for affordable housing. But it would take two years for construction to begin, and when it did it was without any sort of government subsidy. According to Kajeer Yar, the city began setting requirements that would have essentially turned GreenArch into Section 8 apartments.[103]

"We said, 'Are you guys nuts? Why in the world would you—first of all, do you know the message that would send? That you're building a subsidized housing project on Greenwood? That was never the deal from the beginning. You guys understood what we were doing, why we were doing it, and to kind of pull the rug out from under us at the end like this, just is B.S'"[104]

So the Yars did something unexpected. They took out a bank loan and built GreenArch—all $9.5 million of it—on their own. It opened a year later, with first-level retail space and seventy apartments geared for downtown workers who could not afford the high-end digs a few blocks away. In all of the shuffle, though, the Greenwood Community Development Corp., had to give up its equity position in exchange for $476,000, a fair deal from a business standpoint but one that ended Black participation in ownership.[105]

Asked in 2022, Gant said he was "not displeased" with the way things turned out but bemoaned what he said is the "red tape" that dictates development of TDA property.

"The plan that I [originally] envisioned . . . was going to be challenging," he said. "I would have had to raise the funds to do it, and it was a $25–$30 million project. You are talking condominiums and a hotel and commercial businesses. That would've been a daunting task. And in talking with the [Greenwood] Chamber's board, when the ballpark concept came up, that's the way we looked at it."[106]

Once the ballpark was announced, financing for other projects began to line up, including—eventually—the six-story Vast bank building on the northwest corner of Elgin and Archer. By 2020, criticism of the decision to build ONEOK Field in what had historically been part of Greenwood tended to be couched in terms of a ballpark used and financially benefitting mainly whites versus Black-owned businesses and homes. But in 2008, with capital disappearing into the maw of the Great Recession and not much happening in Greenwood, Gant thinks a more likely scenario would have been a ballpark versus nothing.[107]

"There probably wouldn't be anything on that property right now, or very little," he said.[108]

More generally, Gant is frustrated by a system that, from his perspective, uses opaque rules to rig the game in what he calls the establishment's favor. In 2011, an unfavorable US Department of Housing and Urban Development report on Greenwood Community Development's management of a grant caused it to be frozen out of HUD programs. Gant claimed the city had essentially sandbagged him; he sued, but the lawsuit was dropped, and he left the Greenwood Chamber in 2013.[109]

"They put these properties up for sale," Gant said, "and then you have all kinds of red tape that you have to go through in order to develop the property. I understand they don't sell property based on speculation, but that's a bunch of B.S. too, because they do that all the time."[110]

Kajeer Yar, who has also had his disagreements with the city, said he has the same impression. "I don't have any facts to back this up, but I think that's kind of the way the city of Tulsa has always tried to control what happens in Greenwood and in North Tulsa," Yar said. "Sort of force people that want to do business with them . . . to do it their way."[111]

The Tulsa Development Authority was set up in 1959 under state laws intended to keep urban renewal decisions as independent of local government as possible. From the initial wave of condemnation and demolition to the present, that independence sometimes has been interpreted as insufficient oversight. About the same time Reuben Gant was trying to bring Franklin Square to life, TDA's spending and recordkeeping was under scrutiny by the US Department of Housing and Urban Development. In 2009, the Tulsa city council proclaimed outrage at the amount of land TDA held, some of it since 1966, without any apparent plans for disposing of it. Whether the city of Tulsa and the Tulsa Development Authority are much different than their counterparts across the United States is hard to say, but judging from nationwide criticism of urban renewal and much of what sprang from it, they probably are not. Dwain Midget, a Black man who became one of Tulsa's most respected civil servants over a forty-year career with the city, said people tend to forget the city's involvement in initiatives that work. He made his point by ticking off neighborhoods, businesses, and street projects improved or made possible by TDA or some other city, state, or federal agency. But for the people at ground level, it can all seem like a rolling confusion of regulations, politics, and aggravation. A confusion they do not have the money or knowledge or connections to sort out. A confusion that, given frequent outcomes, can seem intentional and, again, look a lot like the systemic (if not necessarily conscious) racism whose existence so many Oklahomans in authority adamantly deny.[112]

Ground was broken for Greenwood Rising in August, with a completion date of right around the centennial. Money was rolling in. For Matthews, Armstrong, and the others involved, the best and worst days were ahead.[113]

As a legal argument, the petition filed in Tulsa County District Court on September 1, 2020, was widely viewed as a stretch. As a polemical and public relations statement, it hit the bullseye.

Filed on behalf of 105-year-old Lessie Randle and others, including Vernon AME, the Tulsa African American Ancestral Society, and several descendants or other relatives of Black Tulsa residents of 1921, the suit sought damages from the city of Tulsa and six other entities for not only the race massacre but for what it said was a continuing pattern of abuse up to the present. To get around statutes of limitations, which had proved a roadblock to similar previous lawsuits, the plaintiffs' attorneys adopted a strategy that Oklahoma's attorney general used to win a $572 million judgment against opioid manufacturer Johnson & Johnson. In that case, Attorney General Mike Hunter and a legal team hired by the state on a contingency basis argued the company's marketing of the drugs constituted a continuing public nuisance, in which case statutes of limitations would not apply.[114]

"They went back forty years talking about how the (opioid) nuisance was created and continued," lead attorney Damario Solomon-Simmons said at a press conference announcing the race massacre lawsuit. "That's the theory we are working with."[115]

Although sometimes referred to as the "survivors' lawsuit," it was really about Greenwood as a whole. The petition alleged a one-hundred-year pattern of both exploitation and neglect led by the city and what had become the Tulsa Regional Chamber of Commerce, while also naming as defendants the Tulsa Development Authority, the Tulsa Area Metropolitan Planning Commission, the Tulsa County Commissioners, the Tulsa County Sheriff, and the Oklahoma Military Department. Its audacious demands included an accounting of:

> All money received by the Defendants, from public and private sources, for use in the Greenwood neighborhood and community from June 1, 1921 to 1960.
>
> All money received by the Defendants from public and private sources for use in North Tulsa from 1960 to the present. . . .
>
> All money dispersed by the Defendants to residents of the Greenwood neighborhood and North Tulsa, or their descendants, to abate the nuisance from May 31, 1921 to the present. . . .
>
> All money dispersed to directly benefit the Greenwood neighborhood and community, subsequently North Tulsa, from May 31, 1921 to the present.
>
> The value of the loss of life in the Greenwood neighborhood and subsequently North Tulsa, as determined by licensed professional actuaries based upon published mortality tables that can be reasonably attributable to Defendants' actions in causing the nuisance, including those who were killed on May 31 and June 1, 1921 to the present.
>
> The value of the loss of private personal property stolen and looted from Greenwood residents by Defendants from May 31, 1921 to the present. . . .
>
> The value of emotional and psychological trauma inflicted on the residents of Greenwood, subsequently North Tulsa, by the Defendants, by the nuisance created by the Defendants.

> The difference in property values pre-Massacre and every ten (10) years subsequent to the Massacre of property owned by residents of Greenwood and North Tulsa.
>
> The value of property lost due to defendants' actions, including Defendants' policies and practices, from May 31, 1921 to the present.[116]

Clearly, these demands were nearly or entirely impossible to meet, but they underscored the enormity of the wrongs alleged. One of the issues raised by Solomon-Simmons rang remarkably true to a report from a few days after the massacre stating that Greenwood lots were worth $500 as Black residences but $1,700 for industrial use. In court documents, including a deposition, Solomon-Simmons traced the history of the house where Mrs. Randle remembered living with her grandmother at the time of the massacre, and which Mrs. Randle herself had sold to the urban renewal authority in 1980 during creation of Lansing Industrial Park. According to court documents, the authority had paid Mrs. Randle for the house and given her additional money to buy a replacement several miles away, but Solomon-Simmons' point was that Mrs. Randle had not had much choice in the matter and that the property had been combined with others to become the site of a "white-owned business" that substantially increased the value of Mrs. Randle's former parcel.[117]

The lawsuit challenged precedent and legal interpretation and would be thrashed out by judges and lawyers for years to come. Whether *Randle v. City of Tulsa* could prevail as a legal argument remained to be seen, but the polemic arising from it successfully stirred national attention. From the first petition through subsequent revisions and pleadings, with the three elderly plaintiffs in attendance at nearly every court hearing, press conference and television appearance, Solomon-Simmons and his team were on the attack. And two of the targets were the centennial commission and Greenwood Rising. This was no surprise. On June 1, 2020, the ninety-ninth anniversary of the massacre and three months before filing the first *Randle* petition, Solomon-Simmons told a YouTube panel discussion: "The same people who destroyed Greenwood, the same people who oppress black people in this city every single day are now trying to capitalize on the story of Greenwood." [118]

In that same vein, the first paragraph of the petition concludes with "The Plaintiffs also seek to recover for unjust enrichment for the Defendants' exploitation of the Massacre for their own economic and political gain."

Later, the petition went into greater detail.

> Defendants have appropriated the history of the Massacre, using the names and likenesses of the survivors and descendants of Massacre victims, to exploit the horrific event in which they actively participated and the subsequent trauma they caused and which continue to this day. Their purpose is to promote tourism and economic development by appropriating the name "Black Wall Street," along with its cultural and historical significance and through the use of names and likenesses of survivors—predominantly for the benefit of white-owned or controlled Tulsa businesses and organizations. Their appropriations not only result in their unjust enrichment; but rather than offering an apology and compensation for the damages they caused, they are exacerbating the pain of the continued trauma they caused.[119]

The petition then attacks Bynum for recounting the murder of Black surgeon A. C. Jackson without apologizing to Jackson's great-nephew, one of the original plaintiffs and described as Jackson's heir and closest living relative. The petition lays claim to any "benefits" derived from "marketing Black Wall Street" and asks for an injunction preventing the defendants "from receiving any money or other material benefits from the Greenwood Rising facility." Anything that would have gone to the defendants should instead go into a "Victims Compensation Fund."[120]

An interesting aspect of all this is that none of the named defendants in *Randle v. Tulsa* had then or has now a direct financial interest in Greenwood Rising. The city and county could potentially reap some tax revenue if the history center proves successful, but it is the history center that sells tickets and receives contributions. The building, its assets, and the land it sets on are owned by a foundation controlled by unpaid trustees. Museums are not generally big moneymakers, but why the entities through which the money for and ultimately from Greenwood Rising flow—the centennial commission and the museum itself—were not included as defendants is unclear. Similarly excluded were nearby businesses and property owners who conceivably could benefit from a successful Greenwood Rising.[121]

Beyond rattling some cages in Tulsa, *Randle v. Tulsa* challenged age-old practices concerning the preservation and examination of history, who owns it and how it's presented. If Greenwood Rising is exploitive appropriation, is the same true of the National Holocaust Museum? Gettysburg? Dachau? Do images of historical figures belong to the people who create them or to the subjects' descendants and heirs? Certainly it is understandable that people whose history has been so distorted, when not outright ignored, now want to control it. It is also reasonable to wonder whether history is a commodity or community property. Or both. Or something else entirely.

Solomon-Simmons formed a nonprofit, Justice for Greenwood, to solicit donations for the lawsuit, to assist plaintiffs and Greenwood families, and for other related programs, and also to spread the narrative that tens of millions of dollars were being raised for a museum controlled by whites who would determine how the story of the massacre and Greenwood was told. This claim found a ready audience. According to the nonprofit monitor GuideStar, Justice for Greenwood received contributions in excess of $1.4 million in its first year and reported assets of almost $850,000. It also began wresting the role of storyteller away from the centennial commission and set the two sides on a collision course in the months ahead.[122]

The lawyers said Greenwood Avenue's Black Lives Matter sign had to go. The city attorney, David O'Meilia, said it was a "constitutional issue."

"If you permit that kind of thing . . . then you would open any street in your community to any type of message that wasn't pornographic or inciting a riot," O'Meilia told the city council in late July 2020.[123]

But that was not the real issue. The real issue was that some Tulsans, and especially some white Tulsans, simply could not abide what the sign symbolized. They said it was an attack on the police, and that the Black Lives Matter organization, such as it was, harbored socialists and anarchists and just plain outlaws.

In July, Republican county chair Bob Jack emailed Bynum and City Councilor Ben Kimbro, saying, "A group has approached me with a plan to paint on a city street in large letters 'BACK THE BLUE' and 'BABY LIVES MATTER.' As you are aware, the city did not intervene in the painting of 'BLACK LIVE [*sic*] MATTER' on Greenwood, just north of Archer, and the group is requesting the same right to voice their opinion."[124]

A few weeks later, Jack claimed the group was "all good" with the idea that Black lives matter. It was Black Lives Matter they found objectionable.

"That is the biggest problem we have with this," Jack told a reporter. "It represents a Democratic (Party), radical Marxist, anti-American organization. That is the prime reason why we object. Not the message. We are all good with the message; we are not good with the organization."[125]

What they and many others did not understand, or perhaps refused to believe, was that the message *was* the organization. At least that was the case in Tulsa. To be sure, the people marching under the Black Lives Matter guidon saw themselves as disrupters of the social, economic, and political status quo. For Black lives to truly matter, they believed, change was necessary. That message unified them, not any particular political philosophy or party loyalty. Mareo Johnson, who claims credit for starting Black Lives Matter in Tulsa, laughed when asked if it was a Marxist organization.

"Black Lives Matter is not trying to overthrow the government," he said in the summer of 2020. "We just [want] a fair government."[126]

That is not to say some attached to the movement were not more radical than others, or that the movement did not attract some people itching for a fight. The small-scale riots that followed Tulsa's 2020 protests like aftershocks demonstrated that. Almost all of those arrested were from out of town and white.[127]

In an interview for this book, Jack acknowledged he was "upset" about the sign painted on Greenwood Avenue but was also pressured to act by those "with total disdain for Black Lives Matter."

"I was hearing a lot," he said. "I had people call me up, 'I've got enough paint, and people and rollers. We're ready to go. We're ready to go. We're ready to go. We got the paint and rollers, we're ready to go.'"[128]

In late July, the city's legal department told the mayor's office and city council that allowing the Black Lives Matter mural to remain would invite anybody to paint anything on any street.

Several years earlier, the city had denied an application from a local LGBTQ organization to paint rainbow crosswalks near its downtown headquarters, citing federal regulations. Now it invoked similar reservations about the Greenwood sign and the one Bob Jack's group wanted to paint near city hall. Bynum's chief of staff, Jack Blair, said the consensus within city government was that finding a way to permit "this kind of use" was insurmountably difficult.

"It won't be popular, but I think we have all heard there is just not an alternative from a legal perspective," Blair said.

This sounded like doubletalk to the people who painted the mural and those who wanted it to remain. Some, like Nehemiah Frank of the digital publication *Black Wall Street Times*, accused Bynum and the city of trying to create cover by splitting the Black community on the issue. The Greenwood Chamber of Commerce, as owner of the historic buildings on either side of Greenwood Avenue, had been approached about taking over responsibility for the mural. Barely able to keep the doors open as it was, the Greenwood Chamber declined, which prompted Bynum to say the "The property owner (the Greenwood Chamber) indicated they do not want the mural to remain."[129]

Frank was among Greenwood Chamber critics who suspected it of complicity in a scheme to squeeze out Greenwood's remaining Black entrepreneurs. This view was not universal among Black Tulsans, but it was and is pervasive. Forced into a difficult if not impossible business model, the Greenwood Chamber had for years told tenants to be patient with leaky roofs and substandard plumbing, electrical, and air handling systems, while raising rents that often go unpaid, either out of protest or financial difficulty. Although things seem to have improved in recent years, the Greenwood Chamber remains controversial among Black Tulsans.[130]

"Having been aware of the odd relationship Tulsa Black leaders and Black entrepreneurs had with the Greenwood Chamber board for years, it can only be assumed that Mayor Bynum seized the opportunity to gain the approval from a Black minority in *blackface* [italics in original] to justify his acts of anti-Blackness through legal means," wrote Frank, whose site's national audience and influence were growing rapidly. "The pitting of Black people against one another is a racist tactic that White politicians have used since the beginning of institutional and racialized enslavement of Africans in America."

Safe to say, most white Tulsans were unaware of this perspective, and probably would not have understood or agreed with it had they been. But many did regard the mural's removal as wrong or at least unnecessary, and at some level an example of the law being used to silence dissent.

"I would have preferred they would have had a town hall meeting and we do a community vote on it, but we didn't get that opportunity," said Briana Shea, a white woman involved in organizing the mural's creation. "Having that painted there as Trump flew into Tulsa and he was able to see that, I think it says a lot about Tulsa and our history here and how we are not proud of the history but we wanted to make it known that ninety-nine years later we're still healing from it, and I thought that mural that we did did bring healing."[131]

At a rally a few days after the council vote, Reverend Turner commented:

> [They] said it didn't follow legal procedure. When did this government ever care about legal procedure? How in the heavens did they get this land in the first place? So don't lecture me about legal procedure. . . . They didn't go through a legal procedure when they kidnapped Black men and women

> and children from Africa. They didn't go through a legal procedure when they went through Greenwood and dropped bombs and looted. How dare they hide behind a legal procedure when people declared in asphalt that Black lives matter?[132]

Tiffany Crutcher organized a group that put up cardboard tombstones on the street, each bearing the name of someone killed in the race massacre or by law enforcement. Several churches and a synagogue painted Black Lives Matter murals in their parking lots. But there were other, less supportive reactions. Somebody painted a blue stripe through the Greenwood sign. Drivers tried to "burn rubber" on it. Some people were still itching to paint "Blue Lives Matter" somewhere. And, right on cue, Westboro Baptist Church—the splinter Kansas congregation known for outrageously picketing everything from the funeral processions of military personnel killed in action to services for victims of the Sandy Hook shootings—served notice it intended to paint messages such as "All lives are nothing before God," and "God sent the coronavirus in fury" in the streets outside Tulsa hospitals.[133]

With elections for mayor and city council approaching, Bynum told the street department to leave the sign alone for the time being, giving Hall-Harper and fellow city councilor Kara Joy McKee, in whose district the mural was actually located, some time to find an alternative. One idea was to have the Historic Greenwood District Main Street program obtain a right-of-way and occupancy permit for the 250 feet occupied by the sign. Another was to designate the mural "government speech"—basically, to adopt the sign's message as an expression of city policy—until at least the 2021 centennial.[134]

But none of it panned out, and in early September even McKee gave up. She joined all of the councilors except Hall-Harper in voting eight to one to move up a planned mill and overlay resurfacing of Greenwood Avenue that would literally erase the mural. Maggie Hille Yar, in a last-minute appeal, suggested painting a new sign one block south, between Greenwood Rising and the Yar's GreenArch building, with the history center and the Yars taking responsibility for that section of street. Hall-Harper, now fully aligned with those opposed to the museum, shot that down, saying she would "not support any entity privatizing or vacating the street unless they are willing to sign the deed over to a Black organization and continue to maintain it and commit to the continued maintenance of that space. If that is not going to happen, I am not going to support more white people gentrifying more land in Greenwood."[135]

Just as the mural was laid down in the wee hours of the morning, so it was removed. A city contractor began the job at 3 a.m. on the morning of October 5 and was finished by 6:15 a.m. Quite openly, Bynum said the project was scheduled "so it could proceed without interference." The *Black Wall Street Times* compared the decision to the draining of whites-only swimming pools during the desegregation of the 1950s and 1960s.[136]

The mural, Shea had said earlier, "didn't solve any problems whatsoever. But at least we put the time and effort in it to give love back to the community, and that love was felt by the community."[137]

When another flash crew hastily painted "BLM" in front of city hall a few days later, this time in broad daylight on a Saturday afternoon, it was quickly scrubbed off. Unlike with the original mural, the city made a show of trying to track down those involved.

"Vandalism of public property is not a peaceful protest," Bynum said. "It is a criminal act."[138]

The *Oklahoma Eagle* gave that an editorial eyeroll.

"Yes, you can pursue painters of Black Lives Matter on a city street, or you can station a cop to watch Greenwood night and day to make sure no one has the nerve to paint BLM on city property," wrote the *Eagle* editorialist. "Or you can find a way to address why BLM is painted on city streets in the first place. One way is a lot more effective and cheaper."[139]

Three people were arrested, two for refusing to leave the street when ordered and a third for running from police with paint on her clothing. The district attorney chose not to pursue charges against the latter.[140]

Two weeks later, in a show of even-handedness, city crews painted over an American flag painting that had been maintained in a south Tulsa cul-de-sac for eighteen years.[141]

The archeologists returned in October. Confident of finding remains this time, their primary concern was whether any could be positively linked to the race massacre.

With no ready alternative, the grave search committee decided to move a short distance south of the summer's excavation to where records, remaining grave markers, and earlier field work strongly indicated burials existed, and where researchers suspected the "Original 18" had been interred. These eighteen were listed, albeit sometimes namelessly, in records and reports from immediately after the massacre. Those same sources indicated the eighteen had been buried individually in caskets—which, of course, did not necessarily make it so. And just because eighteen were listed as buried in Oaklawn did not mean there were not more besides. So perhaps finding the eighteen would lead to others. At the very least, it would solve one mystery and perhaps allow identification of individual remains.[142]

The work began on October 19. The next day the team began encountering remains, but whether they were connected to the massacre could not be immediately determined. The plan all along had been for a preliminary examination that might yield sufficient evidence to obtain exhumation orders. Kary Stackelbeck, the state archeologist, acknowledged that scientists in her line of work were not used to such close scrutiny from an impatient public and press.

"Normally, we like to have an opportunity to absorb all of the information, to digest it, and do our interpretations before we turn it around," Stackelbeck said.[143]

Stackelbeck, Phoebe Stubblefield, and others involved in the project held daily press conferences in the Fire Alarm Building, a restored art deco gem adjoining Oaklawn Cemetery's northwest corner. After the false promise of the first excavation, Stackelbeck was cautious at the October 20 briefing.

"Clearly, we're in a cemetery, and we have many other people buried here who were not massacre victims. We're very mindful of that," she said. "We're kind of premature in being able to provide a lot of details, but clearly the main thing we'll be focusing on is whether the remains are in a condition that allows for any indication of trauma."[144]

Stackelbeck described the condition of the remains as "variable," but said the day's developments gave her "reason for optimism because our field methods are proving out . . . [and] the fact that we have human remains that are discoverable and potentially recoverable."[145]

The team and city officials, in fact, had hoped to minimize contact with the press and public by erecting a high screen around the excavation site, but if anything, that only intensified curiosity—and, for some, suspicion. The discovery of a single burial on the morning of October 20 quickly became known and necessitated resumption of the press conferences. And press near and far was eager for something to report.

"Scientists May Be Days Away from Solving a 100-Year-Old Mystery to the Whereabouts of Missing Black Victims from the 1921 Tulsa Race Massacre," the *Black Wall Street Times* told its readers.[146]

"Scientists Find Human Remains That Might Be from Tulsa's 1921 Race Massacre," read a *Washington Post* headline.[147]

That the remains were determined to be those of a woman heightened interest. No women's deaths from the massacre had been documented, but there exists some evidence to the contrary. Proof of that evidence would have indeed been an explosive development. Ultimately, such was not the case; the first remains uncovered were eventually set aside as likely unrelated to the massacre. They did, however, point the way to something more promising.[148]

On October 21, one day after the backhoe inadvertently broke open the single burial, the archeologists began uncovering nearby what they said was evidence of coffins stacked in pairs along a trench. An eleventh was found the next day. Stackelbeck declared the trench a mass grave (she later backed off that assessment) and said there might be more burials still stacked in the trench or nearby. With their work mostly blocked from public view, the researchers described the coffins as badly decayed, with some hardly more than outlines in the tightly packed soil and a few rusted metal fittings. The human remains—essentially bones and teeth, as best Stubblefield could determine without an exhumation—were similarly degraded. No one could say with certainty the site was related to the massacre but given the unusual manner of burial and the location, such did seem likely.[149]

"We have a high degree of confidence that this is one of the locations we were looking for," Stackelbeck said. "But we have to remain cautious because we have not done anything to expose the human remains beyond those that have been encountered."[150]

As she had before, Stubblefield cautioned reporters that one hundred-year-old remains could be quite fragile when exposed to air and sunlight.

"When you go to remove something like this, you only get one chance," she said.[151]

Scott Ellsworth, after decades of literal and figurative digging for answers, said, "This has been a hugely important week for the city of Tulsa, but more than that, for our country. This is the only time any level of [American] government has gone out to search for the hidden remains of victims of racial violence. This is an amazing event that's happened here in Tulsa, and Tulsa is to be complemented for its leadership."[152]

Brenda Alford, the granddaughter of massacre survivors, had spent many days at the Oaklawn worksites as chair of the oversight committee. She was, she said, "truly beyond words."

"I don't believe my grandparents and other members of the community could have ever imagined this time in history," she said.[153]

Lacking legal authority or a definite plan for safely removing and preserving the remains, and with bad weather moving in, the discovery that seemed to bring the search to the literal edge of at least a partial solution to the great mystery was hastily covered with dirt, leaving the secrets buried beneath for the centennial and 2021.[154]

A headline in the September 3, 2020, *Tulsa World* reported that the Black Lives Matter mural on Greenwood Avenue would be "gone by Election Day." While there may have been some grumbling about the painting constituting a gigantic city-sponsored bumper sticker message, in fact it was unlikely to have made much difference in the November 2020 general election. Nothing had for decades. The Republican Party's hold on Oklahoma politics at almost all levels was such that most offices were decided in the summer primary and runoff elections, if not at the moment filing closed in April. Democrats still had a few pockets of strength, mainly in African American communities, and had seen their influence grow somewhat within the Oklahoma City and Tulsa city limits, but for the most part government was run by white male Republicans aligned with evangelical Christians.

The November 2020 elections did not figure to change that much. Some of the elected Republicans, including Stitt, held tribal citizenship, and a few were of Hispanic or Asian heritage. That fall, state senator Stephanie Bice, an Oklahoma City Republican, would become the first Iranian American elected to Congress. But Oklahoma politics is almost entirely a white man's game. Bice is only the third woman, all Republican, to represent Oklahoma in Congress. One of those, Mary Fallin, is also the only woman elected governor. It had been exactly thirty years since former University of Oklahoma football star J. C. Watts, a Republican, won a seat on the Corporation Commission to become the first and still only African American elected to statewide office; later he became the state's first and only Black member of Congress.

There has not been another J. C. Watts. Some Republicans thought they had one with T. W. Shannon, a promising young state representative of African and Chickasaw ancestry. Elected from Lawton, in southwestern Oklahoma, Shannon in 2013 became the first person of color to serve as speaker of the Oklahoma House of Representatives. But as a statewide candidate, in a special election for the US Senate in 2014, Shannon had no chance against Lankford, a Southern Baptist preacher who had built up an influential statewide network as director of Falls Creek Youth Camp.

Kojo Asamoa-Caesar knew all of that but decided to run for Congress anyway. He filed in the Tulsa-based first district, which had not elected a Democrat since 1984, and had not really had a close general election in more than twenty years. His opponent was one-term incumbent Kevin Hern, a multimillionaire who first made it big as a McDonald's franchisee and then expanded into manufacturing, construction, banking, and other endeavors. Hern and Asamoa-Caesar both grew up poor: Hern in rural Arkansas, Asamoa-Caesar a generation later in Washington, DC. Hern overcame his childhood poverty, early career disappointments, and hard times in young adulthood. Asamoa-Caesar's parents were Ghanaian immigrants whose dreams and ambitions never quite overcame not only some of the same obstacles as Hern faced, but also those encountered by immigrants and especially immigrants of color. Their son, though, flourished. He graduated from Old Dominion University and the College of William and Mary's Marshall-Wythe Law School. He pursued his own American Dream, different from his parents' dream, and different from Hern's. Instead of a legal career, Asamoa-Caesar came to Tulsa with Teach for America and migrated to the nonprofit realm. In Asamoa-Caesar's dream, the opportunity is more evenly distributed, and a person is measured by their character instead of their color—or political affiliation.[155]

During his 2020 campaign, Asamoa-Caesar learned how distant that dream is from reality. Republicans and Democrats alike snubbed him, often for reasons that had nothing to do with him or his ideas.

> We decided, if we were going to have any chance of winning . . . we would have to 'cross the street' and talk to Republicans," Asamoa-Caesar said. "And so we did that. I got a chance to go speak at Oral Roberts University and to speak with people from Life Church [a large, multisite evangelical congregation] and started to get to know people.
>
> I'm very genuine and I answer questions directly and I share my story and I tried to find that common ground with folks, and we were able to actually do that successfully. But the barrier that we kept running into was the fact that I was a Democrat. Republicans could just not get over the fact that I was a Democrat. . . . A lot of people would say, "Kojo, I like you, I like your story, it's inspiring, but I just can't vote for a Democrat."[156]

At the root of that irreconcilable opposition, Asamoa-Caesar concluded, was religion. Although he is upfront about his Christianity, the reluctance of many

Democrats, even in Bible-belt Oklahoma, to engage on the matter reinforces perceptions upon which Republican messaging capitalizes, said Asamoa-Caesar.

> A lot of Republicans are very religious, and they just feel as if Democrats are antireligion, anti-God, they want to kill babies, they have this agenda to change and transform our culture with transgender stuff. So even though they like you and you're finding common ground, the fact that you have a 'D' in front of your name is just a nonstarter. It almost feels as if they're making a deal with the devil, and God is going to be mad at them if they vote for you.

During a debate, Asamoa-Caesar said, he was asked what he most disagreed with the Democratic Party about.

> My answer was that I am a Christian, I'm a born again Christian . . . and I don't think I should leave that at the door. I think that's okay for me to talk about in the public square. It's not me promoting religion. It's not breaching the separation of church and state. We should be able to talk about our faith in the public square. Because we cede ground for Republicans to call the Democrats basically antireligion, anti-God, and they have an anti-God agenda. And that got a huge applause line from a crowd that had been booing me the whole night.
>
> I don't think a lot of Democrats are anti-God, but they don't realize how, a lot of times, the things they've advocated for, coupled with this desire to remove religion [from political discussion] because they feel like it's a corrupting influence, what that communicates to a lot of people in Tulsa.

Of course, Asamoa-Caesar expected resistance from Republicans. What he did not expect was the reaction of some Democrats. After launching his campaign in November 2019, a full year ahead of the election, and encountering what he felt was encouraging early response, he ran smack dab into opposition within his own party.

> I'm a newcomer to this. I've gone out and kind of done the legwork and started to make some noise and I'm expecting the Democratic Party and the powers that be to say, "Wow, this is awesome!. Look at this guy, let's help him out." Instead, I received the opposite. It was, "Who is this guy? Who does he think he is? How come he didn't even come and talk to us before he ran?" And basically ask permission, you know?

Even in its diminished state, the Oklahoma Democratic Party had a hierarchy, and Kojo Asamoa-Caesar was not part of it.

"People who I've never heard of, who apparently are powerful people, are upset with me and are basically trying to find a way to get me out of [the race]. So that was very disheartening," said Asamoa-Caesar.

Even after he and the party leadership "kind of made peace," they continued to disagree about his campaign. Asamoa-Caesar wanted to just be himself; the "experienced hands," as he called them, told him that would not work.

> They're coming in and saying, "Okay, this is how it's going to go. This is the part of your story that you should emphasize, and this is the part you should de-emphasize." I kind of played that game for a little bit, because obviously you need resources. But that also did not sit well with me. Obviously I'm a Black candidate, and even though it's the first time running, a lot of what everybody came to see later on with the civil unrest, we were feeling before that and made it a part of our platform. And these people were trying to tell me now that's too controversial. "Social justice and stuff like that, take that out. Don't talk about those things. You don't want Oklahomans to feel bad about themselves."

This is a constant theme in Oklahoma politics. Do not make us feel bad about ourselves, even if it means ignoring reality. Asamoa-Caesar was not pounding tables or firing off incendiary manifestos, but he was saying what he believed needed to be said. Yet, in some ways he was arguably more conservative than those trying to coach him.

"Basically, I decided I was kind of going to go my own way, and I was going to value authenticity and the freedom to speak the way that I wanted to over trying to please somebody just to get resources from them. I was freed from that and it became a lot more fun," he said. When the George Floyd stuff and all those things happened, we were rewarded for that because now all of a sudden it seemed on that path. And we started getting people calling us."

Asamoa-Caesar said the low political ceiling for Black Oklahomans is more complicated than skin tone. People of color, especially African Americans, tend to be more liberal and more Democrat than Oklahoma as whole, which generally makes them less electable regardless of race; Black Republicans, he said, often take a hard conservative line that winds up not winning over many white voters and alienates minorities.

Still, a common thread in that explanation is race.

"It came back to me from very credible sources that [a Democratic Party leader] said, basically, 'Kojo is not the kind of face that Oklahomans can get behind.' That was very distressing. That's the point he was trying to make in a sense, that 'Yeah. This Black guy, he's just not going to make it in Oklahoma.'

> Obviously there is this discomfort with race in Tulsa and in Oklahoma. Race is a touchy issue to begin with, and the black candidates that have been successful in the past in the state have been Republican and they've kind of downplayed race. But I wasn't even coming at the race issue from anger or resentment. I even got some backlash from certain folks in North Tulsa. On the one side, there's this central committee Democrat saying I'm not the face, and then there's somebody in North Tulsa saying, "Well, you know, Kojo, his parents are from Africa, so he's really not African-American like us. He really doesn't understand the Black struggle."

The general election in Oklahoma produced no great surprises and was laden with portents of what was to come in 2021. President Donald Trump carried the state with more than one million votes, the first presidential candidate to break that barrier in Oklahoma, and nearly two-thirds of the total in a field of six. Democrat Joe Biden received only 32 percent. The results were such that a great many Oklahomans could comprehend Biden's national victory only through the conspiracy theories peddled like medicine show elixir by Trump and his acolytes.[157]

Remaining authentic may have recruited some voters to Asamoa-Caesar's banner, but not nearly enough. He received less than 33 percent in a three-way race, eight percentage points less than 2018 Democratic nominee Tim Gilpin, a white attorney, attracted in a head-to-head with Hern two years earlier. There were some other differences: 2020 was a presidential election year, 2018 was not (although turnout was relatively heavy because of a contested gubernatorial election); Kevin Hern was an incumbent in 2020, Oklahoma congressional district 1 was an open seat in 2018. Gilpin's access to resources was considerably greater than Asamoa-Caesar's. But in Tulsa County, Asamoa-Caesar underperformed Biden by four points, suggesting that perhaps the Democratic Party leader was correct.

Kojo Asamoa-Caesar was not a face Oklahomans could get behind.

"Black Lives Matter" painted on Tulsa's Greenwood Avenue ahead of President Donald Trump's June 20, 2020, rally. *Photo by Tom Gilbert, © Tulsa World.*

President Donald Trump speaks to an unexpectedly small crowd at his June 20, 2020, rally in the BOK Center. *Photo by Ian Maule, © Tulsa World.*

Tiffany Crutcher in 2018. *Photo by Matt Barnard, © Tulsa World.*

U.S. senator James Lankford preaches at Vernon AME Church in 2019. Reverend Robert Turner is at left, state senator Kevin Matthews at right. *Photo by Joseph Rushmore, © Tulsa World.*

Oklahoma governor Kevin Stitt speaks to reporters outside the BOK Center prior to President Donald Trump's appearance on June 20, 2020. *Photo by Matt Barnard, © Tulsa World.*

Tulsa Police chief Wendell Franklin, Mayor G. T. Bynum, Tiffany Crutcher, Gregory Robinson, and Damario Solomon-Simmons speak to the press on June 1, 2020. *Photo by Matt Barnard, © Tulsa World.*

Kavin Ross surveys exhumed remains waiting to be reburied at Oaklawn Cemetery in 2021. *Photo by Mike Simons, © Tulsa World.*

State senator Kevin Matthews addresses reporters following the cancelation of the Remember and Rise event. *Photo by Michael Noble Jr., © Tulsa World.*

Attorney Damario Solomon-Simmons, flanked by co-counsel and surrounded by Justice for Greenwood supporters, following a status conference for a lawsuit stemming from the 1921 Tulsa Race Massacre. *Photo by Mike Simons, © Tulsa World.*

Hughes "Uncle Red" Van Ellis *(left)*, Lessie Benningfield Randle, and Viola Fletcher, believed to be the last living survivors of the 1921 Tulsa Race Massacre, ride in the Black Wall Street Memorial March on May 28, 2021, in Tulsa. *Photo by Mike Simons, © Tulsa World.*

PART TWO

TULSA, 2021

5

UNHAPPY NEW YEAR

The *Oklahoma Eagle* began the New Year with an editorial headlined "2020 Was No Friend to North Tulsa." In truth, 2020 was no friend to anybody, thanks in large part to COVID-19 and the weaknesses and divisions it exposed and exacerbated. But North Tulsa had reason to feel particularly hard done by the old year. The momentary exhilaration of late spring and early summer, when people of all races united in the streets and painted Black Lives Matter on Greenwood Avenue, had faded by late autumn. The mural was gone, scoured off in the wee hours of the morning, another signal to Black Tulsans that when head winds rose Oklahoma's white political leadership headed for the lifeboats. With dissatisfaction in Bynum growing, centennial preparations rent by bickering and strife, and Trump refusing to concede defeat, Black Tulsans had more reasons than most to bid 2020 an unfond farewell. The *Eagle*, in its editorial, no doubt spoke for many of them:

> Tulsa has wildly failed in [its] preparation for the recognition of the 100-year anniversary of the Tulsa Race Massacre. It's clear, from the response to the ugly removal of the Black Lives Matter street art to its continued parochial treatment of the Greenwood district, that Tulsa has a long way to go in equal rights. Funds have been resourced in preparation of the world looking at Tulsa during this grim anniversary. But the hope that local government and political views have changed is sadly not the case.

> Those historical views have hardened and seem baked into the fabric of the power structure of Tulsa. . . .
>
> America and Tulsa still must grapple with the national shame of racism that is not dying off with the passing of old bigots but is being passed down. We must not only vaccinate a global pandemic, but also address ails that continue to haunt us with love and forgiveness. Happy New Year.[1]

The New Year, in fact, brought Black Tulsans more disappointment. The one member of Oklahoma's congressional delegation who had put much effort into connecting with them was headed toward what many considered a betrayal. In trying to serve two masters—the truth and constituents enraged by it—Senator Lankford pleased no one. The result would be painful for him and the Oklahomans, including Black Tulsans, who trusted Lankford even when they disagreed with him.

At issue, of course, was the Trump inner circle's attempts to discredit the 2020 presidential election, but that only brought to a crisis Lankford's dilemma over Trump's ascent to the leadership of the Republican Party. Political life, requiring as it does a constant weighing of means and ends, is difficult enough for those espousing a finely tuned moral code. For lawmakers, always voting one's conscience over the clamor of the multitudes may make for sounder sleep, but it also leads to defeat in the next election—more times than not by a member of their own party.

Trump, therefore, was a particular problem for Lankford, a straight-arrow Southern Baptist preacher whose church-going constituents wholeheartedly embraced an irreligious, womanizing New York businessman not known for a commitment to the Beatitudes. Sometimes it was more than Lankford could take. He did not endorse Trump in the 2016 primary and did so grudgingly for the general election. Speaking in Tulsa a few days before Election Day, Lankford said he would "go to bed grieved" regardless of who won. "We're not voting for pastor," he said. "We're voting for a president. We're voting for the direction of policies. We're voting for the direction of the Supreme Court. We're voting for how the agencies are going to be run."[2]

Do not think of it as voting for Donald Trump, Lankford was saying. Think of it as voting for a Supreme Court that will overturn *Roe v. Wade*, for an Environmental Protection Agency friendly to our state's oil and gas industry, and for school vouchers. Most of all, think of it as a vote against Hilary Clinton. It was a deal with the devil from which Lankford got most of what he wanted politically.

But in a 2018 interview for a *Christianity Today* podcast, Lankford admitted that reconciling his faith with now-President Trump's behavior was not always easy.

> What I look for in a presidential candidate is a great role model, and I didn't get that this time. I was very frustrated. I didn't have a good option. I didn't have that person who I would say is a great role model for my daughters and for my family and the next generation based on choices and values and those sorts of things. From either party.
>
> I've had conversations with the President and some of his staff, and I've had conversations with other people, and I've said when I disagree with him I'm going to say it. . . . I don't respond to all of his tweets or I'd get nothing else out. There are some times that he'll make a statement that is just a jarring, dishonoring statement that I feel like the right thing to do is to push back on that and say, 'That's not who we are.' One of the goals I have is to bring dialogue down to a level that we can actually have dialogue rather than just shouting at each other.[3]

But Trump articulated, more effectively than anyone else, the concerns and anxieties of many Oklahomans. He also reflected their biases and ultimately their fundamental values. Devoted conservatives, Christian and otherwise, found ways to rationalize Trump's breaches of their religious and political orthodoxies. Not even Lankford's revered predecessor, former senator Tom Coburn, could dissuade them. Speaking to future Trump ally Steve Bannon on *Breitbart News Daily* in early 2016, when the Republican presidential nomination was still in question, Coburn said Trump "reminds me of a carnival barker. 'Come on in, come on in and buy this.' So tell me what I'm buying! That's what I want to see."[4]

The interview occurred ten days after Trump finished second in Oklahoma's Republican presidential primary, six points behind Texas senator Ted Cruz and two points ahead of Coburn's preference, Florida senator Marco Rubio. By November of that year, however, Trump had thoroughly won over Oklahoma, and carried the state by about the same margin in 2020. With Biden support concentrated in Oklahoma City and Tulsa—Biden may have even carried the city of Tulsa, but the truth is hopelessly obscured by the state's method of tallying absentee ballots—many Oklahomans knew virtually no one who admitted to supporting anyone except Trump. His loss was an incomprehensible shock that could be explained only by the sort of treachery he and his lieutenants claimed.[5]

Some in Oklahoma's congressional delegation seemed taken aback by the ferocity with which their constituents echoed Team Trump's election fraud allegations.

Confronted by immediate and growing pressure, Lankford sought some form of conciliation by repeating, and thus giving agency to, unproved or demonstrably false allegations, all the while downplaying their effect on the election and telling constituents that trying to block certification of the election would be pointless.[6]

As a member of the Homeland Security and Government Affairs Committee, Lankford had been involved in investigating foreign influence in the 2016 election and cited public concern over that as reason to investigate the 2020 results. At a December 16, 2020, committee meeting, Lankford said nearly half of Americans and 80 percent of Republicans believed fraud affected the presidential election results.

"After this election all kinds of issues have come up and . . . and everyone seems to be saying 'move on,'" Lankford said. "One side is now saying let's just move on and ignore this."[7]

Lankford cited Oklahoma's record for delivering accurate results on election night and said that not doing so "gives opportunity for fraud and questions and problems." Lankford had to know the reasons some states take longer to finalize results, and that most of those reasons have to do with counting as many eligible votes as possible. He had to know Oklahoma's election system is generally fast and accurate in part because of policy decisions that value security over access, and because Oklahoma elections are generally so lopsided they do not get much attention—including from the voting-age population. But most Oklahomans do not know these things, and by saying what he did, Lankford repeated what many Oklahomans were thinking: If we had our election results within hours of the polls closing, why are states still counting? Amplification by the Trump campaign and allies—and minimization by the Biden campaign and center to left media—only deepened their suspicions. [8]

Lankford raised questions about ballot harvesting—the practice, legal in some states and not in others, of collecting and submitting absentee ballots on behalf of others—and some states deciding during the pandemic year to mail ballots to every registered voter. Both are legitimate points of discussion. The few cases of actual voting fraud discovered every election cycle more often than not involve absentee ballots. Even so, no one has demonstrated that organized fraud occurred in the 2020 presidential election, by mail ballots or anything else. And even as Lankford tacitly encouraged election conspiracists, he intervened as a member of the Senate Intelligence Committee to get the Biden transition team the daily security briefings refused it by the Trump administration. Ever the conciliator, Lankford was trying to satisfy everyone.[9]

On January 2, he said he believed he had found a way to do it.

While insisting before and after January 6 that he had no intention of denying Joe Biden the presidency, Lankford announced he had signed on to Cruz's attempt to delay certification for ten days so a "commission" of members of Congress and the US Supreme Court could look into the alleged irregularities.[10]

"We're trying to get the facts out," Lankford said in an interview with the *Tulsa World*. "We want to be able to say those questions were answered to the best of our ability.[11]

"I've got three groups of folks," he said. "I've got folks in the state who are saying, 'Move on, Biden won.' I have folks who say, 'Trump won, obviously. Do whatever it takes, including run over the Constitution.' And I have folks who say, 'Something just doesn't smell right.'

"We're not trying to overturn an election," Lankford said. "The commission is only pulling the facts out and handing them to the states to decide. We're not making the decision. The states would make the decision about what they want to do with their electors."

The last two sentences were the tip-off. The commission was not going to overturn the election, but it might make it possible for others to do so.

How much Lankford knew about Cruz's true objective is unclear. Bits and pieces of the scheme would come out over the next year before the *Washington Post*'s Michael Kranish tied them all together in a March 2022 story that revealed the commission was not intended to clarify facts but to create more confusion and delay the election's certification until Trump loyalists in the legislatures of key states could declare their elections tainted, throw out the results and somehow find a way to switch electoral votes from Biden to Trump. It was unlikely but not impossible.[12]

How much Lankford knew and how much he approved of is unclear. He readily admitted the commission was a long shot, and perhaps he hoped, consciously or unconsciously, that supporting an initiative likely to fail would enable him to finesse his way through a tight spot. In the January 2 interview, Lankford seemed to suggest he was of two minds, saying the commission "gives us the opportunity as a country to start healing" while almost in the same breath scraping off whatever scab might have formed on the wound by again suggesting Biden had not been fairly elected.

"The [worst] situation," Lankford said, "is that you get to April and you have a President Biden and suddenly information comes out and people say, 'Oh, he didn't really win.'"[13]

This may have made sense to the two-thirds of Oklahomans who voted for Trump and the sizeable share whose information intake consisted largely of *Fox News* and the *Epoch Times*, but for those who did not, and especially for Black Oklahomans, it was horrifying. As much as they disliked Trump, they feared him and what he represented more; beyond that, the subtle and not-so-subtle implication that "voter fraud" was synonymous with "urban Black voter," especially in Philadelphia, Milwaukee, and Atlanta, infuriated African Americans. The *Black Wall Street Times*'s Nehemiah Frank said "how Lankford questions the integrity of Black voters" proved he had no real interest in Black Tulsans.[14]

Meanwhile, white Tulsans on their way to Washington took credit for forcing Lankford's hand.

"I think he's doing it because of us," one of them, Stacie Cannon, said about Lankford's move to stop certification of the election results.[15]

"I think there are a lot more votes out there and that's what he's trying to get at."[16]

On January 3, Cannon said she knew of at least seventy Oklahomans who planned to be in Washington for the January 6 rally on the day Congress was to certify the election results. A resident of Bixby, a Tulsa suburb, Cannon said she put no stock in the US Department of Homeland Security's statement that the 2020 election was the fairest and most secure in the nation's history.

"They're afraid of antifa," Cannon said, referring to the amorphous "anti-fascists" who as an organized movement seemed to exist more in the minds of a few anarchists and a lot of conservatives than in reality. "They're afraid of the extreme left. They're afraid of putting their families in danger. And there's a lot of hate. Our president has not done a lot to make friends."[17]

On January 5, the *Tulsa World* published an op-ed by Lankford in which he explained his rationale for delaying certification of the election. He said the past year had exposed weaknesses in some states' election procedures but did not claim they materially affected the final results. He said objections lodged after the 1968 and 2004 elections led to needed reforms, but he did not mention that those were not intended to prevent certification. The first involved a white "faithless elector" from North Carolina who cast a ballot for segregationist George Wallace instead of Republican Richard Nixon. The second objection was by an Ohio congresswoman trying to draw attention to what she said had been suppression of Black voters in her home state.[18]

"The cornerstone of democracy is free and fair elections that encourage everyone to vote, ensure all legal votes are counted correctly, and ensure illegal votes are not counted," Lankford wrote. "We shouldn't stop working to restore the confidence that our elections are secure and the results can be verified. It's vital to who we are as a free nation. Oklahomans want to have confidence in our election system and in the election results. That's not too much to ask."[19]

Again, Lankford seemed of two minds. On the one hand, he said he just wanted to tighten up some states' election laws. No big deal. But to do that he wanted to hold up certification of an election—an election that both Trump's Department of Justice and Department of Homeland Security said exhibited no signs of organized fraud or system failure.

"Challenging the results is an ill-conceived last-ditch effort to undo the results of the Nov. 3 presidential election," the *World* editorialized after Lankford's op-ed. "It's a partisan act of psychological denial that puts the interests of party over those of the nation. It flies in the face of the clearly expressed will of the majority."[20]

That majority, however, did not vote in Oklahoma, and on the afternoon of January 6, six of Oklahoma's seven members of Congress arrived at the Capitol prepared to object to some states' electoral votes, either because they actually believed Trump's claims or because a substantial number of their constituents did.

The exception was the delegation's senior member, US senator Jim Inhofe, who had just won reelection to a fifth full term, one he had promised would be his last. Trump had not been Inhofe's first choice for president in 2016 but the senator warmed to him until they fell out over some policy decisions in the final stages of Trump's term. Still, Inhofe certainly preferred Trump to any Democrat. Inhofe, though, said doing anything except certifying the election would violate his oath of office.

"My job . . . is clear," he said in a written statement. "There are only two things I am permitted to do under the Constitution: ensure the electors are properly certified and count the electoral votes, even when I disagree with the outcome. To challenge a state's certification, given how specific the Constitution is, would be a violation of my oath of office—that is not something I am willing to do and is not something Oklahomans would want me to do," he said.[21]

On that last count Inhofe was wrong. Oklahomans—a good many of them, anyway—wanted him to stop Joe Biden from taking office and were not particular about how it was done. After nearly sixty years of carrying the Republican flag into battle, Inhofe was roundly denounced as a traitor and worse. Old friends abandoned him. Red hots in the state party wanted him formally censured.[22]

As unpleasant as things were for Inhofe, they were more so for Lankford. Before January 6 was over, almost everyone in the state seemed to be mad at him.

Standing before his Senate colleagues on the afternoon of January 6, making the case for Cruz's commission, he was interrupted by a rap of the gavel and the sound of rioters in the Capitol halls. The chamber was evacuated; six hours later, order restored, Lankford returned to the lectern and withdrew his objection to Arizona's election results. Some of the same people he had been defending had invaded Congress like a lynch mob.

"Why in God's name would someone think attacking law enforcement and occupying the United States Capitol is the best way to show you're right?" Lankford said. "Why would you do that? Rioters and thugs don't run the Capitol. We're the United States of America."[23]

Those upset with Lankford for the first half of his January 6 speech were not mollified by the second half of it; those convinced the election had been stolen or who were just dead set against a Biden presidency were furious by what they viewed as Lankford's desertion. If anything, they were angrier at him than they were with Inhofe. The *Black Wall Street Times* started an online petition demanding Lankford resign or be removed from both the centennial commission and the US Senate. Jackson Lahmeyer, an entrepreneurial Tulsa pastor associated with a businessman named Clay Clark who had hawked conspiracy theories at the January 6 rally in Washington, quickly hooked up with Trump loyalists Michael Flynn and Roger Stone and in mid-March 2021 launched a primary challenge to Lankford.[24]

"I saw fear all over him on Jan. 6," said Lahmeyer. "He caved in like an absolute coward, and that let me know he is not the man to represent our state in the fight our country is in right now."[25]

Lahmeyer had led a counter-demonstration to the October Black Lives Matter march that coincided with the painting of "BLM" on the street in front of Tulsa's city hall; now he criticized Lankford for apologizing to Black Tulsans for failing to consider their perspective as he attacked the integrity of the presidential election and, by extension, the integrity of those who voted for Joe Biden.[26]

Lankford's apology came in mid-January, a few days after several Tulsans, Black and white, made public their belief Lankford should no longer be on the centennial commission because of his words and actions since the November election.

"I do believe Lankford has some integrity," said Nehemiah Frank. "I do. And I think he tries to be strategic in how he moves." But, Frank said, he could not defend Lankford "at the price of Black people being harmed."[27]

"This is a great example of Black people voting in record numbers, with a coalition of people who look different, who are being told, 'No, their votes didn't count,'" said state representative Monroe Nichols.

Lankford said such reactions surprised him—which speaks to the gulf separating not only Tulsans' but Americans' understanding of each other.

"I was shocked (when Black friends) said to me, 'This was about keeping African Americans from voting,'" Lankford said. "My comment to them was, 'That never crossed my mind. Why would I do that? Why would I think that?'

"I've had some time now to visit with them and to hear them out, and I understand where they're coming from," Lankford said. "Some people caught me and said, 'Let me describe it to you this way'—and they were spot on with this—'You hear the president say, Georgia, Michigan and Pennsylvania are problems. We hear the president say, Atlanta, Detroit and Philadelphia are problems.'"

"And I said, 'You're exactly correct. I hear what you're saying now.'"

Lankford's friend state senator Kevin Matthews knew all too well the frustration of those who could not believe such naiveté.

"Let me tell you what racism feels like to Black people," Matthews said. "When you tell us the rules and why we can't be president before [Barack] Obama, or vice president [before Kamala Harris], we have to jump through these hoops, and as we're jumping through the hoops you move the goalposts. And you keep moving them. And when we get to the goalposts, you want to check our ID and our credentials over and over and over.

"We have a Black woman [Harris], the first Black woman with an opportunity to be vice president and possible opportunity to be president—she's at least next in line—and now is when we want to put out all of these extra alarms? That's what Black people think."

Nevertheless, Matthews fought to keep Lankford on the commission. Having spent twenty-five years in the Tulsa Fire Department—a government agency dominated by conservative white men, and eight years in a legislature dominated by conservative white men, he understood what would happen if the commission split along party lines.

"We don't want this to end up being a political us versus them," said Matthews. "I think that takes away from the work of reconciliation."

In a letter dated January 14 and addressed "To my friends in North Tulsa," Lankford offered a mea culpa—of sorts.

> There is . . . too little cultural understanding between people of different races and backgrounds in the communities of Oklahoma, which is something I was reminded of just last week. When I announced my support for an Electoral Commission to spend 10 days auditing the results of the 2020 Presidential Election, it was never my intention to disenfranchise any voter or state. It was my intention to resolve any outstanding questions before the inauguration on January 20. I believe Congress cannot legally ignore any state's electors or change any state's vote, but we can work to get answers. . . .
>
> But my action of asking for more election information caused a firestorm of suspicion among many of my friends, particularly in Black communities around the state. I was completely blindsided, but I also found a blind spot. . . . After decades of fighting for voting rights, many Black friends in Oklahoma saw this as a direct attack on their right to vote, for their vote to matter, and even a belief that their votes made an election in our country illegitimate.
>
> I can assure you, my intent to give a voice to Oklahomans who had questions was never also an intent to diminish the voice of any Black American. As a United States Senator representing almost four million Oklahomans, I am committed to hearing from all Oklahomans, answering questions, and addressing our challenges to strive toward a more perfect union. In this instance, I should have recognized how what I said and what I did could be interpreted by many of you. I deeply regret my blindness to that perception, and for that I am sorry.
>
> Today, I am asking my friends in North Tulsa for grace and an opportunity for us to show the state what reconciliation looks like in moments of disagreement.[28]

That Lankford even bothered to respond to the outrage of people who likely would not vote for him anyway received national attention but did little to placate Black Tulsans (or, for that matter, the sizeable number of all Tulsans who voted for Joe Biden). Reading the fine print, they pointed out that Lankford apologized for insulting them, but not for participating in a ploy whose ultimate goal—whether Lankford's or not—seemed to be reversing the results of a presidential election. The bottom line: he had a choice, and he had not chosen them.

"[T]he letter relies on a longstanding theme in the perpetuation of white-supremacist culture: the non-apology apology," said the *Black Wall Street Times*. "Senator Lankford, an undoubtedly thoughtful man who is careful with his words, chose not to directly apologize for his actions or their dire and deadly consequences. Instead, he simply apologized that Black Tulsans interpreted his actions as racist while maintaining that his intentions were pure."[29]

It then cited former GOP national chair Michael Steele's Twitter thread:

> @SenatorLankford what exactly did you think was going to happen when you sought to throw out the votes in Ga., MI. or Pa.? What did you hear exactly when we pleaded with you and your colleagues not to pursue this course of action? And while you ignored our plea, what evidence did you present to justify your decision to overturn this election? And now you say "After decades of fighting for voting rights, many Black friends in Oklahoma saw this as a direct attack on their right to vote." And that reaction surprised you? Now, imagine taking the vote away from White Oklahomans, would you still be surprised? After all of your "fighting for voting rights" (a) you didn't think disenfranchising black voters in other states would be a problem with Black voters in OK? and (b) it didn't occur to you to call one of your Black friends and ask? It's not like the rest of us didn't tell you[.] What is disheartening @SenatorLankford is you are known for your good work with Black Tulsans, but toeing the line for Trump was more important than your relationship with the Black community you represent. Like my mama would ask "so, what comes after 'sorry'?"[30]

James O. Goodwin, publisher of the *Oklahoma Eagle*, was more tempered in his response but the message was much the same.

> While knowing all along Congress could not legally ignore any state's electors or change any state's vote, [Lankford] claims he was not trying to disenfranchise black voters "but to resolve any outstanding questions (regarding voter fraud) before the inauguration on January 20 . . . in order to strengthen the confidence of all Americans . . . in their electoral system . . . and knows their vote matters." His act was an act of futility. He put politics over principle.[31]

As Goodwin pointed out, citing as precedent for the proposed commission one that decided the contested 1876 election did not exactly instill confidence in anyone familiar with it, especially African Americans. That commission contributed to the ultimate disenfranchisement of millions of Black voters, which is what many feared a second one would do. But while the *Black Wall Street Times* wanted Lankford off the centennial commission, Goodwin thought it better in the long run for him to remain.

"Senator Lankford, as cumbersome as his attempts have been, is a person with a genuine interest in experiencing our shared humanity," Goodwin wrote. "But we, too, must remember we also are flawed. Senator Lankford has much to learn about the Black experience, and the Commission should be eager to engage him. For Senator Lankford to be immersed in the Black experience is a sure way to expose the malady of white privilege."[32]

For many Tulsans, and especially Black Tulsans, the situation looked and felt and sounded a lot like another of those "Yeah, you may be right, but you'll just have to wait" instances described by Kevin Matthews. And this was not just true for Tulsa, of course. It was a message reverberating among minority groups—whether racial, economic, political or social—throughout the United States and, indeed, the world.

Lankford's letter of apology did not win many points from Trumpites either. For many of them, Lankford had kowtowed to people who, at best, did not matter, and at worst were intent on upsetting the status quo. About the latter, they were not entirely wrong. Many Tulsans, including many Black Tulsans, did want to change the status quo—a status quo that, as the Equality Indicators had shown, was not working out too well for a lot of people. Those comfortable with the way things are do not want them to change. Disruption makes them nervous, even angry. As far as they are concerned, and usually with some reason, they have worked hard to get where they are and to have what they do, be it a little or a lot. They do not want to give it up through taxes or diminished status to "other people" deemed less deserving, less enterprising, less patriotic, less Godly, less morally upright. And so, they turn to leaders who promise to make America—their America—great again. They lavish unqualified praise on local (but not federal) law officers, whose job is almost by definition the protection of the status quo.

Complaints are often expressed in material terms—money, jobs, property—but the underlying fear is loss of power. This is the "white privilege" Goodwin mentioned: a system that, consciously or not, weighs skin tone (and often gender) differently. It is the often unacknowledged reality that, when push has come to shove in America, one group has always gone first and more often than not still does, and everybody else goes after. It is the polarizing truth that when the hard choice is between white and Black, Republican and Democrat, white Republican (and often white Democrat) politicians, even well-intentioned ones, are going to say, in effect, "Sorry, I hear what you're saying but I can't or won't help you."

After days of discussion, the commission issued a statement saying that Lankford would remain on the commission.

"We considered the repercussions [the decision] carries," the statement said. "We understood at the outset that it would not be unanimous. Instead we sought consensus—a well-reasoned decision that all members of the Centennial Commission could support."[33]

> At its core, the Centennial Commission is about reconciliation. For the purpose of achieving that goal, we must continue to harness our connective tissue—even when we are not in absolute agreement. Senator Lankford, despite clear differences (some of them profound), stands on common ground with us in terms of the importance of reconciliation as well as educating all United States citizens about Tulsa's Historic Greenwood District, the storied "Black Wall Street," including the massacre and its impact on Oklahoma and the nation.

In the interest of reconciliation, the statement said, "we must continue to extend an olive branch. It is our inherent duty to show our partners the way. For those reasons, we choose not to request Senator Lankford's removal from the Centennial Commission, but instead, accept his apology and embrace his desire to reaffirm his commitment to help bring vital resources and opportunities to the Greenwood District, Black Tulsans and Black Americans from coast to coast."

By all accounts, the decision came at the end of some very acrimonious arguments; several members resigned, others just stopped participating. It also turned up the volume on assertions that the commission was a front for "white Republicans" trying to control the centennial's narrative and "commodify" Black history and suffering.

"He is a white man who essentially won't be held accountable for attempting to snub Black voters," said Nehemiah Frank, who was not a member of the commission. "It is impossible for a white politician to be held accountable by Black people in Oklahoma, where we make up just 7.8 percent of the population."

Lankford quietly resigned from the commission in mid-May, saying it had become too partisan. By that time the Republican-led legislature had passed and Gov. Kevin Stitt had signed several bills prompted by the previous year's Black Lives Matter rallies—especially the ones in Tulsa—and intended to suppress dissent. Stitt, who had lent his endorsement to the Greenwood Rising project, was expelled from the commission when he refused to veto the legislation. State representative Nichols also resigned, saying he feared his criticism of Stitt might cause repercussions for the commission.[34]

The affair illustrated the cost of involvement. Lankford and Matthews took beatings from all sides while those who chose to stay on the sidelines came through without a scratch. The easy lesson would be to conclude such abuse is not worth the effort. But in 2023, as Matthews's term-limited political career wound down, he appeared to be on the verge of getting Oklahoma's almost all-white legislature to agree to the creation of a state civil rights trail. And, when Lester Shaw formally reopened the Big 10 Ballroom in February, Lankford was there to help cut the ribbon.[35]

6

POLITICS

At the same time the Black Lives Matter crew hastily painted "BLM" on the street in front of Tulsa's city hall on October 20, 2020, a different kind of demonstration—a sort of "Blue Lives Matter" march—was in progress a few blocks away. It had been organized by Jackson Lahmeyer in conjunction with the Tulsa Police Department as part of the first national "Faith and Blue" weekend, an event formulated by Georgia-based evangelist and civil rights activist Markel Hutchins through his MovementForward nonprofit and adopted by the Trump Justice Department. Its stated purpose was to connect law enforcement and faith communities, something Hutchins had been working on in the Atlanta area with his "One Church—One Precinct" program since 2009.[1]

The Tulsa march, though, was a little out of character for Faith and Blue and for Markel, who has said he does not believe "marching and protesting" does much good. Markel's approach emphasizes interaction of law officers and the community through such things as ice cream socials, picnics, basketball games, and discussion groups; few of the Faith and Blue events involved marches, walks, or parades. Tulsa's Faith and Blue schedule that year included a cookout, community forum, and soccer game with the Islamic Society of Tulsa; a cookout and basketball game with an independent church other than Lahmeyer's; and police visiting a congregation whose services included a Sunday night meal. Tulsa Faith and Blue weekends since have involved similar community activities but not marches, according to the Faith and Blue website.[2]

Lahmeyer, whose church obtained the permit for the march, said it was intended as a counterdemonstration to Black Lives Matter, but differentiated (again) between Black Lives Matter "the terrorist organization" and peaceful Black Lives Matter demonstrations.[3]

"They're winning the war. . . . They've got a lot of momentum. They own the narrative right now. We've got to change the frequency of what's going out," Lahmeyer said in a Facebook Live video, apparently referring to the "bad" Black Lives Matter.

Three demonstrations were actually planned for that day. The Faith and Blue march intended to go down Greenwood but changed its route to avoid conflict with a group called Tulsa Anti-Racist Action, which planned to meet at the Greenwood Cultural Center to protest "white supremacy and police brutality." Instead, Faith and Blue started at John Hope Franklin Reconciliation Park and walked to police headquarters about three-quarters of a mile away. In so doing, it passed within a block of a local landmark called Center of the Universe, where Nehemiah Frank and the *Black Wall Street Times* had gathered the "'Good Trouble' Black Lives Matter" rally that would culminate in the quick paint job at City Hall.

Tulsa Police Chief Wendell Franklin, who participated in the Faith and Blue march, had told the city council it was "nothing more than to unite people, not to divide people, and my hope is it goes off as such." On the day of the event, however, officers struck a different note. Lt. Chris Witt, an officer nearing retirement after more than thirty-five years on the force, warned the crowd of "fifty or sixty protesters"—Frank's group—"gathered up at the Center of the Universe," and implied the Faith and Blue group should expect trouble.[4]

"They stay on the sidewalk, that's great," said Witt. "If they don't, what I need you guys to do is fire up your phones and start recording it and move to the back. These officers are going to go to the front. Don't panic. Don't run. Just go to the back. [The officers] will form a line to protect you. We have other officers to come up from behind to reinforce us. . . . I know [the Black Lives Matter protesters] have some shoulder-mounted recording equipment. They edit. We won't. Whatever happens, we're going to make sure the truth is told.[5]

The truth was, not much happened.

"I don't want to hear anybody boo," Frank told his group, and they applauded when the Faith and Blue marchers passed nearby. The closest thing to a conflict occurred a little later, after the Black Lives Matter group finished its painting just as the Tulsa Anti-Racist Action group arrived from Greenwood.[6]

"They are not with us," Frank said, in telling his troops to disperse. "We have made our point."[7]

The Black Lives Matter protesters returned to the Center of the Universe while the second group chanted "No justice, no peace" and similar slogans. Watching all of this were several heavily armed civilians, faces covered, who refused to identify themselves or talk to reporters.[8]

It was a strange, confused, at times unsettling day, and in all of the commotion almost no one recognized the significance of Jackson Lahmeyer's arrival as an avatar of the coming year's politics. To most Tulsans he was one of many ambitious, charismatic preachers building a parochial empire on a catechism of God, capitalism, and the American flag. A product of Oral Roberts University, a cradle of prosperity gospel theology, Lahmeyer had taken over a congregation in midtown Tulsa and built it along the general lines of the independent mega churches for which Tulsa and its suburbs had become known. During COVID-19, Lahmeyer and his church made a point of ignoring the city's mask ordinances and other precautions, ultimately joining with Clay Clark on podcasts and in personal appearances to proclaim the pandemic a hoax and vaccines some sort of death serum. Whether through God's blessing or otherwise, Lahmeyer's endeavors seem to have been profitable. The financial disclosure statement he filed with the US Senate in December 2021 listed income of more than $400,000, including salaries of $120,000 from his church, $84,000 from the Billy Graham Evangelistic Association (of which he was listed as a state director), and $200,000 in self-employment income. This last was attributed to "real estate, lawn care & junk removal services," although during this time Lahmeyer was also among the headliners for Clark's ReAwaken America Tour, a traveling show of Christian Nationalists, election and COVID-19 conspiracy hawkers, government haters, and Trump cheerleaders that played more than a dozen dates from Tampa, Florida, to Anaheim, California, in 2021, and continued through 2022 and into 2023.[9]

Lahmeyer epitomized the most vocal malcontents after the election of 2020. Trump was the rightful winner. Black protesters are terrorists. Critical race theory—by which was really meant any notion of systemic racism—is a scam, and a dangerous one. God, country, and the Republican Party are all one, as Kojo Asamoa-Caesar had learned in his quixotic congressional campaign. Not every conservative or every Republican agreed but in the aftermath of Trump's loss, the persistence of the pandemic and the arrival of COVID vaccines, and more importantly COVID vaccine mandates, they were shouted down.

This unease was understandable and even warranted. People tend to resist sudden, drastic change, whether it is in the basic precepts by which they live their lives or the lives themselves. And drastic change seemed to be coming at Americans, and especially white Americans, faster and more jarringly than anyone could remember. Ideas and demands that were easily ignored or snuffed out in the past were growing louder and more insistent. Americans were being told they had to give up their way of life, from their fossil fuel-burning cars and pickup trucks to the freedom to say anything about anybody anywhere. Some of their most basic beliefs about themselves and the United States as a nation built on hard work, virtue, and equal opportunity were being challenged with a ferocity they could not imagine. Close to home, vilification of the oil and gas industry not only threatened Tulsans' and Oklahomans' economic security but an important aspect of their identity. To working- and middle-class white Americans, the idea of their fairly earned money going to people they did not know for wrongs, in their view, not of their making sounded a lot like theft. That the exploitation of the minorities demanding restitution also sounded a lot like theft—and worse—was beside the point. That was in the past. The threat to the order of things in the here and now is what so unsettled so many Tulsans, Oklahomans, and Americans.

In Tulsa and elsewhere, most of those alarmed by this upheaval went to war politically under the Republican banner. Bob Jack, the Tulsa County GOP chair in 2020 and early 2021, said in 2022 that local Republicans were divided into three groups. The first is relatively quiet: "They go along, get along, they're pretty perfectly fine," Jack said. The second is "fairly active" in the party and politics in general. "And then there's this rabid group that's out there that's really, uh, they're just nuts," Jack said. "The election board is fraudulent. And the jab is, you know, 'I'm never going to get a [COVID-19] vaccination.' I've been called a murderer because I've told people that they should consider getting the vaccination."[10]

Even before COVID-19, opponents of vaccination mandates—anti-vaxxers—had been growing in influence, in Oklahoma and elsewhere, as part of a broader resistance to being told what to do, by government or anybody or anything else. Scientific and medical credentials not only did not matter, but they were often seen as further cause for suspicion.[11]

"That was one of the [biggest] flare ups," Jack said. "And then the biggest, or one of the bigger flare ups, was the issue about absentee ballots and how they were being handled."[12]

Even in Oklahoma, which Trump won by thirty percentage points and absentee voting procedures are among the tightest in the country, people became obsessed with mail-in ballots. Election officials reported fewer than sixty such ballots were cast illegally statewide in 2020, mostly by elderly people who absent-mindedly also voted in person. In the most publicized case, an adult daughter pleaded guilty to submitting her recently deceased father's ballot. Still, one legislator claimed as many as 100,000 people could have voted illegally, while conceding he did not know of any who actually had. [13]

The skeptics, said Jack, "think it's all tied together. COVID was a way of manipulating the election, a way to lower the guard, lower the threshold [for absentee voting] and therefore manipulate the outcome. And therefore it was an invalid election. That's still rampant."

In early 2021, this same fear, anger, and anxiety fed political turmoil the way hot air and atmospheric instability feed tornadoes, and with the same potential for destruction. It is easy to blame Donald Trump and his allies' misinformation carpet bombing, but arguably Trump's political rise was more effect than cause. His rhetoric, while often outlandish, would have echoed in empty halls had it not resonated with a sizeable percentage of Americans. Certainly, Trump sometimes spoke and acted irresponsibly, especially after the election, but he was not alone. Hyperbolic speechmaking from the left may have succeeded in rallying the troops and drawing attention to legitimate issues, but slogans like "defund the police" (which almost no one seems to have meant literally) and "white privilege" (valid as the concept behind it may be) seemed more designed to poke people in the eye than to help them see the inequities still systemic in America, no matter how vociferously they are denied.

"It's a very small portion of the party," Jack said, referring to the most disaffected Republicans. "It's not the big party. It's a very small portion. The vocal activists. They just totally distrust government because government is not ruling in a way . . . they want it to rule. They don't want G. T. (Bynum). If there's an equity issue, an inclusion issue, anything like that, they don't want . . . the city to have anything to do with that. You put a gay pride placard on a street sign, they go nuts. They want the city to rule as a far right city. And they can't handle the middle.

"One of the things that I've always told people is Tulsa is not a red city," said Jack. "Tulsa is not a blue city. Tulsa is a purple city. And the mayor has to be a purple mayor because he represents everybody. And people forget that."[14]

Historically, Tulsa's city government has tended to be more centrist and sometimes liberal than the state as a whole, a disparity that seemed to be growing. In 2021, the city council's nine members ranged from decidedly liberal to moderately conservative, and it sometimes struggled to find a balance among constituents' disparate views.

State government was much less constrained. With super majorities in the House and Senate and control of every statewide elected office, Republicans could do just about whatever they pleased. The only real impediment was coming to agreement among themselves as to what that was. Disagreements, some rancorous, were inevitable. Usually, though, they involved matters of degree rather than direction: how aggressively to further limit abortion rights, deregulate guns, stifle public health measures, and reconcile Republicans protective of their hometown schools while adhering to an agenda that prioritized tax-supported religious schools and undermining the principle of public education. Also on the 2021 agenda was a response to the marches and protests of 2020 and anything conservatives deemed "woke."

Nationally, an increasing number of state legislatures have come under the control of veto-proof majorities, a trend many consider disturbing and detrimental to representative democracy. This seems to apply regardless of party. In that context, Oklahoma's supermajority has not been as autocratic as some others or as it could be. As small as it may be—or perhaps because it is so small—the minority generally gets to have its say, even if it is ignored. But when the supermajority chooses to exercise its muscle, it can be ruthless. The only real brake on its absolute power is not an opposition party, but the thirty-eight tribal governments headquartered in the state.[15]

All but eliminated at statehood in 1907, the tribal governments slowly regained standing until by 2021 they were among the most powerful forces in the state. Some considered Bill Anoatubby, the soft-spoken, long-time Chickasaw Nation governor, the most influential person in Oklahoma. The tribes' strength was not as a voting bloc, but as an economic powerhouse and social services provider. The larger tribes—Cherokee, Muscogee Creek, Chickasaw, Choctaw, and Osage—carried most of the weight statewide, but the smaller tribes were enormously important to both tribal members and the general population of their local communities. This growing influence was largely driven by a series of federal court and policy decisions that gave the tribes a foothold in casino gaming and other enterprises. Revenue from these was shared with the state through a series of compacts. In fiscal year 2022, for example, Oklahoma tribes paid the state $191.5 million in what are called exclusivity fees on gross gaming revenue of $3.19 billion, and also shared revenue on tobacco fuel sales and in some cases motor vehicle tags.[16]

Stitt took office in 2019 determined to renegotiate the compacts on more favorable terms for the state. He soon found that easier said than done, however, and his aggressive and often condescending approach quickly alienated tribal leaders. They retaliated with a public relations campaign that highlighted the jobs and services the tribal governments brought to their communities. With the money from their casinos, the tribes had invested in broad portfolios of businesses, from meat processing plants to high tech industries, and in schools, hospitals, housing, and an array of social services that in many cases also assisted nontribal populations. The tension between Stitt and the tribes escalated in 2020 with the US Supreme Court's conclusion, in *McGirt v. Oklahoma,* that the Muscogee Creek Nation's physical reservation was not properly dissolved at statehood. The ruling was subsequently applied to several other tribes, including the Cherokees, Choctaws, and Chickasaws, which meant almost half the state was, in effect, reservations. Oklahoma's Native American population mostly celebrated Justice Neil Gorsuch's opinion as a victory for tribal sovereignty and identity, but the ruling also created jurisdictional and administrative headaches for tribal leaders and federal, state, and local officials.[17]

Oklahoma has one of the highest proportions of tribal citizens in the country, a result of federal policies that through most of the nineteenth century moved native people to what was then Indian Territory from all over the continental United States. Only the Panhandle and the far southwest corner of the present state were never part of a formal reservation. But by 1890 there were more non-Indians than Indians on tribal lands, and under pressure the Indian nations agreed to individual allotment of their reservations with "surplus" land open to nontribal settlers. Within a few years of statehood, most of the allotments had passed into white ownership, leaving the Indians in many cases landless and penniless. In the 1930s, the federal government reversed course and began encouraging the preservation and recovery of tribal land and placed it in trust. This began accelerating during the Nixon administration, which restored authority to tribal governments.[18]

All of this created a complex set of relationships involving traditional tribal boundaries, a jigsaw puzzle of trust, restricted allotment, and nontrust lands, and a tribal citizenry based on family history and tribal culture. Although citizenship requirements vary by tribe, they generally come down to tracing one's lineage to a forbearer on pre-statehood membership rolls. Over generations, this resulted in a portion of tribal citizens—including Stitt, a Cherokee citizen—who do not "look Indian" and an interweaving of tribal and nontribal society. In taking on the tribes, Stitt attempted to portray them as Oklahomans claiming special privileges based on race—and in many cases a tenuous connection to Indian ancestry. The tribes argued their citizenship was less about race and more about laws and treaties between their ancestors and the US government. Some of these had granted tribal citizenship to freedmen and descendants of Blacks enslaved by the Cherokees, Muscogee Creeks, Choctaws, Chickasaws, and others in pre–Civil War Indian Territory. Thus, among tribal citizens who did not "look Indian" there were a sizeable number of African descent. One of those is Damario Solomon-Simmons, whose ancestry includes freedman and Muscogee Creek lines, and whose practice includes representing Creek freedmen in ongoing action to reacquire full citizenship status.[19]

Over the years, a system of municipal, state, tribal, and federal courts developed that, while at times complicated, was well understood by those who used it. McGirt changed that. The case itself involved Jimcy McGirt, a Seminole citizen convicted in state court of raping a Seminole girl in Tulsa County. McGirt argued he should have been tried in federal court because Congress never explicitly dissolved the Muscogee Creek Nation, which included the place where the alleged crime occurred. This argument had been made before, but the US Supreme Court had never ruled on it. Gorsuch's opinion, while limited to major criminal cases in the Muscogee Creek Nation, was soon determined to apply more broadly on issues ranging from state and local governments' ability to enforce everything from speeding tickets to state income taxes. Gorsuch expected these issues to be worked out among the various governments, but Stitt instead worked to have the ruling modified or overturned. After a year railing against tribal compacts, he was not inclined to embrace them as a solution to the situation. While many tribal and local governments entered into cross-deputization agreements and other arrangements, Stitt complained loud and long about eroding state authority. And McGirt did disrupt the system. Federal courts and US attorney offices, which usually handled mostly civil cases, had to be retooled for the surge of criminal cases coming from state courts. Tribal court systems and law enforcement agencies also had to be beefed up. And all of this was happening with courts already in chaos because of COVID-19.[20]

But Stitt's claim that McGirt was the state's single greatest threat never seemed to convince the general public—or the legislators of his own party. Stitt and his fellow Republicans in the legislature often differed, and sometimes sharply, but on few if any issues did they butt heads more forcefully than the governor's Indian policy. More than a few lawmakers were tribal citizens and almost all of them had a significant tribal presence in their districts. Arguably, the tribes were doing things the state should have been but was not. So, when Stitt signed gaming compacts with four smaller tribes in 2020, Speaker of the House Charles McCall and President Pro Tempore Greg Treat—both Republicans—sued. They won, with the Oklahoma Supreme Court's final decision coming just days before the opening of the 2021 legislative session.[21]

And yet it never seemed to occur to the same lawmakers that the legislation they introduced in reaction to Black Lives Matter and the fear that children might learn something about racial exploitation could be as offensive to their Native American colleagues, family members, and allies as it was to African Americans. While excitedly anticipating Martin Scorsese's *Killers of the Flower Moon,* a movie being made in Oklahoma about one of the most craven examples of racial exploitation on record—the systematic murder of Osage Indians for their oil money—lawmakers fretted that schools might "indoctrinate" kids into thinking race had a lasting influence in this country. It must be said that the Republican majority had undeniably done some good work in areas such as criminal justice reform, child welfare, family services, and mental health, and it had taken some very tough votes on taxes when the state was close to broke in 2018. But when it came to matters of race, the majority often seemed utterly at sea—or perhaps just unconcerned. In any event, several bills filed for the 2021 legislative session revealed the level of consternation and even anger aroused by the rising voices of dissent. Many lawmakers insisted claims of systemic racism were overstated if not outright invented; all heard from constituents who, while trapped at home by COVID-19 for the better part of a year, had watched the unrest of 2020 unfold on television, often to the accompaniment of commentary calculated to alarm and outrage. Locally, Tulsans had seen and heard about the confrontation between protesters and the pickup driver on the inner dispersal loop. They knew that malcontents, most of whom seemed to be Black, were criticizing law enforcement and wanted something called reparations, the exact nature of which sounded vague but decidedly ominous.

State representative Monroe Nichols, the Black Democrat from Tulsa, said he found the 2021 session disillusioning. He thought he had built personal relationships with some white Republicans, despite differences of opinion. But the legislation introduced that year, and more importantly the words (or in some cases silence) that defended it, caused Nichols to reevaluate that assessment. The response of his colleagues, Nichols said in a 2022 interview, was "more overt than I would have expected."

"I probably somewhat disagree with what the majority [party] chooses to do," Nichols said, "but I've always maintained that the character of the folks who serve is way better than the product that we produce. Twenty-twenty and 2021 really challenged me in that it was the first time that I started to think that maybe the people I've worked with aren't better. . . . Maybe they are exactly what they support and choose to vote for. Because you wonder, in a political environment, why do you choose to do that kind of stuff?"

"That stuff," ultimately, was mostly encapsulated in two bills: House Bill 1674, which among other things granted immunity to motorists who run over demonstrators, and House Bill 1775, prohibiting schools from creating "discomfort" by teaching about race or gender. Both bills were inspired, wholly or in part, by events in Tulsa.[22]

HB 1674 was a direct result of the inner dispersal loop confrontation between Black Lives Matter demonstrators and two motorists, and that left a man paralyzed when he toppled off an overpass in the confusion. A day earlier, another demonstrator was injured trying to block Interstate 44. The incidents raised obvious questions about the risks and to some extent the ethics of using pedestrians to block highway traffic, even in relatively controlled situations like these, but that was not the issue addressed by HB 1674. Its concern was with the people wrapped in a ton or two of steel.

"People may not think of it this way, (but) would it be legal for me to grab somebody by the shoulders and keep them from doing what they want to do in order to get my point across?" one of the bill's sponsors state representative Kevin McDugle, a Republican whose Broken Arrow district adjoined Tulsa, told the *Tulsa World*. "No, it wouldn't be. But when we step in front of a vehicle on a road and we block it with ten or fifteen people, and [motorists] can't go where they want to go, that's equivalent to that. And so what I am trying to do is just say, 'Guys, peaceful protests are great, let's stick to the peaceful side of it.' When you are impeding on the freedoms of others, this is no longer peaceful."[23]

Rep. Regina Goodwin, D-Tulsa, predicted mayhem. "It's these kinds of bills that encourage folks to plow through the crowds," she said.[24]

McDugle, in the *Tulsa World* interview, disagreed.[25]

"Do I think that somebody is going to swerve off a road and go through a crowded group of protesters because they might not like their cause? If they do that, they are going to be criminally charged," McDugle said. "Because it all comes down to intent, and a judge is going to be able to see an intent based on what happened."

"If they were in their vehicle and firebombs are being thrown at it and people are stomping on [the vehicle] and they run over three people on the way out, they are not going to be charged."

In its final form, HB 1674 granted immunity "[f]or a motor vehicle operator who unintentionally causes injury or death . . . if: 1. The injury or death of the individual occurred while the motor vehicle operator was fleeing from a riot . . . under a reasonable belief that fleeing was necessary to protect the motor vehicle operator from serious injury or death; and 2. The motor vehicle operator exercised due care at the time of the death or injury."[26]

This may have seemed reasonable to McDugle and many others both inside and outside the legislature, but to others it sounded more like open season on protesters. Goodwin, in an op-ed cowritten with the NAACP's Puneet Cheema, called HB 1674 "a horrific anti-protester law that provides cover for motorists to hit and kill people while evading accountability."[27]

The law was, in effect, a stand-your-ground law for cars and trucks. In theory, stand-your-ground laws give people in threatening situations a stronger legal justification for defending themselves with deadly force. In practice, they allow people to be a little quicker on the trigger—or gas pedal—than necessary. Many believe stand-your-ground laws disproportionately protect whites; the data is inconclusive, but for some the message was clear. [28]

"While the law seems to create parameters that limit its reach," Goodwin and Cheema wrote, "Black people are often deemed suspicious and criminal, even when going about the most banal activity. This statute is ripe for misuse by law enforcement, prosecutors and judges, whose biases—implicit or explicit—already contribute to the disproportionate incarceration of Black people."[29]

Did any of the Republicans who voted for HB 1674 want African Americans (or anyone else) run over? Almost certainly not. What they wanted was for them to stay out of the streets—literally and figuratively. To emphasize the point, HB 1674 included a provision creating a misdemeanor for "unlawfully obstruct[ing] the normal use of any public street, highway or road within this state by impeding, hindering or restraining motor vehicle traffic or passage thereon, by standing or approaching motor vehicles thereon, or by endangering the safe movement of motor vehicles or pedestrians traveling thereon."[30]

The bill also made those convicted of the misdemeanor "liable for all damages to person or property by reason of the same," and created a new category of conspiracy for organizations found to have organized or facilitated a smorgasbord of riot-related offenses. Protest all you want, the majority was saying, but stay out of my way. Chant all you want, just not so loudly as to disturb us. Such is the power of a supermajority.[31]

From one perspective, HB 1674 was about maintaining law and order. From another, it was about intimidation and squelching unwanted criticism. A majority that stood with anti-vaxxers during a pandemic, citing First Amendment religious freedom, was not as keen on the First Amendment free speech rights of Black Lives Matter protesters upset about deaths occurring at the hands of law enforcement. On a more personal level, HB 1674 seemed like a deliberate gesture to the minority in the legislature and across the state signifying that what they said and who they were did not matter.

"When there's someone who can't walk [because of the IDL incident] . . . why would you choose for your response to be let's . . . almost embolden and encourage people to take that same action in a similar situation?" Nichols said. "I think what it really did for those of us serving in the Legislature, particularly those of us Black legislators, is really increase the divide. Not just the partisan, but the racial divide. The trust in the building. And I think there's a lot of those relationships that are changed. I know that's true for me. It doesn't mean that I treated anybody horribly or anything like that, but it certainly has changed my view of folks. It challenged my internal, almost optimism around the (belief) that the folks who serve are better than our product. And I'm not sure I've returned to believing."[32]

While HB 1674 sought primarily to discourage dissent by limiting actions, HB 1775 zeroed in on words and ideas. Its list of things that could not be discussed in public school classrooms included anything that caused any student "discomfort, guilt, anguish or any other form of psychological distress." In full, that section of the new law read:

> No teacher, administrator or other employee of a school district, charter school or virtual charter school shall require or make part of a course the following concepts:
>
> a. one race or sex is inherently superior to another race or sex,
> b. an individual, by virtue of his or her race or sex, is inherently racist, sexist oppressive, whether consciously or unconsciously,
> c. an individual should be discriminated against or receive adverse treatment solely or partly because of his or her race or sex,

d. members of one race or sex cannot and should not attempt to treat others without respect to race or sex,
e. an individual's moral character is necessarily determined by his or her race or sex,
f. an individual, by virtue of his or her race or sex, bears responsibility for actions committed in the past by other members of the same race or sex,
g. any individual should feel discomfort, guilt, anguish or any other form of psychological distress on account of his or her race or sex, or
h. meritocracy or traits such as a hard work ethic are racist or sexist or were created by members of a particular race to oppress members of another race.[33]

HB 1775 also banned mandatory diversity and bias training for students at public colleges and universities. In other words, it sought to discourage if not eliminate any and all suggestion that discrimination still exists in the United States, or that the racism of the past remains a factor in American life. The bad old days are over, and nothing is left to be seen. Discussion of present inequities was to be limited to Horatio Algerish moral tales in which industriousness and virtue overcome all obstacles. This was made clear during discussion and debate of the bill in the legislature and in the manner it would be enforced in the coming years.[34]

As often is the case, HB 1775 started out as something completely different—legislation requiring schools to have in place procedures for dealing with medical emergencies at athletic events. In that form, it passed the House 93 to 0 early in the session. In the Senate, however, its original sponsors and language were jettisoned by Sen. David Bullard, R-Durant; a section of President Trump's 2020 executive order banning diversity training in the federal government became the bill's new text. A Senate bill with similar wording had been filed but could not get a hearing during the session's February committee work period. By April though, enough pressure had been brought to bear by commentators and constituents to put the revised HB 1775 through the Senate on a party-line vote.[35]

In arguing for the bill, Bullard, a former high school history teacher in southeastern Oklahoma, insisted students throughout the state were being force-fed "critical race theory," but would not or could not give specific examples. It is not clear whether those pressing hardest for HB 1775 knew what critical race theory actually is (the bill itself did not use the term) but it was a convenient phrase for labeling an idea—that racism remains embedded in American economic, social, and political systems—they did not like. In a press release after HB 1775 passed the House on April 29, Bullard said, "Too many schools and institutions have stopped focusing on high quality education and instead have turned to a policy of indoctrination. As someone who is proud of my public-school roots, this shift is very disappointing and is not acceptable for the students of our state. I am resolved to make sure this does not continue in Oklahoma."[36]

Critical race theory, Bullard said, "is poison to the minds of students and promotes racism rather than ending it."[37]

Particularly galling to opponents of the bill, Bullard quoted (improperly, some would argue) both Martin Luther King Jr. and Frederick Douglass.

> I am partial to the words of Dr. King when he said, "The ultimate weakness of violence is that it is a descending spiral begetting the very thing it seeks to destroy, instead of diminishing evil, it multiplies it. Through violence you may murder the liar, but you cannot murder the lie, nor establish the truth. Through violence you may murder the hater, but you do not murder hate. In fact, violence merely increases hate. Returning violence for violence multiplies violence, adding deeper darkness to a night already devoid of stars. Darkness cannot drive out darkness; only light can do that. Hate cannot drive out hate; only love can do that."
>
> I am also moved by the words of another great American, Fredrick Douglas [*sic*], who said, "It is easier to build strong children than to repair broken men. And it's true. You cannot give a child back their childhood."[38]

King and Douglass had never been so popular among conservative politicians, and especially white conservative politicians, as they were in the spring of 2021. Repeated references to nonviolence suggest a threat of violence, and by portraying the Black Lives Matter movement as fundamentally violent and even terroristic, defenders of the status quo could claim—or try to claim—King as a posthumous ally. In so doing, though, they largely equated nonviolence with acquiescence, and there they went astray. King did not advocate nonviolence for the sake of nonviolence itself or to preserve the United States of the 1950s and 1960s. He saw nonviolence as a way to win the moral high ground while outnumbered and outgunned. More importantly, he saw it as a way to effect change. So, while many like Bullard quoted King on nonviolence, few borrowed his observation from a 1957 lecture at Brandeis University: "Peace is not merely the absence of tension. It is the presence of justice."[39]

Besides somewhat of a non sequitur, the Douglass quote is of questionable provenance. It has circulated widely for decades and Bullard no doubt believed it to be authentic, but researchers say they can find no evidence Douglass said or wrote those words. The earliest recorded citation dates from the mid-1990s; some believe it may have somehow been derived from Douglass's 1855 treatise on the moral toll of slaveholding, which includes the passage: "Conscience cannot stand much violence. Once thoroughly broken down, who is he that can repair the damage?" Here Douglass was describing how slaveholding had hardened a white woman's better nature, not the education or treatment of children. In any event, the quotation serves a double purpose for those who, for whatever reason, would like to put to bed or at least soften discussions of race and racism. It allows them to claim a famous Black civil rights figure as one of their own while making whatever it is they are trying to do or not do "all about the kids"—the time-honored ploy of dragging children into the middle of adults' political arguments.[40]

The same is true of displaying the flag and waving it at every opportunity. After quoting King on the virtues of nonviolent rebellion—and having said nothing about the violent attack on the US Capitol a few months earlier—Bullard concluded by citing the American Revolution, a decidedly violent act of rebellion, regardless of one's opinion of its provocation or justification.

"Though I did not choose the number, HB 1775, it is rightly numbered," Bullard's statement read. "1775 was the year of 'the shot heard around the world.' The year that America awoke to her independence. Passage of this bill is a declaration of Oklahoma's independence against false teaching, pushing back against those who would divide us. I will not stop fighting until our students are free of this indoctrination."[41]

HB 1775 passed the state senate 38–9 on April 21 and was brought up for a house vote on April 29. Under other circumstances, the house would not have even considered HB 1775 in its final form; even the parliamentarian, who is hired by the majority party, agreed the senate's new language clearly violated house rules that require amendments be germane to the original bill. In any setting controlled by a supermajority, however, rules often apply only to the minority; the house Republicans' supermajority simply voted to suspend the rules and proceeded.[42]

The bill initially passed 70 to 19, with eleven Republicans and one Democrat not voting. Rep. Daniel Pae of Lawton, the son of South Korean immigrants, was the only Republican in either chamber to vote against it. The bill had to be brought back several days later following revelations that someone—it was never revealed whom—had pressed an absent Republican's green button on April 29 in order to get the decisive 68th "yea" vote on the motion to suspend the rules. A member of a caucus ostensibly obsessed with voter fraud apparently had committed what amounted to voter fraud. It did not matter. After a few procedural votes, the bill passed again.[43]

Again, the bill's proponents claimed "Marxist ideology" was rife in the state's public schools but provided no specifics. Hate and divisiveness, said one representative, was being peddled as social justice, and must be stopped. The bill's house sponsor, Rep. Kevin West, R-Moore, tried to sell the idea that HB 1775 was to protect minorities.[44]

"I wouldn't want anybody to be taught that because their ancestors were slaves, that they should be slaves," he said.[45]

Goodwin would not have it.

"Your whole concept, [that] somehow . . . you're trying to help Black folks not feel inferior, flies in the face of the very language," she said. "Would you agree that a white person [West], who we see as white, has brought this language, which really is trying to absolve white folks from feeling guilty and feeling discomforted by the heinous acts that have occurred yesterday and today? Would you agree that's why you're bringing that language?"

"I would totally disagree with that," West said.

But consciously or not, that was pretty clearly the intention. As the discussion ranged far and wide, West and others argued that white children, and especially boys, were being taught to "hate themselves" because of things in the past over which they had no control, such as slavery, segregation, discrimination, the dispossession and near-annihilation of Native Americans, and the treatment of women and nonconformists. Rep. Justin Humphrey, like Bullard a Republican from southeastern Oklahoma, a place known as Little Dixie, no doubt represented many throughout the state when he compared Black Lives Matter to the Ku Klux Klan and suggested all debts were paid by the 600,000 white Americans who died in the Civil War. When Humphrey said, "This is about the story of America," he was spot on, although perhaps not precisely in the way he imagined.[46]

For many Oklahomans, and especially white Oklahomans, the struggle for equality and equity was a fight that had already been fought. To this way of thinking, suggesting otherwise was dishonest, a play for "retribution," as Humphrey put it.

"This is about whether the civil rights movement has failed or whether it was successful," Humphrey said. "How much blood does it take to buy restitution? How much blood does it take in America to say we have tried?"

Yes, Humphrey allowed, racism still showed itself on the floor of the Oklahoma House of Representatives—and implied it was all directed at whites.

An argument can be made that the passion behind the legislation arose from anger and fear at the prospect of being on the receiving end of some measure, however small, of what others had endured for centuries, and the related fear of losing some measure of the almost absolute control exercised for centuries by people like them in Oklahoma and much of the world. To be sure, racism has always been an expression of power. But as the exercise of that power in the most obvious forms has diminished, many people, and especially people with power and position to lose, have tried to convince themselves that race no longer matters, and that the lingering and more subtle effects of racism are an illusion concocted by race baiters and opportunists. We do not have slavery, we do not have state-sanctioned segregation or discrimination, so therefore we have equality or something close to it. America had a problem and fixed it. That is what people behind legislation such as HB 1775 and HB 1674 believed, or desperately wanted to believe.

According to the best evidence, virtually no one, and certainly not in Oklahoma, was shaming white school children as hereditary racists or encouraging Black or Hispanic or LGBTQ kids to riot in the streets. But school children were learning that America has not always been the shining city on a hill. And that is what people found alarming. It might not have been the academic definition of critical race theory, but it was a questioning of the fairness of the system and the subtle and not-so-subtle ways that keep some people in power and others out. With power comes the ability to make the rules (or ignore them) and to decide who gets what. Power, relatively speaking, is a finite commodity. For one person or group to gain power, another person or group must lose it. That is what "critical race theory" really means to the people who worry about it the most.

So, when West said, in defending HB 1775, "We know that this is something that's out there," he was not altogether wrong or disingenuous. What West failed to state or perhaps even recognize was that preservation of power, not the feelings of eight-year-old white boys, really drove the likes of HB 1775 and HB 1674.[47]

Back in Tulsa, the centennial commission was beside itself. After years of trying to cultivate Tulsa's and the state's Republican leadership, Matthews and many of the other members were bitterly disappointed—although not necessarily surprised. They begged Stitt to veto the bill but to no avail; he signed it on May 7, three-and-a-half weeks before the race massacre centennial. Bynum, too, supported the measure, saying, "I think the governor did the right thing on that. I don't support the teaching of critical race theory in schools, either." So once again, when push came to shove, the opinions and concerns of Black Tulsans were pushed and shoved to the back.[48]

"We are extremely disappointed that Oklahoma Legislators, including Governor Stitt, chose to support HB 1775[,] which diametrically opposes the work of the 1921 Tulsa Race Massacre Centennial Commission," the commission said in a written statement. "No matter how poorly written, the intention of the bill clearly aims to limit teaching the racial implications of America's history. The bill serves no [other] purpose than to fuel the racism and denial that afflicts our communities and our nation. It is a sad day and a stain on Oklahoma."[49]

Referring specifically to Stitt, the commission wrote, "As a fellow Commissioner we thought our Governor would do better."[50]

But Stitt and HB 1775's other supporters, and even the commission, noted the new law did not exclude the teaching of specific topics or issues; it even specified HB 1775 "shall not prohibit the teaching of concepts that align to the Oklahoma Academic Standards." In an executive order issued at the same time he signed HB 1775, Stitt wrote: "These standards include important topics in America's fraught history with race from the Dred Scott decision and the Civil War to segregation and Oklahoma's own history, including the Trail of Tears, the Tulsa Race Massacre of 1921, and the courage of Clara Luper. These topics should and will be taught in Oklahoma schools so that we may reckon with our history."[51]

That so many people did not believe Stitt should not have been a surprise and need not have been, but it was. Rep. Monroe Nichols had a simple explanation why.

"They don't come to us and say, 'All right, Monroe, this is what we think' or 'Monroe, how does this sound to you? Is this good or bad for people who you represent? How does this impact you?' We don't get those kinds of conversations in the policymaking space," Nichols said. "Political leaders in Oklahoma are the worst examples when it comes to these kinds of conversations."[52]

In other words, while Black lives might matter under some conditions, Black opinions do not.

Using HB 1674 as an example, Nichols said McDugle's apparent disinterest in anyone else's perspective was indicative of the House majority in general, and especially on anything related to race.

"The question that I would ask Kevin is, 'What's been your conversation with Black elected officials in the Legislature about this?' Nobody presses them on 'Who have you talked to that doesn't look or think like you about this particular issue, and what do they say about it?' And so people get away with it. And I think that's the kind of stuff that we really have to start doing to make people accountable for making decisions that can be quite detrimental to a whole segment of the population."

The major decisions concerning African Americans and other minorities, Nichols said, were being made without "any engagement with communities of color [or] legislators of color . . . [or] thinking deeply about what's the best pathway forward for Oklahoma."

> They've all been done as a knee-jerk response to something people are watching on TV. And so we have this vilification of folks . . . who have real concerns about stuff and have only expressed it in peaceful ways, and what the legislative body taught them is that if you speak up, we'll do something to you. . . . if you speak up, we're going to ignore you. And there's not a time, as best I can tell, in the history of our wonderful democracy that's really worked out well, where folks who felt unheard were either retaliated against or ignored and that it didn't fester and lead to at best a significant amount of distrust. So that means that everything happening subsequently is going to be a lot worse.

HB 1775 worried and bewildered many people. In one breath, the bill's supporters, including Stitt, said they did not want to impede the teaching of hard truths. In the next, they insisted no one feel discomfort at these truths or receive any sort of instruction or training on how to understand people affected by them. In his executive order, Stitt wrote:

> To ensure clarity in the implementation of House Bill 1775 and to provide guidance for the State Regents for Higher Education and the State Board of Education, I declare that it is my intent that no topic of our history or present inequalities are to be hidden from view. Rather, it is my intent that

> we teach about Oklahoma's diversity in light of its fundamental unity. We must come together as one people and refuse to be divided by those who would profit from fringe theories.[53]

But one person's fringe theory is another's gospel. And who decides which is which? Who decides what is divisive? It is easy to hint at dark motives of those who challenge the status quo, but what about those who profiteer from it? None of those questions were answered. Bynum said he did not understand why "this is even a subject of controversy." The legislation was clear, he said. "The bill doesn't say you can't teach uncomfortable facts." But those in a minority know that the intent behind words matters more than the words themselves. They understand better than others that the people who enforce the laws are more important than the shalls and shall nots in the statute books—as borne witness by the manner in which HB 1775 went through the legislature to become law. We call ourselves a nation of laws, not men, but there are exceptions for those with large enough majorities or good enough lawyers.[54]

For the centennial commission, HB 1775 was another crisis. Intentionally or not, the new law was a direct rebuke to the commission's aims and endeavors and a blow to its credibility. Already riven internally and ridiculed from without because of the Lankford dilemma, the commission now had to decide what to do about Stitt. Unlike Lankford, Stitt had never been much invested in the commission or its work, but he was the governor, and some were loath to risk his enmity so close to the finish line. Matthews, especially, was playing a long game. He still had things he wanted to accomplish in the legislature and would need Stitt's signature to achieve them. But in the end there really was not much choice. When neither Stitt nor a representative participated in a May 10 meeting to discuss the situation, the commission sent what amounted to a breakup letter over Phil Armstrong's signature:

> Dear Governor Stitt:
>
> We are gravely disappointed that neither you nor your representative chose to join the special meeting of the 1921 Race Massacre Centennial Commission ("Centennial Commission") last night to discuss the signing of HB 1775 into law. Indeed, your office failed to even extend the courtesy of a reply to the Centennial Commission's invitation.
>
> As a Centennial Commission member, surely you know that the vigorous exchange of ideas through education lies at the heart of our

mission. Telling the story of 1921 requires confronting and sharing the facts about this horrific period in Oklahoma's and Tulsa's history. It also demands an exploration of the underlying causative factors.

HB 1775 chills the ability of educators to teach students, of any age, and will only serve to intimidate educators who seek to reveal and process our hidden history.

You know that. We delivered this message to you before you signed. We were joined by educators, school boards, universities, faith, and community leaders, all of whom vigorously objected to HB 1775. You seemingly disregarded and dismissed this chorus of voices aligned against HB 1775.

In your public address last week you stated, "We need policies that bring us together, not rip us apart," and described HB 1775 as a bill that "encourages honest and tough conversations" by codifying the concepts of Dr. Martin Luther King, Jr. How does this law bring us together and codify the concepts of Dr. Martin Luther King, Jr.?

How do you reconcile your membership on the Centennial Commission with your support of a law that is fundamentally contrary to the mission of reconciliation and restoration?

The Centennial Commission has shared nationally and internationally the unvarnished and difficult truth about 1921. Our community and state will be stronger for telling the story through the lens of those whose lives were lost or forever changed because of racism, hatred, and violence. It has been our collective mission to offer a path for repairing that which was destroyed.

The Centennial Commission feels that your signature on the bill at this critical time when Oklahoma should embrace its history is diametrically opposite to the mission of the Centennial Commission and reflects your desire to end your affiliation. If you would like to contact us to discuss this further, please do so immediately. If we do not hear back from you, we will consider your lack of response as a further disavowal of the stated goals of the Centennial Commission and an official resignation from its membership.[55]

When Stitt's communications office answered a *Black Wall Street Times* request for comment with a terse "our policy is to respond to journalists, not activists pretending to be reporters," the Twittersphere exploded.[56]

"Based on this interaction, it is the *Black Wall Street Times* Editorial Board's opinion that Governor Stitt and his communications team are operating with a segregated media policy," the news site said. "The governor is a frequent guest on *Fox News*, a far-right activist cable network. BWST is a Black-owned, Black-managed and Black experience-centered media outlet based out of Tulsa, Okla.—home of the original Black Wall Street. If *Fox News* has access to the governor, BWST readers deserve access, too."[57]

Belatedly, Stitt's office issued a statement insisting the governor and his wife Sarah Stitt "both strongly support reconciliation, healing and the rebirth of Tulsa's Greenwood District," and that they had worked faithfully with the commission "on multiple productive events." It asserted that Armstrong "does not speak for the entire Centennial Commission" and insisted HB 1775 was a "common-sense law preventing students from being taught that one race or sex is superior to another [which] is contrary to the mission of reconciliation and restoration.[58]

"Gov. Stitt issued Executive Order 2021–12 as a signing statement to expressly direct that the Tulsa Race Massacre, and all historical events included in the Oklahoma Academic Standards, must still be taught in our schools," the statement continued. "The governor believes that any other interpretation of this legislation is misguided and fundamentally inaccurate, and that position was expressed to the Centennial Commission before the bill was signed into law."

This may have been true insomuch as it reflected Stitt's thinking on the matter; if so, it also reflected either a lack of understanding of what many people read between the lines of HB 1775 or an indifference to it. Armstrong, in an email to a reporter, explained why he and so many others were offended by not only the bill but the way it became law.

"I believe the political maneuvering that is taking place . . . to sign such a bill . . . on the threshold of this [centennial] speaks volumes to the continual work that must be done," he said.

Meanwhile, Monroe Nichols decided he had had enough and submitted *his* resignation.

"I'm proud of the work the commission has done," Nichols said at the time. "I wasn't upset that many of the commissioners didn't share my views."

Long a vocal critic of Stitt, Nichols said he quit because he did not want that criticism to further complicate the commission's job.

"I don't think so," Nichols said when asked if the controversies would wreck the centennial. "I trust my fellow commissioners. There's been drama here and there, but I think the personal beefs, the political beefs, will fade. I have more faith in the citizens of the city than I do the leadership. I think this will be a special time for the city and state, but it won't be because of the leadership."

In the weeks ahead, however, the bitterest conflicts were not between Black Tulsans and white political leadership. They were about three centenarians and a one hundred year-long argument over the past, present, and future of Greenwood.

7

SURVIVORS

The first 5,800 doses of the Pfizer-BioNTech COVID-19 vaccines arrived in Tulsa on December 15, 2020; the first shot, administered by the Tulsa County Health Department in a drive-thru setup, went to Dr. Jeffrey Goodloe, Hillcrest Medical Center's emergency department director.[1]

"The opportunity to have this vaccine is just incredible," said Goodloe. "What an amazing accomplishment in a series of a few months. I have studied this extensively as an emergency physician, and I am completely comfortable in the safety of this vaccine. This is something that for me is something very exciting to be a part of, to see what the scientific community can do, in less than a year."[2]

With Tulsa and Oklahoma approaching their pandemic peaks for hospitalizations and deaths from the virus, and the state's hospitalization rate among the top five nationally, one might think the vaccines would have been received with unbounded elation; after ten months of unprecedented upheaval, of suffering, fear, uncertainty and conflict, money and science had delivered what seemed to be a way back to normal. And many Tulsans did think that to be the case.[3]

"Today is an amazing day for us," said Alicia Etgen of the Tulsa Health Department. "While we know that there's still a lot of work to do and we still have to practice good social distancing and mask-wearing, a vaccine is the first step toward getting hold of this public health crisis."[4]

Some of the doctors, nurses and other health professionals lined up for Tulsa's first vaccinations sounded nothing short of ecstatic.

"I was excited to get the first vaccine," said Dr. Jeff Johnson. "I've been talking about it for a while. I was like 'I want to be one of the first people to get it.' I've just been hopeful, you know, that if we can start getting the people vaccinated, we can start kind of moving out of this period and start getting more back toward normal."[5]

For an intensive care unit nurse, Rachel Shields-Carnley, the vaccine offered the prospect of relief from almost unbearable physical and psychological strain.

"It has been a very complicated and heartbreaking season for us because we're not only the nurses, but we're the family," said Shields-Carnley. "We're the support. We have to support each other and support the patient and support the families that are home because they have limited visitation. So we have to be all the things, and it gets heartbreaking when the patients are with us so long. We love them as families love them."[6]

The reality, of course, was that while many in Oklahoma and elsewhere eagerly accepted the COVID vaccines, many others did not, and something that could have been reasonably expected to mitigate the stress on American society and the world at large in some cases exacerbated it. This was true not just for Tulsa. From the Florida Keys to the Aleutian Islands, many of the same people who were convinced that the pandemic was a hoax, that masks were more dangerous than the virus, and that the 2020 presidential election had been rigged, were not inclined to trust a vaccine made from who-knew-what and pushed on them by, in their view, a pharmaceutical industry concerned only with making a buck and a government bent on controlling every aspect of their lives.

"It's not necessarily that Republicans are opposed to COVID vaccines, it's that Republicans, or conservative people, are skeptical of the government," said state senator Greg McCortney, a Republican from Ada in rural south-central Oklahoma.[7]

Polling by Oklahoma City-based Amber Integrated as vaccinations began in mid-December 2020 found 38 percent of respondents did not want to be vaccinated. Two-thirds did not want vaccination mandated. Republicans were more likely to oppose or be skeptical of vaccination, but many Democrats and independents were, too. Amber Integrated's polling proved a pretty accurate predictor: more than two years later, only 61 percent of Oklahoma's population five years old and older was considered fully vaccinated. True, 75 percent had received at least one dose of a vaccine, and 93 percent of the vulnerable sixty-five and older group was fully vaccinated, but groups such as the vaccine-averse Oklahomans for Health and Parental Rights had grown in size and influence.[8]

The overwhelming majority of medical and public health officials were dumbfounded by the resistance of people who, in many cases, idolized Donald Trump but rejected one of his administration's greatest achievements.

Dr. Aaron Wendelboe, a University of Oklahoma researcher who was one of several state epidemiologists Stitt went through during the pandemic, said he did not know how "to reach the conservative white males—that only forty percent of them are willing to get vaccinated. Maybe somebody else is poised to do that research or do that outreach. Who's going to be the voice that those folks will listen to? I'm not sure exactly who that is yet."[9]

Every state—every country—struggled with COVID. But Tulsa does present a case study, particularly in the context of everything else happening there. It both accentuated disagreements and diverted attention from them. Under other circumstances, all eyes might have been turned to the approaching race massacre centennial when the calendar flipped to January 2021. Instead, Tulsans were bombarded with a cacophony of conflicting messages and crises, and so was the rest of the world. Most of this turmoil was caused or amplified by COVID-19.

As Bob Jack pointed out, even the election fraud claims were tied into COVID; both even reached their apex at the same time as the pandemic. COVID, the narrative ran, was the reason—or pretext—for changes in voting laws, especially for mail-in ballots; doing so had let in thousands if not millions of bogus ballots. That is one reason why so many people, including Oklahomans, were skeptical of both the pandemic and the vaccine. Ultimately, though, COVID most highlighted Oklahoma's urban-rural-suburban divides. According to the CDC COVID Data Tracker, more than 70 percent of Tulsa County residents over five years old were fully vaccinated by the spring of 2023. The city of Tulsa was likely higher, given the resistance in some suburbs. Oklahoma County, which includes most of Oklahoma City and a large military installation, Tinker Air Force Base, was at 75 percent. But four of the seven counties adjoining Tulsa County had not made it to 50 percent, and the remaining three barely had. Sparsely populated Osage County, whose Republican Party voted to expel Senators Lankford and Inhofe for not trying to stop certification of the 2020 election, did not get to even 40 percent. The same pattern held statewide. More than forty of the state's seventy-seven counties failed to reach 50 percent fully vaccinated and many were below 40 percent. One, in western Oklahoma, was below 30 percent. And the figures likely would have been lower had not some of the state's thirty-eight tribal governments and most of the state's Black leadership not aggressively encouraged vaccination—an interesting twist given both groups' histories with public health officials and medical researchers.[10]

The geographical divisions highlighted by COVID-19 also reflect the state's politics, and thus bear on every calculation of its elected leaders. With a little over a quarter of the state's population within their city limits, Tulsa and Oklahoma City are divided more or less evenly between Republican and Democrat with significant independent components. The rest of the state, including Oklahoma City and Tulsa suburbs, votes overwhelmingly Republican. In 2018 and 2022, Stitt lost or narrowly won the state's most populous counties but won big elsewhere. Trump won all seventy-seven counties in 2016 and 2020 but by smaller margins in Tulsa and Oklahoma Counties—just one point his second time around in Oklahoma County. Some believe Trump lost in Oklahoma City and Tulsa in 2020, but a definite determination is impossible because of the way absentee ballots are tabulated.[11]

So when Republican-voting rural communities and suburbs such as Broken Arrow, a city of more than 115,000 adjacent to Tulsa, said they did not want mask or vaccine mandates, the elected leadership listened. The same applied to school closures. It was as if any sort of adjustment in routine because of COVID-19 was a form of surrender. Stitt himself encouraged preventative measures such as vaccination and masks but not always with much conviction. He was particularly critical of school districts such as Tulsa's, which remained closed to most in-person instruction for more than a year. This worked a hardship on parents and no doubt affected the children and their learning, but Tulsa Public Schools (TPS) leadership maintained it was better than the alternative. As it turned out, many other districts and individual schools were open only sporadically because of COVID outbreaks and insufficient staff. [12]

The result of this politicization of public health was more conflict and more bitterness. Stitt was at odds with healthcare professionals in general and the Tulsa County Health Department in particular, so much so that a move to strip it and its Oklahoma County counterpart—the state's only two locally controlled health departments—of their independence was initiated in early 2021. Stitt regularly blasted Tulsa Public Schools and Superintendent Deborah Gist, ostensibly because of TPS's COVID policies but also because Gist was frequently critical of Stitt's education ideas and policies. After Stitt attacked TPS in his State of the State address to open the 2021 legislative session, Gist called him a "bully" who had done little to address the pandemic. "We are a district that is managing the effects of his failed leadership" Gist wrote in a Facebook post. Tulsa and Broken Arrow city officials feuded over each other's public health policies, with other nearby municipalities sometimes pushed and pulled by the nearly opposite forces of their larger neighbors. COVID even became an issue in the existing rift between Stitt and the legislature; a legislative report issued days into the 2021 session claimed the administration mishandled and perhaps misspent some of the state's $1.26 billion share of CARES Act funds.[13]

Like muscles straining beneath the skin, the opposing tensions of American society and politics tightened into stark relief during the pandemic. Individual freedom versus collective responsibility. Commerce versus personal or public health. God versus science. Theory versus practicality. Us versus them. In seeking a balance among these elements, Americans often look to religion for guidance. Tulsans have probably been more so inclined than most. The city that gave Oral Roberts his start is also home to one of the country's largest Unitarian congregations. It is a city of churches—and synagogues and mosques and temples. But even here, COVID's icy tentacles reached into existing cracks and opened them wider.

First Baptist Church North Tulsa is one of the city's oldest historically Black churches. Founded in 1899 as the Macedonian Baptist Church, its building at the time of the race massacre, at 902 E. Archer St., on the southeast corner of what was then the city's African American neighborhood, is said to have survived the race massacre because the looters and arsonists mistook it for a white church. In 1953, it moved a mile north to 1414 N. Greenwood Ave., where it remains. Martin Luther King Jr. preached there during his only Tulsa appearance, in 1960. Thurgood Marshall, who as a young lawyer with the NAACP Defense Fund had worked with Tulsa attorney Amos Hall on desegregation cases, visited. So did Ralph Abernathy and Jesse Jackson, among others. It is part of a network of churches that for generations has been a foundation of Tulsa's Black community. The churches' sanctuaries have been the meeting halls; their pastors have been looked to as leaders and spokesmen and sometimes as diplomats, not only by their parishioners but by white Tulsans as well. In crises, everyone looked to the Black pastors.[14]

"That's something we've shared with our white colleagues," said Rev. Anthony Scott, First Baptist North Tulsa's long-time senior pastor. "Whenever there's a . . . shooting in south Tulsa, white faith leaders are not asked to address the situation or calm the community. They're in a different realm. In the black community, no matter what takes place, we are expected and have historically had that role of giving voice for our community."[15]

That can be problematic. For one thing, pastors are humans. Like all humans, they do not all think alike or analyze situations alike or have the same motivations and goals. They do not all interpret scriptures the same way. So it can be difficult presenting a uniform message and united front. More broadly, a lot of people, and especially white people, do not want to hear that message. As much as white conservatives praise King today, he was not so widely admired by even moderate whites of his day.

> There are some within the white faith community who would say to us . . . "Just stick to your church and stop speaking about all this." It's like when [basketball star] LeBron James was told to be quiet and just dribble. There are those, even in the white faith community who would say to us, "You're really stirring stuff up. Why do you speak to it?" Well, if [we] don't speak to it, then you just have maybe some voices speaking to it that are not responsible. And it winds up being a worse situation.

Black pastors, of course, are not the only faith leaders to have ever involved themselves in social and political issues. Senator Lankford is a Baptist minister who speaks frequently on the right to practice one's faith in the public square. Jackson Lahmeyer has his own church and is not shy about mixing politics and religion. But Black pastors have historically filled the void almost all minorities must deal with—underrepresentation in positions of power. Scott noted that typically one and sometimes two of Tulsa's nine city councilors and from five to seven of the 149 legislators are Black.

"That's not a voice," he said. "The Black church, and the Black faith leaders, are still the most sought-after voice when it comes to addressing issues. Even beyond just the church: politically, socially, just across the board."

With all of the changes in society, Scott said, churches remain "the strongest institution still in the Black community," in part because they are self-sustaining. The Black church, he said, "doesn't depend on anyone or anything else for its existence or survival, so it's kind of free to speak. . . . Black faith leaders are not dying for votes to stay in office."

COVID and the national strife of 2020 and 2021 were challenges "a lot of pastors in my generation have never really experienced," Scott said. "We've had to respond to local shootings, but we haven't had to respond as clergy in the black community to national crises like this, maybe since the sixties. Something that affected and impacted everyone. George Floyd impacted Minneapolis, and us vicariously; but the pandemic, like the civil rights movement, affected us all across the nation. So it was almost having to move into this role of crisis leadership and making decisions you've never had to make before."

One of those decisions—one of *the* decisions–was how to continue functioning while contending with a deadly virus. This was true for everyone around the world, and for all of the institutions that define human societies, from religion to schools to jobs and even to the basic family level. For some, masks and social distancing, and later vaccination, were badges of honor signifying commitment to shared duty and responsibility. For others, compliance equaled surrender. Defiance, of course, does not impress a virus, but if one believes said virus is no more dangerous than the common flu, or exists only as a mind-control ploy, or that prevention measures are pointless, that does not matter. The defiance is against the people trying to tell you what to do, not some microbe.

This question, which some chose to frame as a matter of faith in God versus faith in man, and others as God-given reasoning ability versus magical thinking, divided the religious realm just as it did every other aspect of life. In Tulsa, church memberships politically aligned with conservatism stayed open and were disinclined to enforce preventative measures such as mask-wearing and social distancing. Moderate to left-leaning congregations curtailed or eliminated in-person meetings and turned to live streaming. During the pandemic's early stages, some congregations met in parking lots. One held services at a drive-in movie theater. By early 2021, though, local officials had given up trying to keep houses of worship closed. Each group had to decide for itself what was more important, the safety of communing virtually or the comfort and comradeship of personal interaction.[16]

First Baptist Church North Tulsa (FBCNT), like many Black churches, perceived COVID-19 as a serious threat and proceeded accordingly. It was completely closed for more than a year and not fully reopened for two, Scott said. From a public health standpoint, and for the safety of not only its members but everyone with whom they came into contact, it was the right thing to do. FBCNT's services, streamed live for the first time, developed a strong audience. But the churches pastored by the Jackson Lahmeyers and attended by people pushing for legislation to ban schools and universities from teaching critical race theory, or their notion of it, and worried about armies of phantom liberal voters and transgender athletes taking over girls' and women's sports, kept their buildings locked for only a few weeks in the spring of 2020. The significance of this divergence, if any, to the state and nation's deteriorating political climate for racial and cultural minorities during the pandemic is difficult to gauge. In Tulsa, at least, it is perhaps worth considering.[17]

As Scott put it, "The church, by definition, is a gathering of people." Without a gathering in person, some felt, religious communion ceased to exist."

First Baptist Church North Tulsa, like many churches that were not already doing so, began streaming its services. Gathering through the wizardry of modern telecommunications was not the same as gathering in person, but it did have some advantages. Scott said his church's overall reach may have actually grown during the pandemic. But from March 2021 to Easter Sunday 2022, First Baptist Church's 1,200-seat sanctuary mostly sat dark, silent, and empty. On Sunday mornings, said Scott, "It was just me and the singers and a camera."[18]

Similar scenarios played out in churches across America, but not in Lahmeyer's Sheridan Church or ones like it. During the pandemic's early stages, Lahmeyer preached from the flat roof of his strip mall church while the congregation gathered in the parking lot; by May 2020, though, at least some services had moved back inside. As the pandemic dragged on, Sheridan Church and others became progressively less likely to enforce even basic prevention measures. In November, video surfaced of a packed house for a Christian music concert at one of the city's most influential evangelical churches, Victory Christian Center. By the time Lahmeyer announced his candidacy for US Senate in March 2021, he was bragging about flouting the city's COVID ordinances and had joined forces with Clay Clark to, in effect, market conspiracy theories about the pandemic. And they had the right target audience. In what some might interpret as a commentary on the concept of white privilege in terms of a sense of invincibility, Pew Research polling found white evangelicals less likely than other groups to believe COVID-19 a serious threat and to be vaccinated; Black Americans were more likely to view COVID-19 as a serious threat to their own health, and to be concerned about spreading the virus to others.[19]

"There was really no kickback in [Tulsa's] Black community" to COVID-19 precautions or restrictions, said Scott. "There was no resistance. In fact, once we fully opened and the mask mandate was lifted . . . we had some, they really didn't want to stop wearing masks. So even now, I have members who still wear them."[20]

By contrast, the Victory Christian concert-goer had said, "In reality, we just need to enjoy life, go forward with life, live by faith, and go forward."[21]

It is difficult to say this was the majority view, but it was a vocal one and it drove a lot of the politics and public policy of 2021. Meanwhile Scott and the folks of First Baptist Church North Tulsa, and others like them, tried to follow the best evidence on how to keep people alive and well. Scott later reflected that:

> It really caused me a great deal of pain and agony, in that, as a pastor, I had members who were passing away that I couldn't touch, that I couldn't go see in the hospital. We were so disconnected that a lot of times people had gone through crises and I didn't know they had gone through it until it was over. So as a pastor, that really made me feel a great deal of guilt, almost negligent, in my pastoral duties. That was a tough part, not just for me but for a lot of pastors.
>
> I remember participating in a press conference [at another church] that centered on the Floyd situation. A few ministers, a few of our black politicians speaking to that issue. We had masks on and we really tried to calm the community and assure them that these issues would be addressed. We were having to keep angry people calm from a distance. We couldn't look into their faces, to ascertain their emotions. We couldn't actually see who was upset, who was wanting to respond, so we just had to throw out a blanket, general call to calm, and pray and hope for the best.
>
> Now, things being shut down helped to quell a great deal of it, because it was not in your best interest, physically and from a health standpoint. From a church leadership standpoint, what we did see around the country, particularly during that summer [of 2020], when there were a lot of the protests for social justice, was a concern not only for physical safety, but even from . . . just a health standpoint. . . . So what you mean to be a good thing can really lead to a loss of life in another way.[22]

And that presented a dilemma for Black (and other) clergy who may have supported the cause but concluded their more immediate responsibility was the health of their congregants and the public at large.

"We couldn't be out there in the middle of all of this because it was not safe from a COVID standpoint," Scott said. "We had to be dependent on . . . others to give us information and knowledge that we didn't have."

Deaths, Scott said, were particularly difficult.

> We didn't experience hardly any in 2020, but when 2021 rolled around we had a flurry of seven or eight in the first few months, including a husband and wife. So the impact of death from COVID didn't really hit us until 2021. Doing funerals without members being able to come together

> was pretty tough. So much so that when we did finally open there was a great deal of joy and grief sort of intermingled, because everybody had this unprocessed grief that was just sort of lingering. So you just had an outpouring of emotion on all extremes.

Later, Scott reflected on how the pandemic and factors it elevated had affected the communications and leadership dynamic.

> Social media and the whole virtual experience has exposed our people to so many competing voices that whenever there is a crisis, we're not the only voice that our people are listening to. So it's become extremely important that we find ways to recreate our voice so that we're able to reach people, have an impact on people, but it also means we've got to be listening to these other voices so we know how to address those other voices while putting our voice out.

These developments were not unique to Scott or Black clergy or even religion in general. These shifts affected everyone and everything. But the singular role of Black churches and clergy, and specifically in Tulsa, put additional pressure on Scott and others.

"I have a role to lift my community, but also to keep us connected to the larger community," he said. "I can't be divisive. It's not that I don't address truth or reality. But we have to be bridge builders, even in catastrophic and traumatic situations. Those who are on the fringe and have no accountability can just be reckless and speak just to one side. I can't do that."

Scott's assessment of Black Tulsa's relationship with the city's broader power and leadership structure is less critical than that of some others.

> I really think our city has been a great model of how faith communities and political leaders have forged relationships over the years that allows us to speak critically to one another in a civil way," Scott said. "I think what we've lost in the political arena is the ability to have a difference of opinion in a healthy public discourse. But in the city of Tulsa, at least locally, we're able to have public discourse over difference of opinion in a very civil way. Speaking our own truth. That has allowed the larger community, particularly those in north Tulsa who would be upset about these issues, to know our Black leadership, whether faith or political, has the ability to walk into city hall, to go to the faith community citywide, and have an ear of someone who will listen. That helped quell a lot of what was going on.

At the height of racial tension and violence nationwide, Scott was invited to speak at Tulsa's other First Baptist Church—one of the large, predominantly white downtown congregations—and other churches about what the members were seeing on television news almost nonstop. The invitations also raised some questions about the level of awareness, even among people who want to understand their neighbors.

> They wanted us to come and basically speak to the history of social unrest and the history of Black people in our nation, from the past all of the way up to the present, and to speak to why these communities were so upset. I had quite a few opportunities to go into churches like that. And a lot of the pastors said to me, "I want to address this, but a lot of the time I feel more like I put my foot in my mouth than anything else. Will you come?"
>
> I would tell them a lot of times, "As much as I appreciate coming to speak to you in this sanctuary, those of you who are [here] are really not the ones that I need to be speaking to. There's buttons being pushed on both sides, and you're not necessarily the ones on your side who are pushing buttons. Just like the ones who come to First Baptist Church North Tulsa are not necessarily the ones pushing the buttons on this side. We've got to be able to reach those who are out on the fringes . . . that is the challenge."

On February 2, 2021, Viola Fletcher and her brother Hughes Van Ellis were added as plaintiffs in *Randle et al v. City of Tulsa et al.* Damario Solomon-Simmons had mentioned Mrs. Fletcher as a survivor when he announced the lawsuit six months earlier, and she was deposed by teleconference video, as was Mrs. Randle, in October 2020, but she does not seem to have formally joined the lawsuit until the second amended petition was filed on February 2. Until then, Hughes Van Ellis's name had not come up at all. Mrs. Fletcher's half-brother, he had been a few months old at the time of the massacre.[23]

The amended petition adding Ellis and Fletcher did not get much attention when it was filed, but a formal announcement at a February 23 press conference did. Then, on March 31, the plaintiffs sued the city of Tulsa, the Metropolitan Area Planning Commission, and the Tulsa Development Authority individually over Oklahoma Open Records Act requests related to the Greenwood lawsuit. The requests were broad, in some instances seeking information from as far back as 1908. The original request demanded the records within fifteen days or an explanation of why they had not been produced, but TDA said the request involved scanning 550,000 pages—which it eventually did. The city and the agencies involved may have considered the requests unreasonable and an attempt to get the city to do the Greenwood plaintiffs' legwork for them, but for someone with the time, patience, and skill to properly mine those mountains of paper lay the documentary history of how so much of the old Greenwood neighborhoods were lost to Black ownership.[24]

The records dispute would drag on for more than two years, largely out of public earshot. The immediate effect of the lawsuits, and the addition of Viola Fletcher and Hughes Van Ellis as plaintiffs, was to build an argument for the moral high ground. In this version of what was unfolding in Greenwood, the city and the centennial organizers were greedy opportunists trying to exploit the suffering of past generations while ignoring the three remaining massacre survivors and the descendants of the thousands of Black men and women who lost everything—including, in some cases, their lives—and who continued to be affected by ongoing inequities. Given the wording of the initial records requests, it is not unreasonable to think the plaintiffs' legal team expected and perhaps even counted on the city and its agencies' resistance. The Greenwood plaintiffs may have had a right to the documents—no court has said otherwise—but as journalists and others who regularly seek government records can attest, requests such as this one can take weeks, months, or even years to fulfill. In the meantime, any real or perceived delay bolstered the narrative that people in power were stonewalling a crusade for truth and justice. Images of the three elderly plaintiffs further reinforced their lawyers' message and Justice for Greenwood's shaming of the centennial commission for spending $30 million on a museum and not a cent on people.[25]

Not surprisingly, the objects of this scorn and ridicule voiced many of the same opinions about the other side, and especially its most visible and vocal protagonist, Damario Solomon-Simmons. And it was not only people who had been directly attacked or who were involved in Greenwood Rising or the centennial commission. Some massacre descendants grumbled about their exclusion from the Greenwood lawsuit after decades of documenting their claims, while Randle had not been generally identified as a survivor until about 2018, and Ellis and Fletcher after that. This did not mean anything in itself; many formerly unknown survivors had come forward over the previous decades. But it was one more thing to rankle those who felt pushed aside or badly used. The questions and complaints were voiced quietly and off the record, at least until the late spring of 2021. No one wanted to say anything that could be interpreted as critical of the three elders, who after all had survived not just a single cataclysmic event but more than a century of grinding systemic racism and, in the case of the two women, sexism too. Beyond that, no one wanted to get in an argument with the implacable Solomon-Simmons.[26]

A former University of Oklahoma football player, Solomon-Simmons looked in his forties to still be in playing shape. With his shaved head, powerful build and intense eyes, he could take on a fierce demeanor when the situation called for it. He could also flash a winning and disarming smile. His formidable national network of supporters and allies included the noted civil rights and plaintiffs' attorney Benjamin Crump and Harvard Law professor Charles Ogletree. As his filings in the Greenwood and Crutcher lawsuits and his run-ins with the city over policing demonstrated, Solomon-Simmons could be a relentless advocate and unsparing opponent. His crusades won him the praise and admiration of many and the enmity of others. In 2019, Mayor G. T. Bynum said of Solomon-Simmons: "Do I think [he] jumps in front of the cameras every chance he gets to belittle the Tulsa Police Department and to belittle the hard work of so many people in our community who are trying to do work on community policing? Yeah, I do."[27]

To others, Solomon-Simmons was a champion of the exploited, the ignored, the downtrodden. He grew up in Tulsa, raised by a single mother. He's described himself as an indifferent student at Booker T. Washington High School, where he played football and aspired to the National Football League. When it became apparent, after a knee injury, that was not going to happen, Solomon-Simmons dropped out of Northeastern State University and lived for a while in Dallas. In a 2014 interview, Solomon-Simmons said that was a pivotal time in his life.

> I was on my own, working and paying bills, just really experiencing what life was like as an adult and . . . without an adequate education. It . . . motivated me to come back to this state, take education seriously, have the motivation to walk on (to the OU football team) and to be successful. I wanted to be a role model for my younger peers. I was a lot more seasoned because of that "semester of life."[28]

Solomon-Simmons finished law school at roughly the same time Ogletree and a team of lawyers filed a 2003 federal lawsuit on behalf of more than three hundred survivors and descendants seeking reparations from the massacre.

Solomon-Simmons seems to have caught Ogletree's eye, and in 2005 they both spoke at an event in Tulsa headlined by California congresswoman Maxine Waters. Solomon-Simmons joined a prestigious law firm but ultimately went out on his own. He became highly visible for his work with Black youth and often spoke about his own fatherless upbringing. A fairly early client was Felix Jones, a former Booker T. football player who made it big in pro ball and, with a pointed sense of irony, bought the mansion of early Tulsan Tate Brady, a great booster of the city but also a defender of the Confederacy and a one-time Ku Klux Klan member who had patterned his home on the Arlington, Virginia, residence of his hero, General Robert E. Lee. Two other early clients were Fred Johnson and Ron Graham, who were among the hundreds of Oklahoma's "Black Indians" trying to reestablish their citizenship in one of the Five Tribes. As Solomon-Simmons' career progressed, he took on a series of progressively higher-profile cases involving torts, civil rights, and excessive force. One of those, with Crump joining the plaintiffs' team, was the 2015 shooting of a young Black man, Monroe Bird III, by an apartment complex security guard after Bird reportedly backed his car into the guard. Bird was paralyzed by a bullet to the neck and later died. A year later, Solomon-Simmons became the attorney for Terence Crutcher's family after Crutcher was shot and killed by Tulsa police officer Betty Shelby. As his reputation grew, Solomon-Simmons articulated a truth older than Hammurabi: the law and justice are two different things, and one does not always lead to the other. After federal prosecutors declined to charge Shelby in Crutcher's murder following her acquittal in state court, Solomon-Simmons said, "the system is set up to protect officers like Betty Shelby," and placed the entire episode in a broader context.[29]

"This is one of the reasons why we, from the very beginning, discussed and have been working daily and diligently to change the system, to reform the laws on a local level but also a national level," Solomon-Simmons said. "We know what happened on Sept. 16, 2016, was wrong. It was unnecessary. It was unjust."[30]

Just as Solomon-Simmons tried to leverage the Crutcher case, including the family's civil lawsuit against the city, to advance broader goals, the Greenwood lawsuit took on much more than the damages inflicted during the race massacre. It sought to correct what the pleadings claimed were a century of abuse and exploitation, and to challenge the established order of who makes the rules and who tells whose story. In this approach, winning cases is important, but so is advancing ideas in the battlefield of public opinion and probing for weaknesses in the defenses of the status quo. A courtroom loss is proof the system is rigged. A victory is the system finally admitting to injustice.[31]

In April, Solomon-Simmons chastised Greenwood Rising and project manager Phil Armstrong because Armstrong had mentioned Mrs. Randle during a panel discussion at the Oklahoma City National Memorial. Solomon-Simmons warned Greenwood Rising to desist "further unauthorized use of Mother Randle's name or likeness in promotion of the Greenwood Rising project and all other activities of the Commission," and issued a statement attributed to Mrs. Randle in which she said she was "shocked to hear that the commission is 'dedicating' much of their work to me since they have refused to meet with me, did not allow me an opportunity to participate in the Commission's planning, and declined to enter discussions on how I, a living survivor of the massacre, feels about their activities around the centennial."[32]

In his letter to Armstrong, Solomon-Simmons said, "You are also aware that the Commission rejected Mother Randle's request that the Commission utilize some of the $30M the Commission raised 'leveraging the rich history of the Tulsa Race Massacre' and/or revenue generated by the Rising museum to directly benefit the living survivors and descendants of those who suffered because of the Massacre." The letter goes on to say that Mrs. Randle "still lives in poverty because of the Massacre and its continued harm."[33]

Solomon-Simmons' insistence that Greenwood Rising had improperly used Mrs. Randle's name in a way that could be interpreted as an endorsement by her of the museum, or promote it in any way, echoed faintly a national conversation about college (and later high school) athletes' rights to their names, images, and likenesses, something with which Solomon-Simmons would have been familiar. In this case, he was claiming similar rights for public figures—and to portray Armstrong's remark that the commission and Greenwood Rising were "dedicating much [of] this work" to Randle and others like her as a form of exploitation. It proved a popular narrative and raised some interesting questions about priorities and appropriation. It also may not have been entirely accurate.[34]

The idea of a Greenwood museum and memorial went back to at least the early 2000s and probably earlier. It was something almost everyone, including many of the survivors, had agreed on at that time, but for various reasons it had never come about. As mentioned earlier, the centennial commission was formed in 2017 and the successful push for what became Greenwood Rising began in 2018, before Mrs. Randle and later Mrs. Fletcher and Mr. Ellis came forward, and about two years before the Greenwood lawsuit was filed. The impetus for the history center seems to have come mostly from the Tulsa exhibit at the Smithsonian Institution's National Museum of African American History and Culture, although it is true that state senator Matthews and a few others had been working for several years on the idea of cultural tourism as a way to bring economic activity to north Tulsa. Commemoration of the race massacre was to have been part of that, but the bigger picture included the full history of Black Wall Street, including music, food, churches, and its entrepreneurial heritage.[35]

Contrary to what is sometimes said or implied, the $30 million that went into the center came from individuals, foundations, and corporations. Much of that was from sources in Tulsa, but the city of Tulsa, as a corporate entity, contributed none of the $30 million and has no ownership in Greenwood Rising. Through a trust, the city does own the Greenwood Cultural Center, and two days before Solomon-Simmons sent the cease-and-desist letter to Greenwood Rising, one of the nation's largest Black-owned architectural firms was hired to oversee $5.3 million in renovations to the center as part of a citywide bond package.[36]

Greenwood Rising is owned by a nonprofit with a nine-member board of directors of whom six were Black in 2023. The non-Black members were Maggie Hille Yar, a tax accountant, and the superintendent of Tulsa Public Schools. As of 2023, Greenwood Rising has sole title to its building and the land it sets on. Whether the museum softens or tries to deflect attention from the unpleasant aspects of Greenwood's and Tulsa's history is, like all such undertakings, in the eye of the beholder. In any event, it is a tangible reminder of an important element of not just local but American history. Whether $30 million, or some portion thereof, could have been better or more ethically spent elsewhere is certainly open to debate—but Armstrong and others have argued it could not have been the $30 million raised for Greenwood Rising. That $30 million was contributed for a specific purpose, they argue, and to have done otherwise would have been dishonest and likely illegal. [37]

All of that said, the question remains: Why was it possible to raise $30 million for a museum—albeit after almost twenty years—but not reparations? Construction of Greenwood Rising did not preclude reparations; the centennial commission, before it ceased to exist, supported reparations. Greenwood Rising's backers have argued that the museum makes some form of reparations ultimately more likely because its education component is designed to build awareness and understanding. But a lot of folks have lost patience. They want something tangible in their hands, not vague promises of something down the road. For hundreds of years, they and their ancestors have been told to wait just a little bit longer. They are tired of waiting—and perhaps they sense a tipping point. [38]

"They want to talk about healing and reconciliation," Solomon-Simmons said several months before filing the Greenwood lawsuit in 2020. "You cannot have reconciliation without reparations, period."[39]

Money and control—which usually enter the equation when millions of dollars, pride, reputations, and careers are at stake—were a factor in the disputes between the centennial commission and the Justice for Greenwood orbit. But so were the priorities, tactics, and strategy each employed in pursuit of similar objectives. The centennial commission sought to effect change through persuasion and reconciliation, and reparations and equity primarily through the imprecise tools of economic development. It did not oppose cash payments to individuals as a form of reparations, but as a practical matter thought them unlikely given political and judicial conditions and precedent. It is difficult to conceive of an elected body in Oklahoma, including the Tulsa City Council, voting for them. Pursuing direct restitution through the judicial system is a well-worn path that has led nowhere hundreds of times since 1921; while the 2020 lawsuit took a new angle, it still ran into the same long-standing obstacles. The first is that no definite legal responsibility for the massacre has ever been attached to anyone or anything, including the city of Tulsa. Indisputably, the city's response to the crisis of June 1–May 31, 1921, was, at best, shambolically inadequate. Ample evidence shows police officers joined in the destruction of Greenwood. National Guardsmen reported killing African Americans, allegedly in exchanges of gunfire. But whether the city's apparent ineffectualness was intentional and the law officers' involvement directed by city officials, as many have suspected over the years, or a combination of ineptitude and individual actions, as others maintained, has never been proved.[40]

The other barrier is time. Every race massacre-related lawsuit since the mid-1920s has been dismissed on statute of limitations grounds. The Greenwood lawsuit tried to get around that by claiming a continuing public nuisance, but in 2022 District Court Judge Caroline Wall narrowed the issue to the damages suffered by the three plaintiffs as a direct result of the massacre. In any event, time remains an issue. After more than one hundred years, the plaintiffs must not only prove damages, but fix responsibility for paying them. The defendants are essentially the taxpayers of the city of Tulsa, all of whom can argue that the passage of time prevents them from presenting a proper defense. Witnesses are dead. The record has become muddied. While some of those taxpayers likely are descendants of the massacre's perpetrators, others are known descendants of massacre victims. Conceivably, some could be descendants of both. And the lines of cause and effect, perpetrator and victim, grow every more difficult to untangle and easier to dispute.[41]

"The problem is, where does the cash come from?" Bynum said in 2021, explaining why he did not support direct payments. "The most commonly mentioned way is some sort of legal judgment that would be paid from the city's sinking fund. That raises property taxes for everybody."

Instead, he said, the city had "shifted our economic strategy to north Tulsa. There is over $1 billion of new investment there during this administration."[42]

Whether that investment is actually benefitting Black Tulsans is part of the debate.[43]

Time works against the Greenwood plaintiffs in another way. Aside from the obvious one, that the three survivors are quite elderly, is the difficulty of proving in a court of law where the three were in 1921. This is not a commentary on the survivors' credibility. It is a simple statement of fact. Documenting anyone's location, let alone the location of three children—and especially three Black children—one hundred years after the fact is not easy. Justice for Greenwood, the nonprofit set up by Solomon-Simmons, reported in its 2021 tax filing that it had hired "two world class genealogists" to "research, identify and document the lineage of every individual and entity that experienced the massacre and its immediate aftermath." In May 2021, though, some people had unanswered questions about the three survivors' biographies.

These questions began bubbling near the surface as the centennial approached in spring 2021, and ultimately led to an intense public argument between Solomon-Simmons and the author of this book. I and others had noticed a few inconsistencies we thought deserved to be clarified, and which Solomon-Simmons was reluctant to address.

One of the issues had to do with timing. Keeping track of survivors has been difficult ever since efforts to do so began in the late 1990s. Publicity from the original race riot commission and then the 2003 federal reparations lawsuit helped connect survivors and those wishing to identify them, but neither Mrs. Randle nor Mrs. Fletcher seems to have been identified then and neither was a plaintiff in the 2003 lawsuit. When Hazel Jones died in March 2018, she was thought to be the last survivor living in Tulsa. Still, people were only mildly surprised when Lessie Randle came forward soon after. Over the decades, many survivors had been reluctant to talk about what happened in 1921.[44]

Mrs. Randle had lived in Tulsa most of her life but apparently told few people she had been there in 1921. In her 2020 deposition, Mrs. Randle said she was living with her grandmother Mollie Benningfield at the time. She recalls huddling in her grandmother's home, or possibly that of another relative, until "soldiers" came to take them all to the fairgrounds. Solomon-Simmons suggested Mrs. Randle and her grandmother lived at 1217 N. Iroquois Avenue—where Mrs. Randle was living in 1980—and which at that time would have been on the northeastern edge of Black Tulsa. Solomon-Simmons produced a letter to Mollie Benningfield at that address postmarked 1937, but Mrs. Randle said she could not remember if they lived there in 1921. Taken all together, her deposition was convincing and plausible, if understandably hazy. As she herself mentions several times, she was very young then.[45]

Nevertheless, a couple of other things attracted attention. For some reason, Iroquois Avenue and those living on it were completely excluded from the 1921 city directory, except for a listing in an index of street names and locations. The 1922 directory lists a Black man named John Cash as the sole resident of 1217 North Iroquois Avenue. However, other Benningfields—perhaps the aunt and uncle Mrs. Randle mentions—lived only a few blocks away, so that may have been the house she remembered. Another slight inconsistency had to do with age. Mrs. Randle says in the deposition that she was born November 10, 1914, and sounds quite definite. She goes on to say she graduated Booker T. Washington High School in 1937 and a class photo is provided as verification. That would mean she finished high school at twenty-two, unusual today but perhaps not for a young Black woman during the Depression. In the 1940 census, the age of Lessie Benningfield of Tulsa is given as twenty-one, which would have placed her birthdate as November 10, 1918, rather than 1914, and her high school graduation age at eighteen. But this is not conclusive. Individual census information is notoriously unreliable, especially when it comes to African Americans and other minorities. In any event, Lessie Benningfield Randle would have been born before the massacre and has a long connection with Tulsa.[46]

Mrs. Fletcher's connections to Tulsa were more tenuous than Mrs. Randle's. According to her deposition, documentation, and interviews given after her one hundredth birthday in 2014, Mrs. Fletcher was born in southwestern Oklahoma and moved with her family several times before arriving in Tulsa. Her half-brother, Hughes Van Ellis, was born in Holdenville, about ninety miles southwest of Tulsa, in January 1921; if so, the family may have been living there in December 1920 when a vigilante mob lynched a Black man from a downtown telephone pole. In any event, it seems likely the family lived in Tulsa only a short time before the massacre and, according to Mrs. Fletcher's deposition, did not return after it—although she did live there for a while in the 1930s. After working in a California shipyard during World War II, Mrs. Fletcher and her family settled in Bartlesville, forty-five miles north of Tulsa, and remained there.[47]

According to her deposition, Mrs. Fletcher was living with her mother, stepfather, and siblings in a rented house on the north edge of town in 1921, and fled in a wagon or buggy on the morning of June 1. In her deposition, Mrs. Fletcher says the family went to Claremore, a town about thirty-five miles northeast of Tulsa. She also describes going through the heart of the massacre, which is a little incongruous because it would have meant driving south, toward the fires and gunshots, and in the wrong direction to reach Claremore. But Mrs. Fletcher was quite young at the time, only seven years old, and nearly one hundred years had passed when she summoned these memories for the 2020 deposition. All things considered, Mrs. Fletcher's statements—and those she would make in the coming months—have an authentic ring to them.[48]

But, on their face, they also are inconsistent with Mrs. Fletcher's 2014 interviews. In one recorded by Oklahoma State University researchers, her demeanor changes visibly when she is asked whether she lived in Tulsa at the time of the massacre.

"Well, my family was, but I think they left during that time," she says. Gently prodded by the interviewer, Mrs. Fletcher adds: "Let's see . . . see, I was real young then, about five to six years old. I don't remember anything about that."[49]

In the other interview, with the Dwight Eisenhower Library, Mrs. Fletcher mentions going to school in Claremore and Nowata but not Tulsa. Asked where she lived during the Dust Bowl of the 1930s. Mrs. Fletcher replies: "In Tulsa. We moved from Claremore to Tulsa."

Asked when she moved to Tulsa, Fletcher replied, "I got married in 1932 in Tulsa."[50]

These points were a matter of whispered discussion as the centennial approached, especially the two 2014 Fletcher interviews. After trying for weeks without success to obtain clarification from Solomon-Simmons, I decided to wait for him outside Gilcrease Museum, where he was scheduled to appear for a press conference a few days before the centennial. The result was a loud, angry, and public argument during which I said a few things I wished I had not and made the mistake of placing my hand on Solomon-Simmons' arm. He threatened an assault complaint against me because of it.

But I got an answer.

Mrs. Fletcher had been so traumatized by what she had seen as a child, Solomon-Simmons said, that she only recently had been willing to talk about the massacre publicly. The explanation was not surprising. When Ed Wheeler in the 1970s and Scott Ellsworth in the 1980s began interviewing survivors, they encountered great reluctance, especially on the part of African Americans in the presence of whites. The change in expression and tone of voice in the video-recorded 2014 interview suggest this was a subject Mrs. Fletcher did not want to discuss.[51]

"It is only in more recent years that Mother Fletcher has been willing to openly discuss the massacre and her memories of that terrible night," Solomon-Simmons said in a later written statement.[52]

The American legal system recognizes laches and statutes of limitations to encourage timely action and to avoid situations such as the Greenwood lawsuit, cases in which evidence and witness memories have long gone cold or disappeared entirely. Some, though, are of the opinion that this system serves to protect the powerful and prevent claims long-delayed because of intimidation or discrimination. In this line of thought, victors not only write the history, but they are also in charge of the records that document it. The people in power write the laws and run the courts. There is undoubtedly something to this argument. It can also be a convincing fallback.[53]

Hundred-year-old-plus African Americans are survivors, regardless of where they were on May 31–June 1, 1921. The lives of Viola Fletcher, Lessie Randle, and Hughes Van Ellis, like those of all Black Americans of their generation—not to mention earlier ones—were shaped by a society in which racism was an entrenched component. The Tulsa Race Massacre may have been a brutally singular manifestation of that racism, but separate and unequal education, economic opportunity, justice, and political voice must have been at least as devastating. That is something on which almost everyone agrees, but that is sometimes lost in the arguments over money and power.

8

CENTENNIAL

The first day of 2021 was brisk and overcast. Bundled up against temperatures in the mid-thirties and with the statuary of John Hope Franklin Park as a backdrop, state senator Kevin Matthews, Phil Armstrong, and more than a half dozen others pitched the centennial commission's version of what the one hundredth anniversary of the Tulsa Race Massacre should be about.

"I'm so excited that we're in 2021 and we're going to see it to fruition," Matthews said. "On May 31, 2021, we want the world to come to Tulsa, come to our great history center, come to this area and be part of our efforts to be a beacon of reconciliation around the world."[1]

The speakers included businessmen and women, the executive director of the YWCA, and, via video, actress Alfre Woodard, a Tulsa native. Onikah Asamoa-Caesar, who opened her own small establishment, Fulton Street Books & Coffee, in the midst of the pandemic, summoned Black Tulsa's history of enterprise in the face of adversity.

> So many of our entrepreneurs have made it "in spite of." In spite of [a] lack of access to funding, in spite of [not] being able to access circles of social capital . . . and when they break through those walls, we applaud them. My hope for 2021 is that we use our hands, our voices, our dollars—all the dollars—to break down the barriers that create success "in spite of." And that we build an ecosystem that allows Black entrepreneurs to thrive.

> Because collectively, small businesses are an economic pillar in the Black community and essential to building a thriving city where more people have the opportunity to realize their full potential.[2]

While in some ways obvious, the choice of John Hope Franklin Park as the setting for promoting a vision that included opening a Greenwood museum was also fitting for reasons that had already been largely forgotten. Less than twenty years earlier, the park had been Plan B, a sort of placeholder for the memorial and history center that was supposed to be built and was not.[3]

Don Ross, in convincing the legislature to authorize the original 1921 commission, had leveraged the attention and money directed toward a memorial for the 1995 Oklahoma City bombing—the present Oklahoma City National Memorial & Museum. In 2000, a race massacre memorial design committee was appointed with the understanding that the state would contribute $5 million over several years. An early idea, floated by Mayor Susan Savage in the final months of her ten years in office, was to convert Vernon AME into a memorial and museum using surplus city capital improvement funds and federal grants. The city council, including the African American who represented Greenwood, said no. And design committee chair Julius Pegues had his own ideas. An engineer and meticulous planner whose family had moved to Tulsa after the massacre to help rebuild Greenwood, Pegues envisioned an $18 million library, museum, and memorial. In February 2003, from the Tulsa Development Authority the committee acquired three acres that lay between Detroit and Elgin Avenues and across the inner dispersal loop from Mt. Zion Baptist Church. The land was inside historical Greenwood, although it had been a freight yard at the time of the massacre. Pegues's plan to spend as little as possible until all or most of the fundraising goal had been reached almost backfired; later that year when a strapped legislature looking under every seat cushion for spare change—and not all that enamored of the Greenwood project in the first place—issued what amounted to a spend-it-or-lose-it ultimatum. The committee had received $1.5 million from the state and still had $1.4 million in its account. That was not nearly enough to do what the committee wanted, but it was enough to do something. A memorial park, it was decided, could act as a "phase one" placeholder until the funds for the library and museum could be raised. The city, at the urging of Mayor Bill LaFortune, spent $400,000 to move utilities and otherwise prepare the site, and the committee commissioned nearly $1.5 million worth of art from nationally known sculptor Ed Dwight.[4]

The money never came, or certainly not in the amounts envisioned. The legislature stopped appropriations in 2007, after six years and $3.6 million. Only after the city kicked in another $500,000 in 2008 was ground broken on John Hope Franklin Reconciliation Park, with the great historian himself in attendance at age ninety-three. It would be one of his last public appearances. With the country sliding into the Great Recession and the interest in the massacre stimulated by the commission waning, the park transitioned from placeholder to permanent landmark. With its landscaping and Dwight's dramatic bronzes, Franklin Park wound up succeeding on its own terms, popular with locals and visitors alike as both a place of reflection and a rallying point. Now, on the first day of 2021, the park's original purpose was to be fulfilled less than two blocks away as the bird flies, at the corner of Greenwood and Archer. This event was not about Greenwood Rising per se, but for those who knew the story the connection was unavoidable.[5]

A few days earlier, Matthews told a reporter he wanted Greenwood Rising to be a tribute to "the most resilient people on this earth."[6]

At the rally, Matthews said:

> We believe that we're going to be the place of reconciliation for the whole world. We're the only city in the United States that we know where Americans bombed Americans [from airplanes]. We're the only state in the United States where not one county voted for our first Black president. We're the state where the Oklahoma City bombing has a national memorial where 168 people died—but three, four-hundred Black people died here, and you can't find a tombstone. If we can be that city and come together around race, around reconciliation, we can be an example for the world.[7]

Contrary to what was sometimes portrayed and widely perceived, the commission was not focused solely on Greenwood Rising. One of its earliest efforts was getting a race massacre curriculum into schools, and it spent a good deal of money and effort on the arts as a means of communicating Black Tulsa's story to the community and nation at large. With a $1 million Bloomberg Public Art Challenge grant and $200,000 from the George Kaiser Family Foundation (GKFF), the Greenwood Art Project involved the work of more than thirty local artists in "painting to pottery, onsite installations to spoken-word pieces, multimedia to music, dance to film." Fire in Little Africa, sponsored by the commission and the GKFF-affiliated Woody Guthrie Center and Bob Dylan Center, brought together "more than 50 rappers, singers, producers, poets, musicians and visual artists" for an intensive week of audio and video recording in studios set up at the Greenwood Cultural Center and Skyline Mansion, the name Felix Jones had given Tate Brady's architectural ode to the antebellum South. The project produced an album, a documentary, and a podcast, and was still occasionally performing live in the spring of 2023. Tulsa Opera—again, with the centennial commission's involvement—and the Tulsa Ballet commissioned special pieces to commemorate the centennial.[8]

The arts projects softened some edges but sharpened others, a not unpredictable result of encouraging artists to express themselves. Some say a fundamental purpose of art is disrupting established patterns and ideas. In this case, the commission should not have been surprised—and probably was not—to find itself in awkward situations from time to time. Interestingly, given the passion of the "Black Lives Matter" street painting less than a year earlier, the visual arts produced during the centennial year evoked praise and admiration but very little controversy. Instead, what conflict arose did so from the performing arts.

For instance, amid the commission's internal turmoil over Senator James Lankford's involvement in the attempt to sidetrack certification of the 2020 presidential election, the executive producer of Fire In Little Africa said out loud what a lot of people were grumbling.

"Why isn't Sen. Lankford removed from the Centennial Commission?" Stevie "Dr. View" Johnson said on the Pod 4 Good podcast. "They [the Commission] are saying that this is a non-partisan situation. And I'm like there is no such fucking thing as bipartisan, nonpartisanship when it comes to race. Like, either you're with us [Black people] or against us."[9]

Lankford was playing a role and "not really an ally of Black Oklahomans," Johnson said.[10]

Johnson does not just call himself "doctor." He is a PhD who in 2021 was on staff at the Dylan and Guthrie centers, on his way to a Harvard fellowship and the Ohio State University faculty. His nationally recognized 2019 dissertation at the University of Oklahoma consisted of 250 written pages and a 25-track rap album with the title: "Curriculum of the Mind: A BlackCrit, Narrative Inquiry, Hip Hop Album on Anti-Blackness & Freedom for Black Male Collegians at Historically White Institutions."[11]

"I want to make sure that Fire in Little Africa's brand is in alignment with everything that's going on racially, whether it's in Tulsa or the nation," Johnson said during the podcast. "And if it doesn't fit what we have, I don't care who's in power or who or what money people have given. I [couldn't] care less. It's about the alignment and the values that we represent. And a lot of people have a lot of push back with that. And I don't care.

"I'm calling it what it is," he said. "It's white supremacy. And people are afraid to say these things."[12]

Not long after, controversy arose over Tulsa Opera's planned "Greenwood Overcomes" concert. It featured the work of 22 living Black composers, chosen from among more than 350 considered, performed by 8 African American singers, including Oklahoma native Leona Mitchell of the Metropolitan Opera. Tulsa Opera commissioned four of the compositions, something it had never done before, including an aria by Pulitzer Prize winner Anthony Davis. Local graffiti artist Chris "Sker" Rogers created the backdrops. The two performances in early May were deemed a huge success; PBS later aired a recording of one. But the production was not without controversy. In March, one of the original four commissioned pieces was dropped because of what officials said was a disagreement between composer Daniel Bernard Roumain and mezzo-soprano Denyce Graves.[13]

Roumain blamed Tulsa Opera and Artistic Director Tobias Picker.[14]

Roumain's aria, "They Still Want to Kill Us," concluded with the lines "God bless America / God damn America." Roumain told *Opera Wire* the words reflected "the hypocrisy of our country committing countless atrocities, time and again, in the name of country and under God." He said Picker suggested changing the last lines to "God Bless America" repeated, or "God Bless America / God Help America."[15]

According to Graves, in a statement issued by the opera company, and interviews with Picker and Howard Watkins of the Metropolitan Opera and Juilliard School, who helped put together the program, Graves did not want to sing the final words, and Roumain refused to change them. Picker said the piece was offered to the other performers, but none accepted.[16]

"As a Black woman, I am a huge supporter of all Black Lives, Black expression, and creativity," Graves is quoted as saying in the Tulsa Opera statement. "I don't have trouble with strong lyrics, but I felt that they did not line up with my personal values. I could not find an honest place to express the lyrics as they were presented."

"I thought it was a beautiful song, and I wanted to make it work," Picker told the *Tulsa World*. "So to try to be helpful, I made a suggestion of alternate ways of getting the same point across, to make the ending just as powerful, and make it something that (Graves) would sing. It's something I would have done with any composer in such a situation."

Roumain saw things differently. In a statement to *Opera Wire*, he said:

> The Tulsa Opera has revealed why the operatic field continues to be seen as racist and divisive. When a Black composer must endure the intrusions of a white composer—within a work and a festival built around the death and artistry of Black people—but insists on his words and his way, what are we to think and do? I say we don't bend, or break, or subject ourselves to their ideas. The opera world is full of white stories and perspectives. This is the time for Black stories and our experiences to be on our stages.[17]

The Black Opera Alliance said Tulsa Opera "chose to weaponize the voice of one Black artist to justify the silencing of another" and should have found another artist willing to perform the piece.[18]

Watkins offered a third perspective. A Black man who had recommended Roumain for the program, Watkins said he was "taken aback" by Roumain's public reaction.[19]

"There's not any mention of my involvement (in the project) or Denyce's involvement," Watkins said, referring to Roumain's original statement. "He just presented it as a Black man against the white establishment.

"Daniel is a friend of mine, and the last thing I want to do is hurt him. But the fact of what happened is he wrote a piece for a singer who was not willing to sing it. Daniel has the right to express what he needs to say, but Denyce has the right and the need to believe in what she is saying and express it from a place of honesty, and she wasn't able to do that with this piece."

In May, "They Still Want to Kill Us" premiered as written, sung by J'Nai Bridges with Opera Philadelphia and featured in a companion film directed by Yoram Savion. Among those commenting on the composition and the controversy in Tulsa was Damario Solomon-Simmons. In the opera world, Tulsa Opera's decision to cut Roumain's piece was denounced by some as censorship.[20]

So, while it might not have been exactly in the way Roumain intended, his work did spark discussion about race and racism and whose version of a story is told. In various ways, in various circumstances, the approach of the race massacre centennial and the activities surrounding it prompted similar conversations all over Tulsa and the country. Many of those were stimulated by initiatives of the centennial commission. But, sometimes to its dismay, the centennial commission found it could not control the direction of that conversation. Matthews's hopes for a united message of "triumph over tragedy," of Tulsa as a "beacon of reconciliation," and Greenwood Rising as a significant medium for redefining the nation's perception of its past, present, and future, faded in the cacophony of 2021's competing story lines.

Some of it was unrelated or connected only tangentially to the centennial. Adding to the misery and recriminations from the COVID-19 pandemic was the southern plains' longest, deepest cold snap in nearly forty years. Utilities, caught unprepared, found themselves paying exorbitant fuel prices to meet customer demands for natural gas and electricity, and while Oklahomans fared better than their Texas neighbors, the ten-day deep freeze nonetheless left them with heating bills that would take decades to pay. In May, Tulsa city government was nearly paralyzed by a ransomware attack that for months complicated things as simple as paying a water bill. It also hampered the collection of data needed to measure and implement policing reform measures instituted by Chief Franklin. These had nothing to do with the centennial, but they were irritants that added to the tension of the moment.[21]

As the weather warmed, so did the rhetoric from the state capitol. Whether intentionally or through lack of awareness, the governor and legislative leadership blithely seemed to take every opportunity to insult Black Oklahomans and undermine the commission. Two of the session's proudest accomplishments, legislation that essentially protected white school boys from having their feelings hurt and encouraged drivers to run down protesters, kneecapped their colleague Matthews's efforts to convince skeptics in Tulsa and across the nation that Blacks and whites, Republicans and Democrats, could find common ground on difficult issues of race. In so doing, Oklahoma's white Republican politicians strengthened Solomon-Simmons and Justice for Greenwood, locally and nationally.[22]

In mid-January, with the Lankford controversy still hot, the *Washington Post* published a long piece under the headline "The 'whitewashing' of Black Wall Street" that more or less echoed Solomon-Simmons's claim that most of the centennial activity masked further gentrification of the historic neighborhood.[23]

"[A]s Tulsa authorities provide millions in financial incentives to revitalize the district ahead of an anticipated influx of tourists for this year's centennial of the 1921 bloodshed," reporter Tracy Jan wrote, "Black entrepreneurs say they are being threatened with erasure yet again, shut out of Greenwood's most prestigious development projects and priced out of prime retail locations.

The story pointed out that individual Black ownership had all but disappeared from the Deep Greenwood of 1921. The Black-owned businesses that did exist rented their space, mostly from either the Greenwood Chamber of Commerce in the 100 block or the Yars in the GreenArch Building.

Guy Troupe, whose Liquid Lounge coffee shop is a GreenArch tenant, told reporter Jan he was frustrated that African Americans had been priced out of commercial property in the former Black Wall Street.

"It's hard to stomach the idea that a museum and tourism will fix the challenges of systemic racism. I came to take back what's rightfully ours," said Troupe. "Who owns in there? It's not us. The only thing we own are homes. But big industrial buildings, lands zoned for commercial development? We don't have it."

In truth, Greenwood was never entirely Black-owned. Several businesses on Greenwood Avenue at the time of the massacre were owned by whites, and the land on which GreenArch sets passed through many hands of various skin tones before the Yars acquired it. In 1921, railroad tracks ran through the space occupied by Greenwood Rising. But the concerns of Troupe and others are not unwarranted. Solomon-Simmons was unsparing in his summation of the situation.

"In the historical Greenwood district, large corporations and rich white folks are building high-rises and condos not benefiting the original owners of Greenwood, their descendants or the larger Black population pushed into north Tulsa," he said. "The exact same entities that destroyed Greenwood and perpetrates the continuing harm to Greenwood are now benefiting by selling the brand of Black Wall Street to the world."

He ridiculed the notion that people would "come and walk around what really is nothing because historic Greenwood doesn't really exist anymore."

In any event, Solomon-Simmons said, "How does that lessen the wealth gap? How does that put money back into the pockets of the individuals who lost money, power, assets? It's actually worse to acknowledge the massacre and do nothing to fix it."

As it happened, this was something just about everyone involved agreed upon. Long before he became involved in the centennial commission, Matthews promoted entrepreneurship and mentoring in his community. The commission's centennial events included an "economic empowerment" conference with actor and entrepreneur Hill Harper. The George Kaiser Family Foundation was involved in several initiatives to bring jobs and business ownership to Black Tulsans. And Kaiser himself sounded ambivalent about Greenwood Rising in a 2023 email. He said he contributed to the project because he was persuaded that a large share of north Tulsans wanted it; sometimes, he said, "you hold your nose and kick into the pot to be good community partners if the project is positive, just not the highest priority."[24]

"I was not much enamored with the Greenwood Rising project from the beginning," Kaiser wrote. "It's hard to demonstrate that building a museum is the highest and best use of charitable dollars."[25]

GKFF, in fact, had opened the Woody Guthrie Center in 2013 and in 2021 was preparing to open a second museum, the Bob Dylan Center. But those were viewed as something different, as "fun" places where locals and visitors alike would want to go. Kaiser was not convinced a place like Greenwood Rising, with a more somber tone, would change many minds.

"I cannot imagine many abusive bigots will choose to view the exhibits and have their life transformed by the experience," he said. "Sure, it's an appropriate concept, and can encourage understanding and pride among many people, and shame among others, but it would not and did not rise to the upper end of my priorities or successfully compete with other ways to help improve the lives of Black Tulsans."

And what were those priorities?

Kaiser said his and GKFF's underlying mission is "equal opportunity for very young children," and that everything else flows from that. From simple things like playground equipment in a neighborhood park to complicated ones like recruiting a major employer to the city, everything is intended to create better short- and long-term opportunities for kids, Kaiser said.

He further explained:

> Birth-to-three early childhood education and parenting are the proven best ways to overcome the disadvantaged circumstances of birth. Brain cells are fully formed but functionally undeveloped at birth, gaining cognitive reasoning abilities, social emotional skills and executive functioning, only through processing sensory experiences, especially in the earliest years of life. Those three characteristics, especially the last, are predictive of life success, however defined, much more than genetics. . . . So we highly prioritize ECE and parenting, less so K-12 . . . and less so yet, economic development, though a stable, nurturing household, with adequate income is material to child well-being.

That said, GKFF's lower priority ventures sometimes turn out to be the most controversial. Such was the case with Greenwood Rising as the centennial approached in the spring of 2021. With all that was going on, and all that was planned, the race massacre centennial had turned into a conflict not so much between Black and white but multiracial factions contesting how the story should be told and who had the moral authority to tell it.

In an interview in September 2022, Phil Armstrong said:

> The narrative got so twisted. All of the sudden, the commission is a bunch of politicians and Republicans [who] are telling the story of Black people and creating this amusement park. And it was referred to as that, an amusement park called Greenwood Rising to make money from. And that narrative seemed to have a national following after five, almost six years of very, very substantial conversation, walking through this—to see it be eroded the last three or four months by a false narrative, that was probably the most distressing. We had done so much—we had done a lot of great work of bringing people together, and then [in] a matter of the last few months, national interests came flooding in. And the political divisiveness. You have that much money, you have politics involved, something is going to go wrong.[26]

Armstrong's frustration was mirrored by those on the other side who viewed Greenwood Rising as a symbol of gentrification and the $30 million spent on it an example of misplaced priorities. They were leery of the messages it would ultimately convey.[27]

"I have really made a commitment to myself to no longer be a victim of symbolic gestures of the killing, the oppression and just the horrible treatment of my ancestors," said Kristi Williams.[28]

And it was not just Greenwood Rising. The ballpark, now a decade old, still rankled. High-rise apartments, a new bank building, and a clubby sports bar, with little to no Black ownership stake, had moved into the old neighborhood. The new National BMX headquarters was under construction a few blocks east of Greenwood Avenue. Three parcels totaling fifty six acres, including some North Greenwood Avenue frontage, were tagged for redevelopment with input from the community promised, but nothing tangible had happened and would not for some time.[29]

In April, a group of more than two dozen local partners, including Justice for Greenwood, the Terence Crutcher Foundation, the Gathering Place, and Oklahoma State University-Tulsa, and national organizations such as Human Rights Watch, the Equal Justice Initiative, and FWD.us, announced Black Wall Street Legacy Festival for May 28–30, the weekend ahead of the centennial. Tiffany Crutcher's years of advocacy work opened doors from downtown Tulsa to the White House. Solomon-Simmons's reach was growing, too, especially in the civil rights litigation sphere. By the time the first amended complaint in the Greenwood lawsuit was filed in February 2021, Solomon-Simmons had acquired a team from the New York law firm Schulte Roth & Zabel as co-counsel. A founding partner, William Zabel, became one of Justice for Greenwood's directors.[30]

Legacy Festival billed itself as the only event—or series of events—centered on survivors and descendants. It would grow into a huge, sprawling four-day affair with at least one advantage over anything the centennial commission might try to do: access to the survivors. Solomon-Simmons drove this home with his cease-and-desist letter to Armstrong less than a week after the Legacy Festival announcement.

In some ways, Rev. Robert Turner seemed to be in the middle. The Vernon AME pastor had been a vocal advocate of reparations, and his church was one of the original plaintiffs in the 2020 Greenwood lawsuit, but he was also on friendly terms with Matthews. He was also, in effect, the caretaker of an historic church building in need of about $1 million worth of repairs and updates. Vernon's location across from the Greenwood Cultural Center and the story of its basement surviving the conflagration of 1921, not to mention the free meals it provided during the pandemic, raised Vernon's profile and helped Turner's fundraising campaign. A $150,000 grant, for instance, made possible restoration of the building's stained-glass windows. In the spring of 2021, though, the church still needed a roof. A $200,000 contribution from the centennial commission in early April helped pay for some of those repairs.[31]

"Vernon AME Church is still ministering about love, forgiveness, healing and support to members of this community," Matthews said. "Rev. Turner and his team are providing hot meals to the homeless every single week. They are also providing safety and warmth in the same basement that sheltered survivors in 1921.

"This is why we, as a commission, want to show the Vernon AME Church congregation how much we support, love and need them to keep Greenwood rising."[32]

For Turner, the $200,000 meant fulfilling a little more of his duty to preserve "the grandmother of Greenwood," as he called it. "It'll greatly help this church be here for another 100 years, for other generations to see just this magnificent place built by those who died and survived and rebuilt Greenwood after the worst massacre in American history,"[33]

Two blocks south, construction crews were rushing toward an early May completion of the Greenwood Rising building. The commission hoped to have at least some exhibits in place by early June. [34]

As might be expected, the calendar on and around the race massacre centennial dates was filling up fast. Not all of the events were sanctioned by the commission or Justice for Greenwood's Black Wall Street Legacy Festival. One, announced on May 10, involved a conference, several public meetings, and a march by the New Black Panther Party and some Black Second Amendment groups, including one calling itself the Huey P. Newton Gun Club. The John Hope Franklin Center for Reconciliation's annual symposium lineup featured Cornel West, the Tulsa-born philosopher and social critic. As a sort of grand finale, Wynton Marsalis and the Jazz at Lincoln Center Orchestra, along with the Tulsa Symphony Orchestra and Festival Chorus, were to perform Marsalis's two-hour "All Rise" on June 6 at the BOK Center. This and the two performances of "Greenwood Overcomes" at the Performing Arts Center would be the first concerts in the two venues since the beginning of the pandemic.[35]

And rumors circulated that President Joe Biden would be in town.

The schedule became even more congested—and contentious—on May 14 when the commission announced a major televised event, called Remember and Rise and headlined by Grammy winner John Legend. It was to be at the baseball stadium, ONEOK Field, on the night of May 31; the list of participants grew to include former Georgia Democratic Senate nominee Stacey Abrams, a choice that rankled some as overly partisan but did not seem to diminish general public interest. The event's 6,000 tickets disappeared in a half-hour.[36]

A little less than a week later, on May 19, Mrs. Fletcher, Mr. Hughes, Solomon-Simmons, Tiffany Crutcher, and others appeared before a US House of Representatives subcommittee. Mrs. Randle, to outward appearances the most fragile of the survivors, and state representative Regina Goodwin testified virtually. No longer hesitant, Mrs. Fletcher especially impressed as she read a statement, with Solomon-Simmons at her side, summarizing her memories of one hundred years earlier.[37]

"I will never forget the violence of the white mob when we left our house," Fletcher said in a strong, clear voice. "I still see Black men being shot, and Black bodies lying in the street. I still smell smoke and see fire. I still see Black businesses being burned. I still hear airplanes flying overhead. I hear the screams. I live through the Massacre every day."

The hearing was an appeal for congressional assistance in obtaining restitution for the massacre and the exploitation of Black Americans in general, but it was also an opportunity to jab the centennial commission, the city, and the Tulsa Chamber of Commerce, the latter two of which remained defendants in the Greenwood lawsuit. The $30 million raised by the commission, and that none of it had gone to the survivors or descendants, was mentioned repeatedly.

"All the while the city of Tulsa has unjustly used the names and stories of victims like me to enrich [itself] and its white allies through the $30 million raised by the Tulsa centennial commission while I continue to live in poverty," Mrs. Fletcher said.

Without doubt, the survivors had lived all or most of their lives in modest circumstances, but according to some, those circumstances were improving by the time of the subcommittee hearing. A day or two after the hearing, Matthews told Janelle Stecklein of the newspaper group CNHI that one of Greenwood Rising's donors had agreed to pay the survivors regular stipends and help with their medical costs for the rest of their lives. Later remarks suggest this proposal was not a new one. In the last paragraph, Matthews notes this was not mentioned during the congressional hearing.[38]

Stecklein's story appeared in the *Enid News and Eagle* on May 22, the same day Solomon-Simmons and his team met with representatives of the commission and its funders, including the GKFF and Metropolitan Baptist Church Pastor Ray Owens, who acted as a mediator. Emails obtained by *CBS News*, the *Tulsa World*, the *Oklahoman*, and others indicate Solomon-Simmons was trying to negotiate concessions from the centennial and its funders in exchange for the survivors appearing at Remember and Rise and a "unified Centennial commemoration." One of the emails indicates the parties had agreed on $100,000 for each of the three survivors and $2 million for a descendants' fund.[39]

By the next evening Solomon-Simmons had changed his mind. Citing the last two paragraphs of Stecklein's story, he told the other parties that Matthews's description of the situation had "attacked the credibility and integrity of our survivors." Therefore, he wrote, his group wanted $1 million per survivor, $50 million for the descendant fund, and one-third of everything raised by the centennial commission "to directly benefit survivors and descendants and the North Tulsa community." And that was not all. Solomon-Simmons's email listed a total of seven conditions, some of which had multiple parts. Some of those conditions, it appears, may have been included in the May 22 discussion.

Solomon-Simmons and his fellow lawyers later insisted these were "requests," rather than "demands." The message at the top of the list read "this is where we are and/or what we need in order to come to an agreement."[40]

The money and the accusation that survivors' "credibility and integrity" had been attacked got most of the attention when the story broke after Remember and Rise was abruptly canceled a few days later. Buried in the memo, though, was the statement that GKFF had agreed to provide a "grant" to cover either the survivor payments or all or some of the contribution to the descendants' fund, and that Solomon-Simmons wanted that kept secret.

"GKFF and I agreed that any gift would be strictly anonymous to ensure the gift would not impede our larger reparations campaign," Solomon-Simmons wrote. "In fact, the grant agreement specifically states the grant would be "anonymous and not be announced in any way publicly or privately. Obviously, this confidential agreement was breached, and the proposed gift is now being used to try to put the survivors in a false light to lessen their credibility and undermine our overall reparations fight. As a result, we will decline the grant."

The wording and other clues suggest the "grant" was to help the survivors.

The email excoriates Matthews for what it says was inaccurately stating that the survivors were to be, in effect, taken care of for life. "Sen. Matthews needs to clearly state that no Commission donor has given any funds to Justice For Greenwood or the Survivors," it says, "Despite what Sen. Matthews and others have falsely stated, there was never an agreement to provide for the survivors "for the rest of their life" or "all of their medical needs."

Here, too, Solomon-Simmons emphasizes that there is to be no public connection between the commission and its donors and the survivors and Justice for Greenwood. Whether this condition is a matter of keeping the record straight or connected to his desire for confidentiality is unclear.

Stecklein seems to have interviewed Matthews before the May 22 meeting mediated by Reverend Owens, given that the story was published on the same day as the meeting. Matthews, then, was likely talking about an offer on the table and not the final agreement. Those paragraphs in the Stecklein story are paraphrases, not direct quotes, and say a donor had "agreed" to pay "salaries" and help with medical expenses. The story does not say the offer had been accepted.[41]

Other conditions included expanding the Greenwood Rising Board from nine to fifteen members with the additional six slots reserved to Justice for Greenwood (a condition not unlike the one that ended negotiations with the Greenwood Cultural Center), and for Greenwood Rising and the donors to publicly support the Greenwood lawsuit. Finally, the email says, if the other conditions are met or satisfactorily negotiated, "we would also want to help shape the program of the Remember & Rise event. . . . We want an opportunity to speak and honor the survivors and our work." How much consideration the commission and its funders gave this second list of conditions is unclear, but soon rumors circulated that John Legend and Stacey Abrams had pulled out of Remember and Rise, and on May 27 it was canceled.[42]

The emails leaked almost immediately, especially the lengthy one detailing Solomon-Simmons's conditions for resuming talks. The next day, May 28, Matthews faced reporters in the Greenwood Cultural Center parking lot, with the Black Wall Street mural painted on the side of an inner dispersal loop overpass in the background. He said the commission was approached by the survivors' "legal representation" about being included in Remember and Rise in exchange for a "financial gift" to the survivors. The commission was open to this, Matthews said, because donors "had offered to provide those financial gifts to the survivors in the past." After the May 22 meeting, he said, the commission was "excited." That quickly evaporated with the second list of conditions.[43]

Matthews said:

> We could not respond to those demands. I absolutely want the survivors and descendants to be financially and emotionally supported. However, this is not the way. We do have the funds available. If the [survivors'] legal team doesn't bar us from it again, we will be providing those funds directly to the survivors. It is my hope that what people remember from this weekend is an outpouring of support for survivors, for descendants, for justice and for reparations—not that a concert was canceled.[44]

While the commission's offer does not ever seem to have been accepted, a few days later Justice for Greenwood said it was giving each of the three survivors $100,000 as the result of contributions from "numerous supporters and a national fundraising effort." In mid-June, one of Tulsa's newer mega churches contributed $200,000 to each of the survivors as part of $1 million given to various North Tulsa interests. And, in May 2022, New York philanthropist Ed Mitzen announced a $1 million grant to the three survivors from his foundation.[45]

Matthews took no questions at his May 28 press conference but later that day revealed some of his frustration to a reporter.

"I try not to fight my own people in public, but I couldn't go any longer," he said. "The people working so hard on this for six years are very disappointed."[46]

Solomon-Simmons put the blame squarely on the commission and seemed to suggest that the seven-point set of conditions were the ones agreed to in the May 22 meeting.

"After months of zero communication and under immense pressure that John Legend and Stacey Abrams may no longer participate if the survivors were not centered, a Zoom call with 10 people was scheduled for Saturday. Immediately following that call our legal team submitted a list of seven requests to ensure the survivors' participation with the Commission's scheduled events," Solomon-Simmons said in a written statement on May 28.[47]

"We've been continuously asking for many, many months for the centennial commission to share some of the $30 million in resources that they raised with the survivors and descendants," Solomon-Simmons said. "We never sent them 'demands.' We made requests to them. All the emails that were sent to them said 'request.'"[48]

Jamaal Dyer, who had been the commission's first project manager and left amid disagreements over its direction, told the *Washington Post*'s Brown: "I was very vocal: 'If we are going to do this for the community, we need to allow them to be part of the decision-making body.' That was not welcomed. A year or two later, they went to them, but they had already started making decisions. They are still trying to control the narrative."[49]

In truth, both sides were trying to control the narrative. Matthews and the commission's version was broader and perhaps palatable to more people, but with results more difficult to measure. Solomon-Simmons and Justice for Greenwood's message was sharper and more direct, a demand for immediate, quantifiable results. And few things are more quantifiable than dollars. Interestingly, both camps were accused of limiting input. Both claimed to have community support.

"I am stubborn," Matthews acknowledged. "But I don't care what people think when I believe I'm doing the right thing."[50]

Perhaps Solomon-Simmons would say the same about himself.

President Joe Biden's arrival on June 1, 2021, was considerably less stressful and controversial than President Donald Trump's had been less than a year earlier. To be sure, Biden had at least as many detractors in Tulsa as Trump, and COVID-19 was still a threat. But COVID was not quite the mystery it had been when it seemed 100,000 people might descend on the city. Effective vaccines were available for those who could be convinced to take them, and prevention and treatment were better understood. And Biden just seemed to evoke less passion, from friend and foe alike. Republican Governor Kevin Stitt even met Biden at the airport.[51]

Presidential visits to Tulsa are exceedingly rare. Before Trump's, the last had been nearly thirty years earlier when President Bill Clinton plugged health care reform to the 1993 National Governors Association. Now there would be two such visits in less than a year, and each would be significant in its own way. Trump's essentially restarted the 2020 presidential campaign, however fitfully. The disappointing attendance, accentuated by recklessly inflated expectations, the chaos surrounding it, and Trump's rambling performance caused some to predict the rally would prove a Waterloo from which he would not recover. How much the Tulsa debacle ultimately had to do with Trump's loss in November is debatable, but indisputably it was not the triumphant relaunch envisioned. The purpose and tone of Biden's visit was much different. It was not a campaign event. It was, in a sense, a post-campaign follow-up, the keeping of a promise. The repayment of a debt. Black voters had been integral to Biden's election the previous November; he needed to show his appreciation in ways both tangible and symbolic. The one hundredth anniversary of one of the worst single examples of violence against African Americans was an obvious opportunity to do that.[52]

The race massacre centennial may have made it onto Biden's itinerary anyway, but Tiffany Crutcher, Greg Robinson, Nehemiah Frank, and a few others were able to make a direct pitch to Biden aides at the White House the day of the congressional hearing. It was a moment to which everything had been building. Crutcher had expanded her work from policing reform to a broader social platform that included reparations and economic opportunity. Robinson, who had worked in Hilary Clinton's 2016 campaign, had extensive political contacts and would unexpectedly wind up involved in Raphael Warnock's 2022 US Senate campaign in Georgia. Frank had become a rising media figure through his *Black Wall Street Times*.

With Remember and Rise canceled, Legacy Festival had center stage all but to itself in the days leading up to Biden's visit on June 1. Events began on Thursday, May 27, with the unveiling of a Michael Rosato mural on Greenwood Avenue just north of Vernon AME. Gilcrease Museum, which had recently received a trove of materials from Black Tulsa historian Eddie Faye Gates, opened a new exhibit that allowed interactive conversations with images of Mrs. Randle and Mrs. Fletcher by utilizing hours of interviews with the two women. The next morning began with the two women and Mr. Ellis riding in a carriage at the head of the mile-long Black Wall Street Memorial March from Carver Middle School at Greenwood Avenue and Pine Street to Greenwood and Archer a mile away. Mr. Ellis was in particularly fine form. A World War II veteran, he wore a black leather US Army cap and waved his right index finger to signify, he said, "We are one, one America."[53]

"Feel good about yourself," he told well-wishers. "Be your best in life."[54]

Solomon-Simmons was less magnanimous.

"For some people, this is about concerts. It's about a Disneyland experience. It's about raising money and buildings that will benefit south Tulsa," he said in obvious reference to the Remember and Rise event to whose cancellation he had contributed, and to Greenwood Rising. "But for us, it's about our people. It's about the blood that ran down this street. It's about these people running for their lives.

"This is a crime scene, and we will not tolerate anyone trying to exploit our survivors, our descendants and our community any longer. They can attack me but they cannot attack our movement because our movement is righteous. It's justice. It is timely."

Juxtaposed with this was the dedication that day of Matthews' Pathway to Hope linking the Greenwood Cultural Center and Vernon AME with the John Hope Franklin Reconciliation Park. Among those helping cut the ribbon were Julius Pegues and Reuben Gant, who had worked for so long to create a lasting memorial to the race massacre and the neighborhood that had fought so hard for more than a century to survive. In his eighties and weakened by cancer, Pegues was the first to walk the pathway.

The pathway is intended to honor both the struggles and the successes of Greenwood and Black Tulsans, utilizing the sides of the elevated roadway for installations by photographer Don Thompson, who has captured the mood and spirit of the neighborhood for decades. In so doing, it draws attention to the highway so many believe was the final stake through the heart of the old Greenwood neighborhood.

"This has been a long journey," Pegues told several hundred people at Reconciliation Park. "Looking out over this crowd, I know that work has not been in vain."[55]

Legacy Festival was in full swing, blending entertainment and advocacy. Performance stages were set up on Greenwood three blocks apart, one at the intersection with Archer and the other on the OSU-Tulsa campus. Seminars with such titles as "Who Controls the Narrative?" and "Descended from the Promised

Land: Healing and Transformation after Generational Trauma" attracted audiences to the Greenwood Cultural Center on Friday. That continued on Saturday, with an invitation-only luncheon for survivors and descendants, more music, a parade, and more seminars, including "The Parallel Universe of a Thriving Black Community" and "The Case for Reparations."[56]

The centennial event probably viewed with the most trepidation by city officials as well as some of the Legacy Festival organizers was the Black gun rights demonstration on Saturday evening. The concern was not with the gun rights group or several hundred armed Black people marching through the streets. It was that armed counterdemonstrators might show up looking to start something. Chilling echoes of one hundred years earlier aside, officials were also mindful that just a few months earlier, masked and armed militia-type figures had materialized at the Black Lives Matter march downtown. And Legacy Festival, whose private event permit included control of the festival's stretch of Greenwood Avenue, had banned guns. It did not want the demonstrators testing that authority. But unlike in 1921, when the sight of armed black men in downtown Tulsa sent some whites into an angry and ultimately violent panic, this Second Amendment display proved uneventful. The next day when some of the group showed up at First Baptist Church North Tulsa for a community service, Reverend Scott told them they could stay but their guns could not. They quietly complied.[57]

Legacy Festival concluded on Monday afternoon with a "Descendants and Survivors Town Hall" that included several members of the Congressional Black Caucus. By one estimate, about 25 percent of those present were survivors or descendants. The meeting and Legacy Festival as a whole demonstrated the extent to which Crutcher, Solomon-Simmons, Robinson, and others were able to forge an alliance of people with a direct connection to Greenwood and the race massacre with other interested parties, including influential figures from politics, law, entertainment, and the media. As had been the case for more than twenty years, the lingering issues from the Tulsa Race Massacre were not only about the Tulsa Race Massacre. Success in Tulsa, especially success on reparations, was a pathway to success nationally.

Amanda Jackson, economic justice director of Color of Change, said her organization highlighted historical US race massacres that destroyed Black lives and property. Jackson said her organization has identified about a dozen; in truth, destruction of Black communities—and those of other minority groups, especially when American Indians are included—has been more common in US history than is commonly acknowledged.[58]

"We want to bring attention to all the Black Wall Streets in the nation," Jackson said. "As we seek to remember this centennial of Black Wall Street, this will only amplify these voices."

Human Rights Watch, which had been active in Tulsa for several years, also made an appearance at the final event. It was "here on the ground in Tulsa," said Executive Director Nicole Austin-Hillery, "because the fight for justice is a human rights issue. Some folks think of human rights issues as happening in other parts of the world. Some folks falsely think the human rights [problems] are things [that] happen in foreign countries.

"We are a nation built on slavery, on free labor, on degrading, pillaging and taking from and not giving voice to people," Austin-Hillery said. "Those are human rights issues. We are going to be here with you in Tulsa."

That night hundreds of people stood in the rain at Greenwood and Archer, shielding candles lit in commemoration of the start of the violence that began at almost the same hour and minute one hundred years earlier. People from as far away as California, many with no direct connection to Greenwood or the massacre, were among the participants.[59]

"I just hope this is not what others have said—just an event, just acknowledging the one hundred years and then we go back to normal. That can't happen," said Lana Turner-Addison, a long-time civic leader and North Tulsa economic development executive. "This event provides an opportunity for all races to come together and unite around a common cause, addressing a wrong that was done one hundred years ago and moving forward to build brighter futures for everyone here in Tulsa, Oklahoma."[60]

The candlelight vigil was to have concluded Remember and Rise; as it happened, Remember and Rise would have almost certainly been rained out had it not been canceled. But several hundred people showed up in the rain even after four days packed with activities, which surely says something about what had become a national fascination with the massacre and its centennial.

Air Force One landed at Tulsa International Airport at 1 p.m. the next day—about the same time, exactly one hundred years earlier, that the destruction of Greenwood ended. Biden's entourage included advisers Susan Rice and Cedric Richmond and Secretary of Housing and Urban Development Marcia Fudge, all African American. They were met by Stitt and G. T. Bynum, and a contingent that included City Councilor Kara Joy McKee, Oklahoma Democratic Party chair Alicia Andrews, and the leaders of four tribal governments. Stitt issued a terse, standard statement, but Bynum was a little more substantive in describing his exchange with the president.[61]

"We agreed that this is a painful moment for our city, as we honor our fellow Tulsans who died in the 1921 Tulsa Race Massacre one hundred years ago this week," Bynum said. "It means a lot to have the president of the United States acknowledge this moment in our city."[62]

People congregated around the Greenwood Cultural Center, where Biden was to speak, hoping to get a glimpse of him, but this presidential visit was even more tightly controlled than Trump's. Instead of making an unlimited number of tickets available online, it was invitation-only for a carefully chosen crowd of about 120. Among them were members of the Congressional Black Caucus, civil rights icons Jesse Jackson and Al Sharpton, actor Sophie Bush, and state and local officials—most but not all, Democrats. Biden met privately with the survivors, Tiffany Crutcher, and a few others, and was taken on a brief tour of the center's historical exhibits. During this, he could be heard telling the center's program director, Michelle Brown-Burdex, what happened was a "massacre," not a "riot."[63]

This was just one of several things for which observers had cocked their ears.

Biden had issued a proclamation the previous day, May 31, declaring a "Day of Remembrance" for the massacre. In it, he said "I commit to the survivors of the Tulsa Race Massacre, including Viola Fletcher, Hughes Van Ellis, and Lessie Benningfield Randle, the descendants of victims, and to this Nation that we will never forget. We honor the legacy of the Greenwood community, and of Black Wall Street, by reaffirming our commitment to advance racial justice through the whole of our government, and working to root out systemic racism from our laws, our policies, and our hearts."[64]

Biden called on "the people of the United States" to "commit together to eradicate systemic racism and help to rebuild communities and lives that have been destroyed by it."[65]

The proclamation, along with word from the White House that Biden would announce "new steps to help narrow the racial wealth gap and reinvest in communities that have been left behind by failed policies," fueled speculation that the president might broach the subject of reparations. This was important to reparations advocates—and opponents. A president of the United States acknowledging the issue, much less endorsing the idea, would be monumental. But while Biden delivered a generally well-received forty-minute speech that included what was, for some, the key phrase "this was not a riot. This was a massacre," and references to systemic racism and wealth gaps, he did not use the word "reparations."[66]

But he came close.

"Only with truth can come healing and justice and repair," Biden said early in his speech. A few minutes later, he said: "The only way to build a common ground is to truly repair and to rebuild. I come here to help fill the silence, because in silence, wounds deepen. And only—as painful as it is—only in remembrance do wounds heal."[67]

Biden's appearance, then, was primarily about acknowledgement:

> The events we speak of today took place one hundred years ago. And yet, I'm the first President in 100 years ever to come to Tulsa—I say that not as a compliment about me, but to think about it—a hundred years, and the first President to be here during that entire time, and in this place, in this ground, to acknowledge the truth of what took place here.
>
> For much too long, the history of what took place here was told in silence, cloaked in darkness. But just because history is silent, it doesn't mean that it did not take place. And while darkness can hide much, it erases nothing.[68]

The *Oklahoma Eagle*, which had been fighting decades for this sort of high-level recognition, led with it. "President Biden: 'This was a massacre,'" read the *Eagle*'s top headline. "He becomes the first U.S. president to dispute Tulsa's official 'riot' cause," read the secondary head. A large graphic component listed the more than three hundred plaintiffs in the 2003 federal lawsuit; a text block says, in part, "You know our story of the crimes committed on Greenwood 100 years ago this week. For a century we have demanded justice be served. We will not stop demanding until that day arrives."[69]

The *Black Wall Street Times*—a newer voice on the block—emphasized the reparations angle. "President Biden vows to repair Greenwood in Tulsa but stops short of saying reparations," was its lead headline. The story by Deon Osborne, though, noted Biden "did something White politicians have rarely done for Greenwood; he showed empathy and understanding."[70]

Tiffany Crutcher, in a piece published a few weeks later by *The Progressive*, wrote that Biden "acknowledged what happened. He called out white supremacy. He talked about how you can't bury this truth."[71]

> But there is one thing the President didn't say: the word "reparations." Doing so could have helped to change the prospects and material conditions for Black people in Greenwood and across the United States.

> Reparations are not about taking away from anybody; it's about giving Black people a chance to recover what's been lost, and giving the United States a chance to live up to its promise of creating an equitable society for all. . . .
>
> If we are ever to have racial justice in this country, the U.S. government cannot treat the national crisis of systemic racism as a local problem. My sole motivation in meeting with President Biden was to make sure that the descendants of the Tulsa Race Massacre, the victims of racially biased policing, and everyone else who has suffered under structural racism get the repair and respect that they deserve. President Biden began the important work of acknowledging Tulsa's dark history, but the darkness will continue until there is concrete action at the federal level.[72]

The economic initiatives announced in connection with Biden's centennial visit to Tulsa were not the big, dramatic measures some had perhaps hoped. One addressed the chronic undervaluation of property, and especially homes, owned by Black people. Another sought to even out disadvantaged business owners' ability to win federal contracts. Neither received the attention given direct payment concepts—probably because cash is a lot easier to understand and explain—but each has the potential to get at what seem to be leading factors in the much-discussed wealth gap. Economists and historians say the gap is largely rooted in differences in home ownership and equity that can be traced to federal lending policies beginning in the 1930s, and to minorities' lack of access to capital, markets and expertise.[73]

At about the same time President Biden began his speech at the Greenwood Cultural Center, the centennial commission's Economic Empowerment Summit was wrapping up at the Cox Convention Center on the west side of downtown. Bynum and Lankford were involved but the stars of the show were high-level Black executives and actor-turned-investor Hill Harper. Sponsored by Bank of Oklahoma, Nationwide Retirement Systems, and JPMorgan Chase, it highlighted Black people who had succeeded within the system without losing sight of its inequities.[74]

In acknowledging those inequities, Earl "Butch" Graves Jr., president and CEO of the multimedia company Black Enterprise, said the United States is in the midst of a "pandemic of racism."

In terms of financial inequality, Harper said Black Americans are "actually worse off today than we were back then (in 1921)."

One reason for that, he said, is that Black Americans are less likely than they once were to trade with each other and to cooperate with and depend on each other in businesses.

"If we don't hold up a mirror of how destructive and systemic institutional racism is for everybody, we all are going to miss understanding how to work collectively . . . to solve something so big," Harper said.

Thus, the one hundredth anniversary of the Tulsa Race Massacre came and went. It was not perhaps as some had hoped, but neither was it as some had feared. As Air Force One lifted off from Tulsa International Airport and organizers collapsed after years of working, planning, and sometimes fighting, two quotations came to mind.

One, from William Faulkner: "The past is never dead. It's not even past."[75]

The second, of uncertain origin: "The future is now."

9

UNFINISHED BUSINESS

Greenwood Rising was dedicated on June 2, 2021. It was not completely finished and would not be for several months, but it was close enough for a limited preview restricted to massacre descendants and a program that included Phil Armstrong singing "America the Beautiful" and an invocation by Rev. Robert Turner. "Give us your courage, Lord," Turner said. "We may lose some friends. Give us your courage, Lord, we may lose some elections. Give us your courage, Lord, this community is divided, this city, this state—but you can unite us for such a time as this."[1]

Matthews told the approving crowd spread across the famous intersection of Greenwood and Archer, "Greenwood Rising is not a history center dedicated solely to the tragedy of 1921. No, not just that. It is a history center dedicated to telling the entire history, before, during and after the massacre."[2]

Nearby, a few protestors held "Justice for Greenwood" and "Reparations Now" signs. Later, as the event broke up, they chanted "no justice, no peace" and called for reparations. But this time, descendants—more than one hundred of them—were applauding Matthews and Greenwood Rising. Several spoke.[3]

Tracy Gibbs's grandmother Ernestine Gibbs had been one of the survivors interviewed by Eddie Faye Gates twenty years earlier. Ernestine was seventeen at the time of the massacre. "Even when she was ninety years old, one hundred years old, she could still close her eyes and see it," said Tracy Gibbs.[4]

Ernestine had remained in Tulsa, married a man named Leroy Gibbs, raised a family and taught school for more than forty years. The Gibbses owned a grocery market and were fixtures in the community for decades.[5]

Pulitzer Prize-winning art critic Holland Cotter of the *New York Times* was among those given an early peek at Greenwood Rising. He said it fit a recent "museum-as-monument" trend, and that while two "gee whiz" galleries—a barber shop in which three holographic barbers talk about everyday life in Greenwood, and a special effects recreation of the massacre—were dramatic, they were not the museum's focal point.[6]

"If Greenwood Rising had been conceived as simply the museum equivalent of a docudrama, or as a memorial to a catastrophe, its mission would probably end here," Cotter wrote.

Instead, the massacre reenactment gallery is only halfway through the museum.

"What we get first is a kind of resurrection narrative," Cotter said, "one about a community that, after unspeakable destruction, physically reconstituted itself, and did so despite roadblocks thrown up in its path."

The final galleries, in which visitors are challenged to actively write about and discuss issues of race and community, gave Greenwood Rising dimension and relevance, Cotter wrote.

> For visitors habituated to the conventional don't-talk-don't-touch museum model or the commemorative monument as a statue or plaque—and there are several such monuments in the nearby John Hope Franklin Reconciliation Park—this fluid environment may feel uncomfortable, or negligible. In my view, it's crucial to defining what both a museum of history and a monument to history can be.
>
> Museums are valuable to the extent they link the past to the present and illuminate, and appraise, both. In Greenwood Rising the links are made overt and we are urged to ponder them, to recognize that the white-on-Black violence of 1921 is still with us, and that Black disenfranchisement, like racism, remains entrenched. The very presence of this museum in a neighborhood that is still predominantly Black in population, but now only minimally Black-owned, is a reminder of what a struggle the early risings of Greenwood were, and the present one is.
>
> And there is a rising in progress, in this neighborhood, in this city and in this country. You can read it symbolically in the fact that Greenwood Rising exists in the larger context it does, in a deep-red state, and in a city

> where Donald Trump chose to hold one of his first mass rallies after the coronavirus shuttered most of the country.
>
> Change is happening, nowhere near fast enough, or strong enough, or anything enough, but it's there, and it's complicated as hell. We need museums that will explain it, good and bad, now and then, and monuments that will honor it and call it out. Greenwood Rising does some of all of this.

Others objected. Some, including city councilor Vanessa Hall-Harper, vowed never to set foot in Greenwood Rising.

"It is all a farce to make Tulsa appear not to be the racist-ass city that it is," Hall-Harper said a few days before the dedication.[7]

Quraysh Ali Lansana found Greenwood Rising superficial and exploitive. "Trauma porn," Lansana said in a 2022 interview. "Very, very disappointing."[8]

He wanted more on Greenwood at its peaks before and after the massacre, he said.

"The museum has almost nothing . . . about the Gurleys and the Williamses [early leaders of Greenwood] and about the money and about the prosperity, and about the doctors and the hospitals," Lansana said. After an introductory exhibit of historical and contemporary photos of Greenwood, he said, "You get the beautifully edited video, and then you're in trauma from that point forward. And then when you get out of trauma . . . you're into a hodgepodge collection of things about post-massacre, but not enough information of substance. . . . nothing, to me, that even speaks to the fact that the economic height of the district was 1941."

"There's almost nothing there that speaks to the prosperity," Lansana said. "There's almost nothing that speaks to the truth that it was rebuilt, that two hundred businesses were rebuilt by '23. Where is that? Where is the resilience that built the district? Where is the resilience that *re*built the district? It's not there or it's not there with enough presence that . . . anyone takes away with them in an overwhelming sense."

Greenwood Rising, Lansana said, "certainly wasn't built for us historians of this stuff. I think that museum was built for K-12 student group field trips. I think it was built for folks from outside of Tulsa, and maybe some inside of Tulsa who don't know anything at all about this history, which I guess has its place. And it was built for tourism."

Reuben Gant, who had worked with Julius Pegues for so many years to bring attention to Greenwood and its story, and to create a lasting memorial to it, was also not happy.

"It's a good thing that there is a history center," he said. "It's a good thing that there's a focus on this district in terms of its legacy and history. But I think . . . there's too much of an emphasis on what happens in the inner dispersal loop, to the detriment of the community at large. Development on the north side of the expressway is critical and crucial to demonstrate to the community that somebody cares. There has to be a catalyst for progress on the north side of the expressway. The impression is the Greenwood District is one block, because that's where all the emphasis is. And that one block doesn't define the history and legacy of Greenwood."[9]

Observations such as Lansana's and Gant's are a variation of a central issue in Tulsa and elsewhere. Not only is it a matter of who tells the story and how, but who hears it. For whom is the story intended? And how can the tragedy and loss that is part of so much history, not just Greenwood's, be told in a way that does not come across as exploitive? These questions apply not only to Greenwood Rising but to any attempt (including this book) to tell a piece of Greenwood's story, or any story.

In 2023, two years after the dedication, Greenwood Rising seemed to be still finding its footing. National reviews were generally positive, and attendance was good. Much and perhaps most of it seemed to be from out of town. Raymond Doswell, who came from the Negro Leagues Baseball Museum to become executive director in January of that year, said the museum saw itself as a "facilitator," a place that conveys a basic story and leads further discussion and inquiry prompted by that story.[10]

In the fall of 2021, a few months after Gov. Kevin Stitt signed HB 1775, Tulsa Public Schools (TPS) began requiring most of its eighth-graders to tour Greenwood Rising. The massacre continued to be taught in TPS classrooms and throughout the state, although not without some trepidation.[11]

Cornel West keynoted the centennial commission's final event, a virtual National Day of Learning on June 3. Although he grew up in California, West was born in Tulsa. His grandfather, Clifton L. West Sr., pastored Metropolitan Baptist Church, the same congregation led by Ray Owens. So Cornel West knew Tulsa's story. But he also brought a much broader prospective. A graduate of Harvard and Princeton who has had faculty appointments at both, as well as at Yale and Union Theological Seminary—which is affiliated with a fourth Ivy League school, Columbia—West is something of an iconoclast whose interests and critiques cover a wide swath of the American scene. On this day, West sized up what seemed to be growing friction between whites and a growing nonwhite population, and the test of democratic principles that friction presents.

"With all of these chickens coming home to roost, it's clear that we can lose our whole democratic spirit," he said. "We've got a significant number of fellow citizens who have never believed in democracy and don't believe in it now. They only believe in it when it renders them able to live a life of convenience and comfort. They aren't concerned with citizens on the other side of town, and once you reach that point then it's hard to see how you can sustain a democracy."[12]

"'We don't really care about your plight or predicament.' That's what white supremacy is," West said. "It generates that deep indifference. . . . So when you're indifferent to what has been done, then the very notion of you taking responsibility and providing some type of reparation is alien."

This observation seemed particularly applicable to Oklahoma, where supermajority rule—politically and racially—had been the norm for most of the state's history.

Reparations, West said, involve an honest attempt to identify and fix structural inequities. Too often, he said, those wanting change are so busy fighting each other they fail to make a clear case for that change or explain what exactly it should be. Defenders of the status quo, he said, try to preserve it by limiting education to basic skills and story lines.

"Learning, yearning—deep education, not just schooling" are essential West said. "Schooling is just a bunch of skills and the facts. Education is about formation of persons who are willing to be critical, compassionate and of service to something bigger than them."

The centennial commission ceased to exist on June 30, 2021, but left behind one more project to be fulfilled: the erection of six towering granite-and-concrete markers staking out Greenwood's traditional boundaries. The first was installed that November.[13]

Hours after the Greenwood Rising dedication, the Tulsa City Council convened for an unusual, even historic, meeting. The Reverend Jesse Jackson, who had been in the city for several days, sat on the front row and was at the top of the public comment list. On the agenda was a resolution acknowledging and apologizing for the 1921 Race Massacre. Mayors and at least one police chief had apologized for the massacre, but the city council and its predecessor city commission had not, and so the nonbinding resolution, in most respects as toothless as an old circus lion, filled a void of sorts. Beyond its symbolic significance, though, the resolution put the city government on record promising the framework for a community-led discussion on "tangible amends" for the destruction of Greenwood.[14]

Approaching eighty and struggling with a manifestation of Parkinson's disease that affected his speech, Jackson said, "I urge those in here who have light to speak up. Silence will betray us." One of the council's Republicans hugged Jackson. Two others took selfies with him. Reparations advocates from as far away as North Carolina and Evanston, Illinois, followed him to the microphone. The resolution passed 9–0.[15]

"This resolution is an acknowledgement and apology and a commitment from the Tulsa City Council. It is not a reparations proposal," said Hall-Harper, the council's chair and only Black member. "It's about equity. The resolution is solely a vehicle to create infrastructures, or good policies that will benefit Tulsa citizens who are and who have been adversely affected from long-term systemic racism."[16]

In truth, the resolution was not what most of those in the room wanted. It did not really commit the city to anything, not even the community discussions. But it was more than any previous Tulsa City Council had done and probably the most that could not only pass the city council but with a unanimous show of support and Bynum's endorsement. And, it would not be quickly forgotten, as many assumed. The six-month deadline to launch the initiative came and went, but Hall-Harper said she was raising money and working with Robinson on a proposal. Funding the initiative through the city would not be considered, she said.[17]

"If the community doesn't trust it, it is not going to work," Hall-Harper said. "And historically, when it comes to the Black community in particular, any community, but certainly the Black community, when the city government leads the way in something, to be perfectly honest, we've always gotten screwed."[18]

Such was certainly the belief. No one understood that distrust and the reasons for it better than Hall-Harper. By spring she and Robinson had put together a proposal called Beyond Apology that had the support of the city council and the mayor and independent financial backing. To what Beyond Apology would lead was anybody's guess, but the previous June Cornel West had observed that reparations proponents too often lacked the organization and fully articulated message to be effective. Now, as 2021 ended and 2022 began, the movement in Tulsa had never been more organized or more sophisticated.[19]

The three survivors' court fight, meanwhile, was stuck in the usual exchange of motions and countermotions. The plaintiffs filed a response to the defendants' motion to dismiss on June 1 and followed it up with a press conference that got some publicity but did not do much to change the case's trajectory. In November, the Oklahoma Supreme Court overturned the opioid case decision that had been the basis for plaintiffs' ongoing public nuisance claim. This would result in another round of briefs; by the end of 2021, *Randle v. Tulsa* did not appear much closer to resolution than the day it was filed.[20]

During the June press conference, a lawyer for the plaintiffs reiterated the lawsuit's demands for investment in North Tulsa. Damario Solomon-Simmons called for a "Greenwood Plan" similar to the Marshall Plan that helped rebuild Western Europe after World War II.

"This is why museums, plaques, trees and murals are good, but we must eradicate the wealth gap," he said. "We must eradicate the health gap."[21]

Again, almost no one disagreed; in fact, substantial resources were being put into North Tulsa. Bynum put the total public and private commitment at $800 million-$1 billion over five years, but more than half that was the $550 million invested in American Airlines's maintenance hub at Tulsa International Airport, on the northeast side of the city and miles from what is generally considered Greenwood. One or two other big-ticket items, it could be reasonably argued, had little direct impact on Greenwood either. But Bynum's total did not include millions of dollars in federal economic development grants and philanthropic projects. As Dwain Midget, the long-time city planner and economic development officer said, "Things are happening. They're too incremental, but that's because . . . of systemic, institutionalized racism that has to be overcome. It can still be done, and it's being done, just not fast enough."[22]

Just the opening of a grocery store at Peoria Avenue and Pine Street, a mile and a half northeast of Greenwood and Archer, two weeks before the race massacre centennial, was celebrated as a major achievement. To many, a grocery store may not seem like much to be excited about, but North Tulsans had been without one for more than a decade. According to data cited by advocates, 93 percent of City Council District 1—which included the area now thought of as greater Greenwood—had only "limited" access to fresh, affordable, first-quality food, compared to 19 percent for the rest of the city. For the most part, people in the area relied on "dollar stores" and trips outside the district for groceries and other supplies. That, again, might not seem like much of an issue for most Americans, but it is for communities in which many residents do not have reliable vehicles and public transit is limited. While a mobile grocery had made the rounds of neighborhoods like North Tulsa for years, it was obviously limited by both space and time.[23]

Policymakers, including Bynum and Hall-Harper, regarded the situation as more than an inconvenience. They believed it contributed to North Tulsa's poor health measures. Hall-Harper went so far as to press for a moratorium on small chain retailers such as Dollar General and Family Dollar because she believed they lessened the chances of a regular grocery, preferably locally owned, moving into the neighborhood.[24]

The concept for Oasis Fresh Market, developed over several years, was quite different than the conventional supermarket business model. Although not organized as a non-profit, it operates much like one; it was financed by a combination of philanthropic, public, and private sources through the Tulsa Economic Development Corp., a quasi-governmental agency headed by an African American woman, Rose Washington-Jones. Washington-Jones was also the Tulsa Metropolitan Chamber of Commerce's 2021 chair and a former chair of the Kansas City Federal Reserve. The public face of Oasis, Aaron "A. J." Johnson, came not from the corporate world but from Victory Christian's Dream Center, which for more than twenty years had been providing medical care, after school and youth sports programs, food, and clothing to North Tulsans.[25]

Oasis adapted a similar multipurpose concept. At 16,500 square feet, it was about one-third the size of most contemporary chain supermarkets. It included space for socializing and, on certain days, the likes of basic health care providers, social service agencies offering assistance with such things as job searches and filing for unemployment, legal advice, and family counseling, and other supports.[26]

"It's right there in the name—Oasis," Johnson said six months after opening. "An oasis is a refuge, a safe place, a shelter. It's a place where everyone feels welcome. That's why one of the most important things we do here at Oasis is that we greet everyone who comes into the store. We want them to take a step inside and think, 'Yes—I belong here.'"[27]

A mile west, retired firefighter Terry McGee—the same Terry McGee who had helped steer a young Kevin Matthews to the Tulsa Fire Department decades earlier—was working with the Tulsa Development Authority (TDA) and an affiliate of the local Habitat for Humanity, called Boomtown Development Co., to build twenty-four single-family townhomes on a vacant 1.76-acre tract. Throughout his fire department career and into retirement, McGee had been involved in real estate and development. Over the decades, he had built and renovated scores of houses in North Tulsa. Here the goal was to create housing stock for households whose incomes were too high for Habitat for Humanity's traditional program but not enough to qualify for a regular mortgage, especially with home prices escalating rapidly even in North Tulsa.[28]

The forces buffeting urban redevelopment were all in play for Black Wall Street Square, as the development was called. After hearing concerns about gentrification, the original eight 2,000-square-feet and sixteen 1,600-square-feet townhomes, costing $150,000–$200,000, were scaled back to 16 "affordable" units of 1,152 square feet and eight 1,382-square-feet "market rate" units. Some nearby residents feared the larger units first proposed—and even the smaller ones in the final plan—would drive up property values and taxes and lead to higher rents for those who did not own. This led to discussions about who benefits from investment in a neighborhood and who does not, and the suggestion that the national housing shortage could trigger a repopulation of Tulsa's north side.[29]

"We can't always be like 'Oh, is it going to be enough for the low-income people?'" one area resident said during a meeting with the developers, TDA, and the city. "What about the middle-class people? Why not gentrify our own neighborhoods?"[30]

Alisia Myers, a city of Tulsa neighborhood liaison, told the residents that interest in North Tulsa neighborhoods was increasing.

"These are people with good jobs and wanting to move here," Myers said.[31]

Oasis and Black Wall Street Square each carried price tags of around $5 million. Far grander were several other projects in various stages of development by the second half of 2021, all of which tested Bynum's promise of equitable development in greater Greenwood.[32]

The most visible of these were four long-fallow parcels near downtown, three of which the city and TDA had more or less clawed back from the trust set up in the 1980s for a higher education consortium called the University Center at Tulsa. When Oklahoma State University took over the campus in 1998, it envisioned growing into a two-hundred-acre footprint. It did not, and as time passed, pressure mounted to let someone else develop the land. In 2018, the trust surrendered forty-five acres north of the inner dispersal loop and west of Martin Luther King Boulevard. It had been a white residential neighborhood in 1921 but became mostly Black after World War II when African Americans pushed clear of Greenwood's traditional boundaries. Also returned were six acres adjacent to Vernon AME and eighteen acres used mostly for storm water retention. These two featured Greenwood Avenue frontages.[33]

The fourth parcel had been on the city's books for nearly two decades. Known as the Evans-Fintube site, in 1921 it was an industrial complex looming above Greenwood from atop a hill a few blocks east. Clearly visible in photos of Greenwood during and after the massacre is the hulking form of the Oklahoma Iron Works, at that time one of the country's largest fabricators of oilfield equipment. Closed in 1961 and eventually occupied simultaneously by two different companies, Evans Electric and Fintube Technologies, the twenty-two-acre property passed to the city in 2003 and 2005.[34]

Hemmed in on two sides by highways and a third by railroad tracks and in poor condition, the site attracted little interest until a deal to move the USA BMX Headquarters to Tulsa's Expo Square fairgrounds fell through. The Evans-Fintube parcel was offered as an alternative, with the 120,000-square-foot Oklahoma Iron Works/Evans Building as a potential indoor BMX course. That ultimately proved impractical, but BMX moved to the site anyway, taking up residence in a new facility occupying half the tract. While that construction was in progress, the Tulsa Authority of Economic Opportunity, a new umbrella city agency that included TDA, issued a request for qualifications to develop the remaining eleven acres, including the historic Oklahoma Iron Works facility.[35]

At about the same time, with COVID-19 apparently on the wane, the city restarted Kirkpatrick Heights/Greenwood planning. It and Evans-Fintube were separate projects but the city's approaches to them were much the same. Bynum said his administration would provide technical and financial support but promised unprecedented community involvement. The Kirkpatrick Heights/Greenwood Master Plan, particularly, lent itself to this concept.

"We are not trying to control the decision-making on this from City Hall," Bynum said. "We have one chance to get this right, and we want it to reflect the hopes and aspirations and dreams of north Tulsa residents, and that is why we really put a leadership committee of proven north Tulsa leaders in the driver's seat on this to help evaluate what is the best path forward."[36]

That eleven-member committee consisted entirely of Black Tulsans, including Hall-Harper, Reuben Gant, Dwain Midget, and two former city councilors. Most of the city hall staff assigned to the project were Black.

Referring to the committee, Bynum said:

> They are driving the ship on this. The city is helping facilitate it with financial resources and staff, but from the policy development side the leadership committee of north Tulsa leaders is driving this.

> We also want to know: How do people want to see this space governed? Do they want it within an independent trust or some other mechanism? And what do they want to see (from) any proceeds that this land derives, either from sale or development? How do they want those proceeds to be used? So it is a much larger undertaking than just your typical land-use planning exercise.[37]

In August, the city announced it had hired Philadelphia-based Wallace Roberts & Todd to oversee the project with Tulsa's Black-owned World Won Development as the local engagement partner. In October, the process of gathering public input and shaping it into a blueprint for the three Kirkpatrick Heights/ Greenwood tracts began.[38]

"Where we stand today may very well be one of the most important projects to date in Greenwood's history because what happens with this land could greatly impact the economic, social and political future of the Greenwood community," said Hall-Harper. "We've been talking about this area and what it means for Greenwood and North Tulsa for quite some time. Today, it is so exciting to see that talk move toward action."[39]

Also in August, the city announced four finalists for developing the Evans-Fintube site; among them was a team that included former Dallas Cowboys star Emmett Smith.[40]

All of this created interest and excitement, not only because of its transformational potential but because of the Black-owned businesses and professionals attached to the projects. But in the summer of 2021 it was mostly still talk. Results were years away and far from certain. And that was the difficulty. Achieving equity in the way of Bynum and the George Kaiser Family Foundation (GKFF) takes time. It requires diligence and money, of course, but also the trust of people accustomed to the Charlie Brown treatment—left flat on their backs after yet another broken promise.

That is one reason, George Kaiser said, economic development is one of GKFF's most difficult undertakings. But, he added, it is "arguably the most important element because the basis for the continuing division in Tulsa—physically, socially and financially—is rooted in the wealth and income gap between the communities."[41]

The racial wealth differential, Kaiser said, "is heavily derived from the systemic suppression of the ability of Black Americans to build net worth through the means of most other middle-class Americans—home equity appreciation—which accrued mostly between 1945 and 1980."[42]

Kaiser's analysis is almost identical to the one devastatingly laid out by Ta-Nehisi Coates in his famous 2014 essay for the *Atlantic*. Richard Rothstein in his 2017 book, *The Color of Law*, gives a more detailed account of how federal home loan programs, beginning during the Great Depression, intentionally segregated neighborhoods in ways that rapidly accelerated the value of white neighborhoods while suppressing that of others.[43]

"We still had subtle Jim Crow (or worse) denial of participation in that 'starter kit' through denial of ownership or transfer of new homes in the most attractive areas," Kaiser said. "The Federal Government shares culpability."[44]

By the summer of 2021, GKFF had invested far more in other facets of North Tulsa than in Greenwood Rising and with far less controversy. Its EduCare early childhood education centers, which had at first encountered resistance, were now widely accepted; one, next to Hawthorne Elementary School near 36th Street North and Peoria Avenue, was part of an initiative by GKFF and the Zarrow and Schusterman Foundations, other nonprofits, private business, and local and federal government to literally rebuild one of the city's most depressed neighborhoods. Comanche Park, a dreary government housing project, was slated for demolition, to be replaced by a $200-million mixed use development. A few hundred yards away, a new 250,000-square-foot Muncie Power Products plant had just opened as the first tenant of a 120-acre industrial park, bringing good-paying jobs to the neighborhood. A few hundred yards to the west, a $24 million school and community services complex under the auspices of Crossover Church would soon begin construction. One way or another, GKFF had a hand in all of it.[45]

Kasier said GKFF's economic development ventures involve three elements: New quality starter job attraction, homegrown entrepreneurship, and "enticement of promising entrepreneurial companies."[46]

"The first is pretty easy," Kaiser said in 2023, using Muncie Power's Mohawk Industrial Park plant as an example. "As we expected, it has been difficult attracting companies there because of Comanche Park across the street, the most rundown and 'rough' public housing in the city. But we have attracted one manufacturing plant so far [Muncie] and they have completed their plant and are hiring 150 or so initial employees, building to 700, in jobs requiring relatively light training and paying $60,000 or so. Now that [Tulsa Housing Authority] is making real progress on the rebuild of Comanche Park . . . we have two very promising leads for additional, higher tech companies."[47]

The premise is not original: Better jobs spur housing and retail—and lead to better outcomes for children, which Kaiser says is the ultimate goal.

Less visible—and less subject to criticism—is development of what Kaiser calls "indigenous entrepreneurship" and recruiting Black entrepreneurs and their businesses to Tulsa. For these, GKFF deploys Build in Tulsa (and its in-house business incubators) and an affiliated venture capital company called Atento.

By "indigenous," Kaiser means homegrown. By "entrepreneurship" he means innovative and leading edge. That mostly means technology, but it can also mean something like Silhouette, an art, fashion, and high-end sneaker store in the GreenArch Building. A disgruntled educator with a passion for sneakers, Venita Cooper opened Silhouette in November 2019, just before the COVID-19 veil descended. Her disaffection with education, hastened by the state's politics and their effect on teaching and learning, and her experience creating Silhouette, illustrate some of the best and worst of Tulsa.[48]

"What makes Tulsa really special at this moment in history is our access to one another," she said. One of the first people she met in Tulsa was Kojo Asamoa-Caesar. He introduced her to Brandon Oldham, a senior program officer at GKFF and former Bynum aide; through Oldham, Cooper met city councilor (and at the time council chair) Phil Lakin, whose day job was managing the Tulsa Community Foundation, a GKFF satellite that provides investment and technical support to nonprofits.[49]

"All three of these guys were into sneakers—Phil Lakin and Brandon in particular, huge sneaker heads," said Cooper. "And so, literally the third degree of separation was Phil Lakin for me . . . trying to get in front of him to talk about a sneaker store concept. And they were all fully supportive. And that's really all that I needed."[50]

Kajeer Yar, who would become Cooper's landlord, was also supportive.

"His sons are . . . big sneaker heads," said Cooper. "He understood the vision immediately, and then Rose Washington at TEDC . . . those people would end up being incredibly consequential. . . . So November 2019, November 1, we opened our doors. And my first customer was the mayor, G. T. Bynum."[51]

Cooper even had assists from the Oklahoma City Thunder, especially through COVID-19. The NBA team has become involved in several Greenwood-related endeavors, including a program to expose disadvantaged Tulsa youth to real-world business experiences. And even this has a Kaiser connection—George Kaiser is a minority owner of the franchise.[52]

GKFF is also a funder of Black Tech Street, an initiative conceived by a young Black man named Tyrance Billingsley II as a way to reclaim the spirit of Black

Wall Street in a twenty-first-century setting. Billingsley said he began formulating what became Black Tech Street in high school.

In 2022, Billingsley said:

> When I thought about the level of tenacity that it took for these entrepreneurs to build these incredible businesses during Jim Crow, the smashing through walls and the out of the box thinking reminded me a lot of the tech industry. That kind of ended up leading me to a three-pronged epiphany: One, tech is one of the only verticals in which you can create intergenerational wealth in seven to ten years; two, tech is the core medium through which all global innovation and the creation of new wealth-generating markets takes place pretty consistently; and three, by the year 2030, there are projected to be as many as 4.3 million vacant, high paying tech jobs. So when I thought about these three and I put them together, I not only saw an incredible wealth building opportunity for Black people, but I saw the Black Wall Street vision kind of push to a new horizon.
>
> Our mission is to rebirth Black Wall Street as a Black tech hub, but also to catalyze a movement that sees Black people kind of use the Black Tech Street moniker as a banner to embrace tech and . . . to build wealth and impact the world.[53]

Billingsley is not a techster himself. His job is putting people together. Similarly, but on a larger scale, Kaiser said Atento Capital has brought "literally hundreds of Black Founders, venture capitalists and investors to town for extended weekends during which we proselytize and incentivize them to move their companies here to provide employment, role models and stimulation of followers to help close the wealth and income gap. Slow to develop but lots of interest and some small moves."[54]

"I'm very optimistic that things will be happening," said Billingsley. "How will they be happening and . . . happening the correct way is a fight that we're in every day. It's something we have to be conscious of every day. But will Greenwood, at least in some form, become what it was before? I think the chances are looking good."[55]

Back on what is left of the original Greenwood business district, the struggle continued. The centennial and the opening of Greenwood Rising and new housing along Archer Street seemed to increase foot traffic, which helped. But most of the business center's tenants were not retailers and restaurants; most did not even have a street front presence. They occupied spaces tucked upstairs and in the back of the buildings. Age, deferred maintenance, and an outdated floor plan made for a difficult business model for the Greenwood Chamber of Commerce, the entity charged with operating the center. In June 2021, the Greenwood business center's thirty to thirty-five tenants represented only a 55 percent occupancy rate. Not terrible, but not good enough, either.[56]

Critics accused the Greenwood Chamber of not only mismanaging the historic buildings in the 100 block of North Greenwood Avenue, but of being too cozy with white businesspeople—several were on the board—and not doing enough to foster Black business. One of the loudest voices, Councilor Hall-Harper, organized the alternative Black Wall Street Chamber in 2018 with Sherry Gamble-Smith, a former Greenwood Chamber president. The complaints about the Greenwood Chamber were not without basis but the split also reflected political and ideological divisions within the community. State senator Judy Eason McIntyre accused Hall-Harper of trying to acquire the historic buildings through an intermediary, a crowd-sourced investment scheme called the Tulsa Real Estate Fund (TREF)—which, despite its name, had nothing to do with Tulsa. Hall-Harper dismissed the claim but admitted to talking to TREF founder Jay Morrison, an Atlanta real estate tycoon.[57]

Hall-Harper said she told the Greenwood Chamber's Freeman Culver: "The Greenwood Chamber does not have a good reputation, and I don't trust their board or decision-makers."[58]

Her opinion had not changed nearly two years later, in late 2020, when Hall-Harper and Kristi Williams attended a press conference in the 100 block after a long-time tenant was evicted over $4,200 in unpaid rent.

"We care about maintaining the history and spirit of Greenwood," said Hall-Harper. "To harass and kick more Black businesses out of Greenwood is not the way to do that."[59]

So while one might think an announcement, ten days after the centennial, that the 100 block had been added to the National Register of Historic Places would have been met with unanimous approval, it was not. It was instead another chapter in the long dispute over where and what Greenwood was and is. Reuben Gant and others believed the designation too limited: historic Greenwood had been much larger, and present-day Greenwood was bigger yet. Culver, by then the Greenwood Chamber's president, said he agreed and that he had sought the 100 block's designation only to enhance grant applications and tenant recruitment.[60]

At a community confab on June 17, Eason McIntyre urged everyone to view the National Register designation as a victory for everybody.

"My hope is that we can come together and stop fighting," she said. "Because we're fighting over crumbs. As long as we're divided in this community, we're not going to move forward."[61]

Still, the disagreements continued among those most immersed in Greenwood's history and traditions. For some, nothing less than the return of the historic Greenwood would do. Others thought that unrealistic given that so much of early Greenwood was now occupied by the OSU-Tulsa campus and a city-owned baseball stadium, and that a major highway sliced through it.

In July, state representative Regina Goodwin held a legislative study on the possibility of removing the north leg of the inner dispersal loop, long blamed for contributing to Greenwood's deterioration. President Biden had gotten behind the idea in his June 1 address, in which he mentioned an administration program to reconnect neighborhoods cut off by highways. Some alternatives to the loop were put forward, including taking it underground, but none generated much public enthusiasm. The highway may have been ugly, dangerous, and a barrier to street-level movement, but it routed 90,000 vehicles a day onto multiple major highways spinning off in all directions. And the traffic load would likely increase with the planned upgrade of one of the highways carried by the north loop, US 412, to the interstate system. In any event, at the end of 2021 the highway remained an emotional and unresolved issue for many with an interest in Greenwood.[62]

Also largely unresolved was the definition of Greenwood. Did the intersection of Pine Street and Peoria Avenue count? A century earlier, white real estate investors had tried to push, pull and shove the residents and business owners of Deep Greenwood "out" to Pine and Peoria. Black Tulsans had successfully resisted coerced removal but ultimately spread into the neighborhood on their own. By 2021, several dozen businesses, some Black-owned and some not, occupied the intersection and immediate vicinity. Was the area two miles further north, where Comanche Park was being reimagined on what had been farmland in 1921, part of Greenwood? Or, as some skeptics wondered, was this all just more of the relocation that had been underway since before the embers cooled in the ruins of the original Black Wall Street?

Dwain Midget, the city economic and neighborhood development officer, grew up in Greenwood and spent virtually his entire adult life trying to reconcile its past, present, and future into a better life for Black Tulsans.

"Black Wall Street is to be honored," he said in 2021, just before the centennial. "It's to have continual recognition and acknowledgement in history. But we will never have that Black Wall Street on Greenwood again. To me, you remember it, and then you make a new Black Wall Street."[63]

A few days before the race massacre centennial, three women looked down at a modest headstone in the southwest sector of Oaklawn Cemetery, contemplating the tenuously remembered life it memorialized. Eddie Lockard, the marker said. He was the great-uncle of one of the women, Pearl Alford, and the great-great-uncle of the other two, Alford's daughters Dene' Harjo and Cheri Pearson-Jordan. Lockard's headstone is one of two for known Black massacre victims in Oaklawn Cemetery. The other, for Reuben Everett, is next to it.[64]

Eddie Lockard died at age thirty-two, apparently without children. According to contemporary news accounts, his body was found five days after the massacre in a field east of town near an airstrip—quite possibly the same one where Mary Jones Parrish reported men with guns getting into airplanes—with a bullet hole in his neck and a rifle lying nearby. Family lore has it that Lockard was shot from the air while on horseback. His brother Joe Lockard—Pearl Alford's grandfather and Harjo and Pearson-Jordan's great-grandfather—survived the massacre and played an important role in not only resisting pressure to abandon Deep Greenwood but in rebuilding the community. He seems the person most likely to have placed the headstone in Eddie's honor.

But Eddie Lockard, like many of those killed in the massacre, is mostly a mystery.

"He worked in Joe's restaurant, we think," Harjo told a reporter. "But beyond that we don't know much about him."

"A lot of those details died with our ancestors," said her sister. "I think back then there was a fear sometimes of actually talking about the race massacre."

Among the things not known about Eddie Lockard is whether his remains actually lie at the foot of his headstone. The same is true for Reuben Everett.

Those were among the questions researchers hoped to answer when they returned to Oaklawn one hundred years to the day after Greenwood's destruction. Eight months after the dramatic discovery of what at the time were thought to be badly deteriorated coffins stacked in a trench—it was ultimately decided the burials had not been one on top of another—the archeologists were back to uncover them, extend excavations, and exhume remains thus discovered. With luck, they would be able to extract DNA and get a better idea whether these were, in fact, some of the eighteen Black massacre victims known to have been buried in the cemetery. But the three years since Mayor Bynum launched the project had dispelled all thoughts of swift, definitive solutions. As the researchers warned at the outset, this was not a television program in which the most baffling problems are solved with the help of high-tech gadgets in forty-four minutes plus commercial time. Human remains, especially those buried in cheap coffins, can be badly degraded over a century. Causes of death can be difficult or impossible to ascertain. And differentiating remains of riot victims from others buried in the cemetery can be, too.

On June 3, the city disclosed that eight more burials had been uncovered, bringing the total under examination to twenty. That would grow to thirty-five over the next three weeks, including the graves of several women and children. This was potentially significant because no death certificates for women and children killed in the massacre are known to exist, and the discovery excited those convinced such deaths did occur. The researchers, though, said the manner of burial suggested the women and children were not among those hastily interred after the massacre.[65]

From the thirty-five burials, the team exhumed nineteen sets of remains for examination by Phoebe Stubblefield, the forensic anthropologist, and on which to attempt DNA extraction. A skull among the remains of an African American male not only exhibited gunshot wounds but an actual bullet. These remains, though, were found not in the coffin-packed trench, but beneath a row of children's graves. Ultimately, fourteen sets of remains were judged more likely subjects for further study; seven burial sites were designated "of Archeological Interest." Stubblefield said this section of the cemetery was filled with burials, many of them unmarked. Records for what is labeled "New Potters Field" on the cemetery plat were sparse.[66]

"It's probably wall-to-wall caskets," Stubblefield said. "We didn't hit any blank spots in our excavations. Somebody planned and organized that cemetery, and knew what they were doing, but we don't have any record."[67]

Stubblefield said she remained convinced that "at least the original eighteen are in there," meaning the southwest section of the cemetery. Figuring out exactly where, and proving it, was another matter. Not even the skull with the bullet holes could be definitively linked to the massacre. Extracting DNA from the badly degraded bones and teeth would prove difficult and in many cases impossible; even when quantities sufficient for analysis were recovered, the inquiry advanced only to the extent the results could be matched with DNA on publicly available databases. It was all very technical and for most people tedious, and it did little to satisfy skeptics who doubted the city was ever serious about finding race massacre victims.[68]

Tempers exploded in late July when the city announced that testing and sampling had been completed and the exhumed remains would be reinterred in protective cases exactly where they had been found. This riled a substantial share of the Public Oversight Committee. Dissenters suspected the city of literally covering up whatever evidence had been unearthed and then shutting down the operation. Some argued the remains should not be reinterred without more formal burials. Protestors showed up at the cemetery on the morning of July 30, waving a few signs and shouting through the fence obscuring the public's view of the excavation site.

"Tell the truth! Quit telling lies!" shouted one unidentified man.[69]

Another connected lynching to the reburials beneath a tree.

"You are just burying their bodies right back up," shouted a woman, Celi Butler Davis. "This is a crime."

Phoebe Stubblefield and Brenda Alford tried to reassure the crowd. Stubblefield said the safest, most respectful place for the remains was back in their graves. Each plot had been mapped. They would not be forgotten.

"We don't have our people yet," she said. "We've got one probable. Two suspiciously buried. And that still leaves fifteen (of the original eighteen). We're not done. We have not stopped."

Some people did not believe it. Some thought the decision too cold-blooded.

"We should have been included," said Heather Nash. "We should have been able to stand on those graves and put our spirit in them with them in us."

"The correct thing would have been, if they were going to have a ceremony, to notify the community that there was going be a ceremony and to do it the right way: with pomp and circumstance," said Joyce G. Smith-Williams.

The city pointed out that the Public Oversight Committee had agreed in March to temporarily return any exhumed remains to Oaklawn until identifications could be established. In the event, however, some committee members resisted. On social media, Kristi Williams announced she would not be at the cemetery for the reburial.[70]

"Yesterday we were notified that the City of Tulsa will rebury the remains with or without a ceremony tomorrow," she wrote on July 29. "It didn't matter that we VOTED and ADVISED to postpone this reburial. This is UNACCEPTABLE AND DECEPTIVE!"[71]

Williams wanted the FBI to examine the gunshot victim, and reiterated objections to reburial. "We have not properly identified those remains and family/ next of kin has not been contacted yet," she said. Barring that, Williams said, there should have been "adequate time to create programming for a reburial ceremony."[72]

But a ceremony would have turned into an event, and the city did not want an event. Whether that was because it believed such an event inappropriate or a potential public relations problem, or because it would have signaled the very sort of finality critics said they feared, can be debated. Perhaps it was some combination. Maybe the professionals just understood how far they were from putting names to the bones and teeth recovered from Oaklawn Cemetery. The researchers would return several times over the next two years, and the Utah DNA lab working with the city would periodically issue calls for information based on public database matches to the scant genetic material collected, but by the summer of 2023, not a single positive identification had been reported.

In 1921, the Tulsa Race Massacre was knocked from the top of the nation's front pages by a devastating flood in Pueblo, Colorado. In 2021, the massacre's centennial was replaced on news feeds, websites, and cable networks by something much closer to home.[73]

By that summer, Julius Jones had been behind bars for more than twenty years, sentenced to death for the 1999 shooting death of Paul Howell during a carjacking in Edmond, a northern suburb of Oklahoma City. The murder fit just about every stereotypical scenario imaginable. Jones was a young Black man who had been in trouble with the law; Howell was a white, upper-middle-class insurance executive killed in white upper-middle-class suburbia by a masked carjacker while Howell's sister and two young children watched in horror. The killer wore a bandanna and a stocking cap that precluded a definitive description, but all three witnesses agreed a Black man pulled the trigger. Acting on information from two people who said they'd been approached about finding a buyer for Howell's stolen Suburban, police soon arrested Jones and an alleged accomplice, Christopher Jordan.[74]

Jones always maintained his innocence and eventually persuaded a large and influential group of followers that included Kim Kardashian, basketball stars such as Stephen Curry and Blake Griffin, Heisman Trophy-winning University of Oklahoma quarterback Baker Mayfield, five Republican state lawmakers, the executive director of the American Conservative Union and even the woman Howell was dating at the time of his death. A change.org petition urging clemency for Jones attracted more than six million signatures. But despite all of that and after numerous delays, including more than six years when Oklahoma suspended executions after badly mishandling two, time was running out for Jones. When Oklahoma began preparing to resume lethal injections in 2021, Jones was near the top of the list.[75]

Although it was an Oklahoma County case, Jones's situation attracted the interest and in some cases involvement of quite a few Tulsans, including Tiffany Crutcher. Policing and criminal justice reform had been her first calling as an advocate, and by September 2021 she appeared fully engaged again in that cause. September 16 was the fifth anniversary of her brother Terence's death and a week of activities were planned around it, including attendance at Jones's commutation hearing before the Oklahoma Pardon and Parole Board on September 13.[76]

"I can't bring Terence back," Tiffany Crutcher told a group of Jones's supporters. "But guess what? I can fight like crazy to make sure Julius Jones isn't killed by the same system that killed Terence Crutcher."[77]

Tulsa's *Oklahoma Eagle* and *Black Wall Street Times* had been advocating for Jones for some time, too. They saw in Julius Jones a prototype of young Black men everywhere who, guilty or not, tend to be disproportionately convicted and sentenced to death—"killed by the system," as Tiffany Crutcher put it. Indeed, the Justice for Julius movement was probably as much about the system, or more, than it was about Julius Jones. It highlighted not only the inequities that landed a disproportionate number of Black Americans on death row, in Oklahoma and elsewhere, but also the state's inability to execute prisoners without gruesome complications.[78]

Jones and his supporters staunchly proclaimed, and still do, his unquestionable innocence, but the matter is not so clear cut. A high school honor student and athlete, Jones had dropped out of college during his freshman year and gotten into a series of scrapes with the law, including an armed carjacking just a few days before Paul Howell was shot to death during the commission of a similar crime on July 28, 1999. Witnesses placed Jones in possession of Howell's Chevrolet Suburban within hours of the murder, and the murder gun, ammunition, and a red bandanna like one worn by Howell's killer were found in Jones's house. DNA testing of the bandanna years later, while not conclusive, suggested Jones had worn it—but not when or where.[79]

Jones and his defense team contended he was at home with his family at the time of the shooting, and that the killer was actually Christopher Jordan, who told authorities he was Jones's accomplice in the carjacking. The gun and other evidence, the defense said, had been planted by Jordan, who then directed police to it. The defense also contended the killer's description given by Howell's sister, an eyewitness, better fit Jordan than Jones. As often happens in criminal cases, much depended on the testimony of people with something at stake, and Jordan and two other key witnesses allegedly received lesser sentences for leading law officers to Jones—a claim prosecutors disputed. On Jones's side, three former inmates of various facilities ultimately swore that Jordan had confessed to killing Howell. Suffused throughout Jones's defense, in the courts and in appeals to the public, were common complaints about the American criminal justice system: inexperienced defense council, biased jurors, upper-middle-class white victim and Black suspect, and police and prosecutors more interested in convictions than justice.[80]

The extent to which any or all of those elements applied in Jones's conviction is a matter of bitter debate, but the case served to highlight doubts, difficulties, and failures within the criminal justice system and especially the application of capital punishment. Jones's trial attorneys were overmatched—one had just passed the bar, and the other had never tried a capital case. Bob Macy, the Oklahoma County district attorney when Jones was charged, retired from office in 2001 with a reputation for zealous and sometimes heavy-handed pursuit of the death penalty and a record of reversals and exonerations. Macy was gone and took no part in Jones's 2002 trial, but much of the department he built remained intact. All of this and more the Los Angeles-based nonprofit Represent Justice assembled into a well-planned and realized campaign to raise doubts about Jones's guilt, even in a state that as recently as 2016 voted two to one to confirm the state's authority to impose the death penalty. And while those most readily identified with the Justice for Julius movement probably would be thought of as liberal, an important factor in his case was the extent to which conservatives joined in. One conduit for that was Kelli Masters, a white, Oklahoma City-based attorney and NFL agent who says she became "convinced we were about to execute an innocent man" and began making contacts that Jones's supporters might not have otherwise reached. "I knew we had to bring conservative voices into the discussion and I knew that the faith community needed to weigh in," she said.[81]

The Oklahoma City public policy consultants working with Represent Justice had a long association with conservative and Republican politics. Organizations such as Americans for Prosperity and the American Conservative Union had taken up the cause of reform, arguing the current system was ineffective, unfair, and too expensive. Governor Stitt had also embraced this position. He commuted hundreds of sentences in a single day in 2019 and appointed reformers to the Pardon and Parole Board, which in Oklahoma must recommend clemency before the governor can act upon it. Whether these conservative allies were as convinced of Jones's innocence as the movement's official line is unclear, but they did have doubts and that, it could be argued, was all the law and perhaps conscience required. As *Tulsa World* columnist Bob Doucette wrote in late September: "There's no going back once an execution is carried out, much in the same way you can't recall a bullet after the trigger is pulled. Before you carry it out, you better be damned sure you got this one right."[82]

Jones's cause began gaining national momentum after the 2018 airing of *The Last Defense*, an ABC documentary series executive produced by Oscar, Emmy, and Tony Award-winning actress Viola Davis and her husband Julius Tennon. Three episodes of the series recounted Jones's case; it did not take a position on Jones's guilt or innocence but did carry a sympathetic message to a broader audience. Among those seeing the program was Kim Kardashian, who had become involved in criminal justice reform. She began tweeting about Jones's situation in 2019, and in 2020, she visited Julius Jones in prison, went to church with his family and met with Stitt. Kardashian's involvement undoubtedly raised the case's national profile considerably.[83]

Prosecutors and Paul Howell's family complained bitterly about "celebrity imploration" and a "profusion of misinformation," as then-Attorney General Mike Hunter termed it. Oklahoma County District Attorney David Prater became so upset with the prospect of clemency for Jones that he tried to have two Pardon and Parole Board members removed before they could vote on a recommendation; later, Prater would convene a grand jury to investigate the board and Stitt's influence over it. In a fifteen-page letter to board members, Prater witheringly referred to what he called "a coordinated and alarmingly successful campaign of misinformation, spurred by media frenzy, which is specifically targeted to manipulate and mislead the public through dissemination of half-truths and, frequently, outright lies."[84]

"Not one of these celebrities or athletes [has] tried to reach out to me or my family," said Paul Howell's daughter Rachel, who was nine years old and seated directly behind her father when he was killed.[85]

The Pardon and Parole Board held an unprecedented commutation hearing (technically different from a clemency hearing) on September 13 and, after four hours of testimony, voted 3–1 with one recusal to recommend Jones's death sentence be modified to life with the possibility of parole. "Justice has been subverted by celebrity, money and politics," Prater said afterward. And he was not entirely wrong. Celebrity, money and politics unquestionably were brought to bear on Julius Jones's behalf. But Prater's complaint mimicked what reform advocates had been saying for years: celebrity, money, and politics does often influence the criminal justice system, except usually to the detriment of the poor and people of color.[86]

Stitt rejected the Pardon and Parole Board's recommendation on procedural grounds, noting that no death row inmate had ever been given a commutation hearing. This forced a second hearing under somewhat different rules. During the interim, Prater and Attorney General John O'Connor, who had replaced Hunter in July, each unsuccessfully attempted to have Pardon and Parole Board Chairman Adam Luck and member Kelly Doyle barred from voting on Jones's clemency because of their alleged bias. This hearing, on November 1, also ended with a 3–1 vote for commutation to life with the possibility of parole. That left the decision to Stitt.[87]

The state's first execution in nearly seven years had occurred a few days earlier, on October 28, after the US Supreme Court lifted a stay. Oklahoma's previous two executions, in 2014 and 2015, were badly handled, to put it charitably, and some believed the state had done no better this time. The condemned man, John Marion Grant, began straining, frothing at the mouth and vomiting after receiving the three-drug injection that was supposed to put him more or less quietly to sleep. Department of Corrections officials said the execution was performed "without complications," but Associated Press pool reporter Sean Murphy said it was unlike any of the dozen or more he'd witnessed, save one—the aborted 2014 execution of Clayton Lockett that resulted in his death but only after forty-three agonizing minutes.[88]

For a while, it looked like the Lockett execution might be Oklahoma's last, so badly was it handled. But few states are more committed to capital punishment than Oklahoma. It has the highest per capita execution rate in the country, according to the Death Penalty Information Center, and was the first state to adopt lethal injection. When pharmaceutical manufacturers threatened that mode of execution in the 2010s by withholding or discontinuing the necessary drugs, the legislature okayed nitrogen hypoxia—essentially suffocation—as an alternative should lethal injection be ruled out. This commitment to capital punishment goes back to territorial days, when what is now Oklahoma was mostly under the jurisdiction of Judge Isaac Parker, the "Hanging Judge" of Fort Smith, Arkansas. Over twenty-one years, Parker handed down 160 death sentences, of which about half were carried out. The same attitude toward capital punishment infused the new state, although its second governor, Lee Cruce, opposed the death penalty and from 1911 to 1915 is believed to have commuted every death sentence brought before him except one. That one was of a Black man named Frank Henson, who was convicted in 1911 of killing a Tulsa County sheriff's deputy. Henson admitted shooting the deputy but said the man drew on him without identifying himself as a law officer. Sheriff W. M. McCullough, who ten years later during the Tulsa Race Massacre would barricade himself in the county jail to protect Dick Rowland, is said to have grown fond of Henson and did not want to hang him. Clemency was requested but denied. So McCullough reluctantly turned executioner. In those days, county sheriffs were responsible for carrying out death sentences, and McCullough wound up building the gallows, setting the noose, and dropping the trap door on Henson.[89]

In 1915, an electric chair was installed at the Oklahoma State Penitentiary in McAlester and over the next fifty-one years eighty-two people were put to death in it. For a while in the 1920s and 1930s, two or three executions in a single day were not uncommon. Legal challenges brought executions throughout the United States to a halt in 1967, but in 1976 the US Supreme Court conditionally allowed them to resume. In Oklahoma, a young reform-minded Republican legislator from Tulsa, Bill Wiseman, successfully advocated for something that had never been tried—lethal injection. Wiseman actually opposed the death penalty but knew its reinstatement in Oklahoma was inevitable and believed lethal injection was the most humane method available. He and Dr. A. Jay Chapman, the state medical examiner, came up with a three-step protocol that began with a heavy dose of anesthesia to render the condemned unconscious, followed by a muscle relaxant to paralyze them and finally a drug to stop the heart. Ultimately every death penalty state adopted the procedure.[90]

By 2010, with execution drugs becoming hard to obtain, Oklahoma and other states began looking for substitutes, and may have even tried concocting their own. Most controversial was the use of midazolam, a drug originally developed as an alternative to Valium, as the anesthetic. According to some reports, midazolam did not always thoroughly sedate subjects and in some cases actually agitated them. But pressured by Gov. Mary Fallin's office and ambitious state Attorney General Scott Pruitt, a former state senator from Tulsa County, Oklahoma corrections officials pushed forward without consulting medical or pharmacological experts and scheduled two executions for April 29, 2014.[91]

Lockett was up first. He cut himself on the day of the execution, apparently in an attempt to delay it, and had to be tased before he could be removed from his cell. He refused a final meal after his request for Chateaubriand, fried shrimp, baked potato, garlic toast, pecan pie, and Coca-Cola with ice was denied because it exceeded the state's fifteen-dollar limit. Once strapped to a gurney, Lockett posed another dilemma for his executioners—they could not locate veins to insert the two needles normally used in the procedure. In desperation, a single needle was finally placed in the femoral artery in Lockett's groin. At first the procedure seemed to go normally. The midazolam was administered at 6:23 p.m., and ten minutes later a doctor announced that Lockett was unconscious. Administration of the other two drugs, Vecuronium bromide and potassium chloride, began. Instead of drifting into death, however, Lockett began straining, muttering and cursing. At 6:42 p.m., the witness room blinds were closed so that observers could not see what was happening in the death chamber. The execution was stopped but Lockett died anyway, officially of a heart attack but one most likely brought on by an IV failure that injected the potassium chloride directly into tissue.[92]

The ineptness of Lockett's execution caused officials to delay the day's second scheduled execution, that of Charles Warner. Warner was executed nine months later, the same day the US Supreme Court narrowly rejected a challenge to Oklahoma's lethal injection protocol. Except to complain about a burning sensation before the drugs were administered, Warner's death occurred as expected—until an autopsy revealed the state had used the wrong drug to stop his heart. Officials' insistence that the drug administered—potassium acetate—was not much different than the one called for by the protocol—potassium chloride—made them sound even more cavalier about putting people to death. Fallin immediately shut down all further executions and ordered an investigation. There would be several, in fact, including one by a grand jury and another by a commission that included Fallin's predecessor, Brad Henry.[93]

"If we're going to have a lethal injection process, then we should follow best practices," Henry told the Death Penalty Information Center later. "We make recommendations in our report as to what those best practices are. And, frankly, they are not what the Department of Corrections is currently utilizing."[94]

All of this and John Marion Grant's heaving death a few days before Julius Jones's November hearing weighted the scales as Stitt considered Jones's fate. His own attorney general, John O'Connor, urged Stitt to ignore the parole board's recommendation. So did the Howell family and the state's district attorneys, who seemed just as convinced of Jones's guilt as his supporters were of his innocence. Stitt himself wanted to be seen as a criminal justice reformer without appearing soft on crime or buckling to pressure. Some suspected that he especially did not want to appear susceptible to pressure from African Americans. The underlying philosophy of House Bill 1775 and a good deal of populist rhetoric held that inequities no longer exist. Systemic racism had been eradicated, the thinking goes, so to claim otherwise is itself a form of racism—and probably some kind of scam.[95]

Even before the second parole board hearing, Jones's supporters were holding prayer vigils and courting attention. In late October, Golden State Warriors star Stephen Curry met with Jones's family and some of his supporters before a game in Oklahoma City and recorded a message with Tiffany Crutcher: "I'm Stephen Curry and I stand with Julius and his whole family. I pray that justice is served for our brother and that he is a free man soon."[96]

With Jones's Nov. 18 execution date approaching and Stitt still silent, the advocacy increased. Cable news hosts dedicated segments to the case. Protests in Los Angeles, Washington, DC, Newark, and Saint Paul were planned in the event Jones was put to death. High school students in Tulsa and Oklahoma City organized walkouts and supporters flooded the capitol. Nonessential employees were told to go home. The morning of November 18, a cool bright Thursday, activists including Tiffany Crutcher and Greg Robinson began gathering in a vacant lot a few blocks from the prison entrance. Kelli Masters and others who had spoken with Jones the previous evening were convinced he would not be spared.[97]

"We had already prepared that he was going to die," Masters said later.[98]

But shortly after noon came word that Stitt had taken a middle route, commuting Jones's death sentence but keeping him in prison without the possibility of parole and or even the right to future clemency proceedings. Jones's attorneys questioned whether this latter condition could stand up to a legal challenge. Rev. Cece Jones-Davis, a (unrelated) friend of the Joneses, accused Stitt of "torture" for withholding his decision so long. Someone else called the delay a "tool of white supremacy." The *Black Wall Street Times* said the "state prioritizes white family's feelings over the facts." But in the moment the prevalent emotion among Jones's supporters seemed to be relief. A tearful Robinson said, "This is a breakthrough of the human spirit."[99]

"This is just the beginning," said Jones's sister Antoinette, who had become a powerful advocate during his twenty-two years behind bars. "It should not have taken this long. But I thank God that our governor does have a heart and he is a merciful and gracious man. It was not what we asked, it wasn't what the Pardon and Parole Board voted, but God has a reason and I trust God has a process." [100]

Any thought that Jones's case marked a change in Oklahoma's attitude toward the death penalty or criminal justice quickly evaporated. Three weeks after Jones's reprieve, Stitt ignored a Pardon and Parole Board recommendation and allowed the execution of 79-year-old Bigler Jobe Stauffer to proceed. A few demonstrators showed up outside OSP for Stauffer's execution, but not many. Stauffer, convicted in Oklahoma County for a 1985 murder, maintained his innocence to the end. With a federal trial on the legality of Oklahoma's lethal injection protocol scheduled for February, two more executions were scheduled for early 2022.[101]

In some ways, it might be said that Julius Jones and Dick Rowland, the young Black man whose dubious arrest set in motion the events leading to the race massacre, each personified perceptions and stereotypes that were and are remarkably similar. Both were young Black men who fit, or who were described as fitting, the image of aimless Black youths preying on honest, hard-working white people. In both cases, other African Americans rallied around them in the belief that young Black men could not get fair treatment in the system. Opinion may have differed on Jones's and Rowland's guilt or innocence but not on the fairness of the system.

In 1921, a relative handful of Black Tulsans demonstrated their distrust in law enforcement and the courts by arming themselves and going to the Tulsa County Courthouse to protect Dick Rowland. A hundred years ago, this display of what today would be called Second Amendment rights was seen by many whites as an act of rebellion. They called it the "Negro uprising," an affront to the written and unwritten rules that constrained African Americans to one corner of Tulsa and to a lesser share of the liberty and justice that was supposed to be for all. In retaliation, some portion of Tulsa's white population burned Greenwood to the ground and killed anyone who got in the way while the rest of white Tulsa allowed it to happen.

In 2021, Black Oklahomans demonstrated their distrust of the system by again going to a courthouse, figuratively and literally. Instead of firearms, they bore weapons largely inaccessible to Black Tulsans—and, indeed, most Black Americans—a century earlier. They fought back in the court system. They marched. They exercised their First Amendment rights. They mounted a sophisticated media campaign. They did not fear, as Black Tulsans did in 1921, that a Black man would be dragged from a jail or prison cell for summary execution. But they did fear what many think of as legal lynching: the George Floyds and Terence Crutchers and the people imprisoned and sometimes put to death for things they did not do or because they drew the wrong jury or judge or defense lawyer. But all of that and more also happened alongside lynch mobs and night riders and the coordinated torching of Greenwood's homes and businesses in 1921.

Dick Rowland survived the Tulsa Race Massacre. Kept barricaded in the county jail through the night of May 31–June 1, he was eventually released after the assault charge against him was dismissed at the complainant's request. Rowland seems to have left Tulsa soon after, and while many possibilities have been put forward as to where he went and what became of him, none has been conclusively proven. The rest of Greenwood, though, was made to pay for Dick Rowland's freedom and for its insistence that young Black men had a right to just as much justice as white men.

One wonders what price may be exacted for Julius Jones's life. People of color were not Jones's only advocates, but African Americans nevertheless seem more likely to feel the reaction that generally follows a challenge to the status quo. In 2021, no one's house, much less community, was burned. No one was murdered in the streets. But there was a reaction. The system fought back. The legislature tried to curb the Pardon and Parole Board's ability to advocate for clemency as openly as it did in Jones's case. Across the state, discussion of continuing discrimination, inequity, or racism was officially suppressed to the point of criminalization. Diversity, equity, and inclusion were literally banned. These things did not happen just because Julius Jones's life was spared, or even mostly because of it. His case was just one of the events tumbling together in the avalanche of 2020 and 2021. Tulsans looked about themselves, dazed, angry, afraid, relieved, quarrelsome, and despairing, some because things had not changed enough in the last hundred years to suit them, and some because things had changed too much. The same was true in 1921. On the streets of Tulsa, the irresistible force of aspiration collided with the immovable object of entrenched power.

A hundred years later, the struggle continues.

EPILOGUE

Those hoping for a Kumbaya moment were disappointed. So, too, were those who wanted the Tulsa Race Massacre centennial to be something like a final reckoning. The disagreements that led to the unraveling of the Remember and Rise event precluded the former, however attenuated such a moment might have been. The courts, politics, personalities, and the passage of time kept a resolution of the demands for justice, however imprecise, beyond reach.

That is not to say the tumultuous years leading up to the centennial and its immediate aftermath did not have a profound effect on Tulsa, and to some extent the United States. In Tulsa, many other American cities could see a reality show version of themselves, with all of the competing interests and priorities, long-festering grievances, prejudices, and overweening pride, but also the compassion, generosity, patience, and striving for understanding and conciliation.

When asked one year after the centennial if it had been successful, former state senator Judy Eason McIntyre replied, "Yes and no. Yes, the commission . . . and those that were really [involved] were able to a) raise the funds and b) get the museum completed in time. The 'no' part is the fighting within our community over what the money raised was for."[1]

The Remember and Rise event, McIntyre said, "should have been something where we walked hand-in-hand together in our community and within the larger community."[2]

Others thought such a moment would have been dishonest, or at least premature.

At about the same time, state representative Regina Goodwin said:

> The fight for justice is ongoing. That's every day here. The 100th year, that wasn't anything more significant other than the efforts that are ongoing. . . . I still think strides are being made. We're a long way from where we need to be, but the effort is worthwhile.
>
> We had to honor survivors [and] descendants. We also had to commemorate the 100 years of the Race Massacre. I think we did that. But beyond that, I think it's imperative, I think it's a must, that we see justice.
>
> When all the cameras have left, when all of the documentaries are done, we're still left with a community that has been impacted and has been devastated"[3]

Mayor Bynum, while perhaps differing with Goodwin on some solutions and the means to them, offered a similar long-term view in late 2022:

> The centennial wasn't a finish line, it was an inflection point. The work that was being done for years leading up to [the centennial] was important. And the work that will go on for years after that is important. The actual weekend itself was an important inflection point, but I don't believe that there's a missed opportunity there. Some people probably had unrealistic expectations as to what was going to come out of that specific day. The reality is, you don't fix a century-plus of racial disparities on one day just because it's an important day. It takes a long, committed period of community-wide focus.[4]

Unanswered was what would constitute true justice and how the community, however it is defined, is set right. That discussion, on both the ends and the means, continues.

"We have changed hearts and minds," Phil Armstrong said in May 2022. "I get invitations, even to conservative groups, and when I finish there seems to be this sense of relief. They're saying, 'We thought this was just a way to make white people feel guilty for something that happened a hundred years ago.'"[5]

Making white people feel guilty for something that happened long ago may not be the objective, but there is a strong desire to see the books balanced for centuries of exploitation and discrimination. Many people of color want formal acknowledgement that a system constructed to maintain white social, political, and economic dominance still operates today, even if it is not always as obvious as chattel slavery and Jim Crow.

The best strategy for achieving this is disputed. In withering language, the 2020 Greenwood lawsuit sought direct compensation to the families affected by the Tulsa Race Massacre, but also argued for a broader judgment against the people and agencies in power, not only for complicity in the 1921 destruction of Greenwood but for continued inequities ever since. Such a message does not seem likely to win over a majority of Tulsans or Oklahomans. Certainly it did not win over many judges.

In May 2022, Tulsa County District Judge Caroline Wall issued a rather cryptic ruling that kept the Greenwood lawsuit in play, although in what form exactly was unclear. Ruling from the bench, Wall told a courtroom filled with supporters of the lawsuit, including Texas congresswoman Sheila Jackson Lee, only that she was granting defendants' motions to dismiss part of the case but allowing part of it to continue. The immediate reaction of Solomon-Simmons and his team was celebration, and that was only somewhat tempered by Wall's full written order, which she did not issue until three months later. The case, it turned out, had been substantially narrowed. All of the plaintiffs except the three living survivors were ruled out, and only their claims stemming directly from the massacre remained to be considered. The continuing public nuisance argument was disallowed.[6]

This was not what the plaintiffs' attorneys had hoped for but was perhaps still more than they expected, given the history of similar lawsuits. Solomon-Simmons told the *Washington Post*:

> What we found is that people thought this issue was over with after the big party in 2021. That everybody could just sing "Kumbaya." And they would say all types of things about how the massacre still impacts life today.
>
> But once we had a real, live case, then folks were like, "Wait a minute, wait a minute, let's take that back! We're happy to give you murals, we're happy to do park benches, plant unity trees, we're happy to have little discussion panels . . . but you want us to actually give you your land back? You want us to pay you for the property that was destroyed, the businesses that were destroyed, the lives that were destroyed? You want us to say that, yes, we were actually wrong and we need to atone, for real? Oh, we have a problem with this." All of this was obviously coming from the white power structure.

> But also there are Black people, what I like to call "exceptional Negroes," that they put into positions to give them cover. We saw a lot of these exceptional Negroes saying, "Why are you bringing this lawsuit? Why are you making Mister Charlie mad?"
>
> They were saying this would never work. That this was a waste of time or a PR stunt. So it feels really good to be where we are now.[7]

Some who read Wall's order carefully did not think it left the plaintiffs in that good a position. It did not, as some initially supposed, send the case to a discovery stage. It only allowed the plaintiffs to file an amended petition stating a clear case for restitution to the three survivors under the public nuisance law. Later, in their pleadings, defense attorneys would argue that dismissal of the continuing public nuisance claim subjected the remaining claims to the statute of limitations, which would have tolled when the youngest of the three, Hughes Van Ellis, turned twenty-one in 1942.[8]

Solomon-Simmons was also trying to reopen the estate of Dr. A. C. Jackson, the Black surgeon who was the most prominent person killed in the massacre, and in 2023 Solomon-Simmons sued the city of Tulsa and Greenwood Rising on behalf of Jackson's great-nephew and great-great-nephew. Solomon-Simmons and his clients made an interesting argument, namely that Jackson's heirs—essentially great- and great-great-nieces and nephews—should have exclusive rights to Jackson's image and life story. For this reason, they wanted to reopen Jackson's estate—closed since a few years after his death—to accept any income derived from said image and story. These theories ran contrary to just about all precedent in several areas of law, including copyright and probate, but again pressed the question of who controls history. The arguments did not succeed in district court and by mid-2023 were hanging by a pending appeal to the Oklahoma Supreme Court.[9]

So, too, was the Greenwood lawsuit. Late on a Friday in July 2023, Wall issued a two-sentence order dismissing it with prejudice. Disappointed in the decision and angry about the way it was delivered, the plaintiffs asked the state's highest court to overturn Wall, including the earlier motions to dismiss.[10]

In June 2024, the Oklahoma Supreme Court ruled almost unanimously to uphold Judge Wall's dismissal of the Greenwood lawsuit. "Plaintiffs' grievance with the social and economic inequities created by the Tulsa Race Massacre is legitimate and worthy of merit," said the opinion by Vice Chief Justice Dustin Rowe. "However, the law does not permit us to extend the scope of our public nuisance doctrine beyond what the Legislature has authorized." Because the suit argued a matter of state law, an appeal to the US Supreme Court—which had declined to consider the 2003 lawsuit—appeared unlikely.[11]

Nevertheless, the suit pressed compelling and sometimes novel arguments while invigorating those weary of talk and eager for results, not just in Tulsa but nationwide. It would be easy to frame the discussion as what is most just versus what is most achievable, but that is not accurate. There is no agreement on how justice for the race massacre is best served, or how inequity in general is best resolved. Thus, the search for clarity continued along several lines of inquiry as 2021 turned into 2022 and beyond.

In March 2022, after considerable discussion, the city council approved the Beyond Apology proposal from councilor Hall-Harper and Greg Robinson. When several councilors balked, Robinson said regardless of the council's decision "we are going to have the conversations anyway." Privately funded for that very reason, the program consisted of a series of meetings across the city, during which Robinson and others recapped the findings and recommendations of the 2001 report by the Tulsa Race Riot Commission and took comments from the audience. In early 2024, Beyond Apology submitted to the city council a report recommending, among other things, a city commission "to establish and implement the terms of a reparations program." As of June 2024, no action on the recommendation had been taken.[12]

Federal lawsuits challenging House Bills 1775 and 1674, the two state laws adopted in 2021 in response to the George Floyd and Black Lives Matter protests of a year earlier, and the reparations movement remained in limbo. HB 1674, targeting protesters and protest marchers, had no discernable effect in its first two years, but HB 1775 led to Oklahoma State Department of Education accreditation downgrades for the Tulsa and Mustang public school systems. Both actions were taken on what could only be described as very broad interpretations of the law intended to intimidate the state's other 540 districts. Tulsa's case, given the context of the race massacre and the ethnically diverse student body of Tulsa Public Schools (TPS), was particularly vexing: its basis was a single complaint from one teacher about an optional professional development diversity awareness course. The state board of education voted on the matter without reviewing the material but depended on the education department attorney's assessment that the written material was acceptable, but words used by the online instructor were not. A reporter who saw and heard both said they were identical. Later, state Superintendent of Public Instruction Ryan Walters would launch a verbal assault on TPS and threaten to revoke its accreditation altogether. This resulted in TPS Superintendent Deborah Gist, an outspoken critic of Walters and Governor Stitt, leaving her position.[13]

Meanwhile, a Norman teacher resigned under pressure after criticizing state leaders and giving students a QR code for the Brooklyn Public Library so they could access materials targeted by Walters as "pornography." The extent to which HB 1775 stifled honest classroom discussion of race and gender in Oklahoma classrooms during its first two years in statute was difficult to determine, but the capricious enforcement kept teachers and administrators on edge.[14]

US senator James Lankford easily defeated the Trump acolyte and white nationalist Jackson Lahmeyer in the 2022 Republican primary and that fall won a second full term. In 2024, he lent his support to the creation of a national monument designation for the Greenwood District.[15]

Stitt, too, won reelection, despite heavy tribal financial support for his Democratic opponent, Joy Hofmeister—the term-limited state superintendent whom Stitt had effectively driven out of the Republican Party. With G. T. Bynum committed to not seeking reelection, state representative Monroe Nichols—who had declined to run against Bynum in 2018—announced his candidacy for the open seat.

Policing reform, so much in the spotlight just a few years earlier, all but disappeared from the local stage after Julius Jones's commutation. The Crutcher family's federal lawsuit against the city, which sought substantial changes in the Tulsa Police Department, was dismissed in February 2023, leaving only a state wrongful death claim limited by law to $175,000. In dismissing the federal case, the judge said the plaintiffs had failed to present evidence of the training and supervision deficiencies they alleged led to Terence Crutcher's death.[16]

With the city's search for unmarked burials from the race massacre progressing slowly, criticism mounted. Bynum's fiscal year 2023 budget included $1 million for the project, but his commitment to actually advancing the initiative was increasingly questioned. One Oversight Committee member dismissed the entire undertaking as "superficial, cynical, and inadequate."[17]

Another, Kristi Williams, said, "The city's approach to the graves is further proof that we can't trust a process in which the massacre perpetrators are supposed to be investigating themselves."[18]

Not everyone involved shared that view, but Williams voiced a sentiment heard over and over before, during, and after the centennial: the city and state governments of today are just as invested in obfuscation as they were a century ago.

"The assessment of where we are gives the illusion of some effort," state representative Regina Goodwin said. "But it's been many years, and we still don't have any answers to the key questions. Nor do I see any serious attempt to answer them."[19]

By April 2023, DNA samples had been extracted from twenty-two sets of the remains uncovered in Oaklawn Cemetery. Bynum's office said six had been tied to surnames through public genetic databases. In July, additional test excavations were made near the previous site.[20]

One year later, in July 2024, researchers announced the first identification from those efforts, an African American man named C. L. Daniel.[21]

The multitude of economic and community development projects to come out of the chute postpandemic proceeded—or not—at varying paces, fueled in some cases by the Biden administration's postpandemic spending programs. The combined efforts of the George Kaiser Family Foundation (GKFF), the Osage Nation, the city's higher education assets, the chamber of commerce, and others won a $39 million Build Back Better grant to develop an advanced mobility cluster that included a research center at OSU-Tulsa and testing based at an airport owned by the Osages in northwest Tulsa. GKFF was putting $10 million into the project and OSU $6 million, with the expectation of creating up to 40,000 jobs in the first few years. Separately, Tyrance Billingsley II's Black Tech Street announced an agreement involving Microsoft, the University of Tulsa, and Tulsa Community College to train one thousand African American cyber and technical professionals.[22]

On the same day in 2022 that US Commerce Department officials came to town to announce the advanced mobility grant, US Secretary of Housing and Urban Development Marcia Fudge was a few miles north handing $50 million to the Tulsa Housing Authority for the Comanche Park project. Demolition was completed the next year, and work began on a 545-unit mixed income development with a total cost of $190 million, making it one of the largest public-private housing projects in the country. In December 2022, the Tulsa City Council approved the Kirkpatrick Heights-Greenwood master plan for redevelopment of the three parcels on the city's near north side. Developed by the eleven-member leadership committee with input from several hundred community members, the plan included the possibility of a trust to control future ownership of some or all of the land. An $814 million bond package approved by Tulsa voters in 2023 included $5 million to begin implementing the plan.[23]

Redevelopment of the Evans-Fintube site, on the other hand, was back to square one after the local group given first crack at it came apart. Farther north, a planned $75 million development, including a $35 million hotel named for early Black Tulsa businessman and political activist J. B. Stradford, appeared to be moving slowly after a September 2021 groundbreaking. Terry McGee, the retired firefighter and housing developer, died in a swimming accident in the fall of 2022, but his Black Wall Street Square project continued.[24]

A mile and a half away, in the 100 block of North Greenwood Avenue, maintaining what is left of the original Black Wall Street remains a challenge. Occupancy grew as COVID-19 faded but Greenwood Chamber of Commerce President Freeman Culver said near the end of 2022 that even if full, the operation would barely break even. And that is if every tenant is paying. During the worst of COVID, Culver said, some did not for as much as a year.[25]

"They couldn't," he said.[26]

Some tenants complained about rent increases and lagging maintenance. There were a few evictions, which created bad publicity and hard feelings in the community. But the chamber was also able to help others secure grants to keep them going during COVID and to make improvements to the buildings. Culver said 90 percent of occupants are Black-owned businesses, and pointed out that:[27]

> The legacy of Greenwood is alive and well. But people have to understand that legacy is not just for North Tulsa. People across this world are inspired by Black Wall Street. We need to preserve this place. Even if it's one block, we need to preserve this. This is why we worked so hard to get it on the [National Historic Places] registry. But being on the registry doesn't exempt you from property taxes. It doesn't exempt you from paying bills. Yes, we are historic. . . . But I will say it's difficult. This is not a Wall Street. It's a Main Street of small businesses doing their best to survive.[28]

As controversial as they are within the community, Culver said, the adjoining ballpark and Greenwood Rising have been good for his tenants. So has the revitalization to the west, in what is now called the Arts District, and to a lesser extent the opening of the BMX Center to the northeast. But he also has reservations.

"Everything that grows around us is great," Culver said, "but don't squeeze us like a python. We want to grow with you."[29]

Across Archer Street, Kajeer and Maggie Yar have completed a second building, this one between Greenwood Rising and the railroad tracks. Among the early tenants was Juno Medical, a minority-operated group of clinics committed to equity in health care. Investors included tennis star Serena Williams and GKFF affiliate Atento Capital. After only a few months, though, the national financial backers pulled out and the clinic closed. Meanwhile, strictly local tenants such as a prominent law firm and Onikah Asamoah-Caesar's Fulton Street Books moved in.[30]

Brought into focus by the events of 2020, 2021, and after was the growing cadre of professional African Americans and other people of color in positions of influence, and in some cases decision-making, in the economic development and financial sector. Greg Robinson, for one, had concluded that oratory and passion were insufficient to achieve true equity. By 2022, he had ventured into the deal-making realm, and in 2023 Robinson began pursuit of a graduate degree in urban planning and design. He noted that:

> I am very good at convening people. But what I saw was a lack of people of color on the technical side. That's the skill I want, to be able to expand my company in that way, and to be able to build . . . more equitable communities where economic mobility is really built in for everybody. I'm moving from a place of pure organizing, from a policy advocacy perspective, and moving into a more tangible work. I think that's a natural development, right? I don't want to be the one speechifying forever.[31]

As she considered the transitions in her own life and in the world at large, former state senator Judy Eason McIntyre judged herself moderately optimistic despite the recent racial rhetoric and legislation. McIntyre grew up and spent most of her life in North Tulsa, sheltered in her youth by the cocoon of her family and neighborhood, then roused to anger and activism in young adulthood. As a high school student, McIntyre attended the1963 March on Washington that became famous for Martin Luther King Jr.'s "I Have a Dream" speech. A few years later, as a college student fully aware for the first time of the daily indignities of being an African American woman in a white-controlled world, she became involved in the Black Panthers. As a young social worker, she was sent into rural Oklahoma where some of her white clients made clear their distaste for Black people. She married a state senator and later became one herself, served on the Tulsa school board and from time to time got crosswise with all sorts of people on both sides of the literal and figurative tracks running through Tulsa. Hers is a perspective that sees the present in relation to the last days of Jim Crow.[32]

"When you talk about, have I seen any changes—yeah. I really have," she said at the start of 2023. "There's a heightened awareness. Is it where it should be? No, but from early on in my life to now the positive is the heightened awareness of all ages. And this younger generation of white children. Those two things give me hope."[33]

That, McIntyre said, was not the case in the 1960s and 1970s when she first became politically aware.

"I didn't see hope then because everybody yelling back then was the same color as I was, with a sprinkling of others," she said." Now there's awareness, and young people are taking it to wherever they need to go to be heard and to make the necessary changes. There's always going to be racial tension. But back then I saw no hope."[34]

NOTES

Chapter 1. Setting the Scene

1. Annie Karni, "Trump Will Return to Campaign Trail with Rally in Tulsa," *New York Times*, June 11, 2020; "President Trump Tweets That Almost 1 Million People Have Requested Tickets to Saturday's Tulsa Rally," *Tulsa World*, June 15, 2020; Jimmie Tramel, "Juneteenth: Tulsans Gather to Hear Speakers, Enjoy Music and More in Tulsa's Greenwood District," *Tulsa World*, June 19, 2020; Annie Karni, Maggie Haberman, and Reid J. Epstein, "How the Trump Campaign's Plans for a Triumphant Rally Went Awry," *New York Times*, June 18, 2020; Randy Krehbiel, "With Curfew Lifted, Festival Atmosphere Reigns in Downtown Tulsa near Site of Saturday's Trump Campaign Rally," *Tulsa World*, June 20, 2020; Krehbiel, "Trump in Tulsa: President Attacks China, Biden, Others and Touts US Heritage, Improving Economy," *Tulsa World*, June 21, 2020; Toluse Olorunnipa, Josh Dawsey, and Ashley Parker, "Trump's Anger over Tulsa Rally Underscores Growing Problems within His Campaign," *Washington Post*, June 22, 2020.

2. Olorunnipa, Dawsey, and Parker, "Trump's Anger over Tulsa Rally"; Jonathan Karl, *Betrayal: The Final Act of the Trump Show* (New York: Dutton, 2021); Krehbiel, "Trump in Tulsa"; Tom LoBianco, "Trump's Aides Worried about Empty Seats and Desired Air Force One Turn Around before the Tulsa Rally," *Business Insider*, June 23, 2020.

3. LoBianco, "Trump's Aides Worried about Empty Seats."

4. Karni, "Trump Will Return to Campaign Trail"; Paul Sonne, Fenit Nirappil, and Josh Dawsey, "Pentagon Disarms National Guard Activated in D.C., Sends Active-Duty Forces Home," *Washington Post*, June 5, 2020.

5. Kelsy Schlotthauer, "Thousands Flock to Downtown in Support of Black Lives Matter Movement; At Least Two Injured When Crowds Block Traffic on I-244," *Tulsa World*, May 31, 2020; Samantha Vicent, "Brookside Protest in Response to Minnesota Police Violence," *Tulsa World*, May 31, 2020; "Pickup Rolls through Protesters Gathered on Interstate 244; State Troopers Questioning Driver," *Tulsa World*, June 1, 2020; Tim Stanley, "Tulsa Protest Leaders Praise Participants, Disavow 'Rogue' Vandalism from Sunday Night," *Tulsa World*, June 1, 2020; "Brookside Damage: Consignment Store Owner Says Vandals Caused Estimated $10,000 Damage," *Tulsa World*, June 2, 2020; Vicent

and Schlotthauer, "National Guard Embedded with Tulsa Police as Pepper Balls, Tear Gas Deployed at Protesters Near 71st and Memorial on Monday," *Tulsa World*, June 2, 2020; "Two Men Accused of Inciting a Riot Early Wednesday; Another Jailed on Gun Complaints," *Tulsa World*, June 3, 2020.

6. Oklahoma Commission to Study the Tulsa Race Riot of 1921, *Tulsa Race Riot*, Feb. 28, 2001 (hereafter "Race Riot Commission report").

7. Autumn Brown, "We Don't Want Your Hate Rally Here, Trump," *Black Wall Street Times*, June 11, 2020; Andrea Eger, "Juneteenth's Focus Should be on Important Issues, Not Trump's Visit, Legislative Black Caucus Says," *Tulsa World*, June 13, 2020; Stetson Payne, "Tulsa Health Department Director 'Wishes' Trump Rally Would be Postponed as Local COVID Cases Surge," *Tulsa World*, June 13, 2020; Kyle Hinchey, "'I'm Extremely Concerned': Tulsa Health Department Director Doubles Down on Postponing Trump Rally While Addressing Tulsa School Board," *Tulsa World*, June 15, 2020; "Tulsa Mayor G. T. Bynum Says He Won't Attempt to Block Trump Rally," *Tulsa World*, June 16, 2020; Harrison Grimwood and Stetson Payne, "Legal Challenge Seeking to Enforce CDC Guidelines at Trump Rally Sent to State Supreme Court," *Tulsa World*, June 17, 2020; James D. Watts Jr., "'I, Too, Am America' Celebrates Juneteenth with Music, Presentations and More," *Tulsa World*, June 17, 2020; Stanley, "Tulsa Protest Leaders Praise Participants"; Victor Luckerson, "Juneteenth's Legacy," *Oklahoma Eagle*, June 21, 2020; G. T. Bynum (former Tulsa mayor), interviews by author, Tulsa City Hall, Oct. 27, 2022, and Dec. 14, 2022, transcripts in possession of author.

8. Chris Casteel, "Oklahoma Democratic Party Chair: Trump Visit on Juneteenth a Deliberate Insult," *Oklahoman*, June 11, 2020.

9. Casteel, "Oklahoma Democratic Party Chair"; Kendrick Marshall, "Trump Appearance Has Groups in Tulsa Organizing Alternative Gatherings," *Tulsa World*, June 14, 2020; Krehbiel. "Black Tulsans Apprehensive About Possible Trump Visit to Greenwood," *Tulsa World*, June 15, 2020; John Wagner and Colby Itkowitz, "Trump Reschedules Tulsa Rally Amid Criticism over Juneteenth Date," *Washington Post*, June 13, 2020; Michael C. Bender, "Trump Talks Juneteenth, John Bolton, Economy in WSJ Interview," *Wall Street Journal*, June 19, 2020.

10. Krehbiel, "Black Tulsans Apprehensive."

11. Krehbiel, "Black Tulsans Apprehensive."

12. Krehbiel, "Black Tulsans Apprehensive;" Race Riot Commission report; DeNeen L. Brown, "Trump Rally in Tulsa, Site of a Race Massacre, on Juneteenth Was 'Almost Blasphemous,' Historian Says," *Washington Post*, June 13, 2020; Sarah Kerr, Astead W. Herndon, Ben Laffin, and Emily Rhyne, "Why Trump's Tulsa Rally Put the City's Black Residents on Edge," *New York Times*, video, June 21, 2020, https://www.nytimes.com/video/us/100000007188759/trump-rally-juneteenth-tulsa-oklahoma.html.

13. Eger and Krehbiel, "Oklahoma Leaders Lobbied for Republican National Convention, Instead Got Tulsa Campaign Stop on President Trump's Return to the Trail," *Tulsa World*, June 12, 2020.

14. Eger and Krehbiel, "Oklahoma Leaders Lobbied for Republican National Convention."

15. Rhett Morgan, "Quiktrip Closing Some Downtown-area Stores Temporarily Ahead of Trump Rally Out of Concern for Employees," *Tulsa World*, June 17, 2020; Krehbiel, "Jesse Jackson Advises Trump Opponents That Staying Home Saturday is a 'Form of Protest, Too,'" *Tulsa World*, June 18, 2020; "Downtown Small-Business Owners Take Cautious Approach to President Trump's Visit, Weekend Events," *Tulsa World*, June 19, 2020.

16. Krehbiel, "Jesse Jackson Advises Trump Opponents."

17. Krehbiel, "Black Tulsans Apprehensive."

18. Barbara Hoberock, "Gov. Stitt Says He, Sen. Lankford Now Recommending Trump Not Visit Greenwood District," *Tulsa World*, June 18, 2020; Casteel, "Vice President Mike Pence: Tulsa Can Provide Backdrop for Healing Nation," *Oklahoman*, June 20, 2020; Quraysh Ali Lansana (American poet, book editor, civil rights historian, professor), interview with author, Dec. 2, 2022, transcript in possession of author.

19. Krehbiel, "Barring COVID-19 Outbreak, Tulsa Gets Through Potentially Explosive Weekend," *Tulsa World*, June 22, 2020.

20. Race Riot Commission report.

21. Race Riot Commission report; Amanda Coleman, "A Socioeconomic Analysis of the Greenwood District of Tulsa, Oklahoma: 1940–1980" (master's thesis, Oklahoma State University, 2001); Krehbiel, "Through a Century of Hard Work and Heartbreak, the Spirit of Greenwood Labors On," *Tulsa World*, May 19, 2020.

22. James Lankford, "Senator Lankford Speaks on the Tulsa Race Riot on the Senate Floor," streamed live on May 25, 2016, YouTube video, 15:48, https://www.youtube.com/watch?v=Lezj-fjf-hA.

23. Krehbiel, "Tulsa Race Riot Centennial Commission Announced," *Tulsa World*, Feb. 25, 2017.

24. Kevin Matthews (OK state senator), interview with author, Oct. 18, 2022, transcript in possession of author; Krehbiel, "Legislators Organize Mentoring Program for Black Youths," *Tulsa World*, July 30, 2014.

25. Krehbiel, "Tulsa Race Riot Centennial Commission Announced."

26. Krehbiel, "Tulsa Race Riot Centennial Commission Announced."

27. *Fourteenth Census of the United States Taken in the Year 1920: Statistics for Oklahoma* (Washington, DC: Government Printing Office, 1922). https://www.census.gov/programs-surveys/decennial-census/decade/decennial-publications.1920.html.

28. *Fourteenth Census of the United States Taken in the Year 1920: Statistics for Oklahoma*; Polk-Hoffhine 1921 Directory of Tulsa, Okla. (Tulsa: Polk-Hoffine Directory Co., 1921).

29. Danney Goble, *Tulsa! Biography of the American City* (Tulsa, OK: Council Oak Books, 1997), 13–108; "Evans and Bigger Tulsa Ticket Win," *Tulsa World*, April 4, 1920.

30. 2020 Census Demographic Data Map Viewer, https://www.census.gov/library/visualizations/2021/geo/demographicmapviewer.html; Krehbiel, "For the First Time, Less Than Half Tulsa's Population Identifies as Non-Hispanic White," *Tulsa World*, Oct. 11, 2021.

31. 2020 Census Demographic Data Map Viewer; Krehbiel, "For the First Time, Less Than Half.

32. Goble, *Tulsa!*

33. Goble, *Tulsa!*

34. Goble, *Tulsa!*; J. M Hall, *The Beginning of Tulsa* (Tulsa: Tulsa Tribune, 1933); Angie Debo, *From Creek Town to Oil Capital* (Norman: University of Oklahoma Press, 1943).

35. Tulsa Remote, https://tulsaremote.com/; Prithwiraj Choudhury, Evan Starr, and Thomaz Teodorovicz, "Work-From-Anywhere as a Public Policy: 3 Findings From the Tulsa Remote Program," Brookings Institution, Sept. 15, 2022, https://www.brookings.edu/articles/work-from-anywhere-as-a-public-policy-three-findings-from-the-tulsa-remote-program/; Tulsa's Future, https://www.tulsasfuture.com/workforce-and-talent/community-profile; City-Data.com, Tulsa: Economy, https://www.city-data.com/us-cities/The-South/Tulsa-Economy.html; Matt Trotter, "Electric Vehicle Maker Canoo Betting Big on Oklahoma and Northwest Arkansas," Public Radio Tulsa, Nov. 23, 2021; Sarah Wray, "Tulsa Cyber Scheme Includes Training, Childcare and Transport," *Cities Today*, July 7, 2022, https://cities-today.com/tulsa-cyber-scheme-includes-training-childcare-and-transport/; Stanley, "University of Tulsa gets $6.3 Million Grant for Cyber Students," *Tulsa World*, Sept. 9, 2022.

36. "Should Group Social Agencies," *Tulsa World*, Feb. 20, 1921.

37. Kevin Canfield, "Tulsa's Equality Indicators Program Provides Another Tool to Help Improve Tulsans' Lives, Officials Say," *Tulsa World*, April 15, 2018; Community Service Council, "Tulsa Equality Indicators: 2018 Annual Report," https://okvetunited.org/wp-content/uploads/2020/10/Tulsa_Equality_Indicators_Annual_Report_2018_Web.pdf.

38. Canfield, "Tulsa's Equality Indicators Program Provides Another Tool."

39. Jarrel Wade, "Tulsa's Race for Mayor Is On," *Tulsa World*, Nov. 15, 2015; "Bynum Endorsements," *Tulsa World*, June 24, 2016; Wade, "Five Former Mayors Endorse G. T. Bynum in Tulsa Mayoral Race," *Tulsa World*, June 25, 2016.

40. G. T. Bynum, "G. T. Bynum: Get Ready for Great Things, Tulsa," *Tulsa World*, Dec. 4, 2016.

41. Randy Krehbiel, *Tulsa 1921: Reporting a Massacre* (Norman: University of Oklahoma Press, 2019), 221.

42. Krehbiel, *Tulsa 1921*, 221–22.

43. Krehbiel, *Tulsa 1921*, 225.

44. Notice of Letter, May 19, 2017, *State of Oklahoma v. Betty Jo Shelby*, https://bloximages.newyork1.vip.townnews.com/tulsaworld.com/content/tncms/assets/v3/editorial/c/a5/ca50367f-eafb-5bd2-9d6a-13376a618818/591f762569057.pdf.pdf.

45. Krehbiel, *Tulsa 1921*, 226.

46. Corey Jones, "Officer Betty Shelby's Employment Status Being Evaluated by City and Police Department, Police Chief Says," *Tulsa World*, May 18, 2017.

47. Jones, "Officer Betty Shelby's Employment Status."

48. Ginnie Graham, "Crutcher Family Vows 'To Be Part of the Change That All of America Wants to See," *Tulsa World*, June 22, 2017.

49. Graham, "Launch of Terence Crutcher Foundation Coincides with Birthday and Anniversary of His Death," *Tulsa World*, Aug. 14, 2017.

Chapter 2. Priorities and Perspectives

1. Brent Staples, "Unearthing a Riot," *New York Times*, Dec. 19, 1999; Jim Yardley, "Panel Recommends Reparations in Long-Ignored Tulsa Race Riot," *New York Times*, Feb. 5, 2000; Gail Banzet-Ellis, "Q&A with Don Ross," *TulsaPeople Magazine*, Sept. 21, 2018.

2. Banzet-Ellis, "Q&A with Don Ross"; "Don Ross," UNCROWNED™ community builders, accessed April 21, 2024, https://www.uncrownedcommunitybuilders.com/person/don-ross; Race Riot Commission report.

3. "Don Ross"; Jim Myers, "Legislator Wants Confederate Flag Folded," *Tulsa World*, Sept. 6, 1987; Myers. "Tulsan Criticizes Effort to Reinstate Confederate Flag," *Tulsa World*, Jan. 11, 1989; Brian Ford, "Bill to Seek Compromise to Battle Flag Controversy," *Tulsa World*, Oct. 20, 1998; Juanita Crawford Muiga, "Representative Still Leading the Way for Change," *Tulsa World*, Aug. 19, 1998; Adam Kemp, "Confederate Flag History in Oklahoma," *Oklahoman*, June 24, 2015.

4. Rik Espinosa, "Commission Studies Role of Aircraft in Race Riot," *Tulsa World*, March 28, 1999; Krehbiel, "Tulsa Race Riot: Aerial Bombing Claims Disputed," *Tulsa World*, Dec. 23, 2000; Krehbiel, "Black District Not Bombed, Historian Says," *Tulsa World*, Jan. 6, 2001; Krehbiel, "Pilot's Kin Denies He Bombed Area," *Tulsa World*, Feb. 18, 2001; Krehbiel, "Tulsa Race Riot."

5. Race Riot Commission report.

6. *Polk-Hoffhine Directories of Tulsa, Okla.* (Tulsa: Polk-Hoffine Directory Co., 1913–1923).

7. Melanie Poulter, Research and Data Director, Tulsa Area United Way, US Census data analysis provided to author, 2022.

8. Community Service Council, "Tulsa Equality Indicators," 2018–2021 annual reports, https://www.cityoftulsa.org/equality-indicators/full-reports/; Tulsa Police Department interactive crime map, https://maply.com/maps/february-2022?dm=embed&fbclid=IwAR2n6eFttJ8Loh8F-zP8bClQDKakho8v6sqngnqkreeunDCt7DNfIg3hTgw. As of July 2024, the Maply site indicates the map is "no longer accessible to public."

9. Ray Owens (pastor, Metropolitan Baptist Church), interview with author, Oct. 26, 2022, transcript in possession of author. The following account draws on this source until otherwise noted.

10. Robert Turner (pastor, Vernon AME Church), interview with author, Oct. 6, 2022, transcript in possession of author.

11. Turner, interview.

12. Canfield, "Tulsa's Equality Indicators Program Provides Another Tool to Help Improve Tulsans' Lives, Officials Say," *Tulsa World*, April 15, 2018; Community Service Council, "Tulsa Equality Indicators: 2018 Annual Report."

13. Community Service Council, "Tulsa Equality Indicators: 2018 Annual Report." The account in this and the three following paragraphs draws on this source unless otherwise noted

14. Canfield, "Tulsa's Equality Indicators Program."

15. Community Service Council, "Tulsa Equality Indicators: 2018 Annual Report."

16. Canfield, "Resilient Tulsa: Here Are 41 Steps Tulsa Will Take to Become a Stronger, More Equitable City," June 6, 2018; Mayor's Office, City of Tulsa, "Resilient Tulsa: An Equitable, Action-Oriented and Collaborative Road Map for All of Tulsa," June 2018, https://www.cityoftulsa.org/media/7673/reslient-tulsa-digital-web.pdf; Mayor's Office of Resilience and Equity, City of Tulsa, "Resilient Tulsa: Update," Fall 2019, https://www.cityoftulsa.org/media/12029/rt-implementation-update-fall-2019.pdf. Master website: https://www.cityoftulsa.org/government/resilient-tulsa/.

17. "Resilient Tulsa"; "Resilient Tulsa: Update."

18. Tulsa Police Department (TPD) dashboard and body camera video accessed through *Tulsa World* website, "Videos: Tulsa Police Gang Unit Interacts with Individuals at Town Square Apartments on July 9," posted July 16, 2019, https://tulsaworld.com/news/local/videos-tulsa-police-gang-unit-interacts-with-individuals-at-town-square-apartments-on-july-9/article_a6ec5b38-6473-51a2-bd60-7e97de41966f.html; Marshall, "Officers' Interactions with Towne Square Residents Illustrates Differences in Perceptions about Policing," *Tulsa World*, July 22, 2019; Canfield, "Activist Group Calls for Tulsa to Reconsider Community Policing Practices after Towne Square Encounter," *Tulsa World*, July 16, 2022.

19. TPD, "Videos: Tulsa Police Gang Unit Interacts with Individuals"; Canfield, "Activist Group Calls for Tulsa to Reconsider," *Tulsa World*, July 16, 2022; Canfield, "Police Video Released: Mayor Bynum Says They 'Effectively Capture' What He Saw on Ride-along at North Tulsa Apartment Complex," *Tulsa World*, July 13, 2019; Demanding a JUSTulsa, "A Call to Rethink 'Community Policing' in Tulsa," draft, July 14, 2019, https://bloximages.newyork1.vip.townnews.com/tulsaworld.com/content/tncms/assets/v3/editorial/0/bb/0bb487af-34dd-5dfe-950d-b8a6d697e4ce/5d2d15f6210ee.pdf.pdf.

20. Marshall, "Changing the Culture: Tulsa Activists Are Reshaping the Conversation Around Race and Social Justice," *Tulsa World*, July 29, 2019; "Dr. Crutcher's personal journey towards justice and reconciliation," Terence Crutcher Foundation, https://www.terencecrutcherfoundation.org/news/https-terencecrutcherfoundation-org-news-f-dr-crutcher-e2-80-99s-personal-journey-towards-justice-reconciliation; Canfield, "Police Video Released: Mayor Bynum Says They 'Effectively Capture'"; Canfield, "Activist Group Calls for Tulsa to Reconsider"; Demanding a JUSTulsa.

21. TPD, "Videos: Tulsa Police Gang Unit Interacts with Individuals at Town Square Apartments on July 9." Unless otherwise noted, the following account and dialogue also draws on these videos.

22. Marshall, "Officers' Interactions with Towne Square Residents."

23. Canfield, "Tulsa Mayor Describes Seeing Police Officers' Interactions with Black Youths Differently from Speakers at Council Meeting," *Tulsa World*, July 11, 2019.

24. Canfield, "Tulsa Mayor Describes Seeing Police Officers' Interactions."

25. Demanding a JUSTulsa.

26. Canfield, "Tulsa Mayor Describes Seeing Police Officers' Interactions"; Canfield, "Police Video Released: Mayor Bynum Says They 'Effectively Capture'."

27. Canfield, "Tulsa Mayor Describes Seeing Police Officers' Interactions." The account in this and the following two paragraphs draws on this source unless otherwise noted

28. Canfield, "Police Video Released: Mayor Bynum Says They 'Effectively Capture'"; Demanding a JUSTulsa.

29. Marshall, "Changing the Culture: Tulsa Activists Are Reshaping."

30. Marshall, "Officers' Interactions with Towne Square Residents."

31. G. T. Bynum, interviews; Greg Robinson (community advocate and mayoral candidate), interview with author, Dec. 20, 2022, transcript in possession of author; Payne, "Community Leaders, Activists Push for City Hearing, Accountability on Discriminatory Policing," *Tulsa World*, March 7, 2019; Canfield, "Council Hears from Passionate Residents Before Voting to Hold Public Meetings on 2018 Equality Indicators Report," *Tulsa World*, March 13, 2019; Canfield, "Mayor Responds to Criticism from Terence Crutcher's Sister with Frustration about Portrayal of Police," *Tulsa World*, March 14, 2019; Damario Solomon-Simmons to G. T. Bynum, letter, March 14, 2019, copy in possession of author (hereafter Solomon-Simmons to Bynum).

32. Canfield, "Police Use-of-force Incidents Need Outside Scrutiny, Mayor Says in Proposing Independent Monitor," *Tulsa World*, Jan. 17, 2022; Canfield, "Police Union to Bynum: 'Negotiate with FOP to Create Independent Monitor or Face Lawsuit,'" *Tulsa World*, Jan. 26, 2019; Payne, "Community Leaders, Activists Push for City Hearing, Accountability on Discriminatory Policing," *Tulsa World*, March 7, 2019; Canfield, "Mayor Responds to Criticism"; Canfield, "Mayor Bynum Explains That Controversial OIM Plan Would Do More Than Investigate Police Incidents, Isn't Anti-police," *Tulsa World*, July 1, 2019.

33. *Crutcher v. City of Tulsa, et al*, Northern District of Oklahoma, 17-CV-336-TCK-FHM; Bynum, interviews.

34. Payne, "Community Leaders, Activists Push for City Hearing"; Canfield, "Council Hears from Passionate Residents"; Canfield, "Mayor Responds to Criticism"; Solomon-Simmons to Bynum.

35. Canfield, "City Council Scheduled to Vote on Holding Public Meetings on Equality Indicators Report," *Tulsa World*, March 9, 2019.

36. Canfield, "Council Hears from Passionate Residents."

37. Canfield, "Mayor Responds to Criticism"; Solomon-Simmons to Bynum.

38. TPD, "Videos: Tulsa Police Gang Unit Interacts with Individuals."

Chapter 3. The Plague Year

1. Grimwood, "State's First COVID-19 Death is a Tulsa County Man Who Had Only Tested Positive a Day Earlier," *Tulsa World*, March 19, 2020; Eger, "Wife Of Oklahoma's First Fatal Case Speaks: 'By The Time We Knew It Was COVID-19, His Lungs Were Already Compromised to the Point of No Return,'" *Tulsa World*, April 12, 2020.

2. Eger, "Wife of Oklahoma's First Fatal Case Speaks.'"

3. Centers for Disease Control and Prevention, https://www.cdc.gov/museum/timeline/covid19.html.

4. Jones, "Oklahoma's First Coronavirus Case Is a Tulsa County Resident Recovering Under Isolation at Home," *Tulsa World*, March 7, 2020.

5. Jones, "Oklahoma's First Coronavirus Case."

6. Jones, "Oklahoma's First Coronavirus Case."

7. Hoberock, "Governor Faces Social Media Backlash Following Tweet at Eating Establishment," *Tulsa World*, March 15, 2020; Schlotthauer, "Gov. Kevin Stitt Declares State of Emergency Following Eighth Case of Coronavirus," *Tulsa World*, March 15, 2020; Joe Mussatto, "'Don't Let Them Tip the Ball': Oral History of How COVID Dashed March 11 Thunder-Jazz Game," *Oklahoman*, March 10, 2021; Krehbiel, "Stitt, Hofmeister Make Their Cases for Oklahoma Governor on Dramatically Different Terms," Oct. 2, 2022; Krehbiel, "Stitt Promises Tax Cuts, 'True School Choice' in Second Term," *Tulsa World*, Jan. 7, 2023.

8. Executive Order No. 2020–02, Office of the Mayor, City of Tulsa, Oklahoma, accessed through *Tulsa World* archives, https://tulsaworld.com/document-executive-order-closing-tulsa-restaurants-bars-etc/pdf_7d74889e-ffce-5574-92a8-b6225bfb1151.html; Canfield, "Update: Mayor Orders Tulsa Restaurants, Bars to Close Tonight; Drive-through, Take-out Establishments May Operate," *Tulsa World*, March 17, 2020; G. T. Bynum, "Mayor G. T. Bynum: Bad Part of Pandemic is Yet to Come, but There Are Three Reasons for Optimism," *Tulsa World*, March 31, 2020; Paul Monies, "As Pandemic Widens, Oklahoma Diminishes State Epidemiologist Role," *Oklahoma Watch*, Aug. 3, 2020; Bob Cusack, "Exclusive: Internal Documents Show Officials Waved Red Flags Before Trump's Tulsa Rally," *The Hill*, Sept. 16, 2020; Canfield, "Mayor Bynum Says He's Taking Obama's Advice about Asking Experts Questions in a Crisis," *Tulsa World*, April 16, 2020; Jones, "State Epidemiologist's Analysis Demonstrates Success of Local Mask Ordinances," *Tulsa World*, Nov. 2, 2020; Monies, "After 1,600 Deaths and Counting, Mask Mandate Remains Flashpoint in Oklahoma," *Oklahoma Watch*, Nov. 24, 2020; Kevin Stitt, OKLAHOMA GOV: I Agree With Gov. Abbott—That's Why Oklahoma Reopened Last Summer," *Daily Caller*, March 3, 2021; Schlotthauer, "Watch Now: While State Envisions Return to Normalcy by Summer as Stitt Plans to Lift Virus Restrictions, Experts Caution 'We Are Not There Yet,'" *Tulsa World*, March 12, 2021; Trevor Brown, "Capitol Watch: As Doctors Call For 'All Hands On Deck,' Stitt Remains Largely Quiet on COVID-19 Vaccinations, Rising Cases," *Oklahoma Watch*, Aug. 31, 2021; "Three Key State Health Department Resignations Were Unrelated to Commissioner's Exit, Interim Leader Says," *Tulsa World*, Oct. 28, 2021.

9. Canfield, "Update: Mayor Orders Tulsa Restaurants, Bars to Close Tonight."

10. Schlotthauer, "Stillwater Joins List of Oklahoma Cities Ordering Residents to Shelter in Place, *Tulsa World*, March 30, 2020; "Gov. Stitt Extends Executive Order Through April 30; Says State Peak May be Late April," *Tulsa World*, April 1, 2020; Vicent and Grimwood, "Broken Arrow Ends Emergency Proclamation Following Governor's 'Bounce Back' Plan; Bixby Weighing Options," *Tulsa World*, April 23, 2020; "'Tulsa's Cases Will Not Go Down, They Will Increase,' Mayor Says as Safer-at-home Order Ends April 30," *Tulsa World*, April 24, 2020.

11. "'Tulsa's Cases Will Not Go Down, They Will Increase.'"

12. "'Tulsa's Cases Will Not Go Down, They Will Increase.'"

13. Bynum, interview, Dec. 14, 2022.

14. Bynum, interview, Dec. 14, 2022.

15. "COVID-19: Infections Peak Again for Tulsa County, Oklahoma with More Than 200 New Cases Reported," *Tulsa World*, June 13, 2020; Hoberock, "Gov. Stitt Q&A on Trump Rally in Tulsa: A Venue Change? A Tour of Greenwood? The Danger of COVID?," *Tulsa World*, June 15, 2020; Brian Stelter, "Trump Says Coronavirus Is 'Dying Out;' Dr. Sanjay Gupta Says the Virus Is Not Dying," *CNN Business*, June 18, 2020; Marshall, "Gov. Stitt Says Trump Rally Attendees 'Have Freedom to Stay Home' if Concerned about Contracting COVID-19," *Tulsa World*, June 19, 2020; Bynum, interview, Dec. 14, 2022.

16. Bynum, interview, Dec. 14, 2022. Until otherwise noted, the following account also draws on this interview.

17. Canfield, "Tulsa City Councilors Approve Face Mask Ordinance," *Tulsa World*, July 16, 2020.

18. Election Results, Oklahoma State Election Board, https://oklahoma.gov/elections/elections-results/election-results.html; Casteel, "Trump's Oklahoma County Squeaker, Horn's Grady County Connection and 3 Other Things about the Election," *Oklahoman*, Nov. 15, 2020.

19. Krehbiel, "Trump Embraces 'Angry' Voters at Boisterous Tulsa Rally," *Tulsa World*, Jan. 21, 2016; Wade. "Donald Trump's Rowdy Tulsa Rally: Six Ingredients That Added Flavor," *Tulsa World*, Jan. 21, 2016; Nour Habib, "Area High Schoolers Among Protesters Booted from Trump Rally," *Tulsa World*, Jan. 22, 2016.

20. Amber Integrated, "Amber Integrated Quarterly Poll: Voter Attitudes on Elections, Coronavirus, and Law Enforcement in Oklahoma," Sept. 25, 2020, https://www.amberintegrated.com/news/2020/9/25/amber-integrated-quarterly-poll-voter-attitudes-on-elections-coronavirus-and-law-enforcement-in-oklahoma-88m5c; Casteel. "Poll: Trump, Inhofe Hold Double-Digit Leads Among Likely Oklahoma Voters," *Oklahoman*, Sept. 25, 2020; Election Results, Oklahoma State Election Board.

21. Karni, "Trump Will Return to Campaign Trail with Rally in Tulsa"; Karl, *Betrayal: The Final Act of the Trump Show.*

22. Karl, *Betrayal*; Eger and Krehbiel. "Oklahoma Leaders Lobbied for Republican National Convention"; "Did Oklahoma City Mayor Reject Trump Rally in That City?" *Tulsa World*, June 15, 2020; Hoberock, "Gov. Stitt Q&A on Trump Rally in Tulsa: A Venue Change? A Tour of Greenwood? The Danger of COVID?"; Election Results, Oklahoma State Election Board.

23. Karl, *Betrayal*; Eger and Krehbiel, "Oklahoma Leaders Lobbied for Republican National Convention"; "Did Oklahoma City Mayor Reject Trump Rally in That City?"; Hoberock, "Gov. Stitt Q&A on Trump Rally in Tulsa"; Curtis Killman, "BOK Operator: City, State Officials Notified as Soon as Trump Rally Request Was Received," *Tulsa World*, June 19, 2020; "BOK Center Nominated for Arena of the Year by Pollstar for the 9th Time in Building History," BOK Center, Nov. 19, 2021, https://www.bokcenter.com/news/bok-center-nominated-for-arnea-of-the-year-by-pollstar-for-the-9th-time-in-building-history/.

24. "Trump Rally Attendees in Tulsa Cannot Sue if They Contract COVID-19 at the Event," *Tulsa World*, June 12, 2020; Brooke Singman, "Trump Campaign Touts 1 Million Ticket Requests for Tulsa Rally," *Fox News*, June 15, 2020.

25. Virginia Heffernan, "'Bad Idea' Doesn't Begin to Describe Trump's Tulsa Rally," *Los Angeles Times*, June 18, 2020.

26. Karni, "Trump Will Return to Campaign Trail"; Colbert I. King, "The Most Racist President in Modern History Revels in Violence," *Washington Post*, June 12, 2020; Brown, "Trump Rally in Tulsa."

27. Karni, "Trump Will Return to Campaign Trail."

28. Morgan Phillips, "McEnany Hits Media for Health Concerns Over Rally: 'You Should Exhibit That Same Concern for the Protesters,'" *Fox News*, June 17, 2020; Brie Stimson, "Tulsa Mayor Declares Civil Emergency Ahead of Trump Rally, Stragglers Face Arrest," *Fox News*, June 19, 2020.

29. Hoberock, "Gov. Stitt Q&A on Trump Rally in Tulsa."

30. Krehbiel, "Stitt, Hofmeister Make Their Cases for Oklahoma Governor on Dramatically Different Terms."

31. Hoberock, "Gov. Stitt Q&A on Trump Rally in Tulsa."

32. Payne, "Tulsa Health Department Director 'Wishes' Trump Rally Would Be Postponed as Local COVID Cases Surge," *Tulsa World*, June 13, 2020; Hinchey, "'I'm Extremely Concerned': Tulsa Health Department Director Doubles Down on Postponing Trump Rally While Addressing Tulsa School Board," *Tulsa World*, June 15, 2020; Noah Weiland, "Tulsa Officials Plead for Trump to Cancel Rally as Virus Spikes in Oklahoma," *New York Times*, June 16, 2020.

33. Payne, "Tulsa Health Department Director 'Wishes' Trump Rally Would Be."

34. Hinchey, "'I'm Extremely Concerned.'"

35. Weiland, "Tulsa Officials Plead for Trump to Cancel Rally."

36. Killman, "Oklahoma Supreme Court Denies Last-Ditch Appeal Seeking to Enforce COVID-19 Protocols at Trump Rally," *Tulsa World*, June 19, 2020; "Joshua Partlow, "Threats and Invective Hurled at Health Director Who Sought to Postpone Trump's Tulsa Rally, Emails Show," *Washington Post*, Sept. 21, 2020.

37. Killman, Oklahoma Supreme Court Denies Last-Ditch Appeal."

38. Krehbiel, "Trump in Tulsa: President Attacks China, Biden, Others"; Marshall, "Virginia Man Who Wanted to Intimidate Mayor Bynum into Canceling Trump Rally Charged with Cyberstalking," *Tulsa World*, July 18, 2020.

39. "Letters to the editor," *Tulsa World*, June 26, 2020.

40. Bynum, interview, Dec. 14, 2022.

41. Bynum, interview, Dec. 14, 2022; Killman, "BOK Operator: City, State Officials Notified as Soon as Trump Rally Request Was Received."

42. Killman, "BOK Operator: City, State Officials Notified." The account in this and the following two paragraphs draws on this source.

43. Canfield, "Bynum Says He Told BOK Center Officials He Would Back Decision to not Hold Trump's Rally," *Tulsa World*, June 23, 2020.

44. Bynum, interview, Dec. 14, 2022; Krehbiel, "With Curfew Lifted, Festival Atmosphere Reigns in Downtown Tulsa Near Site of Saturday's Trump Campaign Rally," *Tulsa World*, June 19, 2020; Mayor GT Bynum, Facebook post, https://www.facebook.com/gtbynumfortulsamayor/posts/2564708683857844?__tn__=K-R.

45. Bynum interview, Dec. 14, 2022.

46. Bynum interview, Dec. 14, 2022.

47. Marshall, "Black Wall Street Memorial Covered to Protect Against Presidential 'Photo Ops,'" *Tulsa World*, June 20, 2020; Watts, "Anticipation of the Rally Weekend Inspired Art; At the Peaceful Conclusion Tulsans Danced," *Tulsa World*, June 28, 2020.

48. Lansana, interview.

49. Lansana, interview.

50. Marshall, "Trump Appearance Has Groups in Tulsa Organizing Alternative Gatherings," *Tulsa World*, June 14, 2020; Watts, "'I, Too, Am America' Celebrates Juneteenth with Music, Presentations and More"; Watts, "Rev. Al Sharpton Challenges Trump to Deal With Racism; Juneteenth Organizers Say Sharpton Got Death Threats in Tulsa," *Tulsa World*, June 20, 2020; Tramel, "Tulsa's Juneteenth Celebration Provides Outlet for Fun, Activism, *Tulsa World*, June 20, 2020."

51. Luckerson, "Juneteenth's Legacy"; "President Trump Tweets at 'Protesters, Anarchists, Agitators, Looters or Lowlifes' Today Before Tulsa Rally," *Tulsa World*, June 19, 2020.

52. Lansana, interview; Krehbiel, "Black Tulsans Apprehensive."

53. Michael Overall, "Watch Now: Downtown Turns into Surreal Alternative to Mayfest with Trump Merchandise, Protesters," *Tulsa World*, June 21, 2020.

54. Overall, "Watch Now: Downtown Turns into Surreal Alternative."

55. Bynum, interview, Dec. 14, 2022. The account in this and the following two paragraphs draws on this source unless otherwise noted

56. Karl, *Betrayal*; Michale D. Shear, Maggie Haberman, and Astead W. Herndon, "Trump Rally Fizzles as Attendance Falls Short of Campaign's Expectations," *New York Times*, June 20, 2020; Dave Brooks, "In Tulsa, Trump Campaign Subverted Social Distancing One Sticker at a Time," *Billboard*, June 26, 2020.

57. Krehbiel, "Trump in Tulsa: President Attacks"; Giovanni Russonello, "Trump's Tulsa Rally Attendance: 6,200, Fire Dept. Says," *New York Times*, June 22, 2020; Mark Joyella, "8 Million Viewers Watch Fox News Coverage of Trump's Tulsa Rally," *Forbes*, June 22, 2020; Shane Goldmacher and Rachel Shorey, "Trump's Tulsa Rally Drew Sparse Crowd, but It Cost $2.2 Million," *New York Times*, Aug. 17, 2020; Bynum, interview, Dec. 14, 2022.

58. Eugene Daniels, "Trump Campaign Blames Protesters for Disappointing Turnout at Tulsa Rally," *Politico*, June 20, 2020; Jones, "Tulsa Police Arrest Local Teacher in 'I Can't Breathe' Shirt for Obstruction After Trump's Campaign Asked Officers to Remove Her," *Tulsa World*, June 21, 2020; Ziva Branstetter, "Art Teacher Arrested at Trump Rally Plans to Fight Charge," *Washington Post*, June 21, 2020; Killman, "Photojournalist Says Trump Rally Arrest Unjustified," *Tulsa World*, June 24, 2020.

59. Felicia Sonmez, Josh Dawsey, and Taylor Telford, "Trump Campaign, Democrats Joust Over Tulsa Rally Turnout," *Washington Post*, June 21, 2020.

60. Bynum, interview, Dec. 14, 2022.

61. Bynum, interview, Dec. 14, 2022.

62. Bob Jack (Tulsa County GOP Party chair), interview with author, Oct. 10, 2022, transcript in possession of author.

63. Taylor Lorenz, Kellen Browning, and Sheera Frenkel, "TikTok Teens and K-Pop Stans Say They Sank Trump Rally," *New York Times*, June 21, 2020.

64. Jack, interview.

65. Tulsa City Ordinance 24408, https://www.cityoftulsa.org/media/13782/ordinance-no-24408-face-covering-and-social-distancing-during-pandemic-ordinance.pdf.

66. Bynum, interview, Dec. 14, 2022.

67. "How an Act of Racial Violence Reverberates Across Generations," *CBS News*, June 7, 2020; Eger, "Tulsa Mayor Apologizes for His 'Dumb And Overly-Simplistic' Comment on Terence Crutcher Killing," *Tulsa World*, June 11, 2020.

68. Luckerson, "Tulsa's Hopeful Anger," *New Yorker*, June 16, 2020; Eger, "Tulsa Mayor Apologizes."

69. "Mayor Condemns Tulsa Police Major's Comments; State Representative Calls for His Firing; Police Chief Reviewing Situation," *Tulsa World*, June 10, 2020.

70. "Activist, Ex-candidate Greg Robinson Dies," *Tulsa World*, Jan. 24, 2003; "Pastor Who Helped Lead Saturday's Protest Issues Statement in Response to Mayor G. T. Bynum," *Tulsa World*, May 31, 2020.

71. Turner, interview; Race Riot Commission report.

72. "Mayor Bynum Says 'No,' Ignoring Black Constituents' Concerns Over LIVE PD's Exploitative Nature," *Black Wall Street Times*, Jan. 9, 2020; Canfield, "As Critics Urge Against 'Live PD' in Tulsa, Mayor Stands Behind Participating in the Show," *Tulsa World*, Jan. 13, 2020; Schlotthauer, "Innocent Tulsans Featured on 'Live PD' Lament Becoming Entertainment Fodder in Name of Police Transparency," *Tulsa World*, Feb. 17, 2020; Robinson, interview.

73. Stanley, "Watch Now: 'Angered and Devastated': Pastors, Other Leaders in Tulsa's Black Community React to George Floyd Death in Minnesota," *Tulsa World*, May 29, 2020.

74. Vicent, "Brookside Protest in Response to Minnesota Police Violence."

75. Vicent, "Brookside Protest in Response."

76. Bynum, interview, Oct. 27, 2022.

77. Vicent, "Brookside Protest in Response."

78. Vicent, "Brookside Protest in Response."

79. Marshall, "'Change Can Take Place': Tiffany Crutcher Talks Protests, Progress in Tulsa," *Tulsa World*, June 7, 2020.

80. Mayor GT Bynum, Facebook Post, May 30, 2020, https://www.facebook.com/gtbynumfortulsamayor/posts/2550779351917444/; Vicent, "Brookside Protest in Response."

81. "Pastor Who Helped Lead Saturday's Protest."

82. "Splendid New Colored Church Opened Today," *Tulsa World*, April 10, 1921; Krehbiel, "Land OK'd for Race Riot Memorial Museum," *Tulsa World*, Feb. 22, 2003;

Krehbiel, "Tulsa Race Riot Museum to Start Small," *Tulsa World*, Sept. 5, 2003; Krehbiel, "City to Break Ground on Park, Finally," *Tulsa World*, Nov. 8, 2008; Marshall, "'Signs of Gentrification': Greenwood Community Worries Residents Being Pushed Out, History Disrespected," *Tulsa World*, June 16, 2019; Krehbiel, "Through a Century of Hard Work and Heartbreak, the Spirit of Greenwood Labors On," *Tulsa World*, May 19, 2021.

83. Schlotthauer, "Thousands Flock to Downtown in Support of Black Lives Matter Movement; At Least Two Injured When Crowds Block Traffic on I-244"; Schlotthauer, "Protest Updates: Police Deploy Tear Gas, Pepper Balls for 2nd Time as Protesters Continue Marching in Brookside," *Tulsa World*, June 1, 2020; "Watch Now: Oklahoma House Passes Bill to Protect Drivers Who Hit Protesters," *Tulsa World*, March 10, 2021; Enrolled House Bill 1674, 58th Oklahoma Legislature, https://www.oklegislature.gov; Killman, "Man Paralyzed at 2020 BLM Rally Sues City of Tulsa, Oklahoma Highway Patrol and Pickup Driver," *Tulsa World*, Feb 16, 2022; Ezekiel J. Walker, "Man Who Fell Off Highway During BLM Protest Sues City of Tulsa, OHP," *Black Wall Street Times*, Feb. 18, 2022.

84. Schlotthauer, "Protest Updates: Police Deploy Tear Gas."

85. Schlotthauer, "Protest Updates: Police Deploy Tear Gas"; "Watch Now: Police Deploy Tear Gas, Pepper Balls During Standoff With Protesters in Brookside Sunday Night, Early Monday," *Tulsa World*, May 31, 2022; "Tulsa Protests Lead to Tense Moments with Police, Tear Gas and Vandalism," KTUL, May 31, 2022.

86. "Watch Now: Police Deploy Tear Gas"; Stanley, "Tulsa Protest Leaders Praise Participants."

87. "Watch Now: Police Deploy Tear Gas."

88. Schlotthauer, "Protest Updates: Police Deploy Tear Gas"; "Watch Now: Police Deploy Tear Gas"; Luckerson, "Tulsa's Hopeful Anger"; Bynum, interview, Oct. 27, 2022.

89. Stanley, "Tulsa Protest Leaders Praise Participants."

90. Stanley, "Tulsa Protest Leaders Praise Participants."

91. Canfield, "Watch Now: After Protests, Tulsa Mayor, Advocates for Police Reform Agree to Work Together for Substantial Changes," *Tulsa World*, June 2, 2020.

92. Canfield, "Watch Now: After Protests, Tulsa Mayor."

93. Canfield, "Watch Now: After Protests, Tulsa Mayor."

94. Canfield, "Watch Now: After Protests, Tulsa Mayor"; Krehbiel. "There's a Reason Why Firing Police Officers Can Be Complicated," *Tulsa World*, June 15, 2020.

95. Canfield, "Watch Now: After Protests, Tulsa Mayor."

96. Krehbiel, "There's a Reason Why Firing Police Officers Can Be Complicated."

97. Canfield, "FOP Says It Still Opposes Mayor's Plan for Police Oversight," *Tulsa World*, Aug. 13, 2019; Canfield, "What Happened to Mayor Bynum's Police Oversight Proposal? Tulsa City Council Not Completely Sold on It," Sept. 19, 2019; Canfield, "Latest Proposal for Tulsa Police Oversight Dies in City Council Procedural Vote, *Tulsa World*, March 5, 2020; Canfield, "Tulsa Police Union Opposes Mayor's Renewed Effort to Create Oversight Program," June 3, 2020; Canfield, "Police Oversight: Mayor Bynum Opts for Different Direction, Won't Pursue Denver Model," Aug. 19, 2020.

98. Canfield, "Police Oversight: Mayor Bynum Opts for Different Direction"; Canfield, "TPD, Union Using Incident Involving Judge to Smear Councilor's Police Officer Husband, Vanessa Hall-Harper Claims," *Tulsa World*, March 10, 2019.

99. Canfield, "Police Union Leader Explains How Organization 'Flipped the Vote' on City Council's Oversight Proposal," *Tulsa World*, June 14, 2020.

100. Michael Dekker, "Mayor Bynum, Black Officers Coalition Leader Respond to Video of Officers Handcuffing Black Teens After Jaywalking," *Tulsa World*, June 11, 2020; Payne, "Tulsa Police Release Details About Juvenile Jaywalking Arrest," *Tulsa World*, June 13, 2020; "Charge Filed Against Security Guard in Fatal Shooting Outside Motel," *Tulsa World*, June 11, 2020; Katie Mettler and Brittany Shammas, "Tulsa Motel Guard's Deadly Encounter With Guest Raises Issues Of Race, Private-Security Oversight," *Washington Post*, June 19, 2020; Stanley, "Watch Now: 'We Can't Keep Quiet Anymore': Tulsa Ministers, Faith Leaders Unite for Prayer March on City Hall," *Tulsa World*, June 9, 2020; Schlotthauer, "Prison Term Set for Security Guard Who Claimed Self-Defense in Pepper-Spraying, Fatal Shooting of East Tulsa Motel Guest," *Tulsa World*, March 24, 2022.

101. Stanley, "Watch Now: 'We Can't Keep Quiet Anymore.'"

102. Krehbiel, "Watch Now: Bynum Critics Put Forward a Candidate for Mayoral Race Aug. 25," *Tulsa World*, June 11, 2020.

103. Rose Ann Pearce, "'80s State Newsmakers: Where Are They?," *Tulsa Tribune*, Dec. 29, 1989.

104. Robinson, interview.

105. Stanley, "'Unity Is What We've Been Craving': Mayoral Candidate Ricco Wright Talks About His Vision for a Better Tulsa," *Tulsa World*, June 13, 2020; Canfield, "Mayoral Candidate and Black Wall Street Restaurant Owner Ty Walker Outlines His Priorities," *Tulsa World*, June 24, 2020; "Dr. Ricco Wright Ends Candidacy for Tulsa Mayor Amid Sexual Assault Allegations," KJRH, July 3, 2020.

106. Dylan Goforth, "Mayors of Oklahoma's Largest Cities Reflect on the Challenges of Responding to a Politically Charged Pandemic," *The Frontier*, June 7, 2021.

107. Rfein Rios, "You're Not Coming to Bring Us Justice. So What Are You Coming For?" *Mother Jones*, June 19, 2020.

108. Krehbiel, "Watch Now: Bynum Critics Put Forward."

109. Robinson, interview; Canfield, "As G. T. Bynum Goes for Second Mayoral Term Tuesday, Greg Robinson Seeks to Upend Him," *Tulsa World*, Aug. 20, 2020.

110. Robinson, interview.

111. Canfield, "As G. T. Bynum Goes for Second Mayoral Term."

112. Canfield, "As G. T. Bynum Goes for Second Mayoral Term."

113. Robinson, interview.

114. Bynum, interview, Dec. 14, 2022.

115. Robinson, interview.

116. Robinson, interview.

117. Jack, interview.

Chapter 4. Seeking Justice

1. Canfield, "Mass Graves from the 1921 Tulsa Race Massacre? Mayor Plans to Re-examine the Issue," *Tulsa World*, Oct. 2, 2018; Krehbiel, "Mayor G.T. Bynum Hopes to Have Burial Search Plan by First of Year," *Tulsa World*, Oct. 15, 2018; Canfield, "For Tulsa Mayor, Race Massacre Mass Graves Investigation Is 98 Years too Late, But Still Absolutely Necessary," May 30, 2021.

2. Canfield, "Mass Graves from the 1921 Tulsa Race Massacre?"

3. Brown, "They Was Killing Black People," *Washington Post*, Sept. 28, 2018. Turner, interview; J. Kavin Ross, "Mayor's Mass Grave Investigation|Tulsans Seek Transparency," *Black Wall Street Times*, Oct. 10, 2018; Mayor G T Bynum, Facebook post, Oct. 2, 2018, https://www.facebook.com/gtbynumfortulsamayor/photos/a.1597023863959669/2090781074583943/?type=3.

4. Turner, interview. Until otherwise noted, the following account also draws on this interview.

5. Turner, interview; Ross, "Mayor's Mass Grave Investigation"

6. Turner, interview; Ross, "Mayor's Mass Grave Investigation; Brown, "They Was Killing Black People.

7. Turner, interview; Ross, "Mayor's Mass Grave Investigation; Brown, "They Was Killing Black People.

8. Turner, interview.

9. Race Riot Commission report; "Dead Estimated at 100; City is Quiet," *Tulsa World*, June 2, 1921; Walter White, "The Eruption of Tulsa," *The Nation*, June 29, 1921.

10. "Nine Whites and 68 Blacks Slain in Race War," *Tulsa Tribune*, June 1, 1921; "Bulletins," *Tulsa Tribune*, June 1, 1921.

11. "Dead Estimated at 100; City is Quiet."

12. "Search Cuts Known Death List to 27," *Tulsa Tribune*, June 2, 1921.

13. "Riot Death Toll Reduced to 30 by Re-checking," *Tulsa World*, June 3, 1921; Race Riot Commission report.

14. Bob Hower, ed., *1921 Tulsa Race Riot and the American Red Cross, "Angels of Mercy,"* Tulsa Homestead Press, 1993; White, "The Eruption of Tulsa"; James Leighton Avery, interview, c.a. 1982, Ruth Sigler Avery-Tulsa Race Massacre Collection, Series 1: Tulsa Race Massacre of 1921, Special Collections and Archives, OSU-Tulsa Library, Oklahoma State University, Tulsa (hereafter Avery Collection).

15. Scott Ellsworth, *Death in a Promised Land*, Baton Rouge: Louisiana State University Press, 1982; Ellsworth, *The Ground Breaking: An American City and its Search for Justice*, New York: E. P. Dutton, 2021; Race Riot Commission report; Phillip Rees, interview with author, March 10, 2000, transcript in possession of author; Robert H. Patty, interview with author, June 13–14, 2000, transcript in possession of author; Andrew Wilkes and Margaret Wilsey, interview by Ruth Sigler Avery, July 6, 1972, Avery Collection.

16. Stanley, "50 Years Ago, the 1921 Tulsa Race Massacre Was a Taboo Subject When Tulsan Ed Wheeler Set Out to Write an Article 'To Find Out What Happened.' He

Had No Idea the Threats and Resistance He Would Face Just for Trying," *Tulsa World*, April 12, 2021; Ellsworth, *Death in a Promised Land*; Ellsworth, *The Ground Breaking*; Race Riot Commission report.

17. Ellsworth, *The Ground Breaking;* Krehbiel, "Tulsa Race Riot Commission Looked for Mass Graves 20 Years Ago; Here's What Happened," *Tulsa World*, Oct. 14, 2018.

18. Ellsworth, *The Ground Breaking;* Krehbiel, "Tulsa Race Riot Commission Looked for Mass Graves."

19. Ellsworth. *The Ground Breaking;* Krehbiel, "Tulsa Race Riot Commission Looked for Mass Graves; Ross, "Mayor's Mass Grave Investigation|Tulsans Seek Transparency"; Krehbiel, "Graves Stir Calls for Inquiry," *Tulsa World*, June 30, 2004; Krehbiel, "Headstones Baffle Developer," *Tulsa World*, April 21, 2004.

20. Krehbiel, "Focus: 'Black Indians' Find Roots Well-Hidden," *Tulsa World*, Feb. 4, 2002; Krehbiel, "Family Pasts Fading Away Over Decades, *Tulsa World*, Feb. 4, 2002; Larry O'Dell, "All-Black Towns," *Encyclopedia of Oklahoma History and Culture*, Jan. 15, 2010, https://www.okhistory.org/publications/enc/entry.php?entry=AL009.

21. Amy Latham, "Rentie Grove's Demise," *Tulsa World*, Feb. 16, 1997; Krehbiel, "Graves Stir Calls for Inquiry"; Krehbiel, "Headstones Baffle Developer"; 2022 census data for Tulsa County, OK, tracts 76.31, 76.32, 76.33, 76.34, and 76.49, Census Reporter, https://censusreporter.org/profiles/14000US40143007631-census-tract-7631-tulsa-ok/.

22. Krehbiel, "Graves Stir Calls for Inquiry."

23. Race Riot Commission report; Scott W. Hammerstedt, and Amanda L. Regnier, "Searching for Graves from the 1921 Tulsa Race Massacre: Geophysical Survey of Oaklawn Cemetery, The Canes, and Newblock Park," Oklahoma Archeological Survey, n.d., https://bloximages.newyork1.vip.townnews.com/tulsaworld.com/content/tncms/assets/v3/editorial/e/f5/ef55c53c-3baa-5866-8bc8-a624901fb505/5df85777c0ba4.pdf.pdf; Amy Slanchik, "Archeologists Find Coffins Under Headstones for 2 Known Massacre Victims, Say They Are Outside of Oaklawn's Mass Grave," KOTV, June 10, 2021.

24. Ellsworth, *The Ground Breaking;* Krehbiel, "Race Riot Commission Sets Goals," June 30, 2000; Krehbiel, "Race Riot Digging Canceled," Feb. 1, 2000.

25. Ellsworth, *The Ground Breaking;* Krehbiel, "Race Riot Commission: Panel at Odds on Report Details but Agree Riot was Inexcusable," *Tulsa World*, Jan. 27, 2001; Krehbiel, "Presentation of Findings at Center of Debate," *Tulsa World*, Dec. 16, 2000.

26. Bynum, interview, Dec. 14, 2022.

27. Kavin Ross (writer, journalist, and photographer; son of Don Ross), interview with author, Oct. 21, 2022, transcript in possession of author.

28. City of Tulsa, "Public Oversight Meeting for 1921 Mass Graves Investigation Rescheduled for June 27," press release, June 10, 2019, https://www.cityoftulsa.org/press-room/public-oversight-meeting-for-1921-mass-graves-investigation-rescheduled-for-june-27/; City of Tulsa, "1921 Race Massacre Graves Public Oversight Committee Schedules Next Meeting for July 18," press release, June 28, 2019, https://www.cityoftulsa.org/press-room/second-1921-race-massacre-graves-public-meeting-scheduled/; City of Tulsa, 1921 Graves Investigation website, https://www.cityoftulsa.org/government/mayor-of-tulsa/1921-graves-investigation/.

29. Krehbiel, "Community Engagement Considered Key Element of Search for Race Massacre Burial Sites," May 23, 2019; Kirsten Lang, "Weather Wednesday: A Look Back at the 2019 Historic Flood," *Tulsa World*, May 25, 2022.

30. Marshall, "Meetings Serve as 'Homicide Investigation for Tulsans Who We Believe Were Murdered in 1921,' Mayor Bynum Says of Mass Graves Search," *Tulsa World*, June 28, 2019; City of Tulsa, "1921 Mass Graves Public Meeting - June 27, 2019," public meeting, June 27, 2019, video, 2:10:06, July 15, 2019, https://www.youtube.com/watch?v=7QN62XmWLZc.

31. City of Tulsa, public meeting, June 27, 2019.

32. City of Tulsa, public meeting, June 27, 2019.

33. Marshall, "'Meetings Serve as 'Homicide Investigation'"; Bynum, interview, Dec. 14, 2022.

34. Krehbiel, "Tulsa Race Massacre Mass Graves: 'Be realistic,' Experts Say in Laying Out Plans for Search," *Tulsa World*, July 19, 2019; City of Tulsa, "1921 Mass Graves Public Meeting - July 18, 2019," public meeting, July 18, 2019, video, 1:59:04, July 19, 2019, https://www.youtube.com/watch?v=dAloPcuEDVE.

35. Krehbiel, "Tulsa Race Massacre Mass Graves: 'Be realistic'; City of Tulsa, "1921 Mass Graves Public Meeting - July 18, 2019."

36. Krehbiel, "Tulsa Race Massacre Mass Graves: 'Be realistic'; City of Tulsa, "1921 Mass Graves Public Meeting - July 18, 2019."

37. Krehbiel, "Tulsa Race Massacre Mass Graves: 'Be realistic'; City of Tulsa, "1921 Mass Graves Public Meeting - July 18, 2019"; Race Riot Commission report; Phoebe R. Stubblefield, PhD, faculty biography, University of Florida, https://anthro.ufl.edu/2018/08/29/phoebestubblefield/.

38. Krehbiel, "Tulsa Race Massacre Mass Graves: 'Be realistic'"; City of Tulsa, "1921 Mass Graves Public Meeting—July 18, 2019."

39. Krehbiel, "Search for Graves From the Tulsa Race Massacre to Begin Next Month; Fourth Location Added to Those to be Explored," *Tulsa World*, Sept. 27, 2019; Ellsworth. *The Ground Breaking*.

40. Hammerstedt and Regnier, "Searching for Graves"; Krehbiel, "1921 Tulsa Race Massacre Graves Search Shifts to Newblock Park," *Tulsa World*, Oct. 16, 2019.

41. Hammerstedt and Regnier, "Searching for Graves."

42. Hammerstedt and Regnier, "Searching for Graves."

43. Hammerstedt and Regnier, "Searching for Graves"; Krehbiel, "Tulsa Race Massacre Graves Search: Some Want Inner Dispersal Loop Included among Possible Sites," *Tulsa World*, Oct. 7, 2019; Krehbiel, "Tulsa Race Massacre Graves Search: Scientists Start 'Do-Over' at Oaklawn Cemetery," *Tulsa World*, Oct. 9, 2019; Marshall, "Archaeological Expert Explains Why Unmarked Graves Search Team Can't Explore for Possible Remains Under IDL," *Tulsa World*, Oct. 10, 2019; Natasha Simmons, "Mass Graves Scanning Underway IDL and Crown Hill Search Urged," *Oklahoma Eagle*, Oct. 11, 2019; Krehbiel, "1921 Tulsa Race Massacre Graves Search Shifts to Newblock Park"; Canfield, "A 25-By-30-Foot Pit? Scientists Find Reason to Search Further for Mass Graves from Tulsa's 1921 Race Massacre," *Tulsa World*, Dec. 17, 2019.

44. Nehemiah Frank, "'Truckloads' of Unmarked Black Mass Graves Throughout Tulsa? Investigation Begins," *Black Wall Street Times*, June 28, 2019; Krehbiel, "Tulsa Race Massacre Graves Search: Some Want Inner Dispersal Loop Included"; Simmons, "Mass Graves Scanning Underway."

45. Krehbiel, "Tulsa Race Massacre Graves Search: Some Want Inner Dispersal Loop Included."

46. Doha Madani. "Possible Mass Grave from 1921 Tulsa Race Massacre Found by Researchers," NBC News, Dec. 16, 2019; Canfield, "A 25-by-30-foot Pit?"; Hammerstedt and Regnier, "Searching for Graves."

47. Canfield, "A 25-by-30-foot pit?" The account in this and the following four paragraphs draws on this source unless otherwise noted.

48. Canfield, "Search for Tulsa Race Massacre Graves: Test Excavation to be Done in Oaklawn Cemetery," *Tulsa World*, Feb. 3, 2020.

49. Krehbiel, "Longstanding Distrust, Anger Revealed in Hunt for Tulsa Race Massacre Graves," *Tulsa World*, March 3, 2020. The account in this and the following two paragraph draws on these sources unless otherwise noted.

50. Grimwood, "State's First COVID-19 Death Is a Tulsa County Man"; Krehbiel, "Race Massacre Burial Search on Hold Because of COVID-19," *Tulsa World*, March 23, 2020.

51. Canfield, "City of Tulsa Furloughs Many Employees in Budget-Cutting Plan Through December," *Tulsa World*, April 8, 2020; Grimwood, "'We Need This Community to Come Together': Police Chief Asks for Prayer, Unity After Officers Shot during Traffic Stop," *Tulsa World*, June 29, 2020.

52. Bynum, interview, Oct. 27, 2022.

53. Schlotthauer, "Watch Now: Services for Fallen Tulsa Police Sgt. Craig Johnson Draw Thousands," *Tulsa World*, July 9, 2020; Mike Simons and Ian Maule, "Memorial Service for Tulsa Police Sgt. Craig Johnson," *Tulsa World*, photo essay, July 10, 2020.

54. Bynum, interview, Oct. 27, 2022.

55. Krehbiel, "Watch Now: No Discoveries During First Day of Oaklawn Excavation, but Scientists Remain Optimistic," *Tulsa World*, July 14, 2020; Ellsworth, *The Ground Breaking*.

56. Krehbiel, "Watch Now: No Discoveries During First Day."

57. Ellsworth, *The Ground Breaking;* Krehbiel, "Watch Now: No Discoveries During First Day"; Krehbiel, "Watch Now: Archaeologists Extend Oaklawn Test Site in Search of 1921 Tulsa Race Massacre Victims," *Tulsa World*, July 15, 2020; Krehbiel, "Search for Race Massacre Graves at Oaklawn Remains Fruitless, but Scientists Say They're 'Not Disheartened,'" *Tulsa World*, July 16, 2020; Krehbiel, "Lack of Evidence so far in Tulsa Race Massacre Grave Search Doesn't Deter Commitment, Mayor Says," *Tulsa World*, July 17, 2020; Krehbiel, "Oaklawn Researchers Reassess Potential Race Massacre Burial Sites as Search for Remains Continues," *Tulsa World*, July 18, 2020; Krehbiel, "Next Steps in Search For Unmarked Tulsa Race Massacre Burials to Be Discussed Tuesday," *Tulsa World*, July 21, 2020; Krehbiel, "Discovery Tuesday Creates Some Excitement among Oaklawn Researchers Searching for Race Massacre Graves," *Tulsa World*, July 22, 2020; Krehbiel, "Watch Now: Mass Graves Search Halted at Oaklawn: 'This Is Not the Location We Are Looking For,'" *Tulsa World*, July 23, 2020.

58. Krehbiel, "Watch Now: Mass Graves Search Halted At Oaklawn."

59. Matthews, interview; Krehbiel, "Greenwood Rising is No. 7 on USA Today's Best New Attractions List," *Tulsa World*, Jan. 5, 2022.

60. Matthews, interview.

61. Matthews, interview.

62. Graham, "Ginnie Graham: Renovation of Big 10 Ballroom a Decade in the Making," *Tulsa World*, Oct. 25, 2017; Karen Shade, "Bringing Back the Big 10," *Tulsa World*, Aug. 17, 2008.

63. Matthews, interview. The account in this and the following two paragraphs draws on this source unless otherwise noted.

64. Charles and Lynn Schusterman Family Philanthropies, https://www.schusterman.org/; Anne and Henry Zarrow Foundation, https://zarrow.org/; "Herman Kaiser Dies; Services Set Sunday," *Tulsa World*, Oct. 15, 1992.

65. George Kaiser, email message to author, May 14, 2023 (hereafter Kaiser to Krehbiel).

66. Kaiser to Krehbiel.

67. Kaiser to Krehbiel.

68. Guidestar.org profile, George Kaiser Family Foundation, https://www.guidestar.org/profile/73-1574370; George Kaiser Family Foundation, https://www.gkff.org/; Simon Montlake, "How Tulsa's Bold Experiment is Bringing Families Closer to Stability," *Christian Science Monitor*, Jan. 2, 2019; Jane Thier, "Thousands Of Remote Workers Took $10,000 to Move to Tulsa for a Year. Now They Don't Want to Leave," *Fortune*, Jan. 18, 2023; "The Best City Parks in the US, According to Readers," *USA Today*, March 15, 2021; Bob Dylan Center, Tulsa, OK, https://bobdylancenter.com/; Build In Tulsa, Inc., https://www.buildintulsa.com/.

69. Matthews, interview. The account in this and the following three paragraphs draws on this source unless otherwise noted.

70. Matthews, interview; Graham, "Ginnie Graham: Renovation of Big 10 Ballroom"; Samuel Hardiman, "GKFF Developing Industrial Park in North Tulsa," *Tulsa World*, Aug. 5, 2016.

71. Matthews, interview; Phil Armstrong (former director, Race Massacre Centennial Commission), interview with author, Oct. 10, 2022, transcript in author's possession.

72. Matthews, interview; Armstrong, interview.

73. Krehbiel, "1921 Centennial Commission to Replace 'Riot' With 'Massacre' in Official Title," *Tulsa World*, Nov. 27, 2018; Canfield, "'One of Our Greatest Gifts if We Just Tell the Story': Fundraising Campaign Aims to Expand, Remodel Greenwood Cultural Center," *Tulsa World*, April 1, 2019; Krehbiel, "$9 Million Renovation and Expansion of Greenwood Cultural Center Announced, Coincides with Tulsa Race Massacre Centennial," *Tulsa World*, May 9, 2019; Marshall, "City Leaders, 1921 Centennial Commission Visit National Memorials to Get Ideas for Future Race Massacre Center," *Tulsa World*, May 20, 2019.

74. Marshall, "City Leaders, 1921 Centennial Commission."

75. P. J. Lassek, "Councilors Back Plan for Church," *Tulsa World*, Dec. 21, 2001; Killman, "Councilor Gives Alternative for Riot Memorial Funding," *Tulsa World*, Jan. 4, 2002; Killman, "Third-Penny Tax Use Plan Appears Dead," *Tulsa World*, Jan. 9, 2002;

Krehbiel, "Land for Museum Targeted," *Tulsa World*, Feb 20, 2003; Krehbiel, "'Healing Circle' Is Central Element of Riot Memorial," *Tulsa World*, March 22, 2003; "Dr. John Hope Franklin Greenwood Reconciliation Museum: Program and Conceptual Design Manual," copy in possession of author.

76. Randle, et al, v. City of Tulsa, et al.

77. Matthews, interview; Canfield, "'One Of Our Greatest Gifts if We Just Tell the Story'"; Krehbiel, "$9 Million Renovation and Expansion"; Krehbiel, "Appropriations Bill Includes $1.5 Million for Race Massacre Centennial," *Tulsa World*, May 17, 2019.

78. Marshall, "Tulsa Race Massacre Commission Picks Firms to Design Exhibit Center in Greenwood District," *Tulsa World*, July 12, 2019; Krehbiel, "Plans for Greenwood Museum Unveiled: 'The Past Isn't Really Past at All. It's Part of Our Present,'" *Tulsa World*, Sept. 20, 2019.

79. Krehbiel, "Appropriations Bill Includes $1.5 Million."

80. Krehbiel, "Plans for Greenwood Museum Unveiled"; Canfield, "Greenwood Rising History Center Building Should Be in Place by 1921 Tulsa Race Massacre Centennial," *Tulsa World*, March 10, 2020; Canfield, "1921 Tulsa Race Massacre History Center Won't Be Built on Greenwood Cultural Center Property," *Tulsa World*, April 19, 2020.

81. Canfield, "Greenwood Rising History Center Building"; Canfield, "1921 Tulsa Race Massacre History Center"; Canfield, "'A Hot-Button Issue': Not All Black Tulsans Are Happy about Greenwood Rising," *Tulsa World*, May 26, 2021; "The Oklahoma Eagle Editorial: History Museum to Move, Why Rush to Reopen the State," *Oklahoma Eagle*, April 24, 2020; Armstrong, interview.

82. Canfield, "Greenwood Rising History Center Building."

83. Armstrong, interview.

84. Armstrong, interview.

85. Krehbiel, "People to Watch: Phil Armstrong Is the Man in the Middle of Centennial Preparations," *Tulsa World*, Jan. 4, 2020.

86. Armstrong, interview.

87. Armstrong, interview; Matthews, interview.

88. Armstrong, interview.

89. Morgan, "A Massacre Decimated Black Wall Street, but Driving a Resurgence is the Commemoration of Its Centennial," *Tulsa World*, Feb. 25, 2019; Tracy Jan, "The 'White-washing' of Black Wall Street," *Washington Post*, Jan. 17, 2021; Krehbiel, "Greenwood Chamber Drops Developer Bias Suit Against City, Mayor," *Tulsa World*, Oct. 21, 2013.

90. Armstrong, interview; Matthews, interview.

91. Armstrong, interview; Matthews, interview; Canfield, "1921 Tulsa Race Massacre History Center."

92. Armstrong, interview.

93. Canfield, "1921 Tulsa Race Massacre History Center."

94. Canfield, "Site at Entrance to Historic Greenwood District Donated for Greenwood Rising History Center," *Tulsa World*, April 28, 2020.

95. "The Oklahoma Eagle Editorial: Race Massacre Homerun and Racial Numbers Up," *Oklahoma Eagle*, May 1, 2020.

96. Hille Foundation, https://www.hillefoundation.org/; Canfield, "Tulsans of the Year: Kajeer and Maggie Yar Dedicated to Seeing Greenwood Flourish," *Tulsa World*, Dec. 5, 2021.

97. Krehbiel, "Supporters of E.W. Woods Memorial Push toward Funding Goal," *Tulsa World*, June 1, 2017.

98. Canfield, "Greenwood Investors Happy to Help City Find New Home for Greenwood Rising History Center," *Tulsa World*, May 2, 2020

99. Kajeer Yar (Tulsa attorney and businessman), interview with author by phone, Nov. 28, 2022, transcript in possession of author.

100. Brian Barber, "Downtown Development: Next Step: Tussle Brews Over Site," *Tulsa World*, Aug. 13, 2006; Laurie Winslow, "5 Questions with Reuben Gant," *Tulsa World*, Dec. 21, 2007; Krehbiel, "Through a Century of Hard Work and Heartbreak"; Barber, "Debated Project Clears Hurdle," *Tulsa World*, Jan. 11, 2008; Lassek, "Tulsa Drillers Stadium Coming Downtown to Greenwood District," *Tulsa World*, June 25, 2008; Yar, interview; Reuben Gant (former executive director, Greenwood Chamber of Commerce), interview with author, Oct. 25, 2022, transcript in possession of author.

101. Barber, "Debated Project Clears Hurdle," *Tulsa World*, Jan. 11, 2008; Lassek, "Tulsa Drillers Stadium Coming Downtown to Greenwood District," *Tulsa World*, June 25, 2008.

102. Lassek, "Tulsa Drillers Stadium Coming."

103. Ryan Daly, "Developers Get Go-Ahead for Greenwood Lofts," *Tulsa World*, July 19, 2010; Robert Evatt, "GreenArch Brings Apartments, Retail to Greenwood," *Tulsa World*, July 14, 2012"; Yar, interview.

104. Yar, interview.

105. Yar, interview; Evatt, "GreenArch Brings Apartments, Retail to Greenwood"; Brian Ervin, "Greenwood's Rebirth Underway with Completed GreenArch Development," *Tulsa World*, Sept. 15, 2013; Greenwood Chamber of Commerce, Internal Revenue Service Form 990 for 2013, copy in possession of author.

106. Gant, interview.

107. Gant, interview; "Partnership to Build Lofts, Retail in Brady District," *Tulsa World*, June 18, 2008.

108. Gant, interview.

109. Gant, interview; Lassek, "Greenwood Chamber's Development Arm Criticized in Audit; North Tulsa Project in Jeopardy," *Tulsa World*, June 20, 2011; Lassek, "Mayor Vetoes City Council Allocation of Grant Money," *Tulsa World*, Sept. 1, 2011; Krehbiel, "Greenwood Chamber Drops Developer Bias Suit Against City, Mayor," *Tulsa World*, Oct. 21, 2013.

110. Gant, interview.

111. Yar, interview.

112. Lassek, "Councilors Criticize TDA," *Tulsa World*, Jan. 25, 2009; Krehbiel, "Through a Century of Hard Work and Heartbreak"; Lassek, "Grants for City May Be In Jeopardy," *Tulsa World*, Oct. 8, 2007.

113. Krehbiel, "Watch Now: Long In the Making, Greenwood History Center Finally Breaks Ground," *Tulsa World*, Aug. 22, 2020.

114. Randle, et al, v. City of Tulsa, et al; Jan Hoffman, "Johnson & Johnson Ordered to Pay $572 Million in Landmark Opioid Trial," *New York Times*, Aug. 26, 2019.

115. Stanley, "Success of New Tulsa Race Massacre Reparations Lawsuit Hinges on State's Nuisance Law, Attorneys Say," *Tulsa World*, Sept. 2, 2020.

116. Randle, et al, v. City of Tulsa, et al; Lessie Benningfield Randle, transcript of deposition, Oct. 14, 2020; "To Appraise All Loss by Negroes," *Tulsa World*, June 3, 1921.

117. Krehbiel, "$9 Million Renovation and Expansion"; Krehbiel, "Tulsa Race Massacre: Struggle for Reparations from 1921 Massacre Continue, and so Do the Disagreements," *Tulsa World*, May 25, 2021; Matthews, interview; Judy Eason McIntyre (former Oklahoma state senator), interview with author, Jan. 2, 2023, transcript in possession of author; Randle, et al v. City of Tulsa, et al; "Watch Now: Remember & Rise Event Collapsed After Frantic Week of Meetings, Emails and Talks about Survivor Payments," *Tulsa World*, May 29, 2021.

118. Krehbiel, "'No Reconciliation Without Reparations' Says Race Massacre Panelist," *Tulsa World*, June 1, 2020.

119. Randle, et al, v. City of Tulsa, et al.

120. Randle, et al, v. City of Tulsa, et al.

121. Lassek, "Setup for Ballpark Project Detailed," *Tulsa World*, Dec. 4, 2008.

122. Guidestar.org search for "Justice for Greenwood, March 16, 2023; Justice for Greenwood, https://www.justiceforgreenwood.org/.

123. Canfield, "Black Lives Matter Message To Be Erased, Tulsa Officials Say: 'There Is Just Not an Alternative,'" *Tulsa World*, July 29, 2020.

124. Canfield, "Painted BLM Message Prompts Push for 'Back the Blue' Art from Tulsa Republicans," *Tulsa World*, July 29, 2020.

125. Canfield, "Tulsa Man Challenging BLM Sign in Greenwood Calls Group 'Radical, Left-Wing, Marxist Organization,' Says He Supports the Message," *Tulsa World*, Aug. 10, 2020.

126. Krehbiel, "What's Black Lives Matter About? Combating Police Violence but Also Economic Empowerment, Advocates Say," *Tulsa World*, Aug. 10, 2020.

127. Stanley, "Tulsa Protest Leaders Praise Participants."

128. Jack, interview. The account in this and the following three paragraphs draws on this source.

129. Nehemiah Frank, "Mayor Bynum Seemingly Tries Dividing Black Community on Black Lives Matter Mural," *Black Wall Street Times*, Aug. 3, 2020; Canfield, "Tulsa One of Many Communities Grappling with Implications of 'Black Lives Matter' Street Paintings," *Tulsa World*, Aug. 9, 2020.

130. Frank, "Mayor Bynum Seemingly Tries Dividing Black Community"; Freeman Culver (Executive Director, Greenwood Chamber of Commerce), interview with author, Nov. 10, 2022, transcript in possession of author.

131. Canfield, "Black Lives Matter Message to Be Erased.'"

132. Schlotthauer, "Tulsans March in Solidarity with Black and Indigenous People, Demand Permanent Black Lives Matter Street Mural," *Tulsa World*, Aug. 1, 2020.

133. Canfield, " Tulsa One of Many Communities Grappling With Implications of 'Black Lives Matter' Street Paintings," *Tulsa World*, Aug. 9, 2020; Schlotthauer, "Westboro Baptist Church, Known for Picketing at Soldier Funerals, Wants to Paint Tulsa Streets," *Tulsa World*, Aug. 10, 2020; Grimwood, "Several Tulsa Houses of Worship Display 'Black Lives Matter' on Anniversary of Terence Crutcher's Death," *Tulsa World*, Sept. 17, 2020; Canfield, "Watch Now: City Removes Black Lives Matter Mural from Site of Tulsa Race Massacre," *Tulsa World*, Oct. 6, 2020.

134. Canfield, "Black Lives Matter Message to Be Erased"; Canfield, "Tulsa One of Many Communities Grappling with Implications"; Canfield, "Two Tulsa City Councilors Think Their Proposal Could Keep Black Lives Matter Street Painting in Greenwood," *Tulsa World*, Aug. 8, 2020; Canfield, "Tulsa's 'Black Lives Matter' Sign to Remain While City Councilors Examine Options for Retaining It," Aug. 20, 2020; Canfield, "Council Holds Off on Discussion of 'Black Lives Matter' Street Painting," *Tulsa World*, Aug. 27, 2020.

135. Canfield, "Black Lives Matter Painting to Be Gone by Election Day; Scheduled Repaving of Greenwood Avenue Set for October," *Tulsa World*, Sept.3, 2020; Canfield, "Search for a Home for the Black Lives Matter Street Painting Continues," *Tulsa World*, Oct. 5, 2020.

136. Canfield, "Watch Now: City Removes Black Lives Matter Mural"; "Tulsa Removes Black Lives Matter From Black Wall Street," *Black Wall Street Times*, Oct. 6, 2020.

137. Canfield, "Black Lives Matter Message to Be Erased.'"

138. Schlotthauer, "Police Seek Help Identifying Those Who Painted 'BLM' in Front of Tulsa City Hall," *Tulsa World*, Oct. 13, 2020.

139. "The Oklahoma Eagle Newswire: Defunding Will Not Work, City Finds Itself on the Wrong Side of History Pursuing BLM Painters and Mass Grave Search Uncovers Possible Find," *Oklahoma Eagle*, Oct. 23, 2020.

140. Schlotthauer, "City Mulls Charges Against Tulsa BLM Activists After DA Declines to Prosecute Some Painters," *Tulsa World*, Oct. 21, 2020.

141. Payne, "City Removes Street Painting Honoring Veteran in South Tulsa Neighborhood," *Tulsa World*, Oct. 24, 2020.

142. Overall, "Watch Now: Search For 1921 Race Massacre Graves to Continue with New Excavations, Committee Agrees," *Tulsa World*, Sept. 15, 2020; DeNeen L. Brown, "Tulsa Begins Search For 'Original 18' Black People Killed in 1921 Race Massacre, *Washington Post*, Oct. 19, 2020; Krehbiel, "Tulsa Race Massacre Researchers Begin Uncovering Burial Sites at Oaklawn Cemetery," *Tulsa World*, Oct. 20, 2020

143. Krehbiel, "Watch Now: Researchers Discover Human Remains in Unmarked Grave at Oaklawn Cemetery; Further Examination Needed to Determine Tulsa Race Massacre Connection," *Tulsa World*, Oct. 21, 2020; "Human Remains Found at Possible 1921 Tulsa Race Massacre Mass-Grave Location," *Black Wall Street Times*, Oct. 21, 2020.

144. Krehbiel, "Watch Now: Researchers Discover Human Remains."

145. Krehbiel, "Watch Now: Researchers Discover Human Remains."

146. "Human Remains Found at Possible 1921 Tulsa Race Massacre Mass-Grave Location," *Black Wall Street Times*.

147. Brown, "Scientists Find Human Remains that Might Be from Tulsa's 1921 Race Massacre," *Washington Post*, Oct. 21, 2020.

148. Kary Stackelbeck and Phoebe Stubblefield, "Tulsa Race Massacre Investigation: Oaklawn Cemetery Executive Summary of 2020 Test Excavations," Physical Investigation Committee, December 2020; Krehbiel, "Archaeologists Uncover Additional Coffin as Researchers Close Excavation at Oaklawn Cemetery," *Tulsa World*, Oct. 23, 2020 .

149. Stackelbeck and Stubblefield, "Tulsa Race Massacre Investigation"; Krehbiel, "Archaeologists Uncover Additional Coffin"; Ben Fenwick, "Mass Grave Unearthed in Tulsa During Search for Massacre Victims," *Oklahoman*, Oct. 21, 2020.

150. Fenwick, "Mass Grave Unearthed in Tulsa."

151. Krehbiel, "Mass Grave Found in Search for 1921 Tulsa Race Massacre Victims; 10 Coffins Found in Trench at Oaklawn Cemetery," *Tulsa World*, Oct. 22, 2020.

152. Krehbiel, "Archaeologists Uncover Additional Coffin."

153. Krehbiel, "Archaeologists Uncover Additional Coffin."

154. Krehbiel, "Archaeologists Uncover Additional Coffin"; Stackelbeck and Stubblefield, "Tulsa Race Massacre Investigation"; Krehbiel, "Search for 1921 Tulsa Race Massacre Graves Likely to Expand," *Tulsa World*, Dec. 18, 2020.

155. Krehbiel, "Asamoa-Caesar Hopes to Break 3-Decade Republican Stronghold in Low-Key Congressional District 1 Race," *Tulsa World*, Oct. 18, 2020.

156. Kojo Asamoa-Caesar (2020 candidate for Congress), interview with author, Dec. 23, 2020, transcript in possession of author. Unless otherwise noted, the following account and quotes also draw on this interview.

157. Election Results, Oklahoma State Election Board, https://oklahoma.gov/elections/elections-results/election-results.html.

Chapter 5. Unhappy New Year

1. "2020 Was No Friend to North Tulsa," editorial, *Oklahoma Eagle*, Jan. 1, 2021.

2. Krehbiel, "Presidential Campaign 'Grieves' Lankford, but Vote Anyway," *Tulsa World*, Oct. 27, 2016.

3. James Lankford, "On Being an Evangelical Senator During the Trump Presidency," episode 101, *Quick to Listen* (podcast), March 21, 2018, *Christianity Today*, https://www.christianitytoday.com/ct/podcasts/quick-to-listen/james-lankford-senator-oklahoma-evangelical-trump.html.

4. John Hayward, "Tom Coburn: Rubio 'Trustworthy' and Electable, Cruz Not 'Effective' Working with Others, Trump a 'Carnival Barker,'" *Breitbart*, March 10, 2016.

5. Election Results, Oklahoma State Election Board, results of 2016 presidential primary, 2016 general election, and 2020 general election, https://oklahoma.gov/elections/elections-results/election-results.html

6. "D.C. Digest: Washington Drama Causes Inhofe to Miss 61st Wedding Anniversary," *Tulsa World*, Dec. 20, 2020.

7. James Lankford, "Lankford Defends Americans' Questions Regarding Election Fraud," Dec. 16, 2020, press release, https://www.lankford.senate.gov/news/press-releases/lankford-defends-americans-questions-regarding-election-fraud/.

8. Lankford, "Lankford Defends Americans' Questions"; Krehbiel, "Oklahoma Still Last in the Nation in Voter Participation Despite Recent Registration Surge," *Tulsa World*, Nov. 12, 2020; https://www.electproject.org/election-data/voter-turnout-data.

9. Lankford, "Lankford Defends Americans' Questions"; Jordain Carney, "GOP Senator Says Biden Should Get Access to Intelligence Briefings," *The Hill*, Nov. 11, 2020; Manu Raju and Ted Barrett, "Lankford Argues He Did 'Step In' Friday and Had Private Conversation with GSA Over Biden Transition Process," *CNN*, Nov. 16, 2020.

10. Krehbiel, "Sen. Lankford Joins Effort to Create 'Commission' to Examine Presidential Election," *Tulsa World*, Jan. 3, 2021; Chris Casteel, "Amid Recriminations, Lankford, Bice Say They Weren't Trying to Overturn Biden's Election," *Oklahoman*, Jan. 8, 2021.

11. Krehbiel, "Sen. Lankford Joins Effort"; Casteel, "Amid Recriminations, Lankford, Bice Say." The account in this and the following four paragraphs draws on these sources until otherwise noted.

12. Krehbiel, "Sen. Lankford Joins Effort"; Casteel, "Amid Recriminations, Lankford, Bice Say"; Michael Kranish, "Inside Ted Cruz's Last-ditch Battle to Keep Trump in Power," *Washington Post*, March 28, 2022.

13. Krehbiel, "Sen. Lankford Joins Effort to Create 'Commission' to Examine Presidential Election."

14. Nehemiah Frank, "Bynum and Lankford not Serious about Racial Justice during the Centennial Year of the 1921 Tulsa Race Massacre," *Black Wall Street Times*, Jan. 5, 2021; Krehbiel, "Oklahoma Trump Supporters Heading to D.C. to Continue Pressing Congress to Block Presidential Election," *Tulsa World*, Jan. 4, 2021.

15. Krehbiel, "Oklahoma Trump Supporters Heading to D.C. to Continue Pressing Congress to Block Presidential Election"; Amanda Gilbert, "Oklahoma Woman to Join MAGA Protests in Washington, D.C.," KOKI, Jan. 5, 2021.

16. Krehbiel, "Oklahoma Trump Supporters Heading to D.C."

17. Krehbiel, "Oklahoma Trump Supporters Heading to D.C."

18. James Lankford, "U.S. Sen. James Lankford: Oklahomans and the Nation Deserve Confidence in the Election Results," *Tulsa World*, Jan. 5, 2021; "Congress and the Case of the Faithless Elector," *Whereas: Stories from the People's House* (blog), History, Art & Archives, United States House of Representatives, Nov. 17, 2020, https://history.house.gov/Blog/2020/November/11-17-Faithless-Electors/.

19. Lankford, "U.S. Sen. James Lankford: Oklahomans and the Nation Deserve Confidence in the Election Results."

20. "Joe Biden Won the Election Fair and Square, Even if Members of Oklahoma Congressional Delegation Don't Like that Result," editorial, *Tulsa World*, Jan. 6, 2021.

21. Krehbiel, "Inhofe Won't Protest Electoral College Vote, Says it Would Violate His Oath of Office," *Tulsa World*, Jan. 5, 2021.

22. Casteel, "Amid Recriminations, Lankford, Bice Say."

23. "Watch Now: Lankford Decries 'Rioters and Thugs' in Second Speech from Senate Floor Wednesday After Capitol Breach," *Tulsa World*, Jan. 7, 2021.

24. Krehbiel, "Oklahoma Lawmakers Safe in Capitol Attack; Lucas and Lankford Condemn Violence," *Tulsa World*, Jan. 6, 2021; "Petition Calls for Sen. Lankford to Step Down and be Removed for Sedition," *Black Wall Street Times*, Jan. 7, 2021.

25. Krehbiel, "Tulsa Pastor Challenges Lankford for Senate with Boost from Trump Loyalist Michael Flynn," March 17, 2021.

26. Krehbiel, "Tulsa Pastor Challenges Lankford for Senate; Stanley, "Watch Now: 'There's Power in Unity': Tulsa Church Leaders, Police Officers Come Together for First Faith and Blue Prayer March," *Tulsa World*, Oct. 1, 2020.

27. Krehbiel, "Black Leaders Want Sen. Lankford Exiled from Tulsa Race Massacre Commission after Electoral College Challenge," Jan. 13, 2021. The following account draws on this source until otherwise noted

28. James Lankford, "To my friends in North Tulsa," letter, Jan. 14, 2021, https://tulsaworld.com/document-u-s-sen-james-lankfords-letter-to-residents-of-north-tulsa/pdf_3f0cb70a-56c8-11eb-bed6-2b558d2cd9e6.html.

29. "Sen. Lankford's Non-Apology Does Not Earn Him Another Chance," *Black Wall Street Times*, Jan. 19, 2021.

30. MichaelSteele, (@MichaelSteele), "1/5 "My intent to give a voice to Oklahomans who had questions was never also an intent to diminish the voice of any Black American." @SenatorLankford what exactly did you think was going to happen when you sought to throw out the votes in Ga., MI. or Pa.?," Twitter, January 15, 2121, 7:55 a.m., https://twitter.com/michaelsteele/status/1350109412199968771?s=21.

31. James O. Goodwin, "Should Senator James Lankford Resign from the 1921 Race Massacre Commission? Or Is This a Teachable Moment for Both the Senator and the Commission?" *Oklahoma Eagle*, Jan. 23, 2021.

32. Goodwin, "Should Senator James Lankford Resign from the 1921 Race Massacre Commission?"

33. Krehbiel, "U.S. Sen. James Lankford to Remain on Race Massacre Centennial Commission," *Tulsa World*, Jan. 26, 2021. The account in this and the following four paragraphs draws on this source unless otherwise noted.

34. Krehbiel, "Centennial Commission Scolds Governor; Legislator Says He's Had Enough," *Tulsa World*, May 11, 2021; Krehbiel, "Tulsa Race Massacre Centennial Commission Formally Severs Ties with Gov. Kevin Stitt," *Tulsa World*, May 15, 2021; "Lankford Steps Down from Race Massacre Centennial Commission, Citing Partisan Shift in Goals," May 28, 2021.

35. Alex Cash, "North Tulsa Ballroom Reopens as Home to Nonprofit," KOKH, Feb. 25, 2023.

Chapter 6. Politics

1. Faith & Blue, https://faithandblue.org/; Movement Forward, https://movementforward.org/people/rev-markel-hutchins/; Chris Polansky, "Demonstrations Opposing White Supremacy, Supporting Police Expected Downtown Saturday," Public Radio Tulsa, Oct. 9, 2020.

2. Faith & Blue; Movement Forward; Polansky, "Demonstrations Opposing White Supremacy; Jozsef Papp, "Faith & Blue Weekend Aims to Build Ties Between Law Enforcement, Communities," *Atlanta Journal-Constitution*, Sept. 8, 2022.

3. Polansky, "Demonstrations Opposing White Supremacy." The account in this and the following two paragraphs draws on this source unless otherwise noted

4. Polansky, "Demonstrations Opposing White Supremacy"; Stanley, "Watch Now: 'There's Power in Unity': Tulsa Church Leaders, Police Officers Come Together for First Faith and Blue Prayer March," story and video, *Tulsa World*, Oct. 11, 2020.

5. Stanley, "Watch Now: 'There's Power in Unity.'"

6. Michael Overall, "Watch Now: Demonstrators Paint 'BLM' in Front of City Hall to Protest Systemic Racism, Removal of Greenwood Street Mural," *Tulsa World*, Oct. 11, 2020.

7. Overall, "Watch Now: Demonstrators Paint 'BLM.'

8. Overall, "Watch Now: Demonstrators Paint 'BLM.'

9. Jackson Lahmeyer, https://www.jacksonlahmeyer.com/; Sheridan Church, https://www.sheridan.church/; Krehbiel, "Tulsa Pastor Challenges Lankford for Senate With Boost from Trump Loyalist Michael Flynn"; Thrivetimeshow, https://www.thrivetimeshow.com/reawaken-america-tour/.

10. Jack, interview.

11. Paul Monies, "Vaccines Become Untouchable Issue in Oklahoma Politics," *Oklahoma Watch*, June 3, 2019.

12. Jack, interview.

13. Krehbiel, "Oklahoma House Moves to Raise Barriers for Initiative Petitions," *Tulsa World*, March 1, 2022; Jana Hayes, "Report: No Widespread Fraud in Oklahoma's 2020 Election; Some Lawmakers Seek Forensic Audit," *Oklahoman*, Feb. 21, 2022.

14. Jack, interview.

15. Karen Tumulty, "How State Legislatures Went off the Rails," *Washington Post*, April 24, 2023.

16. "Chickasaw Nation Governor Bill Anoatubby Named Most Powerful Person in Oklahoma," *Native News Online*, July 22, 2022; Gov. Anoatubby "Three-Peats" as Most Powerful Oklahoman," *Chickasaw Times*, August 2023; "Oklahoma Gaming Compliance Unit Annual Report," Fiscal Year 2022, https://oklahoma.gov/content/dam/ok/en/omes/documents/GameCompAnnReort2022.pdf; Tribal Governments, Government, Oklahoma Historical Society, website, https://www.okhistory.org/learn/government6.

17. "McGirt v. Oklahoma: Supreme Court Decision and Aftermath," *Tulsa World*, June 16, 2023; Faye C. Elkins, "What Does a Recent Supreme Court Decision Mean for Tribal, State and Federal Law Enforcement," Office of Community Oriented Policing Services, U.S. Department of Justice, *Community Policing Dispatch* 15, no.1, January 2022, https://cops.usdoj.gov/html/dispatch/01-2022/McGirt_decision.html; Krehbiel, "Analysis: Tribes Send Subtle Message through Advertising Campaign," *Tulsa World*, Dec. 8, 2019.

18. Tribal Governments, Government, Oklahoma Historical Society, website, https://www.okhistory.org/learn/government6.

19. Tribal Governments, Government, Oklahoma Historical Society; "McGirt v. Oklahoma: Supreme Court Decision and Aftermath," *Tulsa World*, June 16, 2023; Elkins, "What Does a Recent Supreme Court Decision Mean for Tribal, State and Federal Law Enforcement"; Native American Tribal Enrollment, National Indian Law Library, https://narf.org/nill/resources/enrollment.html.

20. "McGirt v. Oklahoma: Supreme Court Decision and Aftermath," *Tulsa World*, June 16, 2023; Elkins, "What Does a Recent Supreme Court Decision Mean for Tribal, State and Federal Law Enforcement"; Krehbiel, "Gov. Stitt Concerned About What McGirt Ruling Doesn't Say, Its Far-reaching Interpretations," *Tulsa World*, April 24, 2022; Matt Trotter, "Muscogee Nation Takes Stitt to Task for His Latest McGirt Remarks, Public Radio Tulsa, Aug. 27, 2021; Dillon Richards, "Stitt Believes Historic McGirt Ruling Could be Overturned," KOCO, April 7, 2021.

21. Hoberock, "Oklahoma Supreme Court Tosses Two More of Gov. Stitt's Tribal Gaming Compacts," *Tulsa World*, Jan. 27, 2021.

22. House Bill 1674, House Bill 1775, 58th Oklahoma Legislature, https://www.oklegislature.gov; Canfield, "Bynum Says He Appreciates State Lawmakers' Desire to Protect 'Law-abiding Citizens' During Riots," *Tulsa World*, March 31, 2021.

23. Canfield, "Bynum Says He Appreciates State Lawmakers' Desire."

24. "Watch Now: Oklahoma House Passes Bill to Protect Drivers Who Hit Protesters," video, *Tulsa World*, March 10, 2021.

25. "Watch Now: Oklahoma House Passes Bill." This source also applies to the next two paragraphs.

26. House Bill 1674, 58th Oklahoma Legislature.

27. Puneet Cheema and Rep. Regina Goodwin, "Opinion: Don't Stifle Dissent. Deal with Underlying Issues," *Tulsa World*, June 5, 2021.

28. Michelle Degli Esposti, Douglas J. Wiebe, Antonio Gasparrini, David K. Humphreys, "Analysis of "Stand Your Ground" Self-defense Laws and Statewide Rates of Homicides and Firearm Homicides," *JAMA Netw Open*. 2022;5(2):e220077, doi: 10.1001/jamanetworkopen.2022.0077. Erratum in: JAMA Netw Open. 2022 Apr 1;5(4):e229270. PMID: 35188553; PMCID: PMC8861849.

29. Cheema and Goodwin, "Opinion: Don't Stifle Dissent."

30. House Bill 1674, 58th Oklahoma Legislature.

31. House Bill 1674, 58th Oklahoma Legislature.

32. Nichols, interview.

33. House Bill 1775, 58th Oklahoma Legislature.

34. House Bill 1775, 58th Oklahoma Legislature; Krehbiel, "Oklahoma's House Sends Legislation Intended to Deflect Criticism of White Males in Classrooms to Governor," *Tulsa World*, April 30, 2021; Lenzy Krehbiel-Burton, "Watch Now: Tulsa Public Schools Violated State Law on Race, Gender, History, State Education Department Says," *Tulsa World*, June 24, 2022; Krehbiel-Burton, "Watch Now: Tulsa Public Schools Accredited with a Warning Over HB1775 Violation," *Tulsa World*, June 29, 2022; Krehbiel-Burton, "Audio from TPS Implicit Bias Training Was a Voice Reading Presentation Slides Verbatim," *Tulsa World*, Aug. 7, 2022.

35. Bill history, House Bill 1775, 58th Oklahoma Legislature; Bill history, Senate Bill 803, 58th Oklahoma Legislature; Trotter, "Republican State Senator Revives Bill Modeled on Trump Executive Order Against Bias Training," Public Radio Tulsa, April 6, 2021; Donald J. Trump, "Executive Order on Combating Race and Sex Stereotyping," Executive Order 13950, Sept. 22, 2020, https://trumpwhitehouse.archives.gov/presidential-actions/executive-order-combating-race-sex-stereotyping/.

36. Trotter, "Republican State Senator Revives Bill"; "Sen. Bullard statement on final passage of HB 1775," Oklahoma State Senate Communications, April 30, 2021, https://oksenate.gov/press-releases/sen-bullard-statement-final-passage-hb-1775?back=/press-releases/2021-04.

37. "Sen. Bullard statement on final passage of HB 1775."

38. "Sen. Bullard statement on final passage of HB 1775."

39. "Martin Luther King Jr., "Justice without Violence," lecture, Brandeis University, April 3, 1957, transcript, https://www.brandeis.edu/now/video-transcripts/mlk-transcript.html, video, https://www.brandeis.edu/now/2020/january/martin-luther-king-legacy.html.

40. William Cheng, "The Radical Compassion of Fredrick Douglass," *Pacific Standard*, Feb. 14, 2018; Aryssa Damron, "FACT CHECK: Did Frederick Douglass Say, 'It Is Easier To Build Strong Children Than To Repair Broken Men'?," https://checkyourfact.com, April 30, 2019.

41. "Sen. Bullard statement on final passage of HB 1775."

42. Krehbiel, "Oklahoma's House Sends Legislation."

43. Vote history, House Bill 1775, 58th Oklahoma Legislature, http://www.oklegislature.gov/BillInfo.aspx?Bill=hb1775&Session=2100; Parker Penrose, "Former OU SGA President Daniel Pae Sees Continued Success in Government Leadership as Oklahoma Representative," *OU Daily*, Sept. 15, 2019.

44. Rep. Justin Humphrey, Oklahoma House of Representatives, video, April 29, 2021, 12:04:04 p.m., https://sg001-harmony.sliq.net/00283/Harmony/en/PowerBrowser/PowerBrowserV2/20210429/-1/30671.

45. Krehbiel, "Oklahoma's House Sends Legislation." The account in this and the following three paragraphs draws on this source unless otherwise noted.

46. Humphrey, video. The account in this and the following three paragraphs draws on this source unless otherwise noted.

47. Krehbiel, "Oklahoma's House Sends Legislation."

48. Canfield, "Tulsa Race Massacre Centennial Commission Asks Stitt to Veto Bill on 'Critical Race Theory,'" *Tulsa World*, May 4, 2021; Hoberock, "Watch Now: Stitt Signs Controversial Bill that Limits In-school Instruction on Race, Gender and History," *Tulsa World*, May 7, 2021; April Hill, "Tulsa Mayor Doesn't Mince Words on Critical Race Theory in Schools," KRMG, May 10, 2021.

49. Hoberock, "Watch Now: Stitt Signs Controversial Bill."

50. Hoberock, "Watch Now: Stitt Signs Controversial Bill."

51. House Bill 1775, 58th Oklahoma Legislature; Executive Order 2021–12, Office of the Governor, State of Oklahoma, Oklahoma Secretary of State, https://www.sos.ok.gov/documents/executive/2000.pdf.

52. Nichols, interview. The following account draws on this source until otherwise noted.

53. Canfield, "Tulsa Race Massacre Centennial Commission Asks Stitt to Veto Bill on 'Critical Race Theory'"; Hoberock, "Watch Now: Stitt Signs Controversial Bill."; Executive Order 2021–12, Office of the Governor.

54. Krehbiel, "Pressure Mounts on Centennial Commission as Tulsa Race Massacre Anniversary Approaches," May 11, 2021.

55. 1921 Tulsa Race Massacre Centennial Commission to Gov. Kevin Stitt, May 11, 2021, https://bloximages.newyork1.vip.townnews.com/tulsaworld.com/content/tncms/assets/v3/editorial/a/30/a30ab1f4-b298-11eb-976e-1bea78279870/609aeb12770c8.pdf.pdf.

56. "Governor Kevin Stitt's Segregated Media Policy Takes Shape Ahead of Race Massacre Centennial," *Black Wall Street Times*, May 11, 2021.

57. "Governor Kevin Stitt's Segregated Media Policy Takes Shape."

58. Krehbiel, "Centennial Commission Scolds Governor; Legislator Says He's Had Enough," *Tulsa World*, May 12, 2021. The following account draws on this source unless otherwise noted.

Chapter 7. Survivors

1. "First Doses of COVID-19 Vaccine Given in Tulsa Tuesday," KJRH, Dec. 15, 2020, https://www.kjrh.com/news/local-news/first-doses-of-covid-19-vaccine-arrive-in-tulsa-county; Schlotthauer, "Arrival of COVID-19 Vaccine in Tulsa Renews Health Care Workers' Hope, But Officials Say the Virus Remains a Threat to Others," *Tulsa World*, Dec. 16, 2020.

2. Emory Bryan, "First Covid-19 Vaccines Distributed in Tulsa," KOTV, Dec. 15, 2020, https://www.newson6.com/story/5fd8c859dd57bd0bdea44371/first-covid19-vaccines-distributed-in-tulsa.

3. Jones, "Oklahoma Has 3rd Highest Rate of COVID-19 Hospitalizations in the U.S., According to Latest White House Report," *Tulsa World*, Dec. 10, 2020; "COVID-19: Hospitalizations Reach New High; 22 More Deaths Reported," *Tulsa World*, Dec. 22, 2020; Jones, "White House Ranks Oklahoma No. 1 Nationally in Test Positivity Rate and Top 10 Among States for Three COVID-19 Metrics," *Tulsa World*, Dec. 24, 2022.

4. "Watch Now: 'Today Is an Amazing Day for Us': Tulsa Health Care Workers Receive COVID-19 Vaccinations," *Tulsa World*, Dec. 15, 2020.

5. Schlotthauer, "Arrival of COVID-19 Vaccine in Tulsa."

6. Schlotthauer, "Arrival of COVID-19 Vaccine in Tulsa."

7. Forman, "Oklahoma is in the Bottom 10 States for COVID-19 Vaccines. Could Politics Be to Blame?" *Oklahoman*, July 18, 2021.

8. Casteel, "Poll Shows Majority Support Oklahoma Mask Mandate, Vaccinations," *Oklahoman*, Dec. 24, 2020; Forman, "Oklahoma Is in the Bottom 10 States"; Oklahoma Covid-19 Weekly Report, Weekly Epidemiology and Surveillance Report, Oklahoma State Department of Health, April 23–29, 2023, https://oklahoma.gov/content/dam/ok/en/health/health2/aem-documents/prevention-and-preparedness/acute-disease-service/disease-information/covid-19/weekly-epi-report/2023/2023.05.02%20Weekly%20Epi%20Report.pdf.

9. Jones, "Oklahoma's Diving Vaccination Rate Won't Earn State Herd Immunity this Summer but Could Come 'Pretty Close,'" *Tulsa World*, May 10, 2021.

10. Weekly Epidemiology and Surveillance Report, Oklahoma State Department of Health, April 23–29, 2023.

11. General election results for 2016, 2018, 2020, and 2022, Election Results, Oklahoma State Election Board, https://oklahoma.gov/elections/elections-results/election-results.html; US Census Bureau Quick Facts, https://www.census.gov/quickfacts/fact/table/US/SBO020217; Krehbiel, "Local Elections May Be Where the Action Is in 2022," *Tulsa World*, Jan. 2, 2022.

12. Kyle Hinchey, "Latest Round of Returning Students Heads into Tulsa Classrooms," *Tulsa World*, Nov. 17, 2020; Stanley, "'It's Painful': Tulsa Public Schools' Move to Return to Distance Learning 'Not Something We Take Lightly,' Leaders Say," *Tulsa World*, Dec. 2, 2020; Schlotthauer, "Tulsa-area School Districts Return to Virtual and In-person Learning Following Winter Break," *Tulsa World*, Jan. 5, 2021; Schlotthauer, 'Watch Now: Tulsa Public Schools Delays Return to In-person Learning," *Tulsa World*, Jan. 18, 2021; Lenzy Krehbiel-Burton, "Downward Trend in COVID Cases Could Have Tulsa Students Back in Classrooms Sooner Rather than Later," *Tulsa World*, Jan. 26, 2021; Krehbiel, "Watch Now: Stitt Praises Administration's Handling of COVID, Takes on McGirt Ruling," *Tulsa World*, Feb. 2, 2021; Krehbiel-Burton, "TPS Making Preparations to Bring Students Back to Classrooms Next Week," *Tulsa World*, Feb. 18, 2021; Krehbiel-Burton, "Months of Distance Learning: TPS Families Talk about Changes, Challenges," *Tulsa World*, Feb. 23, 2021; Krehbiel-Burton, "Stitt Staffers' Tweets Criticizing Tulsa Public Schools Get Chilly Online Reception," *Tulsa World*, March 26, 2021.

13. Deborah Gist, Facebook post, Feb. 1, 2021, https://www.facebook.com/deborahagist/posts/10221600394911882; Vicent and Grimwood, "Broken Arrow Ends Emergency Proclamation Following Governor's 'Bounce Back' Plan; Bixby Weighing Options, *Tulsa World*, April 23, 2020; Payne, "Tulsa Clinic's Chief Medical Officer Pens Letter to Gov. Kevin Stitt, Pleading for More Action," *Tulsa World*, Jan. 11, 2021; Canfield, "Tulsa City Councilors Extend Mask Mandate Through April," *Tulsa World*, Jan. 14, 2021; Vicent, "Watch Now: Mask Ordinance Proposal Dies at Broken Arrow City Council Meeting," *Tulsa World*, Jan. 19, 2021; Krehbiel, "Watch Now: Stitt Praises Administration's Handling of COVID, Takes on McGirt Ruling"; Marshall, "Jenks Mayor Expects Expired Mask Ordinance to Be Extended When City Council Meets," *Tulsa World*, Feb. 3, 2021; Hoberock, "Report Criticizes State Spending of Millions in Federal COVID-19 Dollars," *Tulsa World*, Feb. 4, 2021; Krehbiel-Burton, "Area School Districts Resume In-person Classes After COVID-19-induced Distance Learning Period," *Tulsa World*, Feb. 7, 2021; Jones, "Stitt Says COVID-19 Hospitalizations Have Been 'Pretty Flat' for Two Months, But State Data Show a 50% Increase," *Tulsa World*, Feb. 15, 2021; Eger, "Gov. Kevin Stitt Continues Push for Reopened Classrooms Despite Criticism from Pediatrician Association, Local School Leaders," *Tulsa World*, Feb. 15, 2021; Wayne Greene, "Wayne Greene: Legislative Assault on the Tulsa City-County Health Department Should Upset Every Local Taxpayer," *Tulsa World*, Feb. 28, 2021; Jacob Factor, "Broken Arrow Repeals Mask Resolution," *Tulsa World*, April 22, 2021.

14. First Baptist Church North Tulsa History, https://fbcnt.org/members-guests/history/; Mary Noble, "Legacy and Impact: Remembering MLK's Visit to North Tulsa, 50 Years after His Death," *Tulsa People*, April 4, 2018; *Tulsa City Directory 1921* (Tulsa: Polk-Hoffine Directory Co., 1921).

15. Anthony Scott (pastor, First Baptist Church North Tulsa), interview with author, Nov. 17, 2022, transcript in possession of author. The account in this and the following four paragraphs draws on this source unless otherwise noted.

16. Overall, "Drive-in Church Offers Tulsa 'Joy in a Messed-up World,'" *Tulsa World*, April 6, 2020; Bill Sherman, "Most Churches Likely to Remain Closed this Sunday as They Work to Find 'New Normal' For Worship," *Tulsa World*, May 2, 2020; Steve Fair, "Steve Fair: God's Law Trumps Man's Law . . . Even in a Pandemic," *Tulsa World*, Sept. 14, 2020; "Some Tulsans Concerned over Indoor Church Concert Held Tuesday Night," KJRH, Nov. 18, 2020.

17. Claire Gecewicz, "Amid Pandemic, Black and Hispanic Worshippers More Concerned about Safety of In-person Religious Services," Pew Research Center, Aug. 7, 2020, https://www.pewresearch.org/short-reads/2020/08/07/amid-pandemic-black-and-hispanic-worshippers-more-concerned-about-safety-of-in-person-religious-services/; Nichols, interview.

18. Scott, interview.

19. Gustavo Olguin, "Only a Few Churches in Tulsa Plan to Open Back Up on May 3," KTUL, May 3, 2020; "Some Tulsans Concerned Over Indoor Church Concert Held Tuesday Night," KJRH, Nov. 19, 2020; Cary Funk and Alec Tyson, "Growing Share of Americans Say They Plan To Get a COVID-19 Vaccine—or Already Have," report, Pew Research Center, March 5, 2021, https://www.pewresearch.org/science/2021/03/05/growing-share-of-americans-say-they-plan-to-get-a-covid-19-vaccine-or-already-have/; Krehbiel, "Tulsa Pastor Challenges Lankford for Senate"; John Yang, "Pastor reveals the reasons behind COVID vaccine hesitancy in the evangelical community," *PBS Newshour*, April 8, 2021; The Thrive Time Show, 2024, https://www.thrivetimeshow.com/reawaken-america-tour/.

20. Scott, interview.

21. "Some Tulsans Concerned over Indoor Church Concert Held Tuesday Night," KJRH, Nov. 18, 2020.

22. Scott, interview. The following account, until the section end, draws on this interview unless otherwise noted.

23. Randle, et al v. City of Tulsa, et al, CV-2020–1179, Tulsa District Court; Stanley, "Success of New Tulsa Race Massacre Reparations Lawsuit Hinges on State's Nuisance Law, Attorneys Say," *Tulsa World*, Oct. 7, 2021; Lessie Benningfield Randle, video deposition, Oct. 14, 2020, transcript; Viola Fletcher, video deposition, Oct. 16, 2020, transcript; Stanley, "Previously Unknown Tulsa Race Massacre Survivor Added to Lawsuit Plaintiffs," *Tulsa World*, Feb. 23, 2021.

24. Stanley, "Previously Unknown Tulsa Race Massacre"; SolomonSimmonsLaw PLLC v. City of Tulsa, et al, CV-2021–451, Tulsa County District Court; SolomonSimmonsLaw PLLC v. Tulsa Development Authority, CV-2021–452, Tulsa County District

Court; SolomonSimmonsLaw PLLC v. City of Tulsa Metropolitan Area Planning Commission, CV-2021–453, Tulsa County District Court; Factor, "Lawsuit Filed Against City of Tulsa for Denying Access to Tulsa Race Massacre Public Records," *Tulsa World*, April 2, 2021.

25. SolomonSimmonsLaw PLLC v. City of Tulsa, et al, CV-2021–451; Trotter, "1921 Tulsa Race Massacre Centennial Commission Told to Stop Using Survivor's Name, Likeness," Public Radio Tulsa, April 16, 2021; Jacinda Hameon, "'This Issue Isn't Dead': Tulsa Race Massacre Lawsuit Seeks Reparations for Emotional, Physical Damages," *OU Daily*, April 9, 2021; "The Records OHP Didn't Want Us to Have," *Tulsa World*, podcast, Jan. 21, 2022.

26. James D. Watts, "Original Play Highlights the Unquenchable Spirit in Greenwood History," *Tulsa World*, Feb. 9, 2019.

27. Canfield, "Mayor Responds to Criticism from Terence Crutcher's Sister with Frustration about Portrayal of Police"; Randle, et al v. City of Tulsa, et al, CV-2020–1179; SolomonSimmonsLaw PLLC v. City of Tulsa, et al, CV-2021–451, Tulsa County District Court; SolomonSimmonsLaw PLLC v. Tulsa Development Authority, CV-2021–452, Lesa Jones, "Men of Distinction 2015: Damario Solomon-Simmons," *Tulsa Business and Legal News*, Dec. 18, 2015; Marshall, "Security Guard Who Paralyzed Tulsa Man in Shooting Charged with Drug Possession," May 30, 2015; Dylan Goforth, "Attorney Who Represented Families of Trayvon Martin, Michael Brown, Retained in Tulsa Shooting Case," *Tulsa World*, March 31, 2015

28. Lane Clegg, "Five Questions: Damario Solomon-Simmons," *Tulsa People*, April 1, 2014.

29. Vicent, "Betty Shelby Won't Face Federal Prosecution on Alleged Civil Rights Violation in Death of Terence Crutcher, U.S. Attorney Says," *Tulsa World*, April 4, 2019; Krehbiel, "Group Undaunted in Quest for Reparations," *Tulsa World*, Oct. 31, 2005; Ralph Schaefer, "Former Sooner Turns Gridiron Lessons into Success in the Courtroom," *Tulsa Business and Legal News*, Aug. 29, 2015; Goforth, "Attorney Who Represented Families of Trayvon Martin, Michael Brown, Retained in Tulsa Shooting Case"; Marshall, "Tulsa-Area Mentoring Groups Help Shape Young Lives by Offering Positive Role Models," *Tulsa World*, Feb, 27, 2015; S. E. Ruckman, "Freedmen Case May Also Affect Creeks," *Tulsa World*, March 9, 2006; Bill Haisten, "Rising Star," *Tulsa World*, July 7, 2009; Graham, "Ginnie Graham: MVP Fatherhood Weekend Coming to Tulsa," *Tulsa World*, March 30, 2013; Marshall, "Security Guard Who Paralyzed Tulsa Man"; Marshall, "Tulsa Man Shot and Paralyzed by Security Guard Dies," *Tulsa World*, July 2, 2015; Caleb Gayle, "The Black Americans Suing to Reclaim Their Native American Identity," *Guardian*, Nov. 2, 2018.

30. Vicent, "Betty Shelby Won't Face Federal Prosecution."

31. SolomonSimmonsLaw PLLC v. City of Tulsa, et al, CV-2021–451; Trotter, "1921 Tulsa Race Massacre Centennial Commission Told to Stop Using Survivor's Name, Likeness"; Adams v. City of Tulsa, et al, CJ-2023–261, Tulsa County District Court; In the matter of the estate of Andrew Cheesten Jackson, PB-2022–1291, Tulsa County District Court.

32. Trotter, "1921 Tulsa Race Massacre Centennial Commission Told to Stop"; Damario Solomon-Simmons to Phil Armstrong, letter, April 14, 2021, copy in possession of the

author, https://drive.google.com/file/d/1nI38mn4Ve26uxpzrzakj27WFmjRJU95V/view (hereafter Solomon-Simmons to Armstrong).

33. Solomon-Simmons to Armstrong.

34. Solomon-Simmons to Armstrong.

35. Matthews, interview; Armstrong, interview; Krehbiel, "North Tulsans Say They Wanted Input Before Juvenile Justice Center Was Planned for Area," *Tulsa World*, Sept. 29, 2015; Watts, "Original Play Highlights the Unquenchable Spirit."

36. Armstrong, interview; City of Tulsa, "City Selects Award-winning Architecture Firm for Greenwood Cultural Center Renovation," press release, April 12, 2021, https://www.cityoftulsa.org/press-room/city-selects-award-winning-architecture-firm-for-greenwood-cultural-center-renovation/; Derek Major, "Black-Owned Architectural Firm Chosen to Renovate Greenwood Cultural Center," *Black Enterprise*, April 14, 2021; *The ReidOut*, MSNBC, May 8, 2023, https://www.facebook.com/watch/?v=262485202894050.

37. Armstrong, interview; Greenwood Rising, 2024, https://www.greenwoodrising.org/; Yar, interview; Business Entity Search, Oklahoma Secretary of State, https://secretaryofstate.com/oklahoma; Property Search, Tulsa County Assessor, https://assessor.tulsacounty.org/Property/Search .

38. Matthews, interview; Armstrong, interview; Krehbiel, "'No Reconciliation Without Reparations' Says Race Massacre Panelist," *Tulsa World*, June 1, 2020; "The 1921 Tulsa Race Massacre Commission Releases Reparations Position," *Black Wall Street Times*, March 26, 2021.

39. Krehbiel, "'No Reconciliation Without Reparations.'"

40. Krehbiel, "Tulsa Race Massacre: Struggle for Reparations from 1921 Massacre Continues, and so Do the Disagreements," *Tulsa World*, May 24, 2021; Stanley, "'Black Wall Street 100': Tulsa Author-Historian Reviews Century of 'Grappling' with Lingering 'Wound' of 1921 Tulsa Race Massacre," *Tulsa World*, Oct. 13, 2020; "The 1921 Tulsa Race Massacre Commission Releases Reparations Position;" Redfearn v. American Central Insurance, Brief of Plaintiff Error, Oklahoma Supreme Court; Capt. John McCuen to Lt. Col. L. J. F. Rooney, n.d., Case 1062, Attorney Generals Civil Case Files, Governor J. B. A. Robertson's papers, 1919–1923, Oklahoma State Archives, Oklahoma Department of Libraries, Oklahoma City.

41. Randle, et al v. City of Tulsa, et al, CV-2020–1179.

42. Krehbiel, "Tulsa Race Massacre: Struggle for Reparations from 1921 Massacre Continues."

43. Krehbiel, "Tulsa Race Massacre: Struggle for Reparations from 1921 Massacre Continues"; Jan, "The 'Whitewashing' of Black Wall Street."

44. "'She Spoke the Truth': After Years of not Talking about It, Tulsa Race Riot Survivor Hazel Jones Opened Up, Providing a Public Face for Survivors," *Tulsa World*, March 8, 2018; Nora K. Froeschle, "History Key to Better Future," *Tulsa World*, Feb. 16, 2000; Krehbiel, "Tulsa Race Massacre: Struggle for Reparations from 1921 Massacre Continues, and So Do the Disagreements"; Watts, "Original Play Highlights the Unquenchable Spirit in Greenwood History."

45. Lessie Benningfield Randle, video deposition, transcript, Oct. 14, 2020.

46. Lessie Benningfield Randle, video deposition, transcript, Oct. 14, 2020; 1940 U.S. Census entry for Lessie Benningfield; *Tulsa City Directories, 1920–22*, (Tulsa: Polk-Hoffine Directory Co., 1920–22).

47. Viola Fletcher, video deposition, transcript, Oct. 16, 2020; "Woman Recalls Working as Welder During War," July 14, 2014, *Bartlesville Examiner-Enterprise* https://www.examiner-enterprise.com/story/news/military/2014/07/14/woman-recalls-working-as-welder/27379766007/. Transcript of May 21, 2014, interview of Viola Fletcher by Joe L. Todd, of the Dwight D. Eisenhower Library, reference No. EL-VOH-WWII-822; Tanya Finchum and Alex Bishop, "Oral History Interview with Viola Fletcher," Oklahoma 100 Year Oral History Project, Oklahoma State University, Dec. 10, 2014; "Negro Lynched by Holdenville Mob," *Tulsa World*, Dec. 6, 1920; "Oklahoma Disgraced Again by Mob Violence," *Tulsa Star*, Dec. 11, 1920.

48. Viola Fletcher, video deposition, transcript, Oct. 16, 2020.

49. Finchum and Bishop, "Oral History Interview with Viola Fletcher."

50. "Woman Recalls Working as Welder During War," July 14, 2014, *Bartlesville Examiner-Enterprise*.

51. Finchum and Bishop, "Oral History Interview with Viola Fletcher"; Stanley, "50 Years Ago, The 1921 Tulsa Race Massacre Was a Taboo Subject When Tulsan Ed Wheeler Set Out to Write an Article 'To Find Out What Happened.' He Had no Idea the Threats and Resistance He Would Face Just for Trying," *Tulsa World*, April 4, 2021; Krehbiel, "Attorney Says Trauma Impacted Race Massacre Survivor's Memory," *Tulsa World*, May 29, 2021.

52. Krehbiel, "Attorney Says Trauma Impacted."

53. Rodney C. Roberts, "The Morality of a Moral Statute of Limitations on Injustice," *Journal of Ethics* 7, no. 1: 115–38.

Chapter 8. Centennial

1. Payne, "'Beacon of Reconciliation': Tulsa Race Massacre Commission Begins 2021 Campaign as Centennial Nears," *Tulsa World*, Jan. 2, 2021; Tim Landes, "Scenes from Centennial Year Launch Event at John Hope Franklin Reconciliation Park," *Tulsa People*, Jan. 1, 2021.

2. Payne, "'Beacon of Reconciliation'"; Landes, "Scenes from Centennial Year Launch Event."

3. Krehbiel, "Race Riot Memorial Action Urged to Protect Funding," *Tulsa World*, Aug. 20, 2003; Krehbiel, "John Hope Franklin Center Again on Hold," *Tulsa World*, May 2, 2008

4. Krehbiel, "Race Riot Memorial Action; Krehbiel, "John Hope Franklin Center Again on Hold"; P. J. Lassek, "Councilors Back Plan for Church," *Tulsa World*, Dec. 21, 2001; Killman, "Third-Penny Tax Use Plan Appears Dead," *Tulsa World*, Jan. 9, 2002; Krehbiel, "Land for Museum Targeted, "Feb. 20, 2003; Krehbiel, "Land for Race Riot Museum OK'd," *Tulsa World*, Feb. 22, 2003; Krehbiel, "Tulsa Race Riot Memorial to Start Small," *Tulsa World*, Sept. 5, 2003; Krehbiel, "Support for Riot Project Questioned," *Tulsa World*, April 4, 2004; Barber, "Council Oks Funds for Race Riot Park," *Tulsa World*, Oct. 27, 2008; "Dr. John Hope Franklin Greenwood Reconciliation Museum Program

and Conceptual Design Manual"; Krehbiel, "City to Break Ground on Park, Finally," *Tulsa World*, Nov. 8, 2008; Denver Nicks, "Harmony's Park," *Tulsa World*, Nov. 18, 2008.

5. Krehbiel, "John Hope Franklin Center Again on Hold"; Barber, "Council Oks Funds for Race Riot Park."

6. Krehbiel, "People to Watch: Sen. Kevin Matthews Hopes to Turn 1921 Race Massacre Anniversary into Something of Lasting Importance," *Tulsa World*, Jan. 3, 2021.

7. Payne, "'Beacon of Reconciliation.'"

8. "Bloomberg Philanthropies Announces City of Tulsa Will Receive $1 Million for Public Art Project Honoring America's First 'Black Wall Street," Bloomberg Philanthropies, Jan. 15, 2019, https://www.bloomberg.org/press/bloomberg-philanthropies-announces-city-tulsa-will-receive-1-million-public-art-project-honoring-americas-first-black-wall-street/; Canfield, "Artist Rick Lowe Says Community Involvement Key to the Greenwood Art Project," *Tulsa World*, Jan. 17, 2019; Tramel, "Fire in Little Africa: Oklahoma Artists Unite on Project Commemorating Tulsa Race Massacre," *Tulsa World*, April 5, 2020; Tramel, "Oklahoma Hip-Hop Artists Unite for Historic Project on Centennial of Tulsa Race Massacre," *Tulsa World*, March 1, 2021; Watts, "Tulsa Opera to Present 'Greenwood Overcomes' Concert," *Tulsa World*, March 2, 2021; Watts, "Tulsa Opera Concert a Celebration of Black Artistry," April 29, 2021; Watts, "Community Voices, Community Vision: Greenwood Art Project to Unveil Works by Dozens Of Artists," *Tulsa World*, May 26, 2021; Stanley, "Watch Now: Greenwood Art Project Officially Unveiled at Public Event: 'Powerful to See,'" *Tulsa World*, May 27, 2021; Watts, "Review: Tulsa Ballet's 'Breakin' Bricks' Confronts History of Race Relations," *Tulsa World*, Nov. 30, 2021; Fire in Little Africa, https://fireinlittleafrica.com/, accessed Jun 9, 2024; "'Fire in Little Africa' Live Performance," Hutchins Center for African & African American Research, Harvard University, April 26, 2023, https://hutchinscenter.fas.harvard.edu/event/performance-stevie-johnson-fire-little-africa.

9. Jesse Ulrich, "Dr. View and the Fire in Little Africa," *Medium*, Feb. 10, 2021, https://medium.com/rant9-com/dr-view-and-the-fire-in-little-africa-cd3e25cd315c. Links to episode 7, Pod 4 Good, Rant9 Productions, Jan. 28, 2021, https://www.pod4good.com/dr-view-and-fire-in-little-africa/; "Dr. View Says the 1921 Commission Can't Be Nonpolitical When Race is Involved," *Black Wall Street Times*, Jan. 29, 2021.

10. Ulrich, "Dr. View and the Fire in Little Africa"; "Dr. View Says the 1921 Commission Can't Be Nonpolitical."

11. "Dr. View Joins the Ohio State University," *Black Wall Street Times*, March 21, 2023. The text of Johnson's dissertation is available on the UO / UCO institutional repository website SHAREOK, https://shareok.org/handle/11244/319608.

12. Ulrich, ""Dr. View and the Fire in Little Africa"; "Dr. View says the 1921 Commission Can't Be Nonpolitical."

13. Watts, "Tulsa Opera to Present 'Greenwood Overcomes' Concert," *Tulsa World*, March 2, 2021; David Salazar, "Tulsa Opera Removes Composer Daniel Roumain From Concert Commemorating Race Massacre Over One Word," *Opera Wire*, March 21, 2021, https://operawire.com/tulsa-opera-removes-black-composer-from-concert-commemorating-race-massacre-over-one-word/; Watts, "Composer's Work Dropped

From Tulsa Opera 'Greenwood' Concert Over Lyrics," March 24, 2021; Watts, "Tulsa Opera Concert a Celebration of Black Artistry," *Tulsa World*, April 29, 2021.

14. Salazar, "Tulsa Opera Removes Composer Daniel Roumain."

15. Salazar, "Tulsa Opera Removes Composer Daniel Roumain."

16. Watts, "Composer's Work Dropped." The account in this and the following two paragraphs draws on this source unless otherwise noted

17. Salazar, "Tulsa Opera Removes Composer Daniel Roumain"; Watts, "Composer's Work Dropped."

18. Francisco Salazar, "Black Opera Alliance Releases Statement Regarding Tulsa Opera & Daniel Roumain's Removal from 'Greenwood Overcomes,'" *Opera Wire*, March 25, 2021, https://operawire.com/black-opera-alliance-releases-statement-regarding-tulsa-opera-daniel-roumains-removal-from-greenwood-overcomes/.

19. Watts, "Composer's Work Dropped." The account in this and the following two paragraphs draws on this source unless otherwise noted

20. Logan Martell, "Arts Organizations Partner for World Premiere of Daniel Roumain's 'They Still Want to Kill Us,'" *Opera Wire*, May 11, 2021, https://operawire.com/arts-organizations-partner-for-world-premiere-of-daniel-roumains-they-still-want-to-kill-us/; Watts, "Two Tulsa Massacre-themed Works to Debut Online," *Tulsa World*, May 16, 2021.

21. Schlotthauer and Canfield, "Federal Authorities Helping with Investigation of Ransomware Attack That Is Slowing City Services," *Tulsa World*, May 11, 2021; Adam B. Smith, "2021 U.S. Billion-dollar Weather and Climate Disasters in Historical Context," *Beyond the Data* (blog), National Oceanic and Atmospheric Administration, Jan. 24, 2022, https://www.climate.gov/news-features/blogs/beyond-data/2021-us-billion-dollar-weather-and-climate-disasters-historical; Michael Grogan, "Green Country's Record Breaking Deep Freeze Feb. 2021," KOKI, Feb. 13, 2022; Morgan, "OG&E Ratepayer-Backed Bonds to Pay for Last Year's Cold Snap Are Now Hundreds of Millions More than Estimated," *Tulsa World*, July 19, 2022.

22. Krehbiel, "Oklahoma's House Sends Legislation Intended to Deflect Criticism"; Canfield, "Tulsa Race Massacre Centennial Commission Asks Stitt to Veto Bill"; Hoberock, "Watch Now: Stitt Signs Controversial Bill"; Cheema and Goodwin, "Opinion: Don't Stifle Dissent. Deal with Underlying Issues," *Tulsa World*, Jun 25, 2021.

23. Tracy Jan, "The 'Whitewashing' of Black Wall Street," *Washington Post*, Jan. 17, 2021, https://www.washingtonpost.com/business/2021/01/17/tulsa-massacre-greenwood-black-wall-street-gentrification/. The account in this and the following eight paragraphs draws on this source unless otherwise noted:

24. Stanley, "'Revive the Spirit of Black Wall Street': Program for Black Student Entrepreneurs Kicks Off 12th Summer with New $1,000 Prize," *Tulsa World*, June 30, 2020; Morgan, "Closing the Racial Wealth Gap Focus of Summer Economic Empowerment Day, *Tulsa World*, March 18, 2021; Build in Tulsa, Inc., https://www.buildintulsa.com/, accessed Jun 9, 2024; Kaiser to Krehbiel.

25. Kaiser to Krehbiel. The following account draws on this source until otherwise noted.

26. Armstrong, interview.

27. Canfield, "'A Hot-Button Issue': Not All Black Tulsans Are Happy about Greenwood Rising," *Tulsa World*, May 26, 2021.

28. Canfield, "'A Hot-Button Issue.'"

29. Canfield, "Upcoming City Projects in the Works to Commemorate Tulsa Race Massacre, Begin North Tulsa Development," *Tulsa World*, May 31, 2020; Our Legacy, Our Community: A Renewed Vision For North Tulsa, https://www.ourlegacytulsa.org/, accessed Jun 9, 2024.

30. "Survivors and Descendants to Host 'Black Wall Street Legacy Festival' to Commemorate Centennial of the 1921 Tulsa Race Massacre," *Black Wall Street Times*, April 8, 2021; Dr. Tiffany Crutcher, *Black Wall Street Times* 2021 Person of the Year," *Black Wall Street Times*, Dec. 20, 2021; Justice for Greenwood, https://www.justiceforgreenwood.org/, accessed Jun 9, 2024; Randle, et al v. City of Tulsa, et al, CV-2020–1179, Tulsa District Court.

31. Historic Vernon AME Church Needs Help for Renovations," KRJH, Sept. 23, 2019; Overall, "Vernon AME Church to Receive Preservation Help for Stained Glass Windows from National Grant," *Tulsa World*, July 18, 2020.

32. Krehbiel, "'The Grandmother of Greenwood': Vernon AME Church Receives $200,000 Donation for Renovations," *Tulsa World*, April 4, 2021.

33. Hicham Raache, "Large Donation to Help Preserve Historic Church that Survived Tulsa Race Massacre," *Tulsa World*, April 3, 2021.

34. Canfield, "Completed Greenwood Rising Exhibit Now Awaits to Be Filled with Stories," *Tulsa World*, May 10, 2021.

35. Watts, "Wynton Marsalis Will Join Tulsa Symphony to Present 'All Rise' at BOK Center," *Tulsa World*, May 8, 2021; Stanley, "Race Massacre Centennial Events Begin This Week, Continue into Next," *Tulsa World*, May 10, 2021; Schlotthauer, "Watch Now: National Black Power Conference Coming to Tulsa Ahead of Race Massacre Centennial," *Tulsa World*, May 13, 2021.

36. Stanley, "John Legend to Headline Televised Tulsa Race Massacre Commemorative Event May 31," *Tulsa World*, May 14, 2021; Stanley, "Tulsa Race Massacre Centennial: Stacey Abrams Announced as Keynote Speaker for Nationally Televised Commemoration," *Tulsa World*, May 19, 2021; Stanley, "Tickets for Remember & Rise 'Sell Out' Within 30 Minutes," *Tulsa World*, June 21, 2021.

37. "Hearing on Centennial of 1921 Tulsa Race Massacre," *C-SPAN*, May 19, 2021, https://www.c-span.org/video/?511795-1/hearing-centennial-1921-tulsa-race-massacre. The account in this and the following three paragraphs draws on this source unless otherwise noted

38. Janelle Stecklein, "Last Tulsa Race Massacre Survivors Push for Reparations," *Enid News & Eagle*, May 22, 2022.

39. Phil Armstrong to Damario Solomon-Simmons, e-mail #2, author's files, n.d.; Solomon-Simmons to Armstrong, et al, e-mail #1, author's files, May 23, 2021; Carla Hinton, "Attorneys Requested Funds to Go to Tulsa Race Massacre Survivors for Involvement in 'Remember + Rise,'" *Oklahoman*, May 28, 2021 (digital copy of email

#1 imbedded); "Tulsa Race Massacre Remembrance Main Event Suddenly Canceled," *CBS*, May 29, 2021; Canfield, "Watch Now: Remember & Rise Event Collapsed after Frantic Week of Meetings, Emails and Talks about Survivor Payments," *Tulsa World*, May 29, 2021

40. Solomon-Simmons to Armstrong, et al, e-mail #1, author's files, May 23, 2021; Carla Hinton, "Attorneys Requested Funds to Go to Tulsa.'" The account in this and the following four paragraphs draws on these sources unless otherwise noted.

41. Solomon-Simmons to Armstrong, et al, e-mail #1; Hinton, "Attorneys Requested Funds to Go to Tulsa"; Stecklein, "Last Tulsa Race Massacre Survivors Push for Reparations"; Canfield, "Watch Now: Remember & Rise Event Collapsed."

42. Solomon-Simmons to Armstrong, et al, e-mail #1, author's files, May 23, 2021; Hinton, "Attorneys Requested Funds To Go To Tulsa"; Canfield, "Watch Now: Remember & Rise Event Collapsed."

43. Solomon-Simmons to Armstrong, et al, e-mail #1; Hinton, "Attorneys Requested Funds to Go to Tulsa."

44. Solomon-Simmons to Armstrong, et al, e-mail #1; Hinton, "Attorneys Requested Funds to Go to Tulsa."

45. "Foundation Gifts $100,000 to Living Tulsa Race Massacre Survivors," *Tulsa World*, June 4, 2021; Mike Creef, "Transformation Church Gifts Over $1 Million to Tulsa Race Massacre Survivors, Nonprofits," *Black Wall Street Times*, June 22, 2021; Brown, "Three Survivors of Tulsa Race Massacre Receive $1 Million Donation," *Washington Post*, May 18, 2022.

46. Canfield, "Watch Now: Remember & Rise Event Collapsed."

47. Solomon-Simmons to Armstrong, et al, e-mail #1, author's files, May 23, 2021; Carla Hinton, "Attorneys Requested Funds to Go To Tulsa"; Canfield, "Watch Now: Remember & Rise Event Collapsed."

48. Hinton "Attorneys Requested Funds to Go to Tulsa"; Canfield, "Watch Now: Remember & Rise Event Collapsed."

49. Brown, "Tensions Erupt in Tulsa as City Commemorates 1921 Race Massacre," *Washington Post*, May 30, 2021.

50. Matthews, interview.

51. Canfield, "Biden Makes Strong Impression on Local Leaders, Who Praise his Knowledge of Race Massacre," *Tulsa World*, June 2, 2021.

52. Rob Martindale, "Clinton to Launch Push in Tulsa for Health Reform," *Tulsa World*, Aug. 8, 1993.

53. Watts, "Eddie Faye Gates' Collection of Race Massacre History Donated to Gilcrease Museum," *Tulsa World*, Oct. 15, 2020; Vicent, "Visits with Centenarian Tulsa Race Massacre Survivors Will Stay Possible Through Interactive Exhibit Unveiled at Gilcrease Museum," *Tulsa World*, May 28, 2021; Morgan, "Watch Now: Black Wall Street Memorial March Keeps Eye on Justice During Race Massacre Commemoration," *Tulsa World*, May 29, 2021.

54. Morgan, "Watch Now: Black Wall Street Memorial March." The account in the following three paragraphs draws on this source unless otherwise noted.

55. Overall, "'Pathway of Hope': Trying To Heal a Scar Left by the 'Second' Destruction of Tulsa's Greenwood District," *Tulsa World*, May 29, 2021; Landes, "Scenes from the Pathway to Hope Opening," *Tulsa People*, May 28, 2021.

56. Tramel, "Black Wall Street Legacy Festival Announces Full Schedule," *Tulsa World*, May 18, 2021.

57. Dekker, "Watch Now: Armed Marchers Take to Downtown Tulsa Streets in Show of Strength, Solidarity in Honor of Race Massacre Victims," *Tulsa World*, May 30, 2021; Scott, interview.

58. Graham, "Watch Now: Town Hall on Justice for Survivors and Descendants of Tulsa Race Massacre," *Tulsa World*, May 31, 2021. The following discussion draws on this source until otherwise noted.

59. Factor, "Hundreds Gather for Candlelight Vigil to Honor 1921 Tulsa Race Massacre Victims, Survivors and Descendants," *Tulsa World*, June 1, 2021.

60. Factor, "Hundreds Gather for Candlelight Vigil ."

61. Krehbiel, "Watch Now: 'Hate is Never Defeated,' Biden Says on Race Massacre Centennial," *Tulsa World*, June 2, 2021.

62. Canfield, "Biden Makes Strong Impression on Local Leaders, Who Praise His Knowledge of Race Massacre," *Tulsa World*, June 2, 2021.

63. Krehbiel, "Watch Now: 'Hate is Never Defeated'"; Eger and Stanley, "Crowds Turn Out in Hopes of Witnessing Historic Presidential Visit," *Tulsa World*, June 1, 2021; Osborne, "President Biden Vows to Repair Greenwood in Tulsa but Stops Short of Saying Reparations," *Black Wall Street Times*, June 2, 2021.

64. Joseph R. Biden Jr., "A Proclamation on Day of Remembrance: 100 Years After the 1921 Tulsa Race Massacre," presidential action, May 31, 2021, https://www.whitehouse.gov/briefing-room/presidential-actions/2021/05/31/a-proclamation-on-day-of-remembrance-100-years-after-the-1921-tulsa-race-massacre/.

65. Biden, "A Proclamation on Day of Remembrance."

66. The White House, "Press Gaggle by Principal Deputy Press Secretary Karine Jean-Pierre Aboard Air Force One En Route Tulsa, OK," press release, June 1, 2021, https://www.whitehouse.gov/briefing-room/press-briefings/2021/06/01/press-gaggle-by-principal-deputy-press-secretary-karine-jean-pierre-aboard-air-force-one-en-route-tulsa-ok/; "Remarks by President Biden Commemorating the 100th Anniversary of the Tulsa Race Massacre," speech at Greenwood Cultural Center, Tulsa, OK, June 1, 2021, transcript, June 2, 2021, https://www.whitehouse.gov/briefing-room/speeches-remarks/2021/06/02/remarks-by-president-biden-commemorating-the-100th-anniversary-of-the-tulsa-race-massacre/.

67. "Remarks by President Biden Commemorating the 100th Anniversary."

68. "Remarks by President Biden Commemorating the 100th Anniversary."

69. Gary Lee, "President Biden: 'This Was a Massacre,'" *Oklahoma Eagle*, June 4, 2021.

70. Osborne, "President Biden Vows to Repair Greenwood in Tulsa."

71. Tiffany Crutcher, "What I Told President Biden in Tulsa," *The Progressive*, June 23, 2021.

72. Tiffany Crutcher, "What I Told President Biden."

73. "Press Gaggle by Principal Deputy Press Secretary Karine Jean-Pierre"; Ta-Nehisi Coates, "The Case for Reparations," *Atlantic*, June 2014.

74. Morgan, "Financial Literacy, Equal Access to Money Topics of Black Economic Summit in Tulsa," *Tulsa World*, June 2, 2021. The following discussion draws on this source until otherwise noted.

75. William Faulkner, *Requiem for a Nun* (New York: Random House, 1951).

Chapter 9. Unfinished Business

1. Eger, "Greenwood Rising Dedicated: 'A History Center Dedicated to Telling the Entire History,'" *Tulsa World*, June 2, 2021.

2. Eger, "Greenwood Rising Dedicated."

3. Eger, "Greenwood Rising Dedicated"; Holland Cotter, "Greenwood Rising Links Tulsa's Tragic History to Today's Struggles," *New York Times*, June 3, 2021.

4. Eger, "Greenwood Rising Dedicated."; Greenwood Cultural Center, accessed June 11, 2024, https://www.greenwoodculturalcenter.org/.

5. Eger, "Greenwood Rising Dedicated"; Greenwood Cultural Center; Eddie Faye Gates, *They Came Searching: How Blacks Sought the Promised Land in Tulsa* (Fort Worth, TX: Eakin Press, 1997).

6. Cotter, "Greenwood Rising Links Tulsa's Tragic History to Today's Struggles." Until otherwise noted, the quotes that follow are also from this source.

7. Canfield, "'A Hot-Button Issue': Not All Black Tulsans Are Happy about Greenwood Rising."

8. Lansana, interview. Until otherwise noted, the quotes that follow are also from this source.

9. Gant, interview.

10. Raymond Doswell (executive director, Greenwood Rising), interview with author, June 28, 2023, transcript in possession of author.

11. Jillian Taylor and Ari Fife, "After a State Law Banning Some Lessons on Race, Oklahoma Teachers Tread Lightly on the Tulsa Race Massacre," *The Frontier*, Aug 3, 2023.

12. Jones, "Harvard Professor Talks Tulsa Race Massacre Reparations and White Supremacy During 'National Day Of Learning,'" *Tulsa World*, June 4, 2021. Until otherwise noted, the quotes in the following four paragraphs are also from this source.

13. Overall, "'Much Larger Than One Block': Race Massacre Commission's 'Final Project' Will Mark the True Extent of Historic Greenwood," *Tulsa World*, Nov. 8, 2021; "Historic Greenwood District Boundary Markers," Narrate Design (formerly Selser Schaefer Architects), accessed June 11, 2024, https://narratedesign.com/contact/.

14. Osborne, "Tulsa City Council Apologizes for Massacre, Plans for Repair Despite Demands for Reparations Now," *Black Wall Street Times*, June 3, 2021; Canfield, "Council Approves Resolution Apologizing for Tulsa Race Massacre, Committing to Tangible Amends," *Tulsa World*, June 3, 2021.

15. Osborne, "Tulsa City Council Apologizes for Massacre"; Canfield, "Council Approves Resolution Apologizing."

16. Osborne, "Tulsa City Council Apologizes for Massacre."

17. Osborne, "Tulsa City Council Apologizes for Massacre"; Canfield, "Council Approves Resolution Apologizing"; Canfield, "Preparations Underway for Discussions on Possible Reparations, 'Tangible Amends' for Harm Caused by Tulsa Race Massacre," *Tulsa World*, Dec. 26, 2021.

18. Canfield, "Preparations Underway for Discussions."

19. Canfield, "Mayor Bynum Signs Resolution Creating Community-Led Process to Discuss Possible Race Massacre Redress," *Tulsa World*, April 18, 2022; Jones, "Harvard Professor Talks Tulsa Race Massacre Reparations and White Supremacy During 'National Day of Learning,'" *Tulsa World*, June 4, 2021.

20. Randle, et al, v. City of Tulsa, et al, docket; Jones, "Watch Now: Lawyers for Tulsa Race Massacre Survivors Demand Financial Investment Poured into Greenwood," *Tulsa World*, June 3, 2021; State ex rel. Attorney General of Oklahoma v. Johnson & Johnson.

21. Jones, "Watch Now: Lawyers for Tulsa Race Massacre Survivors."

22. City of Tulsa, "City of Tulsa Commemorates 1921 Tulsa Race Massacre; Substantial Investments Made in Economic and Community Development," press release, May 25, 2021, https://www.cityoftulsa.org/press-room/city-of-tulsa-commemorates-1921-tulsa-race-massacre-substantial-investments-made-in-economic-and-community-development; Krehbiel, "Through A Century of Hard Work and Heartbreak, The Spirit of Greenwood Labors on," *Tulsa World*, May 19, 2021; Morgan, "Local Business Sector Ripe With Successes In 2021," *Tulsa World*, Dec. 26, 2021; Erika DuBose, "Public-Private Partnership Plans Multi-Million Dollar Development in North Tulsa," *Black Wall Street Times*, June 30, 2021; Carson Colvin, email to author, July 6, 2023.

23. Morgan, "Watch Now: Fruits of a Long Labor—Oasis Fresh Market Grand Opening Emotional for Advocates," *Tulsa World*, May 17, 2021.

24. Morgan, "Watch Now: Fruits of a Long Labor."

25. Morgan, "Watch Now: Fruits of a Long Labor"; Watts, "Tulsans of the Year: For Oasis' Owner A.J. Johnson, Grocery Store More Than a Place to Buy Food," *Tulsa World*, Dec. 5, 2021; Tulsa Dream Center, accessed June 11, 2024, https://tulsadreamcenter.org/.

26. Morgan, "Watch Now: Fruits of a Long Labor"; Watts, "Tulsans of the Year: For Oasis' Owner; Tulsa Dream Center; Food Marketing Institute, store size data 1994–2021; "How is the Grocery Store Footprint Changing?" *Current*, Sept. 4, 2018, https://www.led.com/inspiration/how-is-the-grocery-store-footprint-changing.

27. Watts, "Tulsans of the Year: For Oasis' Owner."

28. Morgan, "Townhome Development Called Black Wall Street Square Targeted for Dunbar Neighborhood," *Tulsa World*, April 4, 2021; Morgan, "Town Home Project Called Black Wall Street Square Moves Ahead with Land Sale Approval," *Tulsa World*, Jan. 28, 2022.

29. Morgan, "Townhome Development Called Black Wall Street Square Targeted; Morgan, "Town Home Project Called Black Wall Street Square Moves"; "Black Wall Street Square and Gentrification Concerns," *Black Wall Street Times*, July 8, 2021.

30. "Black Wall Street Square and Gentrification Concerns."

31. "Black Wall Street Square and Gentrification Concerns."

32. Morgan, "Townhome Development Called Black Wall Street Square Targeted"; Morgan, "Watch Now: Fruits of a Long Labor."

33. Morgan, "City Seeks Consultant To Help Develop Kirkpatrick Heights Addition and Greenwood Site Master Plan," *Tulsa World*, Nov. 24, 2019; City of Tulsa, "Our Legacy, Our Community: A Renewed Vision for North Tulsa," 2022; Cory Young, "OSU-Tulsa Land Grant Clears Hurdles," *Tulsa World*, April 14, 2004.

34. Lassek, "City Seeks Expert Development Help," *Tulsa World*, Sept. 2, 2007; "Evans-Fintube Site Roadmap to Redevelopment," Council of Development Finance Agencies, September 2015, https://www.cdfa.net/cdfa/cdfaweb.nsf/ord/201509_EvansfintubeRoadmap.html/$file/Evans-Fintube%20Roadmap%20to%20Redevelopment.pdf; Overall, "Michael Overall: It's an Eyesore Today, But the Evans-Fintube Site Used to Be a Symbol of Tulsa's Progress," *Tulsa World*, Sept. 21, 2021.

35. "Evans-Fintube Site Roadmap to Redevelopment"; "Developers Sought to Create 'Cultural Destination' at Evans-Fintube Industrial Site Near Greenwood District," *Tulsa World*, May 2, 2021.

36. Canfield, "Community Input Key to Developing Kirkpatrick Heights/Greenwood Master Plan, Tulsa Mayor Says," *Tulsa World*, Oct. 28, 2021.

37. Canfield, "Community Input Key to Developing."

38. Canfield, "Community Input Key to Developing"; Morgan, "Watch Now: City Officials Hire Consultant for Kirkpatrick Heights/Greenwood Master Plan," *Tulsa World*, Aug. 18, 2021.

39. Morgan, "Watch Now: City Officials Hire Consultant."

40. Morgan, "Watch Now: Finalists Chosen for Evans-Fintube Redevelopment Project in Greenwood District," *Tulsa World*, Aug. 11, 2021; Canfield, "Potential Evans-Fintube Developers Stress Proposals Are Meant to Lift North Tulsa Community," *Tulsa World*, April 6, 2022.

41. Kaiser to Krehbiel.

42. Kaiser to Krehbiel.

43. Coates, "The Case for Reparations"; Richard Rothstein, *The Color of Law: A Forgotten History of How Our Government Segregated America* (New York: Liveright, 2017).

44. Kaiser to Krehbiel.

45. Kaiser to Krehbiel; Hardiman, "GKFF Developing Industrial Park in North Tulsa," *Tulsa World*, Aug. 5, 2016; Morgan, "$100 million Revitalization Proposal Could Transform Parts of North Tulsa," *Tulsa World*, March 6, 2020; Canfield, " City Leaders Working To Address Inequities as Tulsa Race Massacre Centennial Approaches," *Tulsa World*, May 31, 2020; Morgan, "New Plant a First for Muncie Power Products and Peoria-Mohawk Business Park," *Tulsa World*, July 24, 2020; Canfield, "As Comanche Park Apartments Come Down, Former Residents Look Ahead to Brighter Future," *Tulsa World*, May 11, 2023.

46. Kaiser to Krehbiel.

47. Kaiser to Krehbiel.

48. Kaiser to Krehbiel; Venita Cooper (entrepreneur, former educator), interview with author, Dec. 22, 2022, transcript in possession of author.

49. Kaiser to Krehbiel; Cooper, interview.

50. Kaiser to Krehbiel; Cooper, interview.

51. Kaiser to Krehbiel; Cooper, interview.

52. Kaiser to Krehbiel; Cooper, interview; Haisten, "OKC Thunder Invests in Tulsa: New Thunder Fellows Program To Be an Asset for Area Black Students," July 8, 2020; Haisten, "Bill Haisten: Thunder, Chicago Bulls Partner in Classroom Project Involving BTW Students," *Tulsa World*, March 8, 2021; Haisten, "Bill Haisten: Black Students Dream Big with Thunder Fellows 'Opening Doors' for Tulsa Kids," *Tulsa World*, "Dec. 24, 2021.

53. Tyrance Billingsley II (creator of Black Tech Street), interview with author, Dec. 4, 2022, transcript in possession of author.

54. Kaiser to Krehbiel.

55. Billingsley, interview.

56. Culver, interview; Krehbiel, "Greenwood Business District Designated a National Historic Place," *Tulsa World*, June 12, 2021; Krehbiel, "Watch now: Greenwood Stakeholders Hope Historic Designation Will Unite Future Efforts to Revitalize District," *Tulsa World*, June 17, 2021.

57. Canfield, "Ethics Complaint Accuses Councilor Vanessa Hall-Harper of Trying to Stop Work of Greenwood Chamber," *Tulsa World*, Jan. 4, 2019; Krehbiel, "City Councilor Questions Management of Historic Greenwood Buildings," *Tulsa World*, Jan. 28, 2020; Tulsa Real Estate Fund, accessed June 11, 2024, https://www.tulsarealestatefund.com/.

58. Canfield, "Ethics Complaint Accuses Councilor Vanessa Hall-Harper."

59. Krehbiel, "City Councilor Questions Management."

60. Canfield, "Watch Now: National Park Service Considers Nomination to Put Tulsa's Greenwood District on National Register of Historic Places," *Tulsa World*, Jan. 17, 2021; Canfield, "Latest Effort to List Greenwood District on National Register of Historic Places Falls Short," *Tulsa World*, Feb. 9, 2021; Krehbiel, "Greenwood Business District Designated a National Historic Place," *Tulsa World*, June 12, 2021.

61. Krehbiel, "Watch now: Greenwood Stakeholders Hope Historic Designation."

62. Graham, "Interstate 244: 'It Took the Heart Out of Greenwood,'" *Tulsa World*, May 24, 2021; Trotter, "TYPros Urbanists Recommend Plan for Tearing Down I-244 Through Greenwood," Public Radio Tulsa, June 14, 2021; Krehbiel, "Oklahoma House of Representatives Study to Consider Inner Dispersal Loop Alternatives," *Tulsa World*, July30, 2021; Luckerson, "Can Buttigieg's $1B Plan Help Remove I-244 from the Historic Greenwood District's 'Black Wall Street?,'" *Oklahoma Eagle*, Sept. 3, 2022

63. Krehbiel, "Through a Century of Hard Work and Heartbreak."

64. Stanley, "100 years Later, It's Harder Than Ever to Know Much About the Confirmed Dead. But the Families of at Least Two of Them Vow to Never Forget," *Tulsa World*, May 31, 2021. Until otherwise noted, the quotes that follow are also from this source.

65. Canfield, "Watch Now: City Locates Eight More Burials at Oaklawn Cemetery This Week as Tulsa Race Massacre Mass Graves Search Continues," *Tulsa World*, June 4, 2021.

66. Krehbiel, "Watch Now: At Least 27 Coffins Found in Oaklawn Burial Site, Tulsa Race Massacre Researchers Say," *Tulsa World*, June 8, 2021; Krehbiel, "Watch Now: Oaklawn Search Ends with Exhumation of 19 Sets of Remains; At Least One Bears Signs of Violence," *Tulsa World*, June 25, 2021; Stubblefield and Stackelbeck, "Tulsa Race Massacre Investigation, 2020–2021: 2021 Forensic Findings," presentation to Public Oversight Committee, March 1, 2022; City of Tulsa, "1921 Graves Investigation Update—March 1, 2022," March 2, 2022.

67. Krehbiel, "Watch Now: Oaklawn Search Ends with Exhumation of 19 Sets of Remains; At Least One Bears Signs of Violence."

68. Krehbiel, "Watch Now: Oaklawn Search Ends with Exhumation of 19 Sets of Remains; At Least One Bears Signs of Violence;" Stubblefield and Stackelbeck, "Tulsa Race Massacre Investigation, 2020–2021: 2021 Forensic Findings," presentation; City of Tulsa, "1921 Graves Investigation Update—March 1 , 2022."

69. Amy Slanchik, "Confusion, Anger at Oaklawn Cemetery During Reburial Ceremony," KOTV, July 30, 2021. Until otherwise noted, the quotes that follow are also from this source.

70. Krehbiel, Watch Now: Exhumed Remains Reburied at Oaklawn Amid Protests From Greenwood Descendants," *Tulsa World*, July 30, 2021; Osborne, "G.T. Bynum's Administration Rushes to Rebury Potential 1921 Massacre Victims Despite Vote to Postpone," *Black Wall Street Times*, July 30, 2021.

71. Osborne, "G.T. Bynum's Administration Rushes."

72. Osborne, "G.T. Bynum's Administration Rushes."

73. "Pueblo Conscripts All Men for Labor to Clear Flood Area; Death List Drops; Harding Asks People to Help the City; Restoration Work Starts," *New York Times*, June 7, 1921.

74. Justice for Julius, accessed June 11, 2024, https://www.justiceforjuliusjones.com/; Justice for Paul Howell, accessed June 11, 2024, https://www.justiceforpaulhowell.com/; Jones v. State of Oklahoma, Court of Criminal Appeals of Oklahoma, 2006.

75. Justice for Julius; Justice for Paul Howell; "Timeline of Events Involving Capital Punishment in Oklahoma," Associated Press, Oct. 28, 2021; Terry Wallace, "Oklahoma Sets 7 Executions in 6 Months; 1st Since 2015," Associated Press, Sept. 21, 2021; Kim Bellware, "Facing Execution, Julius Jones Seeks Clemency—With Help From an Unlikely Ally." *Washington Post*, Sept. 4, 2021.

76. Dr. Tiffany Crutcher Meets with National Leaders in Washington, D.C. Urging Action On George Floyd Justice in Policing Act on 5th Year Anniversary of the Death of Her Twin Brother Terence Crutcher," *Oklahoma Eagle*, Sept.13, 2021.

77. Osborne, "In Historic Vote, Pardon and Parole Board Recommends Life, Possibility of Parole for Julius Jones," *Black Wall Street Times*, Sept. 13, 2021.

78. Jacey Fortin, "On Death Row Half His Life, Oklahoma Man May Be a Step Closer to Release," *New York Times*, Sept. 16, 2021; Justice for Paul Howell.

79. Justice for Paul Howell; Jones v. State of Oklahoma.

80. Justice for Julius; Jones v. State of Oklahoma.

81. State Question 776, Election Results, Oklahoma State Election Board, Nov. 8, 2016; Ziva Branstetter, "Was 'Cowboy' Bob Macy Product of His Time or 'Deadliest'

DA?," *The Frontier*, July 3, 2016; Michael Levenson, Maria Cramer, and Simon Romero, "Oklahoma Governor Commutes Inmate's Death Sentence Hours Before Execution," *New York Times*, Nov. 18, 2021.

82. The ACUF Nolan Center for Justice, accessed June 11, 2024, https://conservativejusticereform.org/; Americans For Prosperity, accessed June 11, 2024, https://americansforprosperity.org/; Hoberock, "She Saw Her Dad Slain at 9. Now She Sees Celebrities Plead for Convicted Killer Julius Jones' Release," *Tulsa World*, Sept. 13, 2021; Justice for Julius; Bob Doucette, "Bob Doucette: Julius Jones Case Presents Collision of Uncertainty and Finality," *Tulsa World*, Sept. 28, 2021; Nolan Clay, "Gov. Kevin Stitt Asks Judge to Strike 'Smear' from Oklahoma County Grand Jury Report," May 26, 2022.

83. Minyvonne Burke, "Kim Kardashian Draws Attention to Julius Jones Case as Oklahoma Execution Nears," NBC, Nov. 18, 2021; Adam Banner, "ABC's 'The Last Defense' Profiles Julius Jones' Current Legal Battle to Stay Alive," *American Bar Association Journal*, Oct. 25, 2021, https://www.abajournal.com/news/article/abcs_the_last_defense_profiles_julius_jones_current_legal_battle_to_stay.

84. David W. Prater to Oklahoma Pardon and Parole Board, March 1, 2021; Perris Jones, "AG Mike Hunter Releases Documents He Says Prove Julius Jones' Guilt," KOCO, July 6, 2020.

85. Hoberock, "She Saw Her Dad Slain at 9."

86. Fortin, "On Death Row Half His Life."

87. Hoberock, "Watch Now: Julius Jones' Request For Clemency Advances; Board Recommends Commuted Sentence," *Tulsa World*, Nov. 2, 2021.

88. Sean Murphy, "Oklahoma Executes Inmate Who Dies Vomiting and Convulsing," Associated Press, Oct. 28, 2021; Paul Tyrrell, "Oklahoma Executes Its First Inmate Since 2015," *Tulsa World*, Oct. 20, 2021; Associated Press, "Timeline Of Events Involving Capital Punishment in Oklahoma," Oct. 28, 2021, https://apnews.com/article/us-supreme-court-executions-oklahoma-05c84265d553c784eb862321aed2acb8; Rick Green and Graham Lee Brewer, "Botched Lethal Injection in Oklahoma: Independent Autopsy Finds IV Was Not Set Properly," *Oklahoman*, June 13, 2014.

89. Tiana Herring, "Deeply Rooted: How Racial History Informs Oklahoma's Death Penalty," Death Penalty Information Center, October 2022, https://deathpenaltyinfo.org/facts-and-research/dpic-reports/dpic-special-reports/deeply-rooted-how-racial-history-informs-oklahomas-death-penalty; Hoberock, "Oklahoma Moving Toward Gas Executions after Three-Year Death Penalty Hiatus Amid Lethal Injection Controversy," March 15, 2018; Nolan Clay, "Executions by Gas Stalled Indefinitely While State Seeks Willing Seller of Device," *Oklahoman*, Jan. 27, 2019; "Crowd Curious to See Gallows," *Tulsa World*, March 31, 1911; "Henson Has Paid Penalty by Death," *Tulsa World*, April 1, 1911; *Encyclopedia of Arkansas*, s.v. "Isaac Charles Parker (1838–1896)," accessed June 11, 2024, https://encyclopediaofarkansas.net/entries/isaac-charles-parker-1732/.

90. Von Russell Creel, "Capital Punishment," *Encyclopedia of Oklahoma History and Culture*, accessed June 11, 2024, https://www.okhistory.org/publications/enc/entry?entry=CA052; "Oklahoma Man Who Developed Lethal Injection Recipe Lived with Regret,"

KOTV, May 1, 2014; Branstetter, "'Father of Lethal Injection' Talks about History, His Legacy to Oklahoma," *Tulsa World*, May 4, 2014.

91. Alan Blinder, "When a Common Sedative Becomes an Execution Drug," *New York Times*, March 13, 2017; Ziva Branstetter and Cary Aspinwall, "Secrets Still Shroud Clayton Lockett's Execution," *Tulsa World*, May 11, 2014; Branstetter and Aspinwall, "Political Pressure Existed to Find New Execution Drug, Former Oklahoma DOC Official Testifies," *Tulsa World*, Dec. 19, 2014.

92. Branstetter and Aspinwall, "Secrets Still Shroud Clayton Lockett's Execution"; Branstetter and Aspinwall, "Political Pressure Existed"; Branstetter and Aspinwall, "Report: Clayton Lockett Shocked With Taser, Had Self-Inflicted Wounds on Day of Execution," *Tulsa World*, May 1, 2014.

93. Aspinwall and Branstetter, "Oklahoma Executes Charles Warner in 20-Minute Procedure; State Says No Complications," *Tulsa World*, Jan. 15, 2015; Rick Green, "Oklahoma Governor Says Future of Death Penalty Uncertain After Mix-Ups," Oct. 8, 2015; Clay and Green, "Wrong Drug Used For January Execution, State Records Show," *Oklahoman*, Oct. 8, 2015; Herring, "Deeply Rooted: How Racial History Informs Oklahoma's Death Penalty."

94. Herring, "Deeply Rooted: How Racial History Informs Oklahoma's Death Penalty."

95. "Watch Now: Governor Commutes Julius Jones' Death Sentence," *Tulsa World*, Nov. 18, 2021; Hoberock, "She Saw Her Dad Slain At 9. Now She Sees Celebrities Plead for Convicted Killer Julius Jones' Release"; Hoberock, "Watch Now: Julius Jones' Request for Clemency Advances; Board Recommends Commuted Sentence"; David Horowitz, *I Can't Breathe: How a Racial Hoax is Killing America* (Washington, DC: Regnery, 2021).

96. Morris, "Steph Curry Calls for Julius Jones' Freedom as Family Urges Community to Attend Nov. 1st Clemency Hearing," Oct. 27, 2021.

97. Schlotthauer, "Tulsa Students Stage Walkout in Support of Julius Jones Amid Commutation: 'This Isn't Over,'" *Tulsa World*, Nov. 18, 2021; "Watch Now: Governor Commutes Julius Jones' Death Sentence"; Canfield, "Watch Now: Julius Jones' Supporters Celebrate Outside Oklahoma State Penitentiary: 'We Will Continue to Fight for His Freedom,'" *Tulsa World*, Nov. 18, 2021; Hoberock, "Vigil for Julius Jones on Eve of His Execution: 'He Is not This Monster People Have Portrayed Him' to Be," *Tulsa World*, Nov. 18, 2021; Osborne, "Two Days From Julius Jones' Scheduled Execution, All Eyes on State Capitol," *Black Wall Street Times*, Nov. 16, 2021.

98. Canfield, "Watch Now: Julius Jones' Supporters Celebrate.'"

99. Canfield, "Watch Now: Julius Jones' Supporters Celebrate'"; Osborne, "Governor's Delay 'Terrorized' Julius Jones' Family, Traumatized Nation," *Black Wall Street Times*, Nov. 22, 2021; James Beaty and Reese Gorman, "Demonstrators Jubilant after Governor Stops Execution," *Enid News & Eagle*, Nov. 18, 2022; Amir Vera and Dakin Andone, "Oklahoma Governor Grants Clemency to Julius Jones, Halting His Execution," CNN, Nov. 19, 2021.

100. Beaty and Gorman, "Demonstrators Jubilant."

101. Nolan Clay and Jessie Christopher Smith, "Bigler Stouffer Executed in Oklahoma Without Problems of Previous Lethal Injections," *Oklahoman*, Dec. 9, 2021.

Epilogue

1. Krehbiel, "'Fight for Justice Is Ongoing' One Year after Tulsa Race Massacre Centennial," *Tulsa World*, May 31, 2022.

2. Krehbiel, "'Fight for Justice Is Ongoing.'"

3. Krehbiel, "'Fight for Justice Is Ongoing.'"

4. Bynum, interview, Dec. 14, 2022.

5. Krehbiel, "'Fight for Justice Is Ongoing.'"

6. Randle, et al. v City of Tulsa, et al; Schlotthauer, "'History Was Made': Tulsa Race Massacre Lawsuit to Proceed to Evidentiary Stage," May 3, 2022; Anna Codutti, "Watch Now: Tulsa Race Massacre Lawsuit Moves Forward with Another Chance to Seek Reparations," *Tulsa World*, Aug. 4, 2022; Eileen Rivers, "'We're Going to Fight to the Finish': Tulsa Race Massacre Survivor on Lawsuit and Struggle," *USA Today*, June 1, 2022.

7. Karen Atiyah, "In Tulsa, the Movement for Reparations Scores a Historic Victory," *Washington Post*, Aug. 19, 2022.

8. Randle, et al. v City of Tulsa, et al; Krehbiel, "Survivors Plan Appeal after Tulsa Race Massacre Lawsuit Dismissed," *Tulsa World*, July 10, 2023.

9. In the matter of the estate of Andrew Chasteen Jackson, deceased, Tulsa County District Court, PB-2021–487; In the matter of the estate of Andrew Chasteen Jackson, deceased, Tulsa County District Court, PB-2022–1291; Adams v. City of Tulsa, et al, Tulsa County District Court, CJ 2023–261; Krehbiel, "Greenwood Rising Sued by Family of Man Slain in 1921 Race Massacre," *Tulsa World*, Jan. 24, 2023; Krehbiel, "Battle Over Tulsa Race Massacre Victim's Story and Likeness Continues," *Tulsa World*, July 26, 2023.

10. Randle, et al. v City of Tulsa, et al; Krehbiel, "Survivors Plan Appeal."

11. Krehbiel, "State Supreme Court Rules for City, Other Defendants in Tulsa Race Massacre Lawsuit," *Tulsa World*, June 11, 2024; Oklahoma Supreme Court, Randle v. City of Tulsa, 2024 OK 40, https://www.oscn.net/applications/oscn/DeliverDocument.asp?CiteID=496200.

12. Canfield, "Council Starts Talks On Possible Redress for Harm Caused by 1921 Tulsa Race Massacre," *Tulsa World*, Feb. 17, 2022; Canfield, "City Council Advances Process for Providing Redress for Those Harmed in 1921 Race Massacre," *Tulsa World*, March 24, 2022; Canfield, "Mayor Bynum Signs Resolution Creating Community-led Process"; Karoline Leonard, "'We Cannot Bury Our Truth': Tulsa Community Discusses Possible Reparations for 1921 Tulsa Race Massacre," *Tulsa World*, June 14, 2023; Canfield, "Report Recommends City Establish a Commission to Consider Reparations for 1921 Tulsa Race Massacre," *Tulsa World*, Jan. 16, 2024; Gregory Robinson II, Kristi Williams, Tami L. Moore, Cynthia Soto-Rinder, and Landon Wolf, "Beyond Apology Report," n.d., accessed June 19, 2024, https://static1.squarespace.com/static/6582e17065cb6c59f121e854/t/658f4bd94180ea099ea0fb96/1703889925254/The+Beyond+Apology+Report.

13. Osborne, "Groups Sue to Restore Protesters' Rights after George Floyd Backlash," *Black Wall Street Times*, June 24, 2022; Casteel, "Oklahoma Attorney General Defends Controversial Race and Gender Education Law, Pushes for Suit Dismissal," *Oklahoman*, April 9, 2023; Krehbiel-Burton, "ACLU, State Educators File Federal Lawsuit Challenging Oklahoma House Bill 1775," *Tulsa World*, Oct. 20, 2021; Graham, "Ginnie Graham: Brooklyn Library Welcomes Oklahomans' Use of QR Code as Free Speech Symbol," *Tulsa World*, Sept. 22, 2022; Krehbiel-Burton, "Watch Now: State Board of Education Denies HB 1775 Accreditation Challenges from TPS, Mustang," *Tulsa World*, Aug. 26, 2022; Krehbiel-Burton, "Education Department: Implicit Bias Training Audio Consistent in Warning of TPS," *Tulsa World*, Aug. 16, 2022; Nuria Martinez-Keel, "Oklahoma Teachers on Notice after 'Watershed' Vote on HB 1775 Violations in Tulsa, Mustang," *Oklahoman*, Aug. 10, 2022; Krehbiel-Burton, "Audio from TPS Implicit Bias Training Was a Voice Reading Presentation Slides Verbatim," *Tulsa World*, Aug. 7, 2022; Krehbiel-Burton, "Watch Now: Tulsa Public Schools Accredited with a Warning Over HB1775 Violation," *Tulsa World*, July 29, 2022; Krehbiel-Burton, "TPS Board Unanimously Approves Separation Agreement with Gist," *Tulsa World*, Aug. 23, 2023.

14. Osborne, "Groups Sue to Restore Protesters' Rights"; John Thompson, "Which is Crazier: The Onion's Satire? Or Ryan Walters' Ramblings?" *Oklahoma Observer*, August 2023; Graham, "Ginnie Graham: Brooklyn Library Welcomes Oklahomans' Use."

15. "National Park Service Supports Greenwood National Monument, Official Says," *Tulsa World*, May 15, 2024.

16. Killman, "Lawsuit Against City on Behalf of Terence Crutcher Estate Mostly Dismissed in Ruling," *Tulsa World*, Feb. 10, 2023.

17. Gary Lee, "North Tulsans Question Race Massacre Graves Investigation," *Oklahoma Eagle*, May 19, 2022; Lee, "Rift Widens Between Mayor's Office and Tulsa Race Massacre Descendants," *Oklahoma Eagle*, July 3, 2022.

18. Lee, "North Tulsans Question Race Massacre."

19. Lee, "North Tulsans Question Race Massacre."

20. City of Tulsa, "Historic Discovery Made in 1921 Graves Investigation," press release, April 12, 2023, https://www.cityoftulsa.org/press-room/historic-discovery-made-in-1921-graves-investigation/; City of Tulsa, "1921 Graves July Test Excavation Complete; Experts to have Excavation Determination in Coming Weeks," press release, July 14, 2023, https://www.cityoftulsa.org/press-room/1921-graves-july-test-excavation-complete-experts-to-have-excavation-determination-in-coming-weeks/.

21. City of Tulsa, "Major Discovery Made in 1921 Graves Investigation; C. L. Daniel Confirmed as First Victim Identified from City's Yearslong Investigation," press release, July 12, 2024, https://www.cityoftulsa.org/press-room/major-discovery-made-in-1921-graves-investigation-c-l-daniel-confirmed-as-first-victim-identified-from-city-s-yearslong-investigation/.

22. Krehbiel, "Federal Officials Laud Tulsa's Advanced Mobility Plans," *Tulsa World*, Sept. 22, 2022; Morgan, "Tulsa Poised to Become Centerpiece of Drone Corridor in Oklahoma," *Tulsa World*, Dec. 10, 2022; Michael Dekker, "1,000 Black Tech Professionals is Goal of New Microsoft-Greenwood Collaboration," *Tulsa World*, Aug. 1, 2023.

23. Canfield, "HUD Secretary Visits Tulsa to Celebrate $50 Million Redevelopment Grant," *Tulsa World*, Sept. 23, 2022; Canfield, "As Comanche Park Apartments Come Down, Former Residents Look Ahead to Brighter Future," *Tulsa World*, May 11, 2023; Kimberly Marsh, "The $190 Million Envision Comanche: One of the U.S.'s Largest Public-Private Investments in Public Housing," *Oklahoma Eagle*, Sept. 30, 2022; Canfield, "City Officials Unveil Kirkpatrick Heights/Greenwood Master Plan Draft," *Tulsa World*, June 29, 2022; Canfield, "Public Invited to Comment on Final Draft of Kirkpatrick Heights-Greenwood Master Plan," *Tulsa World*, Oct. 15, 2022; Max Bryan, "Tulsa City Council Adopts Master Plan for Greenwood, Kirkpatrick Heights," *Tulsa World*, Public Radio Tulsa, Dec. 15, 2022; "Our Legacy, Our Community: A Renewed Vision for North Tulsa," https://www.ourlegacytulsa.org/; Canfield, "Improve Our Tulsa 3 Capital Improvements Package Passes Easily," *Tulsa World*, Aug. 9, 2023.

24. Morgan, "Watch Now: Picturesque Setting Site of Proposed New $35 Million Boutique Hotel North of Downtown," *Tulsa World*, Sept. 21, 2021; DuBose, "Public-private Partnership Plans Multi-Million Development in North Tulsa," *Black Wall Street Times*, June 30, 2021; Morgan, "Pair of Development Partners Drop Out of Evans-Fintube Project North of Downtown," *Tulsa World*, Feb. 3, 2023; Canfield, "City To Restart Discussions Wednesday on Plans for Evans-Fintube Redevelopment," *Tulsa World*, June 11, 2023; Black Wall Street Square, accessed June 16, 2024, https://www.blackwallstreetsquare.org/.

25. Culver, interview.

26. Culver, interview.

27. Culver, interview; Krehbiel, "City Councilor Questions Management of Historic Greenwood Buildings," *Tulsa World*, Dec. 28, 2020.

28. Culver, interview.

29. Culver, interview.

30. DuBose, "Dr. Jabraan Pasha Brings Healthcare to Greenwood with Juno," *Black Wall Street Times*, Jan. 30, 2023; Franklin, "New Medical Center Offers 'Health Care Meets Apple' Experience in Greenwood," *Tulsa World*, July 29, 2023; Codutti, "National Investor Dropping Out Forces Juno to Shutter Tulsa Clinic, Medical Director Says," *Tulsa World*, March 1, 2024.

31. Robinson, interview.

32. McIntyre, interview.

33. McIntyre, interview.

34. McIntyre, interview.

BIBLIOGRAPHY

Archival Sources

Avery, Ruth Sigler–Tulsa Race Massacre Collection. Series 1: Tulsa Race Massacre of 1921. Special Collections and Archives, OSU-Tulsa Library, Oklahoma State University, Tulsa.

McCuen, Capt. John, to Lt. Col. L. J. F. Rooney. n.d. Case 1062. Attorney Generals Civil Case Files, Governor J. B. A. Robertson's papers, 1919–1923. Oklahoma State Archives, Oklahoma Department of Libraries, Oklahoma City.

Court Cases

Adams v. City of Tulsa et al.
Alexander et al v. City of Tulsa et al.
Cleaver v. City of Tulsa et al.
Crutcher v. City of Tulsa et al.
Birdie Lynch Farmer v. T.D. Evans et al.
M.L. Gilliam v. T.D. Evans et al.
J.S. Gish v. T.D. Evans et al.
Mrs. J.H. Goodwin v. City of Tulsa et al.
W.S. Holloway v. City of Tulsa et al.
In the matter of the estate of Andrew Cheesten Jackson
Lockard v. Evans et al. Case No. 15,780
Redfearn v. American Central Insurance
SolomonSimmonsLaw PLLC v. City of Tulsa
SolomonSimmonsLaw PLLC v. Tulsa Development Authority
SolomonSimmonsLaw PLLC v. City of Tulsa Metropolitan Area Planning Commission
State of Oklahoma v. Betty Jo Shelby
State of Oklahoma ex rel. Attorney General of Oklahoma v. Johnson & Johnson
State of Oklahoma v. Shannon James Kepler

News Outlets

Atlanta Journal-Constitution
Associated Press

Bartlesville Examiner-Enterprise
Billboard
Black Dispatch
Black Wall Street Times
Business Insider
CBS News
CNN
Daily Caller
Enid News & Eagle
Fox News
The Frontier
The Guardian
The Hill
KJRH
KRMG
KOCO
KOKI
KOTV
KTUL
Los Angeles Times
Nation
NBC News
New York Times
Oklahoma Eagle
Oklahoman
Oklahoma Watch
Opera Wire
OU Daily
PBS Newshour
Politico
Public Radio Tulsa
Tulsa Business and Legal News
Tulsa Democrat
Tulsa Star
Tulsa Tribune
Tulsa World
USA Today
Wall Street Journal
Washington Post

Author Interviews

Abode, Phil. December 7, 2022.
Armstrong, Phil. September 30, 2022.
Asamoa-Caesar, Kojo. November 14, 2022.

Billingsley, Tyrance II. November 28, 2022.
Bynum, G. T. October 27, 2022, and December 14, 2022.
Cooper, Venita. December 6, 2022.
Culver, Freeman. November 10, 2022.
Doswell, Raymond. December 1, 2022.
Gant, Reuben. October 25, 2022.
Jack, Bob. October 10, 2022.
Johnson, Hannibal. November 29, 2022.
Lansana, Quraysh Ali. December 22, 2022.
Matthews, Kevin. October 28, 2022.
McIntyre, Judy Eason. January 2, 2023.
Nichols, Monroe. October 12, 2022.
Owens, Ray. October 26, 2022.
Patty, Robert. June 13–14, 2000.
Rees, Phillip. March 10, 2000.
Robinson, Greg. December 20, 2022.
Ross, Kavin. October 21, 2022.
Scott, Anthony. November 17, 2022.
Sims, Ashli. December 19, 2022.
Turner, Robert. October 6, 2022.
Yar, Kajeer. November 28, 2022.

Books and Articles

Alexander, Charles C. *The Ku Klux Klan in the Southwest.* Norman: University of Oklahoma Press, 1995.

Banner, Adam. "ABC's 'The Last Defense' Profiles Julius Jones' Current Legal Battle to Stay Alive." *ABA Journal,* October 25, 2021. https://www.abajournal.com/news/article/abcs_the_last_defense_profiles_julius_jones_current_legal_battle_to_stay.

Banzet-Ellis, Gail. "Q&A With Don Ross." *Tulsa People,* September 21, 2018. https://www.tulsapeople.com/tulsa-people/october-2018/q-a-with-don-ross/article_f88826bc-5be4-5695-8b7c-cb324e64d30b.html.

Barrett, Charles. *Oklahoma after Fifty Years.* Oklahoma City: Historical Record Association, 1941.

Brophy, Alfred L. *Reconstructing the Dreamland: The Tulsa Race Riot of 1921, Race Reparations, and Reconciliation.* New York: Oxford University Press, 2002.

———. "The Tulsa Race Riot of 1921 in the Oklahoma Supreme Court." *Oklahoma Law Review* 54, no.1 (2001): 67–148.

Cheng, William. "The Radical Compassion of Frederick Douglass." *Pacific Standard,* February 14, 2018. https://psmag.com/education/the-radical-compassion-of-frederick-douglass.

Clegg, Lane. "Five Questions: Damario Solomon-Simmon." *Tulsa People,* April 1, 2014. https://www.tulsapeople.com/five-questions-damario-solomon-simmons/article_6b14dda0-ba23-5eec-b76b-d57baf5560b0.html.

Coates, Ta-Nehisi. "The Case for Reparations." *Atlantic,* June 2014.

Comstock, Amy. "'Over There': Another View of the Tulsa Riots." *Survey* 46 (July 2, 1921): 460.

Crutcher, Tiffany. "What I Told President Biden in Tulsa." *Progressive,* June 23, 2021. https://progressive.org/latest/what-i-told-biden-tulsa-crutcher-210623/.

Debo, Angie. *From Creek Town to Oil Capital.* Norman: University of Oklahoma Press, 1967.

Degli, Esposti M., D. J. Wiebe, A. Gasparrini, D. K. Humphreys. "Analysis of 'Stand Your Ground' Self-Defense Laws and Statewide Rates of Homicides and Firearm Homicides." *JAMA Netw Open.* 2022 Feb 1; 5(2):e220077. doi: 10.1001/jamanetworkopen.2022.0077. Erratum in: JAMA Netw Open. 2022 Apr 1;5(4):e229270. PMID: 35188553; PMCID: PMC8861849.

Douglas, Clarence. *The History of Tulsa, Oklahoma.* 3 vols. Chicago: Clarke, 1921.

Du Bois, W. E. B. "Let Us Reason Together." *Crisis* 18, no. 5 (September 1919): 231–35.

———. "Opinion." *Crisis* 31, no. 6 (April 1926): 267–71.

———. "Returning Soldiers." *Crisis* 18, no. 1 (May 1919): 13–14.

Ellsworth, Scott. *Death in a Promised Land.* Baton Rouge: Louisiana State University Press, 1982.

———. *The Ground Breaking: An American City and Its Search for Justice,* New York: E. P. Dutton, 2021.

Faulkner, William. *Requiem for a Nun.* New York: Random House, 1951.

Franklin, B. C. *My Life and an Era: The Autobiography of Buck Colbert Franklin.* Baton Rouge: Louisiana State University Press, 1997.

Franklin, John Hope. *Mirror to America: The Autobiography of John Hope Franklin.* New York: Farrar, Straus and Giroux, 2005.

Gates, Eddie Faye. *They Came Searching: How Blacks Sought the Promised Land in Tulsa.* Austin, TX: Eakin Press, 1997.

Gates, Henry Louis Jr. "The New Negro and the Black Image: From Booker T. Washington to Alain Locke." Freedom's story. TeacherServe. National Humanities Center. https://nationalhumanitiescenter.org/tserve/freedom/1917beyond/essays/newnegro.htm.

Goble, Danney. *Tulsa! Biography of the American City.* Tulsa, OK: Council Oak Books, 1997.

Hall, J. M. *The Beginning of Tulsa.* Tulsa, OK: Scott-Rice Printers, 1933.

Halliburton, R. *The Tulsa Race War of 1921.* Saratoga, CA: R and E Research, 1975.

Hart, Albert Bushnell. "Peonage and the Public." *Survey* 46 (April 9, 1921): 43–4.

Hilton, O. A. "The Oklahoma Council of Defense and the First World War." *Chronicles of Oklahoma* 20 (March 1942): 18–42.

Horowitz, David. *I Can't Breathe: How a Racial Hoax Is Killing America.* Washington, DC: Regnery, 2021.

Hower, Bob, ed. *1921 Tulsa Race Riot and the American Red Cross, "Angels of Mercy."* Tulsa, OK: Homestead Press, 1993.

"*Impact* Raps with W. D. Williams." *Oklahoma Impact Magazine* (June–July 1971): 32–36.

Johnson, Hannibal. *Black Wall Street: From Riot to Renaissance in Tulsa's Historic Greenwood District.* Austin, TX: Eakin Press, 1998.

———. *Black Wall Street 100: An American City Grapples with its Historical Racial Trauma.* Austin, TX: Eakin Press, 2020.

Karl, Jonathan. *Betrayal: The Final Act of the Trump Show.* New York: Dutton, 2021.

Kendi, Ibram X. *How to Be an Antiracist.* New York: One World, 2019.

———. *Stamped from the Beginning: The Definitive History of Racist Ideas in America.* New York: Bold Type Books, 2016.

Krehbiel, Randy. *Tulsa 1921: Reporting a Massacre.* Norman: University of Oklahoma Press, 2019.

Krugler, David F. *1919, the Year of Racial Violence: How African Americans Fought Back.* Cambridge: Cambridge University Press, 2014.

Lampe, William T. *Tulsa County in the World War.* Tulsa, OK: Tulsa County Historical Society, 1919.

Landes, Tim. "Scenes from Centennial Year Launch Event at John Hope Franklin Reconciliation Park." *Tulsa People,* January 1, 2021.

Lichtman, Allan J. *The Embattled Vote in America: From the Founding to the Present.* Cambridge, MA: Harvard University Press, 2018.

Luckerson, Victor. "Tulsa's Hopeful Anger." *New Yorker,* June 16, 2020.

Madigan, Tim. *The Burning: Massacre, Destruction and the Tulsa Race Riot of 1921.* New York: Thomas Dunne, 2003.

Major, Derek. "Black Architectural Firm Chosen to Renovate Greenwood Cultural Center." *Black Enterprise,* April 14, 2021. https://www.blackenterprise.com/black-architectural-firm-chosen-to-renovate-greenwood-cultural-center-in-tulsa/.

Moreno, Carlos. *The Victory of Greenwood.* Tulsa, OK: Jenkin Lloyd Jones Press, 2021.

Noble, Mary. "Legacy and Impact: Remembering MLK's Visit to North Tulsa, 50 Years After His Death." *Tulsa People,* April 4, 2018.

Parrish, Mary E. Jones. *Race Riot 1921: Events of the Tulsa Disaster.* Tulsa, OK: Out on a Limb Publishing, 1998.

Phillips, Kevin. *Wealth and Democracy: A Political History of the American Rich.* New York: Broadway Books, 2002.

Polk's Tulsa City Directories. Kansas City, MO: R. L. Polk, 1923–1956.

Polk-Hoffhine Directories of Tulsa, Okla. Tulsa, OK: Polk-Hoffhine, 1913–1922.

Rios, Edwin, "You're Not Coming to Bring Us Justice. So What Are You Coming For?" *Mother Jones,* June 19, 2020. https://www.motherjones.com/criminal-justice/2020/06/trump-juneteenth-tulsa-rally/.

Roberts, Rodney C. "The Morality of a Moral Statute of Limitations on Injustice." *Journal of Ethics* 7 (March 2003): 115–38.

Robinson, Randall. *The Debt: What America Owes to Blacks.* New York: Dutton, 2000.

Rothstein, Richard. *The Color of Law: A Forgotten History of How Our Government Segregated America,* New York: Liveright, 2017.

Scales, James R., and Danney Goble. *Oklahoma Politics: A History.* Norman: University of Oklahoma Press, 1982.

Thoburn, Joseph L., and Muriel H. Wright. *Oklahoma: A History of the State and Its People.* 4 vols. New York: Lewis Historical Publishing, 1929.

Whitaker, Robert. *On the Laps of the Gods: The Red Summer of 1919 and the Struggle for Justice that Remade a Nation.* New York: Crown, 2008.

White, Walter. "The Eruption of Tulsa." *Nation,* June 29, 1921.

Unpublished Reports and Manuscripts

Albright, Alex, Jeremy A. Cook, James J Feigenbaum, Laura Kincaide, Jason Long, and Nathan Nunn. "After the Burning: The Economic Effects of the 1921 Tulsa Race Massacre." Working Paper 28985. Cambridge, MA: National Bureau of Economic Research, July 2021. http://www.nber.org/papers/w28985.

Coleman, Amanda. "A Socioeconomic Analysis of the Greenwood District of Tulsa, Oklahoma, 1940–1980." Master's thesis, Oklahoma State University, 2001.

Finchum, Tanya, and Alex Bishop. "Oral History Interview with Viola Fletcher." Oklahoma 100 Year Oral History Project. Oklahoma State University. Dec. 10, 2014

Gill, Loren L. "The Tulsa Race Riot." Master's thesis, University of Tulsa, 1946.

Hammerstedt, Scott W., and Amanda L. Regnier. "Searching For Graves From the 1921 Tulsa Race Massacre: Geophysical Survey of Oaklawn Cemetery, The Canes, and Newblock Park." Oklahoma Archeological Survey Research Series 5. n.d. https://www.cityoftulsa.org/media/11899/hammerstedt-and-regnier-2019-searching-for-graves-from-the-1921-tulsa-race-massacre-oasrs-5.pdf.

"Hearing on Centennial of 1921 Tulsa Race Massacre." C-SPAN, May 19, 2021. https://www.c-span.org/video/?511795-1/hearing-centennial-1921-tulsa-race-massacre.

John Hope Franklin Greenwood Reconciliation Museum. *John Hope Franklin Greenwood Reconciliation Museum: Program and Conceptual Design Manual.* Tulsa: EWC, June 18, 2003. Copy in possession of author.

Oklahoma Commission to Study the Tulsa Race Riot of 1921. *Tulsa Race Riot: A Report.* Oklahoma City, February 18, 2001. https://digitalcollections.tulsalibrary.org/digital/collection/p15020coll6/id/449.

Smith, Adam B. "2021 U.S. Billion-Dollar Weather and Climate Disasters in Historical Context." National Oceanic and Atmospheric Administration, Jan. 24, 2022.

Stackelbeck, Kary L. and Phoebe R. Stubblefield, "Archaeological and Forensic Research in Support of the 1921 Tulsa Race Massacre Graves Investigation: The 2020–2021 Field Seasons at Oaklawn Cemetery." 2 volumes and Power Point presentation. Oklahoma Archeological Survey and University of Florida C. A. Pound Human Identification Laboratory, University of Florida Department of Anthropology.

INDEX

References to illustrations appear in italic type.